Abundantly Wild

Collecting and Cooking Wild Edibles in the Upper Midwest

For Your Safety

If you're not sure about the identity of a wild plant, or have any doubt about its edibility, don't taste it and certainly don't eat it. Check with an expert first, or pass it by until you can learn more. Although this book includes fairly detailed information to help you identify plants, it must be stressed that this book is not a field guide. Always consult at least one—preferably two or three—reputable field guides when attempting to identify an unfamiliar plant; see the bibliography on page 428 for some suggestions. Read Chapter 2, Harvesting Wild Foods Safely, for more information on plant identification practices. Also read Safely Eating Wild Foods beginning on page 10 and Foraging Guidelines on page 19 before you begin your search for wild foods.

Photo Credits:

Dudley Edmondson: 104 (all), 128 (shellbark bark, shellbark fruit), 166, 232 (both), 250, 266 (Northern red oak acorn), 328 (birdfoot violet), 338, 342 (both), 343 (oxeye daisy), 345 (wintercress), 348 (both), 349, 402 (evening primrose), 414 (birch trees, black spruce) **Michael P. Gadomski/Dembinsky Photo Associates**: 70 (asparagus spears), 90 (highbush blueberry), 416 (juniper berries) **Richard Haug**: 32 (lady fern), 80 (broadleaf cattail), 118 (giant puffball, common puffball), 142, 170, 181 (unripe ground cherries on plant), 225 (black raspberries), 236, 240 (both), 248, 362, 364, 366, 386, 392 (second-year burdock), 402 (groundnut), 403 (wapato), 404 **Randall B. Henne/Dembinsky Photo Associates**: 160 (red currant) **Adam Jones/Dembinsky Photo Associates**: 301 **Ed Kanze/Dembinsky Photo Associates**: 44 (dandelion field) **Bill Lea/Dembinsky Photo Associates**: 284 (beaked hazelnuts) **Bill Lindner/Bill Lindner Photography**: 56 (cut-open morel), 290, 333, 406 (both), 412 **Teresa Marrone**: 22 (all), 32 (ostrich fern close-up, ostrich fern, bracken fern), 33, 34, 56 (morel in forest, morels on cutting board), 70 (asparagus fern), 80 (emerging cattail, pollen-covered cattail), 90 (lowbush blueberry), 92, 118 (pear-shaped puffball), 131, 147, *160 (currant and gooseberry leaves)*, 165 (both), 176, 177, 181 (ripe ground cherries), 188, *204 (leaves and dragon's beak), 206 (mystery fruit)*, 212, 225 (domestic vs. wild), 286, 306, 311 (both), 323, 345 (plantain), 392 (first-year burdock) **Maslowski Productions**: 396, 416 (spicebush berries) **Steve Mortensen**: 343 (spring beauty) **Richard Shiell/Dembinsky Photo Associates**: 284 (American hazelnuts) **Stan Tekiela**: 44 (close-up), 57 (both), 107 (all), 114 (all), 128 (shagbark leaf, shagbark fruit), 154, 194, 199, 204 (leaves and fruit), 218 (both), 246 (both), 266 (Northern red oak leaves, white oak leaves), 273, 279, 296, 319, 328 (common blue violet), 344 (both), 403 (great Solomon's seal), 414 (basswood, Eastern hemlock)

Book and Cover Design by Jonathan Norberg

Copyright 2004 by Teresa Marrone

Published by Adventure Publications, Inc.
820 Cleveland St. S
Cambridge, MN 55008
1-800-678-7006
ISBN: 1-59193-034-0
Printed in China

Abundantly Wild

Collecting and Cooking Wild Edibles in the Upper Midwest

by Teresa Marrone

Adventure Publications, Inc.
Cambridge, MN

Table of Contents

AN INTRODUCTION TO FORAGING, AND ABOUT THIS BOOK

Wild edibles are found almost everywhere: urban forests and parks; country lanes and byways; public lands such as county, state and national parks; and even in your own back yard. This book is written to help you safely harvest and enjoy some of the best wild edibles that are found in the Upper Midwest.

Often, a person's first experience with wild foods is accidental—some wild raspberries or woodland strawberries are spotted while walking through the woods. These wild foods look exactly like their domestic counterparts—only smaller—so they're familiar and "safe." A quick taste turns the hiker into a forager who eagerly searches for more of the unexpected treasure.

There's something really thrilling in gathering and preparing wild foods. No feeling quite matches that of scouting the woods in early spring and finally spotting the first morel, or the first ramp, or the first cluster of fiddlehead ferns emerging from the brown and barren landscape. And although you may spend a fair amount of time on tasks such as shelling nuts, pitting wild cherries or pulling stems off dandelion flowers, the work is pleasant and satisfying because you are taking something you gathered yourself and turning it into a delicious dish.

Foraging can be a quiet individual activity that offers plenty of opportunity for reflection and calming thoughts, as well as a chance to observe nature on an "up close and

INTRODUCTION

personal" level. It can also be an enjoyable family or group activity; and when it comes to cleaning a gallon of just-picked gooseberries, many hands make light work.

This book is written for people who have a casual to moderate interest in foraging, rather than the live-off-the-land survivalist. Certainly, the foods listed in the book can be used by the survivalist, but the emphasis here is on enjoyment rather than necessity. Sustainability and ecology are also important when gathering wild foods; entire colonies of some plants can be wiped out by over-harvesting, while other gathering techniques such as digging for roots can leave the land open to erosion if not done properly. Many wild foods, however, can be gathered without harming the resource, and this book helps identify proper harvesting procedures in the information presented about each species.

Although this book includes lots of fairly detailed information to help you identify plants, it must be stressed that *this book is not a field guide.* Always consult at least one—preferably two or three—reputable field guides when attempting to identify an unfamiliar plant; see the bibliography on page 428 for some suggestions. If possible, show the plant to an experienced forager or a plant specialist at the local University Extension Service. This is particularly important with mushrooms, which can be confusing and hard to identify; a mistake identifying mushrooms can be fatal, so don't take this lightly. Please read Chapter 2, Harvesting Wild Foods Safely, for more information on plant identification practices.

WHERE I GOT MY INFORMATION AND WHERE TO GO FOR MORE

The plants in the book are those with which I have personal experience; I've learned a lot from some very experienced foragers over the years, and am grateful for the opportunity to learn from others who are willing to share their knowledge. If I've got limited knowledge about a plant, I've stated my sources; I've tried very hard to present only information that I have checked out and know to be true. Most of my information about plant ranges and distributions comes from the Unites States Department of Agriculture and the Unites States Geological Survey. Statements about nutrition of various plants are based on the USDA's Nutrient Database for Standard Reference, Release 15. Other sources are cited throughout the book; for additional information, please see the bibliography and list of sources that starts on page 429.

If you look on the internet or in the library, there are many places to learn more about edible wild plants. Unfortunately, there is a lot of bad information out there, especially on the internet. I've seen internet sites that include toxic plants among those on their list of plants recommended for eating; similarly, I've seen plants listed as dangerous that I personally know to be edible. Information, whether good or bad, spreads very quickly in this computerized and connected age.

In general, information from University Extension Services, arboretums, colleges and other institutions of higher learning is far more reliable than that from other sources; however, there is some excellent information out there from people who are simply interested in the subject and willing to share their observations. If possible, check with an experienced forager when researching a new plant. There are several internet chat groups that talk about nothing but wild foods; these forums are a good place to learn more. The groups change frequently, so I'm not going to list any here; your best bet is to do a search for "wild foods forum" or something similar, and see what you can find.

You may also be able to find a local naturalist or plant specialist who would be willing to offer instruction; check with a nature center or park headquarters to locate someone like that in your area. The Mycological Society of America is active in many areas, and if you're interested in mushrooms, you should join the local chapter so you can learn this difficult subject from the experts. Finally, there are sometimes local foraging experts who offer classes and seminars to help people learn how to identify and use plants from the area.

In closing, I'd like to pass along some advice I heard from Sam Thayer, an expert forager. He suggests learning four or five new wild-food plants each year, rather than trying to learn everything all at once. He points out that if you learn four new plants each year, in five years there will be 20 plants with which you're familiar and comfortable. Sam also talks about knowing a wild plant well enough to have absolute confidence in its identification. An example he uses is that if someone hands you an apple and says, "Please peel this orange for me," you would immediately contradict them by saying that this isn't an orange, it's an apple. Sam calls this "contradictory confidence," and it is a good policy to adopt when working with wild plants. If you're not sure about the identity of a wild plant, or have the slightest doubt about its edibility, ***don't eat it.*** Check with a knowledgeable person first, or pass it by until you have the chance to learn more.

THE BASICS OF HARVESTING WILD FOODS

Frequently, you'll have a well-defined goal in mind when you head out to gather wild edibles. You'll be looking for a specific thing: morels, for example, or raspberries, or cattail pollen. In these cases, you probably have a good idea of what to look for. You've studied the plant, know the type of habitat in which it grows, and are comfortable with identification. Other times, however, you may not really be sure how to find and identify a specific plant, or you may stumble across something in the woods that looks interesting or vaguely familiar. How do you proceed in these cases?

SAFELY EATING WILD FOODS

The first thing to remember is the cardinal rule of foraging: If you're unsure about the identity of a plant, *don't taste it and don't eat it.* Check in several good field guides; show the plant to experienced foragers; contact the local University Extension Service; talk to a farmer in the area (they usually have a pretty good idea of what is growing around their land). Note that many wild plants go by a variety of common names, and that these names may be used for more than one plant. "Pigweed," for example, is used to refer to two different plants: *Chenopodium album,* more commonly called lamb's quarters, and members of the *Amaranthus* clan, commonly referred to as amaranth. It helps to become familiar with the Latin names of the plants when looking them up in books or discussing them with others. I've included the Latin names of every plant discussed in this book.

WILD FOODS BASICS

You may hear of lots of rules that supposedly help you determine if a plant is safe to eat; for example, "all berries of a certain color are safe," or "if you see a wild animal eating the plant, then it is OK to try it." Unfortunately, it isn't that easy. The only little rule like this that I know to be true is that if a berry has a crown on the bottom —like blueberries or huckleberries—it won't be poisonous.

Once you have identified the plant as edible and have no doubts about its identity, you still need to proceed with a bit of caution and common sense. Some foods—both wild and domestic—simply don't agree with certain individuals. Other foods may trigger an allergic reaction. When I was a kid, no one (it seems) had heard about peanut allergies, for example; now, it is a very well-known problem. It took a long time for medical science to identify peanuts as a food that can cause a dangerous reaction in sensitive individuals. Many wild foods haven't been studied, so information about problems is largely anecdotal. Whenever you're eating a new food for the first time, it's prudent to sample just a small amount to make sure you won't have a problem.

It's also important to note that not all parts of an "edible" plant can be eaten; this also changes over the course of a season, and is further affected by preparation methods. For example, elderberries are a well-known and much-used wild berry. However, the stems, leaves and roots of the elderberry plant contain toxins that reportedly cause very nasty digestive problems. The underripe berries will also cause problems, especially if eaten in large quantities; some people get sick from even ripe elderberries that haven't been cooked. So you must learn not only how to identify the plant, but also which parts to harvest and how to prepare them. Throughout this book, I've provided this information in the accounts of each plant.

Even within the realm of plants that are gathered by foragers, there are plants (or parts of plants) that I don't mess with due to safety or edibility concerns. Some plants or parts of plants are technically edible, but their edibility is dependent upon very specific harvesting or preparation techniques. Since I am harvesting wild foods for enjoyment rather than out of necessity, I don't work with plants such as these, and I chose not to include them in this book.

Finally, I'd like to point out that just because a plant can be eaten, does not mean that it should be harvested. For one thing, you might not like the way it tastes; it makes little sense to continue to dig it up just because it is edible. There are other plants that are becoming so rare in the wild—particularly in specific areas—that they shouldn't be harvested "just for fun;" and in fact some, such as Solomon's seal, are protected by laws in many places. Others have fragile reproduction methods, and an overzealous forager can wipe out most of a colony of, say, ramps. Whenever you're foraging, always keep the health of the resource in mind; if you find only a small grouping of a specific plant, pass it by.

Even if you find a good-sized grouping or colony of a specific plant, you should limit your harvest in most cases, taking one plant for every ten you see. This doesn't apply to certain plants: most "edible weeds" such as nettle and dock, which reproduce with vigor even when farmers try to eradicate them; some fruits such as strawberries, which reproduce primarily by underground runners, not by the seeds on the berry; or nuts, because it would be pretty hard for a forager to pick up every nut in the forest. However, keep in mind that wild animals rely on wild foods to survive; you should always leave enough for them. I've included information on sustainability and good foraging practices throughout this book.

PLANT PARTS, AND TERMS USED IN IDENTIFICATION

Even though this book is not a field guide, characteristics of the wild edibles are discussed. It's helpful to be familiar with some of the terms used to describe plants as you're using this book. Other field guides might use slightly different terms, but these are some basics to get you started.

Leaf growth is used to identify many plants, even if the leaves are not the edible part. To use the leaves in identification, look at the following aspects.

| Simple | Simple Lobed | Compound | Twice Compound | Palmate |

Type of leaf: Simple leaves are in one piece and are not made up of multiple leaflets, though they may have lobes. A compound leaf is made up of several individual leaflets attached to the main stem. A twice compound leaf is made up of leaflets attached to a stem, which in turn attaches to the main stem. A palmate compound leaf is made up of leaflets that all attach to the same central point on the stem.

| Alternate | Basal | Clasping | Opposite | Perfoliate | Whorl |

Leaf attachment: Leaves attach to stems and branches in several different ways. Leaves can grow directly across from each other (opposite) or staggered along the stem or branch (alternate). Other leaves have no leafstalks and partially encircle the stem (clasping). Leaves that have no leafstalks and entirely encircle the stem are called perfoliate. Leaves can also grow right next to the ground (basal), often in a rosette pattern. When three or more leaves attach around the stem at the same point, the attachment is called a whorl.

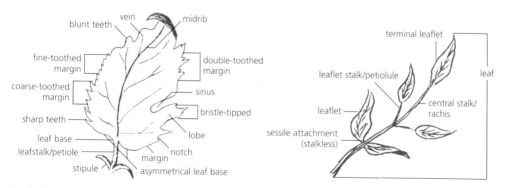

Leaf characteristics: Some things to look for on leaves include the edge of the leaf, which can be wavy or scalloped, toothed or smooth. The leaves themselves can be fuzzy or hairy on either side, or may be smooth. The midrib and venation may stand out sharply, or may be practically imperceptible.

Evergreen needles are also leaves, but the above characteristics don't apply to them. I don't discuss many evergreens in this book; where they are discussed, descriptions are given for the leaf characteristics.

Flowers are a good way to identify plants, but with most of the plants in this book, the flowers are not present when the plant is being harvested for food. If you find yourself in need of information about wildflowers, any good wildflower guide will include lots of information on flower parts and identification. See some suggestions on page 428.

Flowers turn into fruits, which are one of the big categories of wild foods. Some are *pomes:* fleshy fruits containing numerous seeds in the middle, the seeds sometimes surrounded by papery tissue that is not tightly connected to the seeds. When you are trying to identify a fruit, compare it to an apple, which is a well-known pome. If the fruit has just a single seed or pit, it is a *drupe;* plums and cherries are drupes. Some fruits grow as aggregates or *compound fruits,* consisting of many individual drupes clustered together. Raspberries, blackberries and mulberries are examples of compound fruits, which are often called berries. A true *berry* is a thin-skinned fruit with multiple seeds in a soft, fleshy mass; blueberries, ground cherries and gooseberries are all true berries.

PLACES TO GO FORAGING

Many of us look forward all year to a vacation in the country, on the lake, in a woodland cabin or at a favorite campsite. This is a perfect opportunity to get out into the woods and fields and gather wild foods that may not grow closer to home. It also provides a pleasant change from the usual vacation activities; for some people, foraging is the reason to be there in the first place.

If you live in a rural or remote area, you are probably aware of some of the more common wild foods such as chokecherries, asparagus and gooseberries. However, there are many less-familiar plants worth harvesting. In addition, some of the plants that may be considered nuisance weeds have delicious uses.

Another way that many people enjoy foraging is to take a drive in the countryside, looking for areas that are wild or undeveloped. You may see a small woodlot, shelterbelt or windbreak between some farm fields; a quick knock at the door of the nearest farmhouse will usually land you permission to harvest wild foods growing there.

Foraging is also allowed on many types of public land such as river corridors, areas surrounding lakes and ponds, and wildlife management areas; you can locate such spots on maps (be sure to check with the managing authorities for rules about foraging).

THE URBAN FORAGER

Urban foraging is something that many folks don't think of, yet there are dozens of edibles within city limits. I live in a large city, in a very urban neighborhood; yet within walking distance of my house I can harvest crabapples, ramps, watercress, acorns, hackberries, mulberries, wild grapes, dock, and mushrooms including morels and puffballs (and the occasional hen of the woods when I am really lucky). In my own back yard, I gather wood sorrel, violet leaves and flowers, lamb's quarters, wild rose hips (admittedly from a transplanted wild shrub), purslane, plantain, red clover, black walnuts and the ever-popular dandelion. With a 20-minute drive, I can reach areas where I gather cattails, raspberries, blackberries and many other delectable wild foods—all for free.

Small parks are common in urban areas. Walking paths often pass through small patches of urban forest, or former agricultural fields, and these can yield a surprising number of wild foods.

Office parks and corporate offices at the edges of suburbia can be gold mines for the forager. These developments are usually carved out of old agricultural or forested land, and the developers, in an attempt to make the place look "natural," leave belts of trees and other plants around the edges. Some of the best morel picking I've had over the years has come from areas like this. Note that if you're eyeing the woodlot around a corporate office, you should ask for permission to walk in their woods.

CHOOSING A SITE FOR SAFE FORAGING

There is growing concern about chemicals that are used in the production of foods we buy at the store: pesticide sprays, chemical fertilizers, growth hormones given to domestic animals, and genetically altered foods. You may think that by foraging for wild foods, you need have no concerns, but unfortunately that is not always the case. Plants that grow near a highway are exposed to large doses of toxic fumes from automobiles, as well as road dirt and sometimes weed-control spray used by the state or county. Even in the country, vehicle fumes may affect the plants, particularly those next to the road.

Try to get back into the woods or fields before gathering wild foods. A barrier of trees goes a long way in stopping fumes, not to mention dust and dirt. Some plants, such as greens (lamb's quarters and amaranth in particular) and mushrooms, are particularly good at absorbing contaminants; be sure to stay well away from roads when gathering them.

When you're foraging in urban areas, you must always be alert to possible contaminants such as herbicides that may have been sprayed to control weeds. If you see lots of yellowing leaves or dead plants in the area, assume that everything has been sprayed and is unsafe for harvesting. You can also call the park board or whatever group has control of the land, and ask them about spraying; this would be a good time to encourage them to opt for something that is more ecologically friendly.

Some plants are harvested from very wet locations; cattails and watercress are two good examples of this. You should make an effort to ensure that the water is clean and uncontaminated before gathering these plants. For additional safety if you are going to eat the plants raw, you may want to treat the plants with water purification tablets that are used by campers; these will eliminate microscopic parasites such as giardia and cryptosporidium that could cause intestinal problems.

You also need to be concerned with your legal safety when foraging, and avoid trespassing. It takes just a few minutes to knock on the door of the nearest farmhouse to ask permission before tramping into a shelterbelt in an agricultural region. As an added bonus, the landowner might tip you off to an area that you hadn't noticed yet, where more of the plants you're seeking can be found. Foraging and gathering is controlled or restricted on many public lands; on others, foraging is allowed only for immediate consumption (in other words, you can pick a few huckleberries to eat on the spot in some National Parks, but you can't put them in a bag and take them home). Recent regulations put in place by the National Park Service allow harvesting of fruits in specific park areas, but the harvest of mushrooms—which are technically fruiting bodies—is forbidden in the same areas. Check with the rangers or other park personnel before assuming that you have free license to pick whatever you like.

Finally, even when you do have permission to pick from a certain area, always ensure that you leave it in better condition than you found it. Pick up any trash you may find and pack it out with you. Instead of cleaning out an area of all vegetation, harvest as though you were thinning a garden so the plants you've left behind have room to expand and grow (although if you're harvesting "weeds" from an agricultural area, the farmer may ask that you remove all of the plants you find). If you dig up roots, always replace the dirt and pack it down very well to prevent erosion; this is especially important when digging in sandy soil or near flowing water, but it applies to all digging you might do. Don't trample the surrounding vegetation, break shrubs or branches, or uproot nearby plants in your attempts to harvest what you're after.

HABITAT TYPES FOR FORAGING

Throughout this book, I've included information about the range of each plant; this is a listing of the states in our area that are likely to have the particular plant. This information is only part of the picture, because even though a plant may grow in a particular portion of your state, it certainly won't be everywhere you look. That's why I've also discussed the various habitat types required by each plant. This tells you that if you live in northern Illinois, for example, both cattails and hickory nuts grow in your area. After reading the habitat information, you'll learn that you can find cattails in marshy areas, but if you're looking for hickory nuts, you need to head to a hardwood forest. Here is a quick listing of the major habitat types, followed by a listing of some of the wild edibles that you may find in each.

Marshy areas or wetlands generally support few trees except on the fringes. Water may be flowing (from a spring, creek or stream), or stagnant. The ground is spongy, and often consists of mat-like layers of dead vegetation. Reeds, sedges and grasses are the dominant plants. Look for cattails in these areas; elderberries, mushrooms and many wildflowers are often found along the edges.

Streams, rivers, ponds and lakes have water that is generally much deeper than marshy areas, although there can be some overlap. Streams and rivers have flowing water, while lakes and ponds are still (but may be fed by underground springs, keeping the water fresh). Arrowhead tubers (wapato) grow in the shallows of lakes and ponds. Watercress is found in flowing water along the edges of streams and creeks. The banks are rich with wild edibles; look for nut trees, ferns, nettles and other greens, ramps, wild plums, a wide variety of mushrooms, raspberries, strawberries, currant and gooseberry bushes, elderberry shrubs, wild grapes, mulberries, pawpaws and nannyberries.

Hardwood forests in our region are often dominated by oak, ash and maple trees; the area is frequently hilly, and bottomlands have particularly rich soil that supports a wide variety of plants. You'll find nut trees and persimmons in the southern portion of our range, while the northern portion is home to mountain ash, serviceberry and hazelnuts. Wild cherries grow throughout forests in our area. In the clearings and along edges, look for berries and grapes. Ramps, wildflowers and ferns, along with morels and other mushrooms, can be found in shady or partially shaded portions, especially in the bottomlands.

Mixed conifer-softwood forests often have a few scattered hardwoods, but in general are dominated by birch, aspen, pine trees, junipers, spruce, cedars, and tamarack in the north. Some mushrooms such as the cauliflower fungus grow well in these forests. Blueberries and huckleberries thrive in the acidic soil provided by pine needles. Serviceberries and hazelnuts can be found here as well.

Agricultural areas and prairies are host to a wide variety of wild edibles, including Jerusalem artichoke, dock and greens of all sorts, wildflowers, chokecherry shrubs, a wide variety of berries, sunflowers, crabapples and abandoned orchards, asparagus, sumac, and mushrooms including morels and puffballs. In the arid western portions of our region, look for prickly pear cactus.

SEASONS FOR FORAGING

To everything there is a season, and this is certainly the case with foraging for wild edibles. Our region, the Upper Midwest, sees some wide temperature fluctuations, ranging from winter lows in the negative tens and twenties (Farenheit) to summertime highs that can approach or even top 100°F.

We do have a wide variety of plants that survive—and thrive—in our region. Here is a quick summary of various plants and plant parts that can be foraged in each season; note that there may be some overlap between the seasons, so a plant that is found in spring may also be found in early summer. This list, in combination with the Habitat Types for Foraging noted above, should give you some ideas about what to look for when you're headed out the door.

Spring: Blackberry shoots, cattail shoots, curly dock leaves, dandelion leaves and flowers, fiddlehead ferns, lamb's quarters, morel mushrooms, wood and stinging nettles, ramp leaves and bulbs, spring beauty tubers, violet flowers and leaves, wintercress and wood sorrel. In late spring, also look for asparagus, cattail flowering heads, clintonia, elderberry flowers, wild grape leaves, strawberries and watercress.

Summer: Cattail flowering heads and pollen, chamomile flowers, chicken of the woods mushrooms, dandelion flowers and roots, day lily flowers, gooseberries, lamb's quarters, mulberries, plantain, prickly pear pads and fruits, purslane, ramp bulbs, raspberries, red clover flowers, wild rose flowers, sheep sorrel, stinging nettle (tender new growth), strawberries, watercress, wood sorrel. In late summer, also look for blackberries, blackhaws, blueberries, cauliflower mushrooms, wild cherries and chokecherries, crabapples, currants, elderberry fruits, wild grapes, ground cherries, hazelnuts, huckleberries, maypops, nannyberries, oyster mushrooms, wild plums, puffballs, serviceberries and sumac berries.

Fall: Acorns, arrowhead tubers (wapato), blackberry leaves, boletus mushrooms, butternuts, cattail rhizomes, cauliflower mushrooms, chanterelle mushrooms, chicken of the woods mushrooms, chokeberries, crabapples, dandelion roots and greens (new growth), wild grapes, hackberries, hawthorns, hazelnuts, hen of the woods mushrooms, hickory nuts, honey cap mushrooms, Jerusalem artichoke tubers, mountain ash berries, nannyberries, oyster mushrooms, pawpaws, persimmons, plantain seeds, puffballs, ramp bulbs, raspberries (second, smaller crop), shaggy mane mushrooms, strawberry leaves, sumac berries, rose hips, black walnuts, wild rice and wood sorrel.

Winter: Red oak acorns, cattail rhizomes, Jerusalem artichoke tubers, mountain ash berries and rose hips; persimmons may persist, and are edible, through early winter. In late winter or early spring, maple and birch trees can be tapped for sap to make syrup.

Foraging Guidelines

1. If you can't positively identify it, don't taste it, and certainly don't eat it

2. Remember that just because a plant has edible parts doesn't mean that the whole plant is edible

3. Edible parts of a plant may be inedible during some stages of growth or some seasons

4. Harvest in healthy places away from busy roads and polluted water

5. Keep the health of your resource in mind: harvest only 10% of each patch you find, and pass by small patches entirely

6. Ask permission before foraging on private land, and know the rules about foraging on public lands

7. When you try a new wild edible, always eat it in moderation

TOP TEN WILD FOODS

I thought it would be a good idea to start this book by focusing on a limited number of plants, and branching out from there. The ten plants I've chosen for this chapter are often among the first learned by foragers in the Upper Midwest. All of these plants are easy to identify, and are found in most—or all—of our region. They can be safely and sustainably harvested, as long as you follow good identification practices and pay attention to the guidelines in the text. Seasons of harvest range from early spring to late fall, so there is something here for most of the year. Best of all, these foods can be used to make some exciting and delicious dishes. (Species are listed here in the approximate order of harvest, starting with spring, but note that some plants can be harvested across several seasons.)

In addition to basic information about each species, I've included a range map showing plant distribution. As discussed on page 16, these range maps are an approximate guide, intending to show the general areas where the plant might be found. Remember that the habitat must be correct for each species; just because the maps say that asparagus, for example, can be found throughout the area does not mean that asparagus will be growing in every spot you look. Furthermore, even if the habitat is correct, you won't find the plant you're looking for in every spot you check. That's just the way it is with foraging; sometimes, a spot looks perfect for a plant, yet none are to be found.

Finally, each of these Top Ten species accounts include ten recipes for making delicious dishes from your harvest. That's 100 reasons to get out into the woods or fields, so head out there and start enjoying the wild harvest.

Ramps (Wild Leeks) *(Allium tricoccum)*

Although ramp bulbs can be harvested throughout the growing season, spring is the best time to begin your search for these premier wild vegetables. Both the bulb and the greens are used in the kitchen to add zest to any dish that could use a bit of onion-garlic-chive flavor.

HABITAT, RANGE

A native plant, the ramp grows throughout our region in moist, open hardwood forests, along streams and in river-bottoms, on hillsides with dappled shade and in shelterbelts and small woodlots. Ramps prefer moist, rich soil with a fair amount of shade.

Ramp range

PARTS USED

Leaves and "bulb" (underground swelling, not a true bulb)

SEASONS

Leaves, spring; bulb, spring through fall

IDENTIFICATION TIPS, DANGEROUS LOOKALIKES

Ramps are easy to identify in all seasons because of the underground growth and the unmistakable garlic-onion scent. Leaves are broad and smooth, with faint ribs that run from base to tip; the ones I pick are generally about 6 inches long and 2 inches wide at the midpoint, although this varies. Each plant typically has 3 leaves, although many have just 2. Leaves are bright green and a bit rubbery, and have an oniony smell when crushed. The

Freshly dug ramp

Developing flower stalks

Ramps in flower

Flowers gone to seed

leaves come directly from the ground, and are not on any sort of stem (this is important to identification); where the leaves enter the ground, they narrow down to a maroon neck.

If you dig the plant up, you will find that the maroon neck bulges out underground, turning into the white ramp "bulb", which ends in a cluster of hairs like a green onion. (Note that the ramp is not a true bulb but rather a swelling at the base of the plant. However, this swelling is commonly referred to as a "bulb".) Ramps are generally more bulbous than green onions, which tend to be relatively straight. In spring, you'll see other plants such as lilies that have leaves resembling those of ramps; however, none of those plants have the characteristic oniony-garlicky-smelling bulb beneath, and most have stems. Lilies are poisonous, so be certain that the plant has the oniony-garlicky-smelling leaves and bulb before harvesting.

During summer and fall, the ramp loses its leaves and sports a flowering head that resembles those of a number of the other wild onion species. However, most wild onions have purple or pink flowers, making them easy to distinguish from ramps, which have white flowers. Also, most of the other wild onions don't grow in our region. The nodding onion *(A. cernuum)* is somewhat common here, and its flower resembles a ramp flower (although it tends to appear more pinkish when the flowers are fully open); unlike the ramp, however, the nodding onion retains its leaves during flowering. The nodding onion grows taller, and the individual flowering stems are bent back at the top like a shepherd's crook. Most onions, including the nodding onion, have leaves that are narrow and sword-like, in contrast to the broad, soft leaves of the ramp, providing another clue to identity.

One of the most dangerous plants out there is the death camass *(Zigadenus venenosus)*. It resembles a wild onion, with thin leaves and a similar flowering head, so if you find something that you think is a wild onion, be very careful with identification. Death camass do not have the oniony smell. They are generally found in the West rather than the upper Midwest; in our region, they are listed in the USDA Plants Database only in the Dakotas.

HARVESTING TIPS

Ramps can be overharvested; if you find a small patch, take just a few or pass it by entirely. Happily, ramps often grow in large patches; judicious harvesting will not harm the resource.

The greens can be harvested by themselves, leaving the bulb in the ground. It's best to snip just one leaf from each plant, leaving the others to help the bulb grow. If you're after the bulbs (which is generally the case), a dandelion digger is the perfect tool. Push it into the ground next to the ramp, and work it several inches under the soil as you pull gently on the neck of the plant. With luck, the entire bulb will come free; if you've put the dandelion digger in the ground too close to the bulb or at too sharp of an angle, you will end up with a severed bulb (don't worry, you'll get better with practice). However you do it, don't disturb the soil any more than necessary. To avoid overharvesting, take only one bulb from each small cluster of plants, then move on to the next cluster.

MORE ABOUT RAMPS: Ramps are one of the first green vegetables to emerge in our area in early spring. I can easily imagine what a welcome sight they were to native peoples and even to pioneers, who had been surviving on dried or preserved foods throughout the long winter. Perhaps this is why ramp leaves are known as a spring tonic, said to wake up the blood; as the earth was awakening, the first foods it offered were used to awaken the body.

In more recent times, hillfolk and country people have used ramps as both food and medicine; ramps are said to keep away colds and flu. There may be something to this; according to a study published in *Economic Botany* (Zennie and Ogzewalla, Volume 31), ramp leaves have a good amount of ascorbic acid, which is a precursor to vitamin C—a well-known home remedy for colds and flu. Research is also being conducted by Dr. Philip Whanger at Oregon State University to study the possible role of selenium in ramps as a cancer-fighting ally.

Ramps are easy to spot in the spring; they're one of the few green plants poking through the dead brown leaves. The underground bulbs are small at the beginning of the season, so I usually let them grow a bit before digging. Harvesting season for bulbs with greens lasts about a month. The plant sends up a slender, pointed maroon shoot as the season progresses; at this point, the leaves begin to split and fray, eventually disappearing entirely. The shoot turns into a rigid stem, 8 to 12 inches tall, that is topped with an umbrella-like white flower. Soon, the flower petals drop and give way to a cluster of hard berries arranged in umbrella-like fashion. In summer, ramps are difficult to find because this flowering stalk is inconspicuous; the best advice I have is to remember where you got ramps in the spring, and look in the same location during the summer months, until you learn to spot the flowering cluster.

Although hardy souls eat ramps raw, I find that ramps are best when cooked. A few chopped ramps added to a dish add a delightful garlic-onion flavor and aroma. To extend the season, ramp bulbs can be pickled (page 31). Ramp leaves freeze well; simply blanch for a minute in boiling water, then drain, cool and pack into freezer containers or plastic freezer bags.

JUST FOR FUN
Ramp Festivals
If you're down in the South during ramp season, you would enjoy attending one of the numerous ramp festivals that take place. I've seen listings for festivals in North Carolina,

Tennessee, Virginia and West Virginia, generally in late April or early May. Typically a weekend event, these festivals feature cookoffs, recipe sampling and lots of fun activities. For more information, do an internet search for "ramp festival," or contact the local Chamber of Commerce for the city you'll be visiting.

QUICK IDEAS FOR USING RAMPS
- Substitute ramps in any recipe you have for domestic leeks.
- Add a few chopped ramps to scrambled eggs or a skillet of fried potatoes as you're cooking.
- Chopped ramps make an interesting addition to stir-fry dishes and soups.
- Some people sprinkle the flowers over a salad to add a sharp, oniony flavor.

OTHER RECIPES IN THIS BOOK FEATURING RAMPS
- Fiddleheads Sautéed with Ramps (page 39)
- As an option in Wilted Dandelion Greens Salad (page 51)
- Simple Morel Pizza (page 62)
- Grilled Springtime Vegetables with Pasta (page 74)
- Spaghetti with Ramp Leaves and Sunflower Nuts (page 293)
- Homemade Wild Greens Pasta (page 309)
- Nettle and Potato Chowder (page 316)

Candied Ramps

6 servings   Preparation: Under 30 minutes

This unusual accompaniment makes a nice addition to a snack tray or a composed salad. They go particularly well with smoked salmon or any grilled meats. If you've refrigerated the candied ramps for storage, be sure to bring them to room temperature before serving or they will be very stiff and may be impossible to separate (they are very sticky).

2 tablespoons honey	A generous pinch of powdered saffron,
1 tablespoon balsamic-style vinegar	optional
1 tablespoon apple juice or orange juice	1 cup ramp bulbs with neck,* roots trimmed

In small heavy-bottomed saucepan, combine honey, vinegar, juice and saffron over medium-low heat, stirring constantly, until smooth and well blended. Add ramps. Adjust heat so mixture is just simmering. Cook for 15 minutes, stirring occasionally; keep an eye on the heat to be sure the honey doesn't burn. After 15 minutes, remove from heat and cool. Serve at room temperature.

*Cut off the bulbs at the point where the maroon neck begins to branch out into the leaves.

Cheddar-Mashed Potatoes with Frizzled Ramps

4 servings   Preparation: Under an hour

I discovered "frizzled ramps" by accident when I left a pan of sliced ramps on the burner a bit too long. I was distressed to see they had turned golden brown, since many members of the onion family turn bitter if cooked to this state. Happily, the ramps weren't bitter at all; in fact, the taste and texture were fabulous! The ramps would also make a great topping for cooked vegetables, casseroles or grilled meats.

1½ to 2 pounds russet potatoes (about 2 medium)	1 tablespoon butter
	¼ to ½ cup milk
12 ramp bulbs (about 3 ounces), roots trimmed	⅓ cup shredded cheddar cheese
	Salt and pepper

Heat large saucepan of water to boiling. Add potatoes, scrubbed but not peeled, and cook until tender, about 25 minutes. Meanwhile, cut each ramp in half lengthwise. Place halves cut-side down on cutting board, then cut into thin slivers lengthwise. Melt butter in heavy-bottomed small skillet over medium heat, and add ramps. Cook, stirring frequently, until ramps are rich golden and crispy, 7 to 10 minutes; be careful that the ramps don't burn. Set aside and keep warm.

Drain and peel potatoes. Mash coarsely with potato masher. Add milk as needed and mash together until desired consistency. Stir in cheese, and salt and pepper to taste. Serve potatoes with ramps, letting each diner place a spoonful of ramps on top of their potatoes.

Tangy Shrimp and Ramp Sauté

2 servings; easily increased   Preparation: Under 30 minutes

When cleaning ramps for this dish, leave most of the maroon neck of the ramp attached to the white bulb. Use the greens for another dish.

1 tablespoon olive oil	½ teaspoon hot red pepper flakes
½ cup ramp bulbs, roots trimmed	½ teaspoon salt
2 bay leaves	¼ teaspoon coarsely ground black pepper
12 ounces peeled and deveined raw shrimp	½ cup dry sherry or dry white wine
1 teaspoon dried oregano	2 tablespoons lemon juice

In medium skillet, heat oil over medium heat until warm. Add ramps and bay leaves. Cook, stirring occasionally, until ramps are tender and golden, about 10 minutes. Meanwhile, sprinkle shrimp with oregano, pepper flakes, salt and pepper; toss to coat and set aside.

When ramps are tender, pull out and discard bay leaves; add shrimp to skillet. Cook until outsides of shrimp turn pink, stirring once or twice to turn shrimp. Add wine and lemon juice to skillet. Cook, stirring occasionally, until shrimp are cooked through and wine has reduced somewhat; this should take 5 to 10 minutes. Serve immediately.

Ramp Custards

4 servings   Preparation: About an hour

Serve these for a special brunch. For an interesting first course or light entrée, serve the custards on top of sautéed spinach or wild greens that have been tossed with a little balsamic vinegar.

½ cup sliced ramp bulbs (measured after slicing; 20 to 30)

1 tablespoon butter

3 eggs

1 cup milk or half-and-half

2 tablespoons grated Parmesan cheese

½ teaspoon salt

A pinch of nutmeg

5 or 6 drops of Tabasco sauce

Heat oven to 325°F. Spray 4 cups of a popover pan generously with nonstick spray; set aside. In medium skillet, cook sliced ramps in butter over medium-low heat for about 5 minutes, or until lightly colored and tender, stirring occasionally. Remove from heat and set aside to cool slightly. Heat a saucepan of water to boiling; reduce heat slightly and keep at a near-boil until needed in the next step.

In mixing bowl, beat together the eggs, milk, Parmesan, salt, nutmeg and Tabasco sauce. Divide ramps evenly between the 4 prepared popover cups. Place popover pan in baking dish large enough to hold it, then divide the egg mixture evenly among the 4 cups. Return the water to boiling. Set baking dish, with filled popover pan, on oven rack; pour boiling water into the dish to come halfway up the popover cups. Carefully slide the rack into the oven and bake for 30 minutes, or until firmly set.

Place large, thick towel on worksurface. When custards have set, lift popover pan out of the dish of hot water and set it on the towel to dry off and firm up for 5 minutes; turn off oven and let dish of hot water remain in oven until cool enough to remove safely, which can be after the meal (no hurry). After 5 minutes, run table knife around the edges of popover cups to loosen custards. Place baking sheet upside-down over popover pan, then carefully turn baking sheet and popover pan upside-down together so custards fall out onto baking sheet. Be sure to hold the two pans together tightly with potholders or oven mitts while you're flipping them over!

Pan-Fried Walleye with Morel-Ramp Sauce

2 servings; easily increased   Preparation: Under 30 minutes

Flour mixture:
⅓ cup all-purpose flour
2 tablespoons corn meal
½ teaspoon salt
½ teaspoon paprika
½ teaspoon onion powder
¼ teaspoon garlic powder, optional

4 to 6 whole ramps, roots trimmed
3 tablespoons butter (approximate),
  divided
1½ cups coarsely cut-up morels
1 cup half-and-half or evaporated skim milk
Fillets from 1 eating-sized walleye, skin
  and rib bones removed
Salt and pepper

Combine flour-mixture ingredients in plastic food-storage bag; shake well and set aside. Trim and discard root end from ramps. Cut ramp bulbs into ⅛-inch-thick slices; cut greens into ½-inch-wide strips. In saucepan or skillet, melt about 2 teaspoons of the butter over medium heat. Add ramps and sauté for a few minutes. Add morels, and continue cooking until mushrooms are just tender. Push the mushrooms to the side of the pan, and sprinkle 2 teaspoons of the flour mixture into the juices, stirring constantly to prevent lumps. Cook for about a minute, stirring frequently. Add half-and-half to morel mixture. Adjust heat so mixture bubbles very gently and allow to cook while you prepare the fish. Be sure to stir the sauce occasionally while you are cooking the fish.

Shake the damp fish fillets in the flour mixture. Melt 1 tablespoon of the butter in a heavy-bottomed skillet over medium-high heat. Shake excess flour from walleye fillets and add fillets to skillet. Reduce heat slightly and cook until fish is rich golden brown on the bottom. If the skillet seems dry, add a bit more butter, then turn fillets and cook until fish is just done. Sprinkle with salt and pepper to taste. Spoon sauce over fish.

Ramp Flatbread

2 flatbreads (2 or 3 servings each)   Preparation: Under an hour

Ready-made pizza crust dough, found with the tubes of biscuits in the refrigerator case, makes this flatbread easy and quick. It's great paired with soup or a big salad for a tasty lunch.

1 cup minced ramps* (10 to 15 medium)
1 tablespoon olive oil or vegetable oil
1 teaspoon dried marjoram or thyme
1 tube (10 ounces) refrigerated pizza crust
  dough†

¼ cup grated Parmesan cheese
1 egg white, lightly beaten
Sesame seeds, poppy seeds, or coarse salt
  and mixed herbs for garnish

Heat oven to 400°F. Lightly grease baking sheet; set aside. In medium skillet, sauté ramps in oil over medium heat for about 5 minutes. Stir in marjoram; remove from heat and set aside to cool.

On floured surface, unroll dough; roll out slightly to 10 x 12-inch rectangle. Spread cooled ramps evenly over dough, keeping 1 inch away from edges; sprinkle Parmesan cheese over ramps. Starting with wide edge, roll dough up, jelly-roll style. Cut roll in half. Pinch all ends and seams very thoroughly. Roll each half into flat rectangle, about 6 x 9 inches (the dough may burst if you roll too aggressively; if it does, pat back together as best you can and don't worry about it too much). Place flatbreads on prepared baking sheet. Brush with egg white and sprinkle with sesame seeds or other garnish. Bake until golden brown, about 20 minutes. Serve warm or at room temperature.

*Use whole ramps—bulbs and greens—for a more mild ramp flavor. For a stronger flavor, use just half of the greens; for the strongest flavor, use bulbs only (in which case you'll need at least double the count of ramps).

†You can also use homemade pizza crust. Prepare as you would for a regular thin-crust pizza; don't use too much yeast, or the dough will be too springy and hard to handle. Once you have punched the dough down, flatten it slightly and let it rest for 5 to 10 minutes; this makes it easier to handle.

Carrot and Ramp Salad with Indian Flavors

2 or 3 servings; easily increased   Preparation: Under 15 minutes

This simple dish has plenty of flavor, and makes a delicious side salad or accompaniment to roasted meats.

3 or 4 whole ramps	2 carrots, peeled and coarsely shredded
1 tablespoon peanut oil or olive oil	¼ teaspoon salt
1 teaspoon whole brown or yellow mustard seeds	⅛ teaspoon ground cumin
	⅛ teaspoon cayenne pepper

Trim and discard root ends from ramps. Cut ramp bulbs from greens, including the maroon neck with the bulbs. Slice bulbs vertically into slivers; slice leaves across their width into ⅛-inch-thick strips (keep bulbs separate from greens). Heat oil in medium sauté pan or skillet over medium-high heat. Add mustard seeds. When they begin to pop and jump (usually 10 to 30 seconds), add carrots and ramp bulbs. Cook for about 2 minutes, stirring frequently. Stir in ramp leaves, salt, cumin and cayenne; cook for 1 minute longer. Remove from heat and set aside until cooled to room temperature. Serve at room temperature.

Variation: Carrot and Ramp Raita
Use this as a condiment with spicy curries, or add to pita sandwiches. Prepare as directed above; when mixture has cooled to room temperature, stir in 1 cup plain yogurt. Serve immediately, or refrigerate and serve chilled. Makes 4 servings.

White Bean Salad with Ramps

3 or 4 servings   Preparation: Under 15 minutes, plus 2 hours standing time

8 whole medium-sized ramps, roots
 trimmed
2 tablespoons extra-virgin olive oil
¼ teaspoon salt
¼ teaspoon coarsely ground black pepper

1 can (15 ounces) white cannellini beans,
 drained and rinsed; or 1½ cups cooked
 and cooled
3 tablespoons finely diced red bell pepper
Shaved Parmesan cheese and lemon wedges
 for serving, optional

Thinly slice white bulbs and most of the red stems of the ramps; you should have about 2 table-spoons. Place in small mixing bowl; set aside. Slice the ramp greens across the leaves into ½-inch-wide strips. Heat oil in small skillet over medium heat; add ramp greens and cook, stirring frequently, for 1 minute. Stir in salt and pepper. Transfer greens and oil to bowl with sliced ramp bulbs; stir to mix. Add beans and red bell pepper; stir again. Cover and let stand at room temperature for several hours; if it will be more than several hours before serving time, refrigerate the beans, but take them out an hour before serving to allow them to come to room temperature. Garnish with shaved Parmesan cheese, and let each person squeeze a lemon wedge over their portion.

Pesto with Basil and Ramp Leaves

3 or 4 servings   Preparation: Under 30 minutes

Traditional pesto is made with basil, garlic, Parmesan and pine nuts. This wild-influenced version uses ramp leaves in place of the garlic and some of the basil. For a less traditional but equally good version, eliminate the basil leaves entirely, using 1 full cup of ramp leaves.

8 ounces uncooked spaghetti, fettuccini or
 linguini
2 cubes of Parmesan or Romano cheese,
 each about 1 inch square
¼ cup pine nuts, hazelnuts or slivered
 almonds

¼ teaspoon salt
½ cup fresh basil leaves, packed down
½ cup ramp leaves, packed down
2 tablespoons fruity extra-virgin olive oil
Additional Parmesan or Romano cheese for
 serving

Heat a large pot of salted water to boiling. Add pasta and cook according to package directions. Meanwhile, turn on empty food processor (fitted with steel chopping blade). Drop the Parmesan chunks, 1 at a time, down the feed tube onto the spinning blade. Process until chopped to medium consistency. Add pine nuts and salt, and process until fine. Add basil and ramp leaves; pulse on-and-off until coarsely chopped. Turn processor on and add oil in a stream through feed tube; process until mixture is of porridge-like consistency, scraping workbowl once. If mixture is too thick, add up to a tablespoon of cold water and process until proper consistency. When pasta is cooked, drain and return to warm cooking pot. Add sauce and toss well. Serve with additional cheese; the best way is to use a drum grater, which allows each person to grate the desired amount of cheese onto their own serving.

Pickled Ramps

Per half-pint; make as much as you wish   Preparation: Involved

2 cups water
½ cup kosher or pickling salt
1 cup ramp bulbs with neck*
4 quarter-sized slices of fresh, peeled
    gingerroot
1-pint canning jar, with band and new lid

Pickling liquid:
½ cup white wine vinegar
½ cup water
½ cup sugar
1 teaspoon mustard seeds
1 bay leaf
1 dried hot red pepper

In nonreactive saucepan, combine water and salt, stirring to dissolve salt. Add ramps and gingerroot. Heat to boiling over high heat; reduce heat slightly and boil gently for 2 minutes. Remove from heat and set aside until cool. Transfer to ceramic or plastic bowl; cover and refrigerate for 2 days, stirring once or twice each day. The ramps may turn blue during this time; don't be concerned. Like all members of the garlic family, ramps contain sulfur compounds that can react with copper to form copper sulfate, a blue or blue-green compound. Tap water may contain enough copper to cause the reaction; impurities in the salt may also cause this reaction. The blue color will go away during the next step.

After 2 days, drain and discard brine. Sterilize jar and lid as directed on page 418. In nonreactive saucepan, combine pickling-liquid ingredients, stirring to dissolve sugar. Heat to boiling over high heat; boil gently for 2 minutes. Meanwhile, pack drained ramps into prepared jar. Pour hot pickling liquid over ramps, covering completely; for an attractive presentation, arrange bay leaf and hot pepper along the sides of the jar. Cap jar with sterilized lid. Refrigerate for at least 1 week, shaking occasionally, before using; the ramps will turn a lovely pink shade during pickling.

Note: After the ramps have been eaten, use the pickling liquid to make a batch of refrigerator pickles. Slice cucumbers about ⅛ inch thick. Sprinkle with salt; let stand for 30 minutes. Rinse with cold water and drain well, then add to the jar of pickling liquid. Refrigerate for a week before enjoying.

*Cut off the bulbs at the point where the maroon neck begins to branch out into the leaves; trim off and discard the root ends. Save the leaves to use for seasoning another dish.

Fiddlehead Ferns (various)

One of the first wild vegetables to appear in the spring, fiddlehead ferns can be prepared much like asparagus. Blanch them in boiling water for 5 to 10 minutes before serving or using in other recipes, to remove any bitterness or possible stomach-irritating compounds.

HABITAT, RANGE, SPECIES

Ostrich ferns *(Matteuccia struthiopteris)* grow throughout most of our region (with the exception of the Dakotas), in moist hardwood forests and river bottoms, along streams and rivers, and at the edges of swamps. Bracken fern *(Pteridium aquilinum)*, also called brake, is found in the same habitats, as well as areas that are more dry and sunny such as pasture edges and woodland clearings, and in open fields or sparse woods with sandy soil. Bracken fern is the most prolific of wild ferns, and grows throughout our entire area (and, indeed, throughout much of the world). Lady ferns *(Athyrium filix-femina)*, while somewhat less common, grow in the same areas as ostrich ferns, often side by side.

Ostrich fern and lady fern range

Bracken fern range

PARTS USED

Young coiled frond and stem (fiddlehead); cooked

SEASONS

Spring

Ostrich ferns

Bracken ferns

Lady ferns

Ostrich ferns

Grooved stem

IDENTIFICATION TIPS, DANGEROUS LOOKALIKES

Ostrich ferns are the prime fiddlehead fern for eating, and the one that most people think of when the word "fiddlehead" is mentioned. As each individual frond emerges from the knobby brown cluster of roots that pokes above the ground, it is curled in a coil that resembles the head of a violin—hence the name "fiddlehead." As the frond matures, the fiddlehead uncoils and develops numerous opposing leaves, providing the characteristic lush, ferny appearance. Each knobby cluster produces numerous fronds, and each frond may grow at a different rate; so on a single knob, there may be fronds that are at the perfect stage for harvesting, as well as fronds that are too young and fronds that have opened and are too old for harvesting. The bottom portion of the stems is deeply grooved on the inner side, and the stems have a small number of flat brown scales on them.

Lady fern is similar in overall appearance to ostrich fern; however, the stems have numerous small brown stubs rather than scales. The easy way to remember how to identify this plant is that the stem "looks like a lady's legs in need of shaving" (crude, but easy to remember!). The stem is flat or lightly grooved, and often is reddish.

The inedible interrupted fern *(Osmunda claytoniana)* looks a good deal like ostrich fern, except that the frond growth is "interrupted" by a patch of much darker, coarser leaves; these interrupters are dark green in early spring, changing to brown as the season progresses. Mature interrupted ferns are very easy to distinguish, as this interrupted area is quite noticeable; it is a bit less noticeable at the fiddlehead stage when ostrich ferns are edible. One easy way to distinguish the young ostrich fern from the young interrupted fern is that the stem of the interrupted fern is D-shaped in cross section rather than grooved like the ostrich fern. Young fronds of the interrupted fern are also covered with pinkish wooly hairs, especially near the base;

Dark, coarse leaves

Interrupted ferns (inedible)

ostrich ferns have small brown scales, but no hairs. Interrupted fern is found in a line from Minnesota's Arrowhead region down through far eastern Iowa, all the way east to the Atlantic coast and as far south as Tennessee and North Carolina.

Bracken fern is easy to distinguish from other ferns. It has three branchlets atop a central naked stalk, making it look quite unlike the other ferns in the springtime. The "fiddlehead" of bracken is much less curled than that of the ostrich or other ferns; on the bracken fern, the top appears bent over or droopy rather than curled or coiled. In addition, bracken fern has a wooly outer covering on the young shoots.

Cinnamon fern *(Osmunda cinnamomea)* also has a wooly covering, but it is much heavier on the cinnamon fern than on the bracken fern when the plant is at the fiddlehead stage. The brownish white hairs on the cinnamon-fern fiddleheads are so thick that it would be hard to imagine mistaking this plant for another fiddlehead; in addition, each cinnamon fern frond has just a single stalk, unlike the triple branching of the bracken fern. Cinnamon ferns look like an extremely wooly ostrich fern with a brownish cast (hence the name). Cinnamon ferns are considered inedible.

Cinnamon ferns (inedible)

There are many other ferns out there; these are just a few, and the three noted are the only ones that I know are edible. Be sure to consult a reliable field guide to become comfortable identifying ferns.

HARVESTING TIPS

Bracken fern is hard to over-harvest, as it grows from a widespread system of roots. Ostrich fern and lady fern are more sensitive; don't pick an area more than twice in a season, and then only if it is a well-established patch. Take a frond from each clump and move on; don't cut down an entire clump.

Pick ostrich fern when it is still tightly coiled; generally, the frond will be less than 8 inches tall at the peak of edibility. The entire stem is edible at this stage, not just the coiled head. If you're picking bracken fern, remember that it is edible as long as the tops have not leafed out and the stem still snaps easily. The base of the frond may be too tough to snap on a maturing plant; simply snap off the tender part when collecting.

SPECIAL CONSIDERATIONS

Please see below for a discussion of possible problems associated with eating fiddlehead ferns.

MORE ABOUT FIDDLEHEADS: Without a doubt, fiddleheads are the most controversial food covered in this book. Until fairly recently, bracken fern and ostrich fern were considered completely edible in both the raw and cooked stages, and most wild-foods books still contain this information. However, there have been reports of problems with both species eaten raw or lightly cooked that encourage a certain amount of caution—at the least, there are things to consider before eating certain fiddleheads.

Bracken fern has been widely consumed for centuries in many parts of the world, particularly in Japan. It's often available, both fresh and canned, in Asian markets here in the

United States, attesting to its popularity. However, it should be noted that over the years, there have been numerous incidents of livestock being poisoned by eating mature bracken fern. More recently, bracken fern has been questioned as a possible carcinogen. The International Agency for Research of Cancer (a branch of the World Health organization) states that there is "inadequate evidence for the carcinogenicity of bracken fern to humans." Many wild foods are safe to consume at one time of year, but toxic at another, and many foragers believe that the danger posed by bracken fern is no more severe than that from common foods such as bacon and grilled meats, which have also been implicated as possible carcinogens. Bracken fern is bound to be a fairly small part of the diet of any forager; and unlike livestock, we don't eat the plant when it is mature. The choice of whether to eat bracken fern in the springtime, or not to eat it, is a highly personal one.

Ostrich fern fiddleheads have long been considered a prime wild vegetable. But in the 1990s, a rash of food poisoning broke out that was associated with the consumption of lightly cooked ostrich fern fiddleheads. According to information from the Population and Public Health Branch (PPHB) of the Canadian government, more than 60 people became ill in 1999 after eating ostrich ferns gathered in Quebec; similar outbreaks had occurred in New York and British Columbia in 1994. After these incidents, the PPHB put out a recommendation that all fiddleheads be well-cooked prior to eating, as the problems appeared to be associated with lightly cooked fiddleheads.

While the exact cause of these outbreaks is unknown, the PPHB speculated that it may have been due to the particularly dry and warm spring, which may have increased the level of toxins that occur naturally in the plants. Others suggest that the outbreaks were caused by the accidental harvest of inedible interrupted fern, as the symptoms ascribed to the toxic fiddleheads in Canada appear to match those reported by some who have eaten interrupted ferns.

In any event, the solution seems to be simple: cook fiddlehead ferns before eating them, and if they taste extremely bitter, don't eat them at all. Also, do not re-use the water in which the fiddleheads were boiled; it is bitter and may contain compounds which may be the cause of the problems associated with eating lightly cooked fiddleheads. This applies to all three of the species discussed here—ostrich, bracken and lady fern. It's also a good idea to rub off the brown scales from ostrich ferns before cooking; some of the bitterness seems to come from these scales, so the fiddleheads will taste better without them.

By now, you may be wondering why anyone would even want to harvest and eat these ferns. The reason is that they are delicious; they're also one of the very first green vegetables to come up in the woods each spring. It's easy to imagine what a welcome sight the first fiddleheads of spring were to native peoples and early settlers, who had not had a fresh vegetable for many months. Fiddleheads are a delightful sight in the spring, poking through the brown leaves and chaff on the forest floor. Along with ramps and morels, they represent the best of the springtime harvest.

Fiddleheads can be canned by following the procedure given in canning manuals for asparagus. I prefer to freeze any excess I have; I think the texture is better than canned. Freezing is easy; simply boil or steam fiddleheads for 10 minutes, then drain, cool and pack into tightly sealing freezer containers. If you're using frozen fiddleheads in the recipes in this book, remember that they have already been boiled, so they don't need the preliminary boiling that is called for in the recipes.

QUICK IDEAS FOR USING FIDDLEHEADS
- Boil or steam ostrich-fern fiddleheads for 10 minutes (5 minutes for thinner bracken fern or lady fern), then drain and serve with butter, salt and pepper. I like to sauté the drained fiddleheads for a few minutes in butter with a little garlic.
- Add boiled, drained fiddleheads to soup, stew or pasta dishes.
- Chop up boiled, drained fiddleheads to add to salads or scrambled eggs.
- Substitute boiled fiddleheads for asparagus in any recipe.

OTHER RECIPES IN THIS BOOK FEATURING FIDDLEHEADS
- Grilled Springtime Vegetables with Pasta (page 74)

Danny's Favorite Fiddlers

Per 2 servings; make as much as you wish　　　　　Preparation: Under 15 minutes

This simple side dish is named after a video photographer who got his first taste of fiddleheads during a wild-foods shoot we were doing. The Asian-style dressing given below is excellent with the fiddleheads; however, feel free to substitute any Italian- or French-style vinaigrette (you'll need about 3 tablespoons dressing per cup of fiddleheads).

Asian-style dressing:
2 tablespoons soy sauce
2 teaspoons sesame oil
2 teaspoons rice vinegar, optional
1 teaspoon sugar
1 teaspoon sesame seeds
A good pinch of cayenne pepper

1 cup ostrich fern coils, or a bit more, scales rubbed off

Combine all dressing ingredients in a bowl or small container; mix well. This can be done earlier in the day; store the mixture at room temperature. If you want to prepare the dressing further in advance, leave the sesame seeds out until you're ready to serve.

Heat a large pot of salted water to boiling. Add fiddleheads. Return to a gentle boil, and cook for 10 minutes. Drain and refresh immediately with lots of cold water. In mixing bowl, combine well-drained fiddleheads and dressing, stirring to coat. Let stand for at least 10 minutes, or as long as an hour, before serving. This should be served at room temperature.

Easy Fiddlehead Gratin

4 servings　　　　　Preparation: Under an hour

2½ to 3 cups ostrich fern coils and stems (stems cut into 1-inch lengths), scales rubbed off
2 tablespoons cream

¼ cup seasoned breadcrumbs
¼ cup grated Parmesan cheese
1 tablespoon butter, cut into small chunks

Heat oven to 350°F. Spray a small casserole with nonstick spray; set aside. Heat a large pot of salted water to boiling. Add fiddleheads. Return to a gentle boil, and cook for 10 minutes. Drain and refresh immediately with lots of cold water. In mixing bowl, toss drained fiddleheads with cream; transfer to prepared casserole dish. In another bowl, combine breadcrumbs, Parmesan cheese and butter. Rub the mixture together with your fingers (or a pastry blender, if you have one) until the butter is in small bits and fairly well mixed with the crumbs and cheese. Sprinkle the crumb mixture evenly over the fiddleheads. Bake for 20 minutes; for a nice finish, place under the broiler for a few minutes to brown up the topping.

Fiddlehead Pie

2 or 3 main-dish servings; 6 as a side dish   Preparation: About an hour

2 cups fiddlehead fern coils, scales rubbed
   off if using ostrich ferns
½ cup chopped onion
1 cup shredded Gruyère cheese or similar
3 eggs, or ¾ cup liquid egg substitute
1 cup whole milk, light cream or evaporated
   skim milk

¾ cup buttermilk baking mix such as
   Bisquick (reduced-fat works fine)
¼ teaspoon salt
⅛ teaspoon pepper
A good pinch of cayenne pepper or a few
   drops of Tabasco sauce, optional

Heat oven to 400°F. Spray a standard pie plate with nonstick spray; set aside. Heat a large pot of salted water to boiling. Add fiddleheads. Return to a gentle boil, and cook for 10 minutes (5 minutes if using thinner lady fern or bracken fern). Drain and refresh immediately with lots of cold water.

Sprinkle onion in bottom of prepared pie plate. Arrange drained fiddleheads over onion. Sprinkle evenly with shredded cheese. In blender, combine remaining ingredients; process until smooth, about 15 seconds (alternately, combine in mixing bowl and beat for about a minute with whisk or hand beater). Pour mixture evenly over ingredients in pie plate. Bake until top is rich golden brown and egg mixture is cooked through, about 35 minutes; a knife inserted in the center should have no liquid egg on it. Cool 5 minutes before cutting into wedges.

Variation: Asparagus Pie
Substitute 2 cups cut-up asparagus (1-inch pieces) for the fiddleheads. Cook in boiling water for about 2 minutes. Drain, refresh in cold water, and proceed as directed.

Fiddleheads Sautéed with Ramps

2 servings; easily increased   Preparation: Under 30 minutes

1 to 1½ cups ostrich fern coils and stems
    (stems cut into 1-inch lengths), scales
    rubbed off

3 to 5 whole ramps, depending on size
1½ teaspoons butter
Salt and pepper

Heat a saucepan of salted water to boiling. Add fiddleheads. Return to boiling; cook for 10 minutes. Drain and immediately refresh with cold running water; drain well and pat dry with paper towels. This may be done several hours in advance; refrigerate until final cooking if you prepare them more than 20 minutes ahead of time.

When you're ready for final cooking, trim and discard roots from ramp bulbs. Chop white bulbs and maroon stems of ramps; slice green ramp leaves into thin strips. Melt butter in medium skillet over medium heat. Add all parts of the ramps; sauté for about 5 minutes. Add prepared fiddleheads; sauté for about 5 minutes longer. Salt and pepper to taste before serving.

Open-Faced Fiddler Sandwiches

4 servings   Preparation: Under 30 minutes

2 teaspoons butter or margarine, softened
4 slices from large loaf of hearty Italian or
    French bread*
1 cup finely diced ham or smoked turkey
    (about 6 ounces)
3 tablespoons mayonnaise (reduced-fat
    works fine)

1 teaspoon dry mustard powder
¼ teaspoon dried thyme
A few drops of Tabasco sauce
12 to 16 fiddlehead fern coils, scales
    rubbed off if using ostrich fern
4 slices Swiss cheese

Heat oven to 425°F. Spread ½ teaspoon butter over 1 side of each bread slice; arrange in single layer in 9 x 13-inch baking dish, buttered side up. Bake until bread is golden brown, about 5 minutes. While bread is baking, combine ham, mayonnaise, mustard, thyme and Tabasco in mixing bowl; stir well.

When bread is nicely colored, remove from oven and set aside until cool enough to remove from baking dish. Meanwhile, heat a saucepan of salted water to boiling. Add fiddleheads. Return to boiling; cook for 10 minutes. Drain and immediately refresh with cold running water; drain well and pat dry with paper towels. Spread ham mixture evenly over toasted bread, returning to baking dish. Arrange 3 or 4 fiddleheads on each piece of bread. Top each with a slice of cheese. Return dish to oven and bake for about 5 minutes, or until cheese melts. Serve hot.

*Each slice should be about an inch thick, and roughly 4 x 5 inches. Slice the loaf at a diagonal to get larger slices if necessary. If you can't find bread this large, use 2 smaller slices per serving.

Eggs Benedict à la Fiddler

4 servings

12 to 16 fiddlehead fern coils, scales
    rubbed off if using ostrich fern
1 recipe Blender Hollandaise (page 73),
    kept warm
3 tablespoons butter or margarine,
    approximate

4 thin slices ham or Canadian bacon
4 crumpets or split English muffins
4 eggs

Heat oven to 250°F. Heat saucepan of salted water to boiling. Add fiddleheads and cook for 10 minutes if fresh; if previously frozen, they'll only need to cook for about 1 minute, just enough to warm them up, so don't put them in the water until you're almost ready to serve.

While fiddleheads are cooking, make Blender Hollandaise; keep warm by placing blender jar in a pan of hot water. Melt a little butter in medium skillet; and ham and cook until warmed through, turning once. Transfer ham slices to small dish; place in oven. By now, the fiddleheads should be cooked; remove saucepan from heat and set aside. Toast crumpets; spread with butter and place in oven.

Melt a little more butter in same skillet used to fry ham, and fry eggs over-easy; or poach eggs in saucepan of boiling water if you prefer. While eggs are cooking, drain fiddleheads and pat dry with paper towels. Working quickly, place 1 crumpet, or the bottom half of an English muffin, on individual plate. Top each with a slice of ham. Gently place fried or poached egg on each piece of ham; arrange 3 or 4 fiddleheads over egg. Divide sauce evenly between plates; if using English muffins, place muffin top alongside topped muffin. Serve immediately.

Stream Trout with Fiddleheads

2 servings   Preparation: Under 30 minutes

Pack the ingredients for this simple streamside feast when you're going after trout during the spring fiddlehead season.

<u>Cornmeal breading</u>:
¾ cup all-purpose flour
¼ cup yellow cornmeal
2 teaspoons paprika
½ teaspoon salt

1 cup fiddlehead fern coils and stems
    (stems cut into 1-inch pieces), scales
    rubbed off if using ostrich ferns
2 tablespoons butter
2 whole trout (about 1 pound each),
    gutted and gilled
Juice from 1 lemon
Salt and pepper

Combine breading ingredients in plastic bag; shake to mix. Heat saucepan of salted water to boiling. Add fiddleheads and stems. Cook for 10 minutes (5 minutes if using thinner lady fern or bracken fern). Drain and refresh in cold water (if you're streamside, just drain them and set aside).

In skillet large enough to hold the trout comfortably, melt butter over medium heat. When butter stops foaming, add trout to bag with breading; shake gently to coat. Add trout to skillet; cook until golden brown on both sides. Push trout to side of skillet. Add drained fiddleheads and lemon juice. Cook for about 5 minutes, spooning juices over fiddleheads and trout. Check trout for doneness; when flesh is just opaque, it is cooked through. Serve trout and fiddleheads with pan juices poured over; each person can add salt and pepper to taste.

Grilled Fiddleheads

3 or 4 servings   Preparation: Under 30 minutes

For this dish, you'll need a special grilling wok (a square-bottomed pan with 2-inch-high sides; the metal is perforated overall with ¼-inch holes) or vegetable grilling basket. Prepare it when you've got the grill going for another dish; it goes really well with grilled chicken or steak.

2 cups ostrich fern coils, scales rubbed off
Half of a medium onion, cut from top to
    bottom into ¼-inch strips

3 garlic cloves, cut into thick slices
2 teaspoons olive oil
Salt and pepper

Prepare grill. Boil fiddleheads in a saucepan of salted water for 10 minutes. Drain and immediately refresh with cold running water; drain well and pat dry with paper towels. Combine in mixing bowl with onion, garlic, oil, and salt and pepper to taste; toss to coat.

Place grilling wok or vegetable basket on grate over hot coals. Add fiddlehead mixture; cover grill immediately to avoid flare-ups from oil. Cook for 8 to 10 minutes, stirring every few minutes with wooden spoon; fiddleheads and onions should be nicely browned. Serve hot or warm.

Fiddlehead and Tomato Rarebit on Toast

2 or 3 servings; easily increased   Preparation: Under 30 minutes

Serve this for a delicious lunch or light supper; all it needs to accompany it is a green salad. A glass of crisp white wine would be welcome with this dish.

1 cup ostrich fern coils and stems (stems cut into 1-inch pieces), scales rubbed off
2 or 3 large slices hearty bread, or double the amount of regular-sized bread
2 tablespoons butter or margarine
2 tablespoons flour
1 cup flat beer

½ teaspoon salt
¼ teaspoon Tabasco sauce
2 cups (8 ounces) grated sharp cheddar cheese
1 tomato, thinly sliced (preferably peeled before slicing)

Heat a saucepan of salted water to boiling. Add fiddleheads. Return to boiling; cook for 10 minutes. Drain and immediately refresh with cold running water; drain well and set aside. Toast the bread and keep it warm.

In heavy-bottomed saucepan, melt butter over medium heat until foamy. Whisk in flour and cook, whisking constantly, for about 2 minutes; mixture should be rich golden brown and have a nutty smell. Whisk in beer, salt and Tabasco sauce; cook, whisking frequently, until mixture thickens and bubbles. Reduce heat to low and add cheese. Cook, stirring constantly, until cheese melts and sauce is smooth.

Working quickly, place toast on serving plates; top with tomato slices. Top tomato with drained fiddleheads. Spoon cheese sauce evenly over fiddleheads; serve immediately.

Fiddlehead Stir-Fry

4 servings   Preparation: Under 30 minutes

With the hoisin-based sauce, the chopped garlic and hot peppers, and the peanuts, this dish is somewhat reminiscent of the classic Chinese dish, Kung Pao Chicken… without the chicken, of course!

2 cups fresh ostrich fern coils, scales
   rubbed off
2 tablespoons hoisin sauce*
1 tablespoon Chinese bean sauce*
2 teaspoons seasoned rice vinegar
2 teaspoons peanut oil or canola oil
2 medium carrots, peeled and sliced about
   $3/16$ inch thick
Half of a red bell pepper, cut into
   1 x $3/8$-inch strips

1 teaspoon minced garlic
$1/2$ teaspoon minced fresh gingerroot ($1 1/2$
   teaspoons if using wild gingerroot)
$1/4$ to $1/2$ teaspoon hot red pepper flakes
2 tablespoons sherry
$1/4$ cup unsalted dry-roasted peanuts
Hot cooked rice

Heat a large pot of salted water to boiling. Add fiddleheads. Return to boiling; cook for 5 minutes. Drain and refresh under cold running water; set colander aside to continue draining while you prepare other ingredients. In small bowl, blend together hoisin sauce, bean sauce and rice vinegar; set aside.

In wok or large skillet, heat oil over medium-high heat until hot but not smoking. Add carrots. Stir-fry for 3 or 4 minutes. Add bell pepper, garlic, gingerroot and hot pepper flakes; stir-fry for about a minute. Add sherry; stir-fry until sherry has cooked away. Add well-drained fiddleheads and peanuts; stir-fry for about a minute. Add sauce mixture; stir-fry until sauce has reduced and thickened somewhat, about 2 minutes. Serve with hot cooked rice.

*Look in the Asian section of a large supermarket, or at a specialty store, for these Chinese sauces.

Dandelions (Taraxacum officinale)

A plant with many uses! Leaves are a well-known edible that is packed with vitamins, but the flowers and roots can be used as well for delicious and interesting dishes. Always harvest in areas that haven't been sprayed or chemically treated.

HABITAT, RANGE

The dandelion is an opportunistic plant with aggressive growth habits. Common throughout the upper Midwest, dandelions thrive in open areas with normal rainfall; they can also be found in open forests and other shady areas. Lawns, disturbed areas and waste lots are often covered with dandelions.

Dandelion range

PARTS USED

Flowers, leaves, root. The stems are always discarded, as they contain a milky sap that is bitter.

SEASONS

Flowers can be collected from spring through fall. Leaves are best in early spring, before flowers bloom, but are edible throughout the year; late fall growth produces another crop of young leaves that is as tasty as spring leaves. Roots can be dug all year.

IDENTIFICATION TIPS, DANGEROUS LOOKALIKES

Dandelions are so common and familiar that only a brief description is necessary. The long leaves, with edges like teeth, grow in a basal rosette. A single hollow stem with a purplish cast supports a single bright yellow flower cluster with a green base; a few days after blooming, the yellow flower head gives way to a puffy white globe consisting of many seeds. There are no dangerous lookalikes. Coltsfoot (*Tussilago farfara*) and goat's beard (*Tragopogon dubius*) have similar flowers, but the leaves are not toothy like those of dandelions. Field sow thistle (*Sonchus arvensis*) has tooth-edged leaves, but unlike dandelion leaves they

Dandelions

Dandelions

are very prickly; as an added distinction, sow thistle grows from 1½ to 4 feet tall, while dandelions are only 4 to 18 inches tall. Wild lettuces (*Lactuca* spp.) may have leaves similar to dandelions, but the plants are 2 to 8 feet tall. The leaves of all these species are edible, so even if you made a mistake when gathering leaves, it would not be a dangerous one.

HARVESTING TIPS

Pick flowers on a bright, sunny day to avoid bugs that may hide in closed blooms. Light green leaves are less bitter than darker leaves; small leaves are milder than larger leaves. For the biggest roots, dig up the largest flowers you can find.

SPECIAL CONSIDERATIONS

People who are allergic to pollens may have a reaction from eating dandelion flowers. All parts of the dandelion act as a mild diuretic, especially when eaten in quantity. As with all wild plants, be sure to harvest only where you know no pesticides, herbicides or other noxious chemicals have been used, and always wash well before using.

MORE ABOUT DANDELIONS: The bane of suburban lawnmeisters everywhere, dandelions are actually a very useful culinary plant. The young leaves, harvested before the bright yellow flower blooms, are delicious as a raw salad green, and can also be cooked much like spinach. They pack a nutritional wallop, with twice as much vitamin A as red bell peppers or cantaloupe, in addition to respectable amounts of vitamins B, C and D. They're also rich in minerals including iron and calcium (a cup of dandelion greens contains as much calcium as a half-glass of milk), potassium, manganese and phosphorus, as well as useful trace elements such as lutein and potassium (all nutrition information is from the USDA Nutritional Database).

I often find myself with a heap of dandelion plants each year as I prepare my garden beds for tomatoes, peppers and squash. I dig out the whole plant with a dandelion digger and rinse them off with the hose to remove the dirt that is attached to the roots; then it's into the house for final preparation.

By the time I bring them indoors, the greens are usually wilted and limp; however, they can easily be refreshed and crisped for use in salads. Simply snip the greens away from the roots and soak them in a sinkful of very cold water (you may even wish to add a few ice cubes) for 15 or 20 minutes, swishing them around occasionally with your hands. Then, lift the greens out of the water, allowing the dirt and sand to fall to the bottom of the sink. If your soil is particularly sandy or the greens still seem dirty, rinse them again in fresh, cold water.

Spin the greens dry in a salad spinner, and place them into a bowl or container, layering a sheet of paper towelling between each inch or so of greens. Cover and refrigerate for at least an hour. Handled this way, dandelion greens will stay fresh for a week to 10 days.

The flowers have been used for generations to make a strong, sunny-colored wine, which is somewhat of an acquired taste. Dandelion flowers also make delicious fritters, and can be added to soups and stews. I've also found that the flowers are easy to dry; the petals can then be pulled away from the bitter green base and used in pancakes, muffins or other baked goods. If you want to get kids involved in wildcrafting, harvesting and drying a bunch of dandelion flowers—then turning them into pancakes or muffins—would be a good project. As a side note, fresh dandelion flowers are enjoyed by many parrots and other pet birds, and provide them with many important vitamins and minerals as well as chewing fun!

Dandelion roots contain sugars that are easily digested by diabetics (levulose in the spring, which converts to inulin in the fall); they can be boiled as a vegetable, or roasted and used as a coffee substitute. As a vegetable, they are surprisingly bland, with a slight turnip flavor; sometimes, an individual root seems bitter. I find them uninteresting as a solo vegetable, and I don't think they're worth the work involved in preparation unless you are looking for a curiosity (or are in a survival situation). They would be an interesting addition to a wild-foods stew or soup, and perhaps that is the best use for them as a vegetable. Cleaning a mess of dandelion roots is a big job; one spring, I noted that it took me 2 hours to clean 120 roots, yielding a total of just under 5 ounces.

To peel dandelion roots, hold on to the crown (leaf base) and use the thumbnail of your other hand to pick at the skin where the root joins the crown. Once you get the skin started, it peels off easily, taking the fine roots with it. Use your thumbnail or a Scotchbrite-type scouring pad to strip the outer skin off; sometimes it comes off in one long tube, rather like peeling off a stocking. Cut away the crown after peeling the skin off.

Many books recommend boiling roots in two changes of water, with a pinch of baking soda in the first water, apparently to reduce strong flavors or bitterness. I think the baking soda gives the roots an unpleasant, shreddy texture and actually *adds* a bitter flavor. Plain water works better, and I have not found any reason to use two changes of water; the roots are not particularly strong in flavor. Boil the roots until tender (10 to 20 minutes, depending on size), drain and toss with butter, salt and pepper. Or, boil them until not quite tender, then drain and add to a stew or soup with other vegetables to finish cooking.

Dandelion Coffee: To make a coffee substitute, scrub unpeeled roots well and bake at 250°F, stirring occasionally, until the roots are brown and brittle enough to break easily. Small roots, about ³⁄₁₆ inch across, take 45 to 60 minutes to roast; larger roots can take several hours (split larger roots vertically to speed drying). For a more roasted flavor, increase oven temperature to 375°F for 15 or 20 minutes, until the roots are rich brown. When they are brittle, cool and pulverize in a coffee grinder or food processor. Brew as you would coffee, or blend with regular coffee grounds before brewing. Dandelion coffee, incidentally, is caffeine-free.

Dried Dandelion Flowers: Harvest fully open, bright yellow flowers on a sunny day. Cut the flower from the stem at the base of the flower head, avoiding the stem and its bitter juices. Rinse the flowers well in plenty of cold water. Spread on dehydrator trays, or mesh-covered cake cooling racks if you're drying them in the oven (see pages 420-422 for complete information on drying foods). Process at low heat until completely dry, about 1½ hours; the petals should pull freely from the green flower base. When the dandelions are dry, hold a flower by the green base and gently pull the yellow petals away from the base, discarding the base (this is not as tedious as it sounds, as the dry petals pull away from the base quite easily and in large clumps). Two quarts of flower heads will yield about 2 cups of dried dandelion petals, firmly packed.

OTHER RECIPES IN THIS BOOK FEATURING DANDELIONS
- Impossible Greens Pie (page 300)
- Homemade Wild Greens Pasta (page 309)
- Vegetable Terrine with Mushrooms (page 382)

Dandelion Petal Pancakes

3 or 4 servings   Preparation: Under 15 minutes

You can make a batch of dandelion pancakes simply by stirring a handful of the dried petals into your favorite pancake mix. If you prefer to make pancakes the old-fashioned way, try this easy recipe.

½ cup all-purpose flour
½ cup whole wheat flour
1 tablespoon sugar
1 teaspoon baking powder
½ teaspoon baking soda
¼ teaspoon salt
¾ cup firmly packed dried dandelion
    petals (see page 47)

¾ cup plain yogurt (lowfat or nonfat
    works fine)
1 cup water, plus additional as needed
1 egg, or ¼ cup egg substitute
2 tablespoons melted butter or margarine,
    or vegetable oil
½ teaspoon vanilla extract
Nonstick spray or vegetable oil for greasing
    griddle
Syrup, butter, jam etc. for serving

In mixing bowl, combine flours, sugar, baking powder, baking soda and salt; stir well to mix. Add dried dandelion petals and mix with your fingertips to break up petal clumps slightly. In another bowl, combine yogurt, water, egg, melted butter and vanilla; beat with fork or whisk to blend. Add to flour mixture and stir until just mixed; batter will be lumpy and somewhat thick. If batter is thicker than you like, thin with a little milk or water to desired consistency.

Heat griddle or skillet over medium-high heat until a drop of water dances on the surface. Spray with cooking spray, or grease very lightly. Pour batter onto griddle in ¼-cup batches. Cook until edges are dry and bubbles appear on surface. Turn and cook second side until fluffy and dry. Serve immediately with syrup and butter, jam, or whatever you like.

Buttermilk Mashed Potatoes with Dandelion Greens

3 or 4 servings   Preparation: Under an hour

Don't use the buttermilk substitute made by "souring" regular milk with vinegar; stick with cultured buttermilk from the dairy case for this dish.

4 medium Yukon gold or other medium-
    starch potatoes
1 medium sweet potato
2 cloves garlic, thinly sliced
1 cup cultured buttermilk

1 cup cut-up dandelion greens (cut into
    1-inch pieces before measuring)
½ teaspoon coarse salt
Freshly ground pepper

Peel Yukon gold and sweet potatoes, and cut into 1-inch-thick rounds. Combine in nonreactive saucepan with garlic and buttermilk. Heat over medium-high heat until bubbles start to form in the center. Before the milk comes to a full boil, cover and reduce heat so the milk is simmering. Cook, covered, for 5 minutes. Distribute dandelion greens over the top of the potatoes; re-cover and cook for 10 minutes longer, stirring occasionally. Uncover and cook for about 15 minutes longer, or until potatoes are tender and most of the milk has been absorbed (there should still be a bit of milk in the mixture). Mash coarsely with a potato masher, leaving plenty of larger chunks. Add salt and pepper to taste.

Creamed Dandelion Greens

3 or 4 servings   Preparation: Under 30 minutes

Par-boiling takes some bitterness from the leaves, so this recipe works particularly well for large greens (or those from dandelions that are in flower).

8 cups dandelion greens
½ cup chopped onion
2 tablespoons butter
2 tablespoons all-purpose flour
1 cup whole milk, half-and-half, or
    evaporated skim milk

½ teaspoon salt
A pinch of nutmeg
A pinch of cayenne pepper
¾ cup shredded cheddar or Monterey Jack
    cheese

Heat oven to 350°F. Lightly spray 1-quart casserole dish with nonstick spray; set aside. Heat large pot of salted water to boiling over high heat. Add dandelion greens, pushing down with wooden spoon until all greens are submerged. Cook for 1 minute; drain, refresh with cold running water and gently squeeze dry.

In medium saucepan, cook onion in butter over medium heat until just tender. Stirring constantly, sprinkle flour over butter. Cook, stirring constantly, until mixture is bubbly and thick. Add milk, stirring constantly; cook for 2 or 3 minutes, stirring until smooth. Add salt, nutmeg and cayenne; stir to mix. Add drained greens and cheese; stir to combine well. Transfer mixture to prepared casserole. Bake until bubbly, about 20 minutes.

Springtime Torte

4 servings as a main course; 8 appetizer servings   Preparation: About an hour

This type of torte is often served at room temperature in Italy. It makes a great appetizer, luncheon dish or light main course.

Crust:
1 cup all-purpose flour
3 tablespoons grated Parmesan cheese
¼ teaspoon salt
¼ cup cold water
¼ cup olive oil

Filling:
2 cups (about 2½ ounces) sliced radicchio, endive or curly chicory
1 tablespoon white wine vinegar
4 cups (about 2 ounces) mixed dandelion greens and violet leaves, cut into smaller pieces if large
4 eggs
¾ cup shredded cheddar or other cheese

Heat oven to 375°F. Spray a 10½-inch quiche or tart pan with nonstick spray; set aside. To prepare crust: Combine flour, Parmesan cheese and salt in mixing bowl; stir to blend. Add water and stir until incorporated. Add olive oil and stir until fairly well incorporated; mixture will not be smooth. Pour out onto smooth worksurface and knead gently several times, until well blended. Use rolling pin to shape into a circle that is slightly wider than the quiche pan (the pastry is very elastic, so don't worry if it pulls back to a smaller circle). Transfer the crust to the quiche pan. Press the crust slightly up the sides; it doesn't have to go very high, but there should be a rim of crust all around the edges of the pan. Set aside.

To prepare filling: Spray large skillet with nonstick spray and place over medium heat. Add radicchio and cook for about 2 minutes, stirring frequently. Sprinkle vinegar into skillet; it will cook away almost immediately. Add wild greens and cook until wilted, stirring frequently. Remove from heat.

In medium bowl, beat eggs with fork. Stir in cheddar cheese. Add radicchio mixture and stir to blend. Quickly pour into crust, spreading evenly. Bake for 35 minutes; top will be rich golden brown. Allow to cool slightly, or to room temperature, before serving.

Wilted Dandelion Greens Salad

2 or 3 servings; easily increased   Preparation: Under 15 minutes

If you like, you may substitute other tender field greens for some of the dandelion greens in this recipe; or, you could use a mix of wild greens and leaf lettuce. Any way you mix it, this is an absolutely delicious salad. The volume of the greens goes down quite a bit when the hot dressing is added, so the size of each serving isn't as large as you may think.

5 to 6 cups dandelion greens or a mixture of greens (see note above)	3 tablespoons cider vinegar
3 to 4 tablespoons pine nuts	1 tablespoon sugar
4 or 5 slices bacon, diced	1 teaspoon all-purpose flour
¼ cup diced onion*	½ teaspoon salt
¼ cup water	¼ teaspoon dry mustard powder
	¼ teaspoon white pepper

Combine greens and pine nuts in large salad bowl; set aside. In medium skillet, fry bacon over medium heat until very crisp (but don't let it burn). Transfer bacon with slotted spoon to paper towel-lined plate; pour off all but a generous tablespoon of the bacon drippings. Add onion to skillet with drippings and cook over medium heat until tender, stirring frequently. Meanwhile, in measuring cup, combine water, vinegar, sugar, flour, salt, mustard powder and pepper; blend with fork. Sprinkle drained, cooled bacon pieces over greens in salad bowl.

When onion is tender, stir the vinegar mixture again and add to the skillet. Cook, stirring constantly, for about 3 minutes; the mixture should thicken somewhat but should not be as thick as gravy (if it's too thick, stir in a little more water). Pour dressing over greens in bowl; toss immediately and thoroughly with a salad tosser (or 2 large spoons). Serve immediately.

*If you have some ramps on hand, chop up a few of the bulbs and add them to the onion while cooking. Slice the ramp leaves into strips, and stir them into the skillet about a minute before you add the liquid to the skillet. Delicious!

Dandelion Greens with Fried Gingerroot

4 servings   Preparation: Under an hour

Deep-fried gingerroot makes a nice counterpoint to blanched dandelion greens in this adaptation of a classic Chinese recipe.

3-inch length of fresh gingerroot
1 tablespoon hot chili oil
6 cups dandelion greens
¼ cup peanut oil or canola oil

3 tablespoons soy sauce
3 tablespoons seasoned rice vinegar (or plain rice vinegar and ¼ teaspoon sugar)

Peel gingerroot and chop finely. In small bowl, stir together chopped gingerroot and chili oil; set aside while you prepare greens (it should marinate for at least 20 minutes). Heat large pot of salted water to rolling boil over high heat. Add dandelion greens, pushing down with wooden spoon until all greens are submerged. Cook for 2 minutes; drain and refresh with cold running water. Gently squeeze dry; pat with paper towels. Arrange drained greens on serving platter.

In small sauté pan, heat peanut oil over medium-high heat until very hot. Add gingerroot mixture, being careful to avoid spattering; stir-fry until gingerroot is crisp and has turned a rich golden brown, about 45 seconds. Strain mixture through wire-mesh strainer; discard oil (or refrigerate and use for other stir-frying). Sprinkle fried gingerroot over dandelion greens. In small bowl, stir together soy sauce and vinegar. Pour mixture over greens. Set aside at room temperature to marinate for 15 to 30 minutes. Serve at room temperature.

Dandelion Flower Fritters

4 to 6 servings   Preparation: Under 30 minutes

Serve these as an appetizer, as a side dish with meat and vegetables, or, for a change, serve as a brunch dish with syrup and butter, as you would pancakes.

1½ cups dandelion flowers (all trace of stems removed before measuring; green flower bases are OK)
Canola oil for deep-fat frying
1 large egg

¾ cup whole milk
1 cup all-purpose flour
1 teaspoon baking powder
1 teaspoon sugar, optional
½ teaspoon salt

Rinse dandelion flowers quickly in cold water. Spin in salad spinner to dry, or shake in colander; pat dry between paper towels and set aside. Begin heating 1½ inches of oil in deep-fryer or deep skillet; oil should be 350°F-375°F for frying.

In mixing bowl, beat together egg and milk. Combine flour, baking powder, sugar and salt in sifter or wire-mesh strainer; sift into egg mixture. Whisk or stir with fork until smooth. Dip flowers, a few at a time, into batter. Deep-fry individual battered flowers until golden brown, turning if necessary. Drain on paper towel-lined plate. Serve hot.

Dandelion Rosé Wine

5 bottles (750ml each)

Raspberries add a nice flavor and lovely color to dandelion wine. For a more traditional dandelion wine, simply omit the raspberries.

2 quarts dandelion petals* (yellow parts only)

2 pounds sugar (about 4½ cups)

2 cups cut-up raspberries

Juice from 2 oranges

Juice from 2 lemons

½ pound white raisins, chopped (about 1½ cups after chopping)

1 packet (5 grams) wine yeast, such as Montrachet or champagne

1 teaspoon yeast nutrient

Before starting, please read "General Winemaking Procedures" on pages 423-426 if you are unfamiliar with winemaking. You may also be interested in the notes on pages 426, which detail the making of a batch of this wine.

Place dandelion petals in sterilized stoneware crock. Boil 1 gallon water; pour over petals. Cover crock with muslin and let stand in a warm location for 2 days, stirring occasionally with a sterilized spoon. After 2 days, add sugar, raspberries, orange and lemon juice, raisins, yeast and nutrient. Re-cover; let stand in warm location for 4 days, stirring twice each day with a sterilized spoon. On the fourth day, strain liquid through cheesecloth into sterilized jug; discard solids. Seal jug with air lock; let stand in a cool location for secondary fermentation. Rack wine into clean jug whenever it throws ⅛ inch of sediment. When fermentation stops and wine clears (generally 2 or 3 months after primary ferment), transfer into sterilized wine bottles. Cork and let age for at least 1 month before drinking; 3 or 4 months is more traditional.

*Pick the dandelions on a sunny day after the dew has dried off and flowers have opened. Cut or pull off stems and the green petals at the base of the flowers (don't be too fussy about this, but do try to remove the majority of the green material). Pick and clean enough dandelions to yield 2 quarts of just the yellow parts (so you will need more like 3 quarts of flower heads prior to pulling off the green parts).

Salade Sauvage ("Wild" Salad)

Per 2 servings; make as many as you wish   Preparation: Under 15 minutes

Use a mix of greens, with at least 2 types. Dandelion greens should make up half of the amount of wild greens called for; for the remainder, use a mix of violet leaves, watercress, purslane, wood sorrel, ox-eye daisy leaves, clintonia, lamb's quarters or any other mild, tender wild greens.

2 cups mixed young wild greens
2 cups buttercrunch or Bibb lettuce, torn
    into pieces
¼ cup Balsamic Vinaigrette (recipe below),
    or other prepared vinaigrette
Half of a pear (red Bartlett or seckel pears
    are wonderful)

½ cup Honey-Roasted Nut Clusters
    (page 282)
3 ounces top-quality blue cheese
Edible wildflowers for garnish, optional:
    violets, red clover, rose petals,
    redbud flowers

In large mixing bowl, combine wild greens with lettuce; mix gently. Add vinaigrette, tossing gently. Divide between 2 salad plates. Remove and discard core from pear; cut pear into thin wedges and arrange on salad greens. Scatter nut clusters over salads. Crumble blue cheese coarsely over salads. Garnish with wildflowers; serve immediately.

Balsamic Vinaigrette:

½ cup extra-virgin olive oil
3 tablespoons balsamic vinegar
1½ teaspoons Dijon mustard
¼ teaspoon salt, or to taste

1 clove garlic, squeezed through garlic
    press
A few grindings of fresh black pepper
A pinch of sugar, optional

Combine all ingredients in bowl; whisk to blend. Taste for seasoning and adjust as desired.

Salmon with Spicy-Sweet Sauce on Dandelion Greens

4 servings   Preparation: Under 30 minutes

This is definitely a dish in which the sum is greater than the parts. The bitter dandelion greens are a perfect counterbalance for the spicy-sweet sauce; both pair well with the rich salmon.

Sauce:

1 cup sweet (red) vermouth
1 teaspoon hot red pepper flakes
2 tablespoons maple syrup
1 tablespoon soy sauce
1 teaspoon dry mustard
A pinch of ground ginger
2 tablespoons butter, cut into several pieces

3 tablespoons olive oil
4 skin-on salmon fillets or steaks (about
    6 ounces each)
Salt
1 teaspoon chili oil or dark sesame oil
1 tablespoon sesame seeds
3 tablespoons sherry, apple juice or water
6 cups dandelion greens
1 clove garlic, minced

Heat oven to 425°F. Prepare the sauce: In small saucepan, combine vermouth and pepper flakes. Cook over high heat until reduced to ¼ cup, about 10 minutes. Stir in syrup, soy sauce, mustard and ginger; boil for 2 minutes longer. Remove from heat. Stir in butter, a piece at a time, stirring after each addition until butter melts. Set sauce aside.

In large skillet, heat olive oil over medium-high heat until shimmering. Sprinkle salmon fillets with salt; add to skillet, skin-side up, and cook until golden, about 3 minutes. Turn and cook for 3 minutes on skin-side. Transfer fillets to baking dish. Spoon a generous tablespoon of the sauce over each fillet, spreading out with back of spoon. Bake until salmon is just done, about 10 minutes (salmon flesh will become just opaque when done).

While salmon is baking, prepare greens: In same skillet, heat chili oil over medium heat until hot. Add sesame seeds and cook, stirring constantly, until lightly browned. Add sherry, stirring to loosen any browned bits. Add dandelion greens and garlic. Sauté until wilted but still bright green, about 3 minutes. Remove from heat; season to taste with salt. To serve, arrange dandelion greens on individual plates. Top with salmon; spoon any remaining sauce evenly over individual portions. (For a more attractive presentation, lift the salmon fillets away from the skin as you are plating the dish; leave the skin in the baking dish, serving just the skinless fillet. Although the skin can be eaten, the dish is nicer without.)

Morel Mushrooms (Morchella spp.)

One of the premiere wild mushrooms, morels are easy to identify—and hard to beat in the kitchen. They are fabulous simply sautéed in butter, and work well in sauces and casseroles. Don't combine them with strongly flavored ingredients, however; choose simpler preparations to allow their flavor to shine.

HABITAT, RANGE, SUBSPECIES

Four types of choice morels grow in our region: the yellow morel *(M. esculenta)*, the white morel *(M. deliciosa)*, the big-foot morel *(M. crassipes)*, and the black morel *(M. elata, M. angusticeps* and *M. conica)*. They are found throughout our area except in the arid portions of the Dakotas. Look for them in rich, moist woodlands, abandoned woodlots, Boreal forests and old orchards.

Morel range (combined)

PARTS USED

Entire fruiting body (cap and stem)

SEASONS

A few weeks in spring. The season generally starts in mid- to late March in the southern part of our region, while in the northern part the season may start as late as Memorial Day. There are reports of morels growing in the summer and fall on burn sites.

IDENTIFICATION TIPS, DANGEROUS LOOKALIKES

Three basic characteristics identify the true morel mushroom: the cap is honeycombed

A prime morel in the forest

Morels in a variety of colors and sizes

True morels are *completely* hollow

(covered with ridges); the interior is always completely hollow; and on the choice morels, the cap flows smoothly into the stem when the mushroom is cut in half vertically.

Verpa (do not eat)

Half-free morels *(M. semilibera)* and verpas *(Verpa bohemica)* have a distinct "skirt," and reveal an arrowhead-like profile when cut open. Half-free morels are edible but not as good as other morels; verpas cause stomach upset and other problems in many people, and should not be eaten. For the beginner, it is safest to avoid the half-free morels, until confidence is gained in identification.

The false morels *(Gyromitra* spp.) have a cap consisting of brain-like folds, but they have fleshy interiors rather than the completely hollow interior found in true morels; most are inedible. The non-breakable rule to follow in collecting morels is that if there is any flesh inside the mushroom—even if that flesh has pockets or holes—it must be discarded without tasting.

Gyromitra (do not eat)

HARVESTING TIPS

Pinch or cut off the mushroom at its base, avoiding the part that extends underground. If you do get a wad of dirt at the base of a morel, cut it off before adding the morel to your bag; dirt is difficult to dislodge from the ridges, so you don't want to introduce any into your collecting bag.

Much has been written about over-harvesting a morel spot. I've personally picked morels from one particular woods for over 10 years; I've got other spots that have produced for 5 or 6 years. The growing parts of a morel are underground, and the caps disperse their spores shortly after fruiting. You won't damage the resource by carefully picking a few morels; most damage to the resource comes from habitat destruction.

SPECIAL CONSIDERATIONS

Morels must always be cooked before eating. The combination of wild mushrooms and alcohol causes a reaction in some people; this is occasionally reported with black morels in particular. Also, black morels may cause mild digestive problems or lack of muscular coordination in some people if eaten in large quantities, another reason to try any new wild edible in moderation.

MORE ABOUT MORELS: Morels are one of the most well known—and highly sought—wild mushrooms in North America; in fact, they are the official state mushroom of Minnesota.

They are one of the "foolproof four"—a quartet of wild mushrooms that are recommended for beginners because they are easy to identify (others include giant puffballs, chicken of the woods—also called sulfur shelf—and shaggy manes or chanterelles, depending on which list you look at). I've taught kids to identify morels, although I always check their baskets to be sure they've got the hang of it. (Always make it quite clear to children that they are never to eat anything they pick in the wild until a knowledgeable adult checks it out.)

Usually, the biggest problem in identifying morels is finding some to identify! They can be notoriously difficult to locate, and as suburbs expand outward and small towns grow, gobbling up old woodlots and agricultural areas, prime morel habitat becomes more scarce each year. Also, morels require a specific combination of temperature and moisture. In some years, the temperature is just right but there has not been sufficient rainfall; in others, the ground is moist enough but it is too cold. Generally, nights must be 40°F or above; days in the 60s are perfect. Once the weather gets warm in late spring, the morels stop growing; several days of temperatures in the 80s usually shuts them down for the season.

Old-timers and mushroom veterans use other plants as a barometer to indicate the start of the season. "When oak leaves are the size of squirrels' ears" is a common time to begin the hunt. Another saying is that "the time to be 'shrooming is when the lilacs are blooming." Both hold some merit; generally, I consider the peak of the morel season to coincide with the time the lilacs are in full flower. Note that I said "the peak of the morel season." Typically, I am out in the woods looking for morels before the lilacs have even set buds. (Also note that I come back empty-handed quite often in the early season… but I just can't resist the pull of the woods in the spring.)

As many have said, morels grow where you find them; and I have found them in habitats as diverse as a sandy, pine-fringed lakeshore in northern Wisconsin, to a field of tall grass bordering an old woodlot in Illinois, to shelter belts surrounding modern suburban office complexes in the Twin Cities metro area. Recently dead elm are well known as morel magnets, but are becoming increasingly hard to find at the proper stage. The best, in my experience, are those that still have some bark attached; once all bark has fallen off and the tree has been dead for many years, the odds of finding morels diminish. The areas around white ash are noted by some experienced pickers as good morel hunting grounds; others favor poplar, cottonwood, aspen, dead oak or old orchards. In the northern Boreal forests, morels apparently grow in pine forests, although sadly I've never found any during my trips to the Boundary Waters Canoe Area (although I do keep looking). Forests that have burned may produce prodigious crops of morels the following year or two; according to personnel at Glacier National Park in Montana, morel growth was "amazing" after the Redbench fire in 1988 and again after the Moose fire in 2001. I've also read of a similar phenomenon in Yellowstone Park in 1989, the year after the large fires that swept through the Park. (Note that morel picking and other foraging is regulated on public lands and may not be allowed in National Parks; land controlled by the National Forest Service has different regulations that generally allow morel picking, so you should always check with local authorities before harvesting on public lands.)

With their ridged caps, morels are dirt magnets, and I would no sooner cook them without washing than I would a freshly dug beet. I place my morels in a sinkful of cold water and gently swish them around. Then I remove each mushroom, one at a time, and give it a gentle once-over with a soft mushroom-scrubbing brush. I cut it in half vertically, to check for dirt or insects inside (this is also the time to ensure that the mushroom is completely hollow; if it has any internal flesh—even if that flesh is pocketed—throw it out!). I rinse it under a thin stream of cold water, then lay the halves on a towel to dry for a bit. If I have picked more than I can use immediately, I wrap several in a piece of paper toweling and place that into a plastic bag or container, continuing until I've wrapped all the morels. Stored in this fashion in the refrigerator, morels will stay fresh for a week.

For longer-term storage, morels can be dried in a dehydrator or a cool oven; see pages 420-422 for more information on dehydrating. If the ambient humidity is low, you can string them with a stout needle and heavy thread, then hang these ropes to dry; or, lay them out on cake-cooling racks and let them dry on the kitchen counter for a few days. I prefer to freeze morels for storage; when thawed, they taste as though they've just been picked and sautéed. To freeze morels, simply sauté them in a little butter or oil until they release their juices, then pack into plastic containers and freeze.

For more information on morels, visit this fascinating website: http://www.bluewillow-pages.com/mushroomexpert/. I've been picking morels for 20 years, but still found plenty of interesting material on this very thorough website. It includes photos to help you identify not only true and false morels, but also various trees that may harbor morels around their feet. The site's authors have also studied things such as morel growth rates, reproduction of morels, and a host of other fascinating topics. The principal developer of the site is Michael Kuo, Ph.D., a professor at Eastern Illinois University. It is the best of the many morel websites I've seen, and I highly recommend it.

QUICK IDEAS FOR USING MORELS

- For the simplest—and perhaps the best—morel dish, sauté morels, cut as you prefer, in butter (1 tablespoon butter will be enough for 2 cups of fresh morels). When the morels have released their liquid, let them cook for a few minutes longer to re-absorb most of the juices. Season to taste with salt and pepper; devour.

- Dried morels can be powdered in a blender or coffee grinder; the powder can then be sprinkled into scrambled eggs, used to season meats and pasta dishes, or whatever you like.
- Use morels in virtually any recipe that calls for mushrooms; however, respect their delicate taste and don't waste them in heavily seasoned dishes.

OTHER RECIPES IN THIS BOOK FEATURING MORELS
- Pan-Fried Walleye with Morel-Ramp Sauce (page 28)
- Surprise Stuffing (page 126)
- Many recipes in the Wild Mushrooms chaper (beginning on page 350)
- Potato-Mushroom Cake (page 357)
- Dried morels (page 422)

Stuffed Morels

3 or 4 appetizer servings   Preparation: Under 30 minutes

These are best when prepared with the mid- to late-season mushrooms whose caps are at least 3 inches tall (not including the stem). Don't use reconstituted dried mushrooms; they have the wrong texture.

6 to 8 fresh large morels, caps about 3 inches in height	½ teaspoon dried basil
	¼ teaspoon salt
2 tablespoons butter, melted	¾ cup fine breadcrumbs
1 egg	1 to 2 tablespoons chicken broth, apple
2 tablespoons grated Parmesan cheese	juice or dry white wine, as needed
2 teaspoons extra-virgin olive oil	

Heat oven to 375°F. Spray baking sheet with nonstick spray. If morels are still whole, cut in half lengthwise. Place halved mushrooms on baking sheet, cut side down. Brush outsides of mushrooms with melted butter. Turn mushrooms over so cut side is up.

In mixing bowl, combine egg, cheese, oil, basil and salt; beat with fork. Add breadcrumbs and mix well. Add enough chicken broth to make the mixture moist but not wet; if you gently press a small amount in your hand it should hold its shape (depending on the size of your egg, you may not need any broth at all; use your best judgement). Mold a spoonful into a lozenge shape, and pack gently into a mushroom cap and stem; use enough of the breadcrumb mixture to fill the mushroom in a slightly mounded shape that extends to all the edges. Continue until all mushrooms have been filled. (If you have any leftover breadcrumb mixture, it makes a nice topping for any baked casserole-type dish you may be preparing at the same time.)

Bake the filled mushrooms for 15 minutes, or until the crumbs are nicely browned. The mushrooms may be served immediately; or, set them aside and cool until just warm before serving.

Morel Rings in Consommé with Toasts

For each 2 servings; make as much as you wish   Preparation: Under 30 minutes

6 ounces whole fresh morel mushrooms
1 cup canned beef consommé
1 can (14 ounces) vegetable broth, or
equivalent in homemade

2 thick slices stale country-style Italian
bread
1 tablespoon butter or olive oil, optional

Slice the morels into rings by cutting across the caps, separating out the tips, stems and any incomplete rings or broken pieces of mushroom. Chop the stems and other pieces into chunks no larger than ½ inch; keep these separated from the rings (unless you're preparing this dish "family style" as described below).

In saucepan, combine consommé, vegetable broth and 1 cup water. Heat just to boiling. Add chopped stems and other pieces. Reduce heat; cover and simmer for 15 to 20 minutes.

When you're almost ready to serve the soup, strain the broth into another saucepan; reserve the cooked morels for another use (see Note with Grilled Springtime Vegetables with Pasta, page 74; or use them in scrambled eggs or another dish). Add the reserved morel rings to the broth, and heat to a gentle boil over medium-high heat. Cook for about 5 minutes. Meanwhile, toast the bread slices by pan-frying them in a skillet with the butter or oil until golden on both sides; for a lowfat version, toast the dry bread under the broiler or on a grill grate, omitting the butter or oil.

To serve, place a slice of toasted bread into each of 2 soup plates. Use a slotted spoon to divide the mushroom rings evenly over the toasts. Pour the broth around the toasts; serve immediately.

Morel Rings in Consommé, Family Style: Follow instructions above, but don't bother to separate the rings from the rest of the mushroom pieces. Add all mushroom pieces to the consommé mixture, and cook as directed for 15 to 20 minutes (there will be no straining and separate cooking of the rings in this version). Toast bread as directed. Divide mushrooms evenly over the toasts. Pour broth around the toasts; serve immediately.

Simple Morel Pizza

8 slices   Preparation: Under an hour

If you're preparing morels for someone who has never had them before, this is a good dish to serve because it allows the flavor of the morels to shine. The sherry adds a subtle, sweet note to the morels.

12-inch prebaked thin pizza crust, or thin
   focaccia
2 ramp bulbs or 1 shallot, chopped
2 teaspoons olive oil
2 teaspoons butter

2 cups coarsely chopped morels
1 tablespoon plus 1 teaspoon dry sherry
¼ teaspoon salt
1 cup (4 ounces) shredded mozzarella
   cheese

Heat oven to 375°F. Place pizza crust on baking sheet; set aside. In medium skillet, sauté ramps in olive oil over medium heat until fragrant, about 2 minutes. Remove from heat and use a pastry brush to spread evenly over the top of the pizza crust.

Add butter to same skillet and heat over medium heat until melted. Add morels; sauté until they release their juices. Add the sherry and continue to cook until all liquid has cooked away; this will take 5 minutes or a bit longer. Stir in the salt. Spread the mushrooms evenly over the pizza crust. Sprinkle evenly with the cheese. Bake in the center of the oven until cheese is golden with a few brown spots, 15 to 20 minutes.

Light Mushroom Soup

2 main-dish servings, or 4 small appetizer servings   Preparation: Under 30 minutes

This recipe should be considered a starting point for your soup. Feel free to use half-and-half instead of cream, for example, or to use more cream and less chicken broth. For a thicker soup, increase the butter and flour proportionally in the roux, or use less liquid (or more mushrooms).

6 ounces fresh morels, oyster mushrooms
   or chanterelles, well cleaned
1 tablespoon unsalted butter
¼ cup dry sherry

1½ cups chicken broth
½ to ¾ cup heavy cream
Salt and white pepper
Chopped chives or chive flowers for
   garnish, optional

Roux:
3 tablespoons unsalted butter
3 tablespoons all-purpose flour

Cut mushrooms into pieces that are ½ to ¾ inch in size. Melt the tablespoon of butter in saucepan over medium-low heat. Add mushrooms and stir to coat evenly with melted butter. Cook, stirring occasionally, until mushrooms give up their juices. Increase heat to medium and cook until most of the liquid has cooked away, generally 5 to 7 minutes. Add sherry and cook until most of the sherry has cooked away; the mixture should not dry out completely. Remove from heat and set aside.

In a different heavy-bottomed saucepan, melt butter for roux over medium-low heat. (If you want thicker soup, use 4 or 5 tablespoons each of the butter and flour; keep proportions equal.) Whisk in the flour and cook, whisking constantly, until mixture is golden, 3 to 4 minutes. Whisking constantly, add chicken broth. Increase heat to medium and cook, whisking frequently, until mixture boils and thickens slightly (if you have used additional butter and flour for the roux, the mixture will get thicker than if you use just 3 tablespoons). When mixture has boiled for a few minutes, pour mushrooms and any juices, along with the cream, into saucepan with chicken broth. Heat to boiling and cook for a few minutes longer. Taste for seasoning and add salt and pepper as needed. Garnish with chives.

Scalloped Potatoes with Morels

4 servings   Preparation: Over an hour

2 cups chicken broth
1 clove garlic, lightly crushed
1 tablespoon unsalted butter
1 tablespoon minced shallot
½ pound fresh morel mushrooms, cut into
    ¾-inch pieces (3½ to 4 cups cut up)

1 cup dry white wine
Salt and pepper
2 tablespoons snipped fresh chives
1½ pounds Yukon gold potatoes* (about
    6 medium)
1⅓ cups shredded Gruyère cheese

Heat oven to 375°F. Combine chicken broth and garlic in medium saucepan. Heat to boiling over high heat; cook until reduced to about 1 cup. (To help you judge the amount of broth during the reduction process, pour 1 cup of water into the saucepan before you do anything with the chicken broth, and note the level of the water in the pan. Pour out the water, add the chicken broth, and reduce to the level you noted previously.)

Meanwhile, melt butter in large skillet over medium-low heat. Add shallots and sauté for about 3 minutes. Add mushrooms and cook over medium heat, stirring frequently, until the juices from the mushrooms have cooked away. Add white wine and cook until most of the wine has cooked away. Remove from heat; add salt and pepper to taste. Don't forget about the chicken broth during this time; when it has reduced to 1 cup, remove from heat. Remove and discard garlic clove; stir the chives into the reduced broth.

Spray 8 x 8-inch baking dish, or 2 quart casserole, with nonstick spray. Peel potatoes and slice thinly. Arrange half of the potatoes in the prepared dish; salt and pepper to taste. Top with the mushroom mixture; sprinkle with half of the cheese. Top with remaining potatoes, then sprinkle with remaining cheese. Pour reduced broth over the top. Cover with foil and bake for 30 minutes. Remove foil and bake until potatoes are tender, 20 to 25 minutes longer; mixture should be bubbly, and lightly browned on top.

*Substitute russet potatoes for the Yukon gold potatoes; cooking time may be reduced slightly.

Morelle Duxelles

About 1 cup   Preparation: Under 30 minutes

Duxelles is a rich mushroom paste from classic French cuisine. Use it to stuff boneless chicken breasts, to fill savory puff pastries or pastry cups as an appetizer, or serve warm with buttered toast as a first course (for a more specific recipe, see the Tenderloins on Mushroom Toast recipe below). Duxelles keeps for about a week if refrigerated in a tightly covered container, and also freezes well.

1 tablespoon chopped shallot	1 tablespoon finely chopped fresh parsley
3 tablespoons unsalted butter	or tarragon, optional
8 ounces fresh morels, very finely chopped	Salt and freshly ground black pepper

In medium skillet, sauté shallot in butter over medium heat until tender. Add chopped morels. Cook, stirring frequently, until juices released by morels have been completely re-absorbed and the mixture has a pâté-like consistency, about 10 minutes. Remove from heat; stir in parsley, salt and pepper to taste.

Tenderloins on Mushroom Toast

4 servings   Preparation: Under an hour

1 recipe Morelle Duxelles (above), prepared with tarragon	Salt and cracked black pepper
2 tablespoons butter	2 tablespoons olive oil
4 slices hearty French or Italian bread, ¾ inch thick and 5 to 6 inches across	½ cup dry red wine
½ to ¾ pound beef tenderloin, or venison loin (backstrap)	¼ cup beef broth
	1½ teaspoons all-purpose flour
	¼ teaspoon dry mustard powder

Heat oven to 400°F. Prepare duxelles; set aside and keep warm. In large skillet, melt butter over medium heat. Add bread slices; turn quickly to coat both sides with melted butter. Cook until golden on both sides. Remove from skillet; set aside.

Sprinkle tenderloin with salt and pepper to taste; rub in with your fingertips. Heat oil over medium-high heat in same skillet used for bread. Add tenderloin; cook until well browned on all sides. Transfer to small dish; place in oven and roast until desired doneness, 5 to 10 minutes. While meat is roasting, prepare sauce: In small saucepan, heat wine and broth to boiling over medium-high heat. Cook until reduced to about half. Whisk in flour and mustard powder; cook, stirring constantly, until thickened and smooth. Remove from heat; set aside and keep warm.

When meat is desired doneness, remove from oven and let stand, loosely tented with foil, for about 5 minutes. Meanwhile, spread duxelles over prepared bread; arrange on serving platter or individual plates. Slice meat thinly, and arrange a fan of slices over each piece of mushroom toast. Drizzle wine sauce over each portion. Serve immediately.

Rustic Grain with Morels and Fresh Mozzarella

2 main-dish or 4 first-course servings; easily increased   Preparation: Under an hour

Farro (Triticum dicoccum) *is an ancient grain from Italy; it's sometimes called spelt. History tells us that it was used back in the time of the Roman Emperors, and sustained the Roman Legions. Look for it at an Italian specialty store, or with the natural foods in a large grocery store. If you can't find farro, substitute barley. Note: Many instructions say that farro must be soaked before cooking, but I prepare it for this dish without soaking, and it works just fine.*

1 cup farro or barley	¼ cup dry sherry
1 cup dried morels (about ½ ounce)	1 large fresh water-packed mozzarella*
1½ cups water	6 to 8 fresh basil leaves, minced; or
3 cups chicken broth	½ teaspoon crumbled dried
1 shallot, minced	½ teaspoon salt
1 tablespoon extra-virgin olive oil	

Place farro (or barley) in wire-mesh strainer. Rinse under cold running water; set aside to drain well. Crumble morels into small saucepan (the pieces should be no larger than a fingernail). Add water. Heat to boiling; remove from heat and set aside. Place chicken broth in a medium saucepan; heat to simmering over medium heat. Adjust heat so broth simmers throughout entire cooking process.

In heavy-bottomed saucepan, sauté shallot in oil over medium heat until tender. Add drained farro. Cook, stirring almost constantly, until farro is dry and beginning to toast lightly, 3 to 4 minutes. Add sherry to farro, stirring constantly. Cook until sherry has been absorbed by farro. Add about ½ cup of the simmering broth to farro; cook, stirring frequently, until most of the liquid has been absorbed by farro. Repeat with another ½ cup of broth, cooking and stirring until most of the liquid has been absorbed. Add morels and soaking liquid; cook, stirring frequently, until most of the liquid has been absorbed by farro. Continue adding stock, ½ cup at a time, stirring frequently and cooking until each batch has been almost absorbed by farro. Total cooking time will be 15 to 30 minutes; you may not need quite all the stock, or you may need a bit more; use hot water if you run out of stock near the end.

While farro is cooking, cut 2 slices of mozzarella that are about ½ inch thick for 2 main-dish servings (for first-course servings, cut 4 slightly thinner slices); reserve remaining mozzarella for another use. Place each mozzarella slice in bottom of soup plate; set aside. When farro is tender yet still chewy, stir in basil, salt and enough stock or water to make mixture creamy (almost soup-like). Heat to boiling. Divide boiling-hot mixture evenly between 2 soup plates, spooning over mozzarella. Serve immediately.

*Use the fresh mozzarella that is packed in water or a sealed pouch with a little water; American-style mozzarella is not the right texture for this dish. If you find water-packed mozzarella in small balls (about 1 inch across), these work well also; use 2 or 3 per serving in place of the sliced mozzarella for main-dish servings, or 1 per serving as a first course.

Pan-Fried Morel Dumplings (Potstickers)

20 dumplings; 4 to 6 appetizer servings | Preparation: Under an hour

6 ounces fresh morels (or ¾ to 1 ounce dried morels, rehydrated), chopped
2 green onions, chopped
¼ to ½ teaspoon minced fresh gingerroot
1 tablespoon dark sesame oil
Salt
A little cornstarch
1 package (16 ounces) gyoza* or wonton wrappers
Peanut oil or vegetable oil for pan-frying (about ¼ cup)

Dipping sauce:
¼ cup soy sauce (preferably Japanese soy sauce such as Kikkoman)
2 tablespoons rice vinegar
2 tablespoons water
1 teaspoon hot chile oil, optional
½ teaspoon sesame seeds
½ teaspoon sugar
1 green onion, cut into thin rings

In medium skillet, sauté morels, green onions and gingerroot in sesame oil over medium heat until juices released by mushrooms have cooked away and mushrooms are tender, about 5 minutes. Season with salt to taste. Remove from heat; set aside until cool.

Sprinkle baking sheet with cornstarch; set aside. Place a few wrappers on worksurface; brush edges lightly with cold water. Place about 1 tablespoon mushroom mixture in center of each wrapper. Bring wrapper together in a semicircle over filling, pleating edges slightly and pinching to seal. Arrange dumplings on prepared baking sheet as you go, covering with a towel. Continue until all filling has been used up. Dumplings may be prepared to this point and refrigerated or frozen.

When you're ready to cook, heat 1 tablespoon oil in large nonstick skillet over medium-high heat until hot but not smoking. Add a layer of dumplings, pleated side down; cook until bottoms are golden brown, about 2 minutes. Add ¼ cup water to skillet, pouring it along the sides of the skillet; cover immediately and steam dumplings until skins are translucent, about 2 minutes. Remove cover; continue cooking until any water has evaporated. Loosen dumplings carefully with spatula and transfer to serving plate, browned side up; keep warm while you prepare remaining dumplings, using additional oil as needed. Meanwhile, in small bowl, stir together all dipping-sauce ingredients. Serve dumplings with dipping sauce.

To freeze uncooked potstickers: Fill and pleat as directed. Arrange in single layer without touching on prepared baking sheet. Place baking sheet flat in freezer so the dumplings don't slide together; freeze until completely hard, 4 to 6 hours. Once dumplings are completely frozen, remove from baking sheet and transfer to plastic freezer-weight food storage bag or airtight container for storage. Thaw in single layer in refrigerator before cooking.

*Gyoza are round wrappers specifically made for potstickers. You may substitute wonton wrappers; trim corners so wrappers are round before stuffing.

Chicken Breast Stuffed with Morels and Crab

4 servings   Preparation: Over an hour

¼ cup finely diced onion
3 tablespoons butter, divided
1 cup chopped morels (about 3 ounces)
4 boneless, skinless chicken breast halves
    (6 to 6¾ ounces each)
Salt and pepper
¾ cup shredded crab meat (about
    4 ounces)

¼ cup mayonnaise
¼ cup breadcrumbs
¼ cup chicken broth, white wine or water
1 tablespoon chopped fresh herbs (a mix of
    parsley, marjoram and thyme works well)
One of the Morel Cream Sauce recipes
    (page 68), optional

In medium skillet, sauté onion in 1 tablespoon of the butter over medium heat for about 5 minutes. Add morels; cook, stirring frequently, until liquid released by morels has been re-absorbed, about 7 minutes. Remove from heat; set aside to cool completely.

Place each chicken breast half between 2 sheets of plastic wrap. Pound with meat mallet until a uniform ¼ inch thick; it will be about 6 x 7 inches. Sprinkle one side with salt and pepper to taste. In mixing bowl, combine cooled mushroom mixture with crab meat, mayonnaise and breadcrumbs; mix gently but thoroughly. Divide mixture evenly between 4 breast halves, mounding in the center of each breast half. Fold ends over filling, tucking edges up as much as possible. Wrap each rolled breast half tightly in plastic wrap to make a smooth bundle. If possible, refrigerate for an hour or longer, to allow the bundles to firm up; if you like, the chicken can be prepared earlier in the day and refrigerated until you're ready to cook it.

When you're ready to cook, heat oven to 375°F. Spray 9 x 9-inch baking dish with nonstick spray. Unwrap stuffed breast halves; place in prepared dish, seam-side down. Pour broth around edges. In small saucepan or microwave-safe dish, melt remaining 2 tablespoons butter. Mix in herbs. Brush chicken with herb butter. Cover dish loosely with foil; bake until chicken is cooked through (internal temperature should be 165°F), about 25 minutes. When chicken is almost done, prepare one of the morel cream sauces if desired. Serve chicken with sauce.

Variation: Grilled Stuffed Chicken Breasts
Prepare filling and stuff chicken breast halves as directed. Tie each bundle with a cross of wet kitchen twine (as though putting a cross of ribbon on a gift-wrapped box). Wrap each tied bundle in plastic wrap; refrigerate for an hour or longer if possible, as directed. When you're ready to cook, prepare grill for indirect heat. Unwrap stuffed breast halves; prepare herb butter as directed (you will not need the chicken broth). Place bundles on grate away from coals. Brush with herb butter; turn and brush second side. Cover grill; cook for 25 minutes or until cooked through, turning twice and brushing with herb butter. Cut strings and remove before serving. Serve with morel cream sauce if you like.

Three Morel Cream Sauces

If you took a survey on the most common way of preparing morels, cream sauce would surely come out on top. Morel cream sauce is great with fried or grilled fish; it makes a delicious sauce for rice, pasta or mashed potatoes; and it's wonderful poured over hot biscuits or toasted country bread. Here are three variations on this popular sauce.

Simple Morel Cream Sauce

4 servings   Preparation: Under 15 minutes

8 to 12 ounces fresh morels, cut up
1 tablespoon unsalted butter, divided
2 teaspoons all-purpose flour

1 cup cream or half-and-half
1 tablespoon snipped fresh chives, optional
Salt and pepper

In large skillet, sauté morels in half of the butter over medium heat until just tender, stirring occasionally. Push the mushrooms to the side of the skillet. Add remaining butter to center of skillet; when it melts, sprinkle flour over butter, stirring constantly. Cook, stirring constantly, for about 1 minute. Swirl pan so that all the mushroom juices are incorporated into the flour. When the flour thickens and bubbles, stir mushrooms back into mixture and add cream, stirring constantly. Cook until sauce thickens and bubbles. Stir in chives, and salt and pepper to taste.

Morel Cream Sauce with Roasted Shallots

4 servings   Preparation: Over an hour

6 shallots
4 cloves garlic
2 tablespoons olive oil
8 to 12 ounces fresh morels, cut up
1 teaspoon minced fresh rosemary leaves,
     or ½ teaspoon dried

1 teaspoon dried rubbed sage
½ cup dry Marsala wine
½ cup dry sherry
1 cup chicken broth
½ cup cream or half-and-half
Salt and white pepper

Heat oven to 300°F. In small baking dish, combine shallots, garlic and oil. Cover with foil; bake for 1 hour, or until shallots and garlic are very soft. Remove from oven and set aside until cool enough to handle. Slice shallots and garlic; reserve oil. (This can be prepared a day or more in advance; refrigerate sliced vegetables and oil separately until needed.)

In large skillet, heat 1 tablespoon of the reserved oil over medium heat (refrigerate any remaining oil for another use). Add morels, rosemary, sage, and sliced shallots and garlic; cook, stirring frequently, until juices released by morels have cooked away. Add Marsala and sherry; increase heat to medium-high and cook until liquid has reduced to about 1 tablespoon, 5 to 10 minutes. Add broth and cream; cook until liquid has reduced to about half, 10 to 15 minutes. Season to taste with salt and pepper.

Morels with Crème Fraîche

4 servings

8 to 12 ounces fresh morels, cut up
1 tablespoon butter
1 cup chardonnay
1 tablespoon all-purpose flour
½ cup chicken broth

½ cup crème fraîche*
1 tablespoon torn wood sorrel leaves or
   minced fresh parsley
Salt and freshly ground pepper

In medium skillet, sauté morels in butter over medium heat until mushrooms release their liquid. Add chardonnay; increase heat to medium-high and cook, stirring occasionally, until wine reduces to about 2 tablespoons, about 5 minutes. Reduce heat to medium. Sprinkle flour into skillet, stirring constantly; cook and stir for about 1 minute. Add chicken broth while continuing to stir; cook until mixture becomes smooth and somewhat thickened, about 2 minutes. Add crème fraîche and wood sorrel; cook for about 3 minutes, stirring occasionally. Remove from heat. Season to taste with salt and pepper.

*Crème fraîche is a thickened, slightly fermented cream with a nutty flavor; it makes a wonderful topping for fresh berries. It can be boiled without curdling, making it useful for sauces. Look for it in the dairy case of large supermarkets, or make your own by combining 1 cup heavy cream and 1 tablespoon buttermilk in saucepan. Cook over very low heat, stirring constantly, until warmed to 85°F (it will feel cool to the touch). Remove from heat; cover loosely and let stand at room temperature until thickened, anywhere from 8 to 24 hours. Cover and refrigerate for 24 hours before using. Crème fraîche will keep for 10 days in the refrigerator.

Asparagus (Asparagus officinalis)

Wild asparagus is very easy to identify, and can be prepared just like the kind you buy at the store. Look for last year's dead brown asparagus ferns, then check at the base for new growth in spring.

HABITAT, RANGE

Asparagus grows in disturbed areas, on the edges of crop fields, along railroad beds and ditches, and near utility poles in agricultural country. It needs a good amount of sun, and prefers sandy, somewhat moist soil. It is found throughout our area, and grows throughout much of the country.

Asparagus range

PARTS USED

Young shoots, before the flowering head opens; raw or cooked

SEASONS

Spring

IDENTIFICATION TIPS, DANGEROUS LOOKALIKES

Asparagus is unmistakable; the wild variety looks just like the kind you buy in the store. The easiest way to locate asparagus is to look for last year's distinctive fern, which looks like a feathery, yellowed Christmas tree that is 2 or 3 feet tall; new shoots will be at or near the base. During the spring and summer, the fern has soft, feathery branchlets that grow alternately on the central stalk. If you examine the plant closely, you'll see the true scale-like leaves; they're shaped like daggers and clasp the stalk, just like the leaves found on the familiar edible asparagus spear.

HARVESTING TIPS

Cut the spears at ground level with a pocket knife, or use a dandelion digger to cut them just below the surface. If you plan to harvest the same spot more than once, break off any spears that are starting to develop ferns; this will increase the yield of edible stalks because the root

Asparagus spear

Asparagus fern in midsummer

will send up new shoots rather than putting its energy into growing ferns. Don't over-harvest a particular patch of asparagus; after 2 or 3 pickings, leave the patch undisturbed so the plant can grow and replenish the roots for the following year.

Asparagus grows very rapidly once the weather warms, often producing edible spears within a day. Your asparagus expedition may be more productive if you go later in the day rather than first thing in the morning; some say that the spears are more tender if picked late in the day, although I've not been able to verify this.

SPECIAL CONSIDERATIONS

The berries cause gastrointestinal problems and should not be eaten (fortunately, birds seem immune to these deleterious effects because they are the primary seed disperser for the plant). According to the New Zealand Dermatological Society, sap from the young, raw shoots may cause contact dermatitis in sensitive individuals, particularly those such as commercial asparagus pickers who are exposed to the plants for a long time.

MORE ABOUT ASPARAGUS: You're lucky if you find asparagus growing in the wild, because it saves you the time and trouble of growing it yourself. Asparagus is a slow starter; it takes several years before the plants produce enough asparagus to harvest. But once a plant starts producing, it may continue for as long as 20 years, so it pays to remember where you find it in the wild. I've located good stands by driving around in rural areas during summer and fall, when the feathery ferns produced by the plant are easy to see; although the asparagus is not edible at this time, the same area will produce the following spring. With modern clean-tillage practices and ditch-clearing efforts, the distinctive fern may be long gone in spring, when the plants are producing edible spears, so it's very helpful to locate stands you can return to in the spring.

Native to Europe, asparagus has been considered a delicacy since Greek and Roman times. In addition to its culinary uses, asparagus—particularly the root, but also the shoot and seeds—has been used as a folk remedy (and in modern homeopathy) for conditions as varied as gout, urinary infections, rheumatism, high blood pressure, menstrual cramping and arthritis; it is also widely considered an aphrodisiac.

Asparagus found in the wild are escapees from cultivated asparagus. Birds are the primary seed disperser; if you're having a hard time finding wild asparagus, look along right-of-way areas near an asparagus farm, where birds may have deposited asparagus seeds in their droppings. Although asparagus is known as an early-spring crop, remember that the plants won't start producing until soil temperatures reach the low 50s. The temptation to rush the season is great in the spring, but you're wasting your time if you go out when the ground is still too cold.

As with domestic asparagus, the portion of the spear that bends rather than breaks will be tough. Peel the bases of such spears, or snap off the tough portion and save it to peel and cook for cream soups. Asparagus is edible in any size from the thickness of your pinkie up to the size of your thumb, as long as it is still tender. Once it gets thick and tough, starts to flower, or turns into a fern, it is no longer edible; no parts of the asparagus plant other than the young, tender spears should be eaten.

Asparagus is delicious simply steamed and served with butter; it's also excellent when sliced raw into salads. It's best when eaten the same day it's picked, but can be stored in the crisper drawer for a day or two. Don't wash it until you're ready to use it; at that time, simply place it in a sinkful of cold water or rinse under the faucet, then trim off any tough or dried ends.

JUST FOR FUN
Asparagus flower arrangements
In summer and fall, cut a stem of asparagus fern from one of your wild patches. Add it to a vase with daisies, sunflowers and other wildflowers for a lovely table arrangement.

QUICK IDEAS FOR USING ASPARAGUS
- Use wild asparagus in literally any recipe you have for domestic asparagus. It also works well in recipes that call for fiddlehead ferns.
- Asparagus works really well in tempura recipes; try a few spears next time you pepare this Japanese classic.

OTHER RECIPES IN THIS BOOK FEATURING ASPARAGUS
- As substitute in Fiddlehead Pie (page 38)

Simple Steamed Asparagus with Three Sauces

4 servings (sauce recipes each make about 1 cup)   Preparation: Under 30 minutes

Fresh wild asparagus is so good, it doesn't need much in the way of embellishment. Here are basic steaming instructions, along with a trio of sauces; choose your favorite.

1 pound fresh asparagus   **Blender Hollandaise, Mustard-Dill Sauce or Blue Cheese Sauce (recipes below)**

If the asparagus has tough ends at the bottom, snap them off at the point where they break naturally. Rinse asparagus well; place in top half of steamer and set aside. Add 2 inches water to bottom half of steamer; begin heating over medium heat while you make the sauce you have selected. When the sauce is ready, place top half of steamer over boiling water in bottom half. Cover tightly and steam until asparagus is tender-crisp, 2 to 5 minutes depending on thickness. Serve hot, with sauce.

Blender Hollandaise

3 large egg yolks
2 tablespoons freshly squeezed lemon juice
½ teaspoon Dijon mustard

A pinch of cayenne pepper
½ cup (1 stick) butter

Combine egg yolks, lemon juice, mustard and cayenne in blender jar; process just until smooth, about 5 seconds. In small saucepan, heat butter until melted and close to boiling. With blender running, carefully pour butter in thin stream into egg yolk mixture; process until thick and creamy, 20 to 40 seconds. Keep warm by placing blender jar in pan of hot water.

Mustard-Dill Sauce

¾ cup plain yogurt (lowfat works fine)
¼ cup grainy or Dijon mustard
1 tablespoon snipped fresh dill weed

2 teaspoons very finely minced red onion
½ teaspoon honey

Combine all ingredients in small bowl, stirring to blend.

Blue Cheese Sauce

¾ cup sour cream
¾ cup blue cheese crumbles (about 1 ounce)
3 tablespoons milk

1 green onion, sliced
¼ teaspoon salt
A dash of Tabasco sauce

Combine all ingredients in blender jar; process until onion is finely chopped. Transfer mixture to small saucepan or microwave-safe bowl. Heat over medium heat (or at medium power) until sauce is warm; do not boil.

Grilled Springtime Vegetables with Pasta

For each 2 servings; make as much as you wish   Preparation: About an hour

For this dish, you need a special "grilling wok". This metal basket-like container is perforated overall with holes, and is designed to be placed on a grate over coals (or on a gas grill). The basket contains the small pieces of food, while the holes allow the heat—and grilled flavor—to reach the food.

½ cup ramp bulbs,* cut from the stem at the point where the bulb narrows and turns maroon (reserve leaves for another use)

1 tablespoon olive oil, divided

Salt and coarsely ground black pepper

1 to 1½ cups cut-up asparagus (cut into 1-inch pieces before measuring)†

4 ounces (approximate) uncooked medium-sized shaped pasta such as tiralli, shells, orechiette, spirals or penne rigate

¼ cup coarsely grated Pecorino Romano or other hard, salty, full-flavored cheese

Prepare charcoal grill, or pre-heat gas grill. Begin heating a large pot of salted water to boiling; this will be used for cooking the pasta.

In small bowl, toss ramp bulbs with half of the oil, and salt and pepper to taste. Place in grilling wok, and position on grate over prepared coals. Cook, stirring frequently, for about 5 minutes; the ramps should develop some charred spots, but should not burn. Meanwhile, toss asparagus with remaining oil, and salt and pepper to taste.

Add pasta to the water, which by now should be boiling, and cook according to package directions. Meanwhile, add asparagus to grilling wok with ramps, and cook, stirring frequently, for 5 to 10 minutes longer; if vegetables begin to burn before the pasta is done, move them off to cooler area of the grill or remove them completely. Drain cooked pasta. Add grilled vegetables and Romano cheese to pasta, tossing well.

Note: The first time I prepared this, I also had some cooked morel mushrooms from making a batch of Morel Rings in Consommé (page 61). I tossed the morels with the pasta, asparagus and ramps, and it was heavenly. You could sauté a small batch of morels—say, a cup or so—in some butter or oil, and add them to the pasta.

*If you don't have ramps, substitute the white part of green onion bulbs.
†You may substitute fiddlehead fern coils and stems for the asparagus. The ferns should be par-boiled in a pot of salted water for 10 minutes, then drained well before adding to the grill wok.

Spiral-Wrapped Asparagus

Per serving; make as much as you wish   Preparation: Under 15 minutes

4 fresh asparagus spears, at least
⅜ inch in diameter
1 teaspoon olive oil

2 tablespoons grated Parmesan cheese
4 very thin slices prosciutto (see note on
page 77) or Westphalian ham*

Heat oven to 350°F. Use a vegetable scraper to peel the asparagus to within an inch of the budding top. Pat dry with paper towels to remove any clinging moisture; asparagus must be dry. Place in baking dish. Brush asparagus on all sides with the olive oil; some of the oil will rub off onto the baking dish, so there's no need for any further oiling of the dish.

Place Parmesan cheese on a plate. One at a time, roll asparagus in Parmesan. Wrap each asparagus spear with a piece of prosciutto, starting at the top and spiraling down the stem. Place the wrapped asparagus back into the baking dish. Sprinkle any remaining Parmesan over the top. Bake until asparagus is just tender, 10 to 15 minutes.

*The prosciutto must be very thinly sliced—almost shaved. If the slices are very wide, cut or tear them lengthwise into narrower strips; the ideal strip is 1½ to 2 inches wide, and 6 or 7 inches long.

Oven-Roasted Asparagus with Parmesan

Per 2 servings; make as much as you wish   Preparation: Under 30 minutes

Roasting brings out a wonderful depth of flavor in fresh asparagus.

½ pound fresh asparagus
2 teaspoons extra-virgin olive oil
1 clove garlic, coarsely chopped

Salt and freshly ground pepper
A chunk of Parmesan cheese
A few lemon wedges

Heat oven to 450°F. If the asparagus has tough ends at the bottom, snap them off at the point where they break naturally. Rinse asparagus well; pat completely dry with clean towel. In 9 x 9-inch baking dish, stir together oil and garlic. Add asparagus, rolling around to coat. Sprinkle with salt and pepper to taste. Bake until asparagus is bright green and just beginning to turn tender-crisp, 8 to 10 minutes, rolling asparagus over occasionally with spatula. While asparagus is baking, use a cheese plane (or sharp swivel-bladed peeler, being careful not to slice your fingers) to shave a few tablespoons of Parmesan cheese from the block; alternately, shred the cheese coarsely with a grater. When asparagus is just tender-crisp, scatter cheese shavings over top. Return to oven for about 5 minutes longer. Serve with lemon wedges; each person can squeeze as much as they like onto their portion.

Asparagus with Garlic Grits and Eggs

2 brunch or light main-dish servings   Preparation: Under 30 minutes

This sounds unusual, but the combination is delicious. The runny egg yolks create a type of sauce for the asparagus and grits. (If salmonella is a concern in your area, use pasteurized eggs for this dish, since the yolks will be only lightly cooked.) Serve this as a light supper dish; it's also fabulous for a special luncheon or brunch.

1½ cups water
1 small clove garlic, pressed or very
    finely minced
¼ teaspoon salt
½ cup quick-cooking grits (not instant)
10 to 12 asparagus spears (about ¼ inch
    in diameter)

1 teaspoon butter
2 or 4 eggs*
2 ounces crumbled feta cheese (about
    ½ cup)
2 tablespoons finely chopped Parmesan or
    Romano cheese

Heat oven to broil; adjust oven rack so it is 5 or 6 inches away from broiler element. Spray 2 individual oval ramekins with nonstick spray; set aside (you may also use a single larger ramekin, or an 8 x 8-inch baking dish, in place of the individual ramekins, but it is more difficult to serve this if it is prepared in a single dish). In medium saucepan, combine water, garlic and salt. Heat to a vigorous boil over medium-high heat. Stirring constantly, sprinkle grits into water. Reduce heat to medium-low; cover and cook until thickened, about 7 minutes, stirring occasionally. Divide cooked grits evenly between prepared ramekins, smoothing top; set aside.

Add about an inch of water to a large skillet; heat to boiling over high heat. Add asparagus, and cook for 2 minutes; drain and immediately rinse with cold water to set the color. Pat asparagus dry; arrange over grits, dividing evenly between 2 ramekins. Drain water from skillet; wipe dry if necessary. Add butter, and heat over medium-high heat until bubbly. Carefully break eggs into skillet. Cook until whites are just set. Transfer eggs to ramekins, arranging them carefully over asparagus; take care not to break the yolks. Sprinkle feta and Parmesan cheeses over eggs and asparagus. Place ramekins on oven rack under broiler. Cook until egg yolks film over and cheeses are beginning to color, 3 to 4 minutes; eggs should still be runny. Serve immediately.

*The dish is best with 2 eggs per serving, but you may use 1 egg per serving for a lighter meal, or if you are concerned about cholesterol or calories.

Stir-Fried Asparagus with Almonds

3 or 4 servings   Preparation: Under 15 minutes

Oyster sauce is a thick, rich sauce found in the Asian section at large supermarkets. Substitute ½ teaspoon molasses if oyster sauce is unavailable; the flavor will be different, but the dish will still be tasty.

Sauce:

1 tablespoon soy sauce

1 tablespoon chicken broth, white wine or
   water

1 teaspoon oyster sauce

1 tablespoon peanut or canola oil

¼ cup slivered blanched almonds

1 pound asparagus, cut into 1-inch
   lengths*

2 teaspoons minced garlic

In small bowl, blend together all sauce ingredients; set aside. Line a plate with paper towels; set aside. Heat wok or large skillet over medium-high heat until hot. Add oil, swirling to coat inside of wok. When oil is hot but not smoking, add almonds; stir-fry until beginning to color, about 1 minute. Immediately remove almonds from wok, transferring to paper towel-lined plate. Discard all but a thin film of oil from wok; return wok to heat. Add asparagus; stir-fry for about a minute. Add garlic; stir-fry for 30 seconds longer. Add sauce mixture; stir-fry until asparagus is just tender-crisp and most of the liquid from the sauce has cooked away, 3 or 4 minutes. Add drained almonds, stirring to combine. Serve immediately.

*Cut the asparagus at a slight angle for more even cooking and a nicer appearance.

Asparagus with Prosciutto and Mint

4 servings   Preparation: Under 15 minutes

Prosciuto is a specially cured Italian ham that is available in the deli area at larger supermarkets, as well as at Mediterranean markets. It has a nutty taste that is the perfect complement to asparagus; mint adds an unusual but delicious note to this dish.

1 pound fresh asparagus, cut into
   1-inch lengths

2 ounces very thinly sliced prosciutto
   (generally 3 or 4 slices)

1 tablespoon chopped shallots

1 to 1½ teaspoons unsalted butter

1 tablespoon minced fresh mint leaves

Freshly ground black pepper

Steam asparagus until just tender-crisp (see Simple Steamed Asparagus, page 73), 2 to 5 minutes depending on size. Immediately refresh with cold running water to stop cooking and set the color; set aside to drain.

Slice prosciutto into strips that are approximately ½ inch long and ⅛ inch wide; set aside. In medium skillet, sauté shallots in butter over medium heat for about 2 minutes, stirring several times. Add prosciutto; cook for about 2 minutes longer. Add well-drained asparagus and mint leaves. Cook, stirring occasionally, until asparagus is warmed through, about 2 minutes. Season with pepper to taste (the prosciutto is salty, so the dish probably won't need any added salt).

Baked Asparagus with Hazelnut Breadcrumbs

3 or 4 servings   Preparation: Under 30 minutes

Fresh breadcrumbs have better texture and flavor for this dish than dried breadcrumbs, and they're easy to make. Be sure to use freshly grated Parmesan cheese also.

2 teaspoons minced garlic
1 tablespoon olive oil or butter
2 tablespoons white wine, chicken broth
    or water
1 pound fresh asparagus

Salt and pepper
1 cup fresh breadcrumbs*
½ cup grated Parmesan cheese
¼ cup finely chopped hazelnuts

Heat oven to 375°F. In small skillet, sauté garlic in oil over medium heat until just tender. Add wine; cook for about a minute, stirring occasionally. Remove from heat. Arrange asparagus in baking dish large enough to hold it comfortably, no more than 2 deep (a 9 × 12-inch dish works well). Pour garlic mixture over asparagus, turning to coat all spears. Sprinkle with salt and pepper to taste (remember that the Parmesan cheese is salty, so don't use too much salt); toss again. In small bowl, mix together breadcrumbs, cheese and hazelnuts. Sprinkle evenly over asparagus. Cover baking dish with foil or lid. Bake for 15 minutes. Remove cover and bake for 10 minutes longer, until crumbs are browned and asparagus is tender-crisp.

*To make fresh breadcrumbs, remove the crusts from sliced bread. Tear bread into 1-inch chunks. Turn on food processor or blender; add a handful of bread chunks through processor feed tube or open blender top and process until reduced to crumbs (be ready to put the lid on immediately after adding the bread to a blender, as it may jump high out of the blender jar). Day-old French or Italian bread works particularly well for this recipe.

Guiltless Asparagus Guacamole

About 2 cups (6 to 8 appetizer servings)   Preparation: Under 30 minutes

This is much lower in fat than traditional guacamole, and it won't turn brown! For a non-dairy version, simply omit the yogurt; the guacamole will still taste great.

½ pound asparagus spears, cut into 1-inch
    lengths (2 to 2½ cups)
1 clove garlic
2 to 3 tablespoons plain yogurt (low-fat
    works fine)
1 tablespoon freshly squeezed lime juice
½ teaspoon ground cumin

½ teaspoon dried oregano
¼ teaspoon salt
¼ teaspoon Tabasco sauce
⅓ cup prepared salsa; or ½ cup canned
    diced tomato, drained before measuring
Tortilla chips* for serving

Steam, microwave or boil asparagus until just tender. Drain, rinse in cold water and set aside until completely cool. In food processor fitted with metal blade, combine cooled asparagus, garlic, yogurt, lime juice, cumin, oregano, salt and Tabasco; pulse on-and-off just until fairly smooth but not puréed. Add salsa or tomatoes; pulse a few times to blend. Serve with tortilla chips.

*For easy, low-fat tortilla chips, cut burrito-sized flour tortillas into 10 wedges each. Place on baking sheet; spray with nonstick spray on both sides. Bake at 375°F until lightly browned, 6 to 10 minutes. These are best if baked in a single layer, or with minimal overlap; prepare additional batches as needed.

Asparagus Risotto

4 servings   Preparation: Under 30 minutes

Saffron gives the rice a lovely yellow color and subtle taste; the asparagus and roasted pepper make for a really attractive and colorful dish.

1 quart chicken broth or vegetable broth, approximate
A pinch of saffron threads
2 tablespoons chopped shallots
1 tablespoon olive oil
1 cup arborio, carnaroli or other short-grain rice suitable for risotto

⅓ cup dry sherry or white wine
¼ pound asparagus, cut into 1-inch pieces
¼ cup diced roasted red bell pepper, optional
¼ cup finely chopped Parmesan or Romano cheese

In medium saucepan, combine broth and saffron. Begin heating over medium heat; the broth will need to be simmering throughout rice preparation, so keep an eye on it and adjust temperature accordingly.

In heavy-bottomed medium saucepan, sauté shallots in oil until tender, about 5 minutes. Add rice and cook, stirring frequently, for about 5 minutes; the rice will look chalky. Add wine and cook, stirring frequently, until wine cooks away. Add about ¼ cup of the simmering broth and cook, stirring frequently, until the liquid cooks away. Continue to add broth in small batches, stirring frequently, until the rice is almost tender, about 15 minutes. Add asparagus to saucepan with rice and continue to cook, adding broth as needed, until rice is just tender but still firm to the bite in the center. Total cooking time will be about 20 minutes; you may not need quite all the broth, or you may need a bit more (use hot water if you run out of broth near the end.)

Add roasted pepper; cook for about a minute, stirring constantly. Add a bit more broth if necessary, until rice is proper consistency; it should be creamy but not soupy. Remove from heat; stir in Parmesan cheese and serve immediately.

Cattails (broadleaf cattail, *Typha latifolia;* narrowleaf cattail, *T. angustifolia*)

Sometimes referred to as "nature's grocery store," cattails provide food throughout much of the year. Parts used include the young green stalks, as well as the sausage-like flower heads and, later, pollen from the flower heads. Serious foragers even dig the roots in fall and winter, to make a fine flour.

HABITAT, RANGE

Cattails grow in marshes and swampy areas throughout the United States and Canada, with the exception of the Arctic regions. They are one of the most well-known of wild edibles.

Cattail range

PARTS USED

Young stalks, flower heads, pollen, roots (rhizomes)

SEASONS

Young stalks are harvested in spring, before the plants set their sausage-like flower heads. Flower heads are edible in spring, before any part turns brown. Pollen is gathered in early summer in our region. Roots (rhizomes) are dug from winter through early spring.

IDENTIFICATION TIPS, DANGEROUS LOOKALIKES

Cattail stands can always be recognized by the spikes topped with the unmistakable sausage-like flower heads. In winter and early spring, look for last fall's puffy brown flower heads, surrounded by dead reeds and leaves. The new stalks of spring will be in the midst of last year's dead growth, and around the edges of the cattail stand. In late spring, the

Emerging cattail head (narrowleaf)

Pollen-covered heads (narrowleaf)

Male and female heads (broadleaf)

stalks set the characteristic male and female flower heads. A short pollen season follows in early summer; soon after this, the male flower head withers away and the female flower head becomes covered with the familiar downy seeds, which remain on the plant until the following spring.

Cattails are not the only plant growing in the marshes, however, and when harvesting stalks you must take care to avoid harvesting the similar but poisonous iris (*Iris* spp.). Non-poisonous plants like reeds (*Phragmites* spp.), and sweetflag or calamus (*Acorus calamus*) also grow throughout the region, and may be mistaken as cattails by the beginner. When harvesting young cattail stalks in spring, always look for last year's growth as a primary indicator that cattails do, indeed, grow in the marsh you're in. Pay attention to the leaf shape and growth habit of stalks within the cattail bed, and you may notice other plants with lance-shaped leaves that look different. Cattails have long, swordlike leaves that clasp the stalk, while the leaves of iris and other plants grow in a more fan-like fashion.

As spring progresses, cattails grow 3 to 6 feet tall, while iris never grows beyond 2 or 3 feet tall; iris develop a showy flower rather than the sausage-shaped flower head of cattails. Calamus produces a sausage-shaped flower head, but this head grows at an angle to the plant, while cattail flower heads are centered on the stalk as though impaled up the middle. Calamus, which is edible (but has to be prepared quite differently than cattails), has a strong, spicy smell, while cattail is odorless.

HARVESTING TIPS

The thicker, larger cattail stalks have a larger edible heart; smaller stalks may yield nothing but blanched leaves. See the text that follows for more details on harvesting cattails at various times of year.

SPECIAL CONSIDERATIONS

To avoid possible water-borne parasites when eating raw cattail stalks, you may want to soak the peeled stalks for a few minutes in water containing water-purifying tablets used by campers. If you want to use the pollen from male flower heads and you're sensitive to pollens, it would be prudent to sample just a small portion of pollen-containing foods until you are sure you won't have a problem. If you want to experiment with cattail stuffing for toys or pillows (below), you may want to enclose the fluff within thick batting to avoid the allergic reaction reported by naturalist Steve Brill (*Identifying and Harvesting Edible and Medicinal Plants in Wild [and Not So Wild] Places*).

MORE ABOUT CATTAILS: I don't know who first called cattails "nature's grocery store," but the moniker seems appropriate, as the cattail provides a variety of foods throughout the year. In spring, tender young stalks can be eaten raw, or cooked like asparagus. In late spring, cattails develop a sausage-shaped double seed head; the female head is on the bottom and the male head is on the top (on common or broadleaf cattails, the heads are touching, while on narrowleaf cattails there is a space separating them). The male head can be boiled and eaten like corn-on-the-cob, and the cooked "buds" can be scraped from the "cob" and used in casseroles and other dishes. In late spring or early summer, the male head becomes covered in golden pollen, which adds a lovely color and flavor to baked goods. The rhizomes become laden with starch after the growing season, and can be processed from late fall through early spring to yield a sweet, silky flour.

As with all wild-foods harvesting, it's important to keep the welfare of the resource in mind. Cattail swamps provide important habitat and food for wildlife. Cattail debris is used by muskrats for their lodges, and by geese for their nesting platforms. Birds such as red-winged blackbirds nest in the stands. Many animals, including muskrats and geese, feed on the rhizomes. You won't damage a large cattail stand by harvesting the stalks around the periphery; the rhizomes will survive to sprout new shoots, so all you're doing is controlling the spread of the colony. Likewise, harvesting the flower heads and pollen around the edge of the stand won't cause permanent damage. Be sure to leave some flowering heads to go to seed; warblers and other birds use the fluff to build nests the following spring.

To harvest springtime cattail stalks, grasp one near the base and pull straight up. The stalk should pop out fairly easily. If you notice a strong, spicy smell when you pull a stalk, check carefully, as you may have accidentally collected calamus rather than cattail (which have no perceptible odor). I like to peel the hard outer leaves off right away, and to break off the inedible upper green leaf portions at the same time, placing the peeled white-to-pale-green heart of the stalk in my collecting bag (it's much easier to carry a bag of hearts than an armload of 3-foot-long stalks). If I don't get quite all of the tough leaves off, it's easy enough to finish the job at home, so I don't worry overmuch about getting all of the outer leaves off at this stage. Cattail stalks have a mild flavor, somewhat reminiscent of cucumber with asparagus overtones. Please see more complete instructions for peeling cattail stalks with the Cossack Asparagus recipe on page 85.

To harvest the flowering heads, keep a sharp eye on the swamp, inspecting it at close range; the heads will be covered in a sheath of leaves at first, and so are difficult to see from a distance. When the heads are just about to break out of the papery sheaths, snip them off the stalk with a pruning snipper. Cooked heads yield small kernel-like buds whose flavor reminds me somewhat of broccoli, again with asparagus overtones. (To separate the buds for use in recipes, simply rub or scrape them from the boiled heads, discarding the core.)

A week or so after the flower heads have broken from the sheaths, the male heads become covered with golden pollen, which is as fine as talcum powder. Gently bend a stalk over a plastic bucket, and knock the head against the inside walls of the bucket to dislodge the pollen. On average, you'll need to harvest pollen from 40 cattails to get ½ cup. Don't wait too long to gather the pollen; it remains on the heads for only a few days, and a good rain or wind could remove it. Not all plants in a cattail stand ripen at the same time, however, so the harvest can last a week or two. Once you've got the pollen home, sift it with a wire-mesh strainer; freeze for long-term storage. Pollen adds a subtle corn flavor and a lovely golden color to baked goods. When adding pollen to recipes, reduce the flour slightly to compensate, using perhaps ¼ cup less flour for ½ cup added pollen. I've found that ½ cup of pollen is a good amount to use in muffins, cakes and breads; ¼ cup works well for a good-sized batch of pancakes.

I've never dug roots (although I have had the flour made from them, and it is delightful). If you want to try this, I refer you to Euell Gibbons' *Stalking the Wild Asparagus;* this seems to be the standard text to which all other defer. (He also goes into detail about harvesting the young shoots that will soon develop into stalks; again, this is something I've not experienced firsthand.) In harvesting rhizomes, take special care to avoid the poisonous iris, which grow in the same habitat. Iris rhizomes are odorless, but are reported to have an extremely unpleasant taste. Cattail rhizomes are odorless as well, but taste mild. Calamus rhizome, which is edible and can be candied, smells very spicy, so is easily distinguished from cattails. Euell Gibbons writes of getting a yield of several pounds of cattail flour from a square yard of rhizomes (however, he later mentions that he uses it only in its wet state, so we must assume that the yield of dried flour would be considerably less). Other writers, including Steve Brill (*Identifying and Harvesting Edible and Medicinal Plants in Wild [and Not So Wild] Places*) and Kay Young (*Wild Seasons*), offer less-encouraging results; the yields they report were far less, and the work tedious and messy. I've never processed cattail rhizomes. If I were living off the land, I would certainly try it; but since I harvest wild foods for enjoyment rather than out of necessity, I prefer to leave the rhizomes in the swamp, where they will continue to produce tasty foods that are more readily accessible.

JUST FOR FUN
Craft Projects with Dried Cattail Leaves and Seeds (Fluff)
The leaves of cattails can be dried and used in craft projects such as woven toys, baskets, and cane-like seat chairs and backs (soak the dried leaves to make them pliable before weaving; the weave tightens up upon drying). Native peoples wove them into mats, which were even used by the Ioway peoples to build walls for winter dwellings (the Living History Farm in Urbandale, Iowa offers demonstrations of cattail mat building in their re-creation

of an Ioway village; 515-278-5286, info@lhf.org). The fluffy seeds, which cover the female head in late summer and persist through spring, have been used to stuff pillows and toys, and can also be used to make handmade paper. Cattail fluff makes a decent fire starter.

QUICK IDEAS FOR USING CATTAILS

- Add sifted cattail pollen to muffins, quick breads, pancakes etc. You may substitute cattail pollen for up to one-quarter of the measure of white flour in the recipe.
- Slice tender, raw cattail stalks (purified as noted in Special Considerations on pae 00) into salads.
- Add cut-up cattail stalks or cooked, scraped buds to soups or stews.
- Can or freeze cattail stalks for winter use, following the same procedures you would for asparagus.

Cattail and Caramelized Onion au Gratin

4 servings   Preparation: Under an hour

1 large red onion, cut into vertical slivers
   1/8 to 1/4 inch wide
1 tablespoon olive oil
8 to 12 ounces peeled young cattail stalks
   (about 30 average stalks)
2 tablespoons butter
2 tablespoons all-purpose flour

1 cup milk
1 teaspoon dry mustard powder
1/4 teaspoon ground turmeric, optional
1/4 teaspoon salt, or to taste
1/3 cup shredded cheddar cheese
3 tablespoons breadcrumbs

Heat oven to 375°F. Lightly grease 8-inch-square baking dish; set aside. Caramelize onions: In medium skillet, cook onions in oil over medium-low heat until very soft and golden brown, 15 to 20 minutes, stirring frequently. While onions are cooking, heat saucepan of lightly salted water to boiling. Add peeled cattail stalks; cook until just tender, about 5 minutes. Drain thoroughly. Transfer cattails to prepared baking dish. When onions are tender and golden brown, spread onions over cattails in baking dish.

Dry out saucepan used to cook cattails. Melt butter over medium heat. Add flour, whisking constantly to prevent lumps; cook for about a minute, continuing to whisk. Whisk in milk, mustard, turmeric and salt. Cook, whisking frequently, until mixture bubbles and is beginning to thicken. Pour sauce over onions and cattails. Toss together cheese and breadcrumbs; scatter evenly over ingredients in dish. Bake until sauce bubbles and cheese is melted and beginning to brown, about 20 minutes.

Cattail Kernel Pancakes

16 pancakes   Preparation: Under an hour

These make a terrific side dish or a delicious brunch dish. (Try serving some salsa, and maybe a dollop of sour cream, with them; they're also great served plain, hot off the griddle.)

1 cup milk (whole, 2% or skim)	¾ teaspoon salt
½ cup yellow cornmeal	¼ teaspoon baking soda
2 eggs, separated	⅛ teaspoon cayenne pepper
2 tablespoons vegetable oil	Nonstick spray, oil or shortening for
1 to 1¼ cups cattail kernels (see page 82)	greasing griddle
½ cup all-purpose flour	Salsa and sour cream as garnish, optional
1 teaspoon baking powder	

In small bowl, combine milk, cornmeal, egg yolks and vegetable oil. Stir well with fork to blend. Add cattail kernels and stir again. Set aside to allow the cornmeal to soften while you prepare the other ingredients.

Begin heating a griddle or large skillet, as you would for cooking pancakes. Sift together the flour, baking powder, salt, baking soda and cayenne into large mixing bowl; set aside. In another bowl, beat egg whites with whisk or electric mixer until soft peaks form. Working quickly, pour cornmeal mixture into mixing bowl with flour, and stir to combine thoroughly. Add stiff egg whites, and fold in with rubber spatula; do not overmix or the batter will deflate.

The griddle should be hot enough to instantly bead up a drop of water. Spray lightly with nonstick spray, or grease lightly with oil or shortening. Pour about ⅓ cup of the batter onto the griddle for each pancake. When edges become dry and the top is bubbly, turn and cook on second side until just cooked through. Keep warm while cooking remaining pancakes. Serve immediately, with salsa and sour cream if you like.

Cossack Asparagus

General directions; make as much as you wish   Preparation: Under 30 minutes

It takes practice to learn how much to peel away from cattail stalks. If you don't peel enough, the stalks will be too tough to bite through after cooking. No worries, though; if this happens, simply use your teeth to scrape the tender inner flesh away from the tough outer leaves, much like eating artichoke hearts.

Young cattail stalks	**Butter, salt and pepper**

Peel away outer leaves from young cattail stalks until you can break away the green portion, leaving the white bottom portion with just a bit of light green on top; you will be able to dent through the stalk with your fingernail when you have peeled enough of the leaves away. Trim rough ends if desired. Heat pot of salted water to boiling. Add peeled cattail stalks; boil until tender when pierced with a fork, 5 to 10 minutes. Drain and toss with butter, salt and pepper to taste.

Waldorf Salad with Cattails

4 servings   Preparation: Under 15 minutes

The texture and taste of raw young cattail stalks work perfectly in this classic salad.

3 tablespoons sour cream (reduced-fat works fine)

3 tablespoons mayonnaise or salad dressing (reduced-fat works fine)

1 teaspoon honey, optional (good if you're using mayonnaise rather than salad dressing)

2 crisp, juicy apples such as Braeburn, Fuji or Haralson

1 tablespoon lemon juice

1 rib celery

6 peeled young cattail stalks*

1 cup seedless red or green grapes

½ cup chopped walnuts or hickory nuts

Lettuce leaves for serving

In large mixing bowl, stir together sour cream, mayonnaise and honey. Quarter and core apples; peel if you like. Cut apples into ⅜-inch cubes; sprinkle with lemon juice. Add to bowl with dressing. Cut celery into ¼-inch dice; add to bowl. Slice cattail stalks into ¼-inch-wide rounds; add to bowl. Cut grapes in half; add to bowl. Add walnuts to bowl; toss gently but thoroughly. This is best when refrigerated for a few hours to allow flavors to meld, but it can be served right away. To serve, line salad plates with lettuce leaves; mound salad on lettuce.

Variation: Waldorf Salad with Wild Rice

For a more substantial salad, increase sour cream and mayonnaise to ¼ cup each. Add 1 to 1½ cups cooked, cooled wild rice to salad with other ingredients. Serves 4 to 6.

*Wash the peeled cattail stalks with camper's water-purifying tablets as described in cattail text on page 81.

"Kitten Tails" (boiled cattail flower heads)

2 servings; easily increased   Preparation: Under 15 minutes

I don't know who first used the term "kitten tails" for edible cattail flower heads, but it is a delightful name for a delicious dish. This is how I fix them. Eat like corn on the cob, by holding the cooked head and nibbling at the kernels (buds); they pull away from the central stem easily (the stem is not eaten).

12 to 15 male cattail flower heads, picked before pollen develops (see text on page 83)

2 teaspoons butter

Salt and pepper

Heat saucepan of salted water to boiling. Add cattail flower heads; return to boiling. Cook for 5 minutes. Drain, discarding water. In same saucepan over medium heat, melt butter with about 1 teaspoon water. Add drained cattail flower heads, along with salt and pepper to taste. Cook, stirring frequently, for about 5 minutes, or until water cooks away and flower heads are well seasoned. Serve hot.

Summer Sunshine Muffins (with cattail pollen)

12 regular muffins, or 24 mini-muffins   Preparation: Under an hour

2 cups all-purpose flour
1/3 cup sifted cattail pollen
3 tablespoons sugar
1 tablespoon baking powder
1/2 teaspoon salt

1/2 cup sunflower nuts
1 cup milk
1 egg
1/4 cup plus 2 tablespoons butter, melted
2 tablespoons honey, approximate

Heat oven to 425°F. Spray muffin pans with nonstick spray; set aside. Sift flour, pollen, sugar, baking powder and salt together into mixing bowl. Add sunflower nuts; stir to combine. In smaller bowl (or 2-cup measure), combine milk, egg and melted butter; beat with fork to mix well. Pour milk mixture, all at once, into flour mixture. Stir with wooden spoon until just barely mixed, about 15 strokes; batter should still be lumpy (if you over-mix, muffins will be tough). Spoon into prepared muffin cups. Place on center rack in oven; immediately reduce heat to 375°F. Bake for 15 minutes (10 minutes for mini-muffins); right at end of this baking period, heat honey in microwave to make it free-flowing. Remove muffin pans from oven. Quickly brush muffin tops with honey. Return pans to oven, rotating position so that the part of the pan that was in the front of the oven is now in the back (this helps ensure even cooking). Bake until a toothpick comes out almost clean, with a few crumbs, 5 to 10 minutes longer. Remove pans from oven; let cool for 5 to 10 minutes, then turn muffins out onto cake cooling rack. Best served warm.

Curried Cattail Hearts

4 servings   Preparation: Under 30 minutes

8 to 12 ounces peeled young cattail stalks
    (about 30 average stalks)
1/4 cup slivered almonds or unsalted
    dry-roasted peanuts
1 tablespoon vegetable oil
1/2 teaspoon cumin seed
1/2 teaspoon mustard seed
1/2 teaspoon dried thyme
3 green onions, sliced 1/8 inch thick
    (white and green parts)

1/4 cup dried currants or raisins, optional
2 teaspoons sugar (use 1 tablespoon if you
    do not use the currants or raisins)
1/2 teaspoon ground turmeric
1/4 teaspoon cayenne pepper
1/2 cup chicken broth
2 tablespoons chopped cilantro
Hot cooked rice

Cut cattail stalks into 2-inch lengths; set aside. Chop almonds coarsely. In wok or sauté pan, heat oil over medium-high heat until hot but not smoking. Add chopped almonds, cumin seed, mustard seed and thyme; stir-fry for 30 seconds. Add cattail stalks, green onions, currants, sugar, turmeric and cayenne; stir-fry for about 2 minutes. Add broth; cover, reduce heat and simmer for 5 minutes, stirring occasionally. If you prefer a thicker sauce, remove cover and cook for a few minutes at high heat until liquid has reduced. Sprinkle with cilantro. Serve with hot cooked rice.

Golden Scones (with cattail pollen)

12 servings   Preparation: Under an hour

These scones get a beautiful color from the pollen and the Yukon gold potatoes. They're perfect for breakfast or brunch, and make an excellent tea-time snack.

½ pound Yukon gold potatoes
1 cup all-purpose flour, plus additional
  for kneading
⅓ cup sifted cattail pollen
1 tablespoon baking powder
1 teaspoon salt
½ teaspoon ground ginger

¼ cup butter, cut into several pieces
1 egg
¼ cup sugar, plus additional for sprinkling
1 to 3 tablespoons milk
⅓ cup golden raisins, dried blueberries or
  cranberries

In saucepan over high heat, boil potato(es) until tender; drain well. Peel and process with ricer, or mash well. Measure ¾ cup of riced/mashed potatoes and set aside to cool; reserve any remaining potato for another use.

While potatoes are cooling, heat oven to 425°F; lightly grease baking sheet. Combine flour, pollen, baking powder, salt and ginger in food processor fitted with steel blade. Pulse on-and-off until well mixed. Add butter; pulse until mixture resembles coarse meal. In small bowl, combine cooled potatoes with egg and sugar; blend with fork. Add potato mixture to food processor with flour mixture; pulse several times, until just combined. Add milk, a tablespoon at a time and processing briefly after each addition, until soft dough forms.

Turn dough out onto lightly floured board; sprinkle raisins over dough. Knead gently for about a minute, adding more flour if necessary. Divide dough into 2 equal portions. Pat each portion into circle that is ½ inch thick and about 6 inches across. Transfer to prepared baking sheet. Sprinkle with additional sugar. Cut each circle into 6 wedges, separating slightly (a spatula works better than a knife for cutting the wedges). Prick tops with fork at ½-inch intervals. Bake until lightly browned and springy to the touch, 15 to 18 minutes.

Pickled Cattail Stalks

2 half-pint jars; easily increased   Preparation: Involved

1 pound peeled young cattail stalks
1 small white onion, sliced vertically into
  very thin strips
3 tablespoons pickling or kosher salt
1½ cups white wine vinegar
1 cup sugar
½ teaspoon mustard seed
¼ teaspoon celery seed
¼ teaspoon ground turmeric
2 half-pint canning jars, with bands and
  new lids

Place cattail stalks and onion in large ceramic mixing bowl. Sprinkle with salt. Add cold water to cover by 1 inch; mix gently. Let stand at room temperature for 2 hours. Drain, discarding water.

In stainless-steel pot, combine vinegar, sugar, mustard seed, celery seed and turmeric. Heat to boiling. Remove from heat; add drained cattail stalks and onions. Let stand at room temperature for 2 hours.

Prepare jars, bands and lids as directed on page 418; if you are unfamiliar with canning procedures, also read the canning information on pages 418-419. Return cattail mixture to boiling. Pack cattail stalks hot, into hot jars. Fill jars with hot liquid, leaving ¼ inch headspace; seal with prepared lids and bands. Process in boiling-water bath for 15 minutes.

Scalloped Tomatoes and Cattails

4 servings   Preparation: Under an hour

½ cup diced onion
1 tablespoon butter
1 can (14.5 ounces) stewed tomatoes
1 tablespoon all-purpose flour
2 cups croutons, divided
1 cup sliced young cattail stalks (peeled
  and cut into ¼-inch pieces before
  measuring)
2 tablespoons chopped fresh basil, or
  1 tablespoon dried
2 teaspoons (packed) brown sugar
1 teaspoon dry mustard powder
½ teaspoon salt
3 tablespoons grated Parmesan cheese

Heat oven to 350°F. Lightly grease 1-quart casserole; set aside. In sauté pan or large skillet, sauté onion in butter over medium heat for about 5 minutes. Meanwhile, drain tomatoes, reserving juice. Add tomato juice to skillet; cook for about 2 minutes longer, or until tomato juice has reduced to about half. Stirring constantly, sprinkle flour into skillet; cook for about 1 minute, stirring constantly. Remove from heat. Add drained tomatoes, 1 cup of the croutons, the cattail stalks, basil, brown sugar, mustard and salt; stir well. Transfer to prepared casserole. Top with remaining 1 cup croutons and the Parmesan cheese. Bake until browned and bubbly, about 25 minutes.

Blueberries & Huckleberries

Although wild blueberries are smaller than their domestic counterparts, they have far more flavor. Huckleberries are interchangeable with blueberries in recipes, and both are excellent eaten out of hand in the field.

HABITAT, RANGE

Blueberries and huckleberries appear, in combination or separately, throughout our range with the exception of the Dakotas, western Iowa and southwestern Minnesota. Black huckleberries are much more common than highbush blueberries; in most parts of our range, if you're picking "blueberries" from a shrub that's more than a foot high, chances are good that you're actually picking huckleberries.

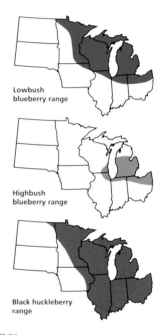

Lowbush blueberry range

Highbush blueberry range

Black huckleberry range

Lowbush or sweet blueberries (*Vaccinium angustifolium*) and black huckleberries (*Gaylussacia baccata*) are found in dry, rocky areas with acidic soil, often at elevation; visitors to the Boundary Waters Canoe Area of northern Minnesota frequently find blueberries along portages, on campsites and on sunny hilltops and ridges. Highbush blueberries (*V. corymbosum*) prefer areas with a bit more moisture; they're found in low areas of forests and woodlots, in sphagnum meadows, and near bogs and swamps, although they are occasionally found in dry areas as well. Blueberries and huckleberries love sunlight, so you won't find them deep in the forest except in clearings.

Lowbush blueberries

Highbush blueberries

PARTS USED
Ripe fruit, raw or cooked

SEASONS
Mid- to late summer

IDENTIFICATION TIPS, DANGEROUS LOOKALIKES

The lowbush blueberry is a native shrub that sprawls along the ground; it's usually less than a foot high, and tends to grow in spreading colonies. Highbush blueberries and huckleberries are taller native shrubs; highbush blueberry shrubs may tower over your head, while huckleberries are typically 2 to 4 feet tall. Leaves on all these plants are oval and light to medium green, with smooth edges; they grow in alternate arrangement on the branches. Lowbush blueberries have small leaves, ½ to 1 inch long; leaves of the taller varieties are generally 1 to 2 inches long.

The fruits of these plants are similar in appearance. Underripe fruits are green at first, turning pink or red before ripening completely. Ripe blueberries are blueish with a light bloom that gives a dusty appearance, while ripe black huckleberries are nearly black with little or no bloom. Blueberries and huckleberries are similar in size, about ¼ inch across or a little larger; they grow in clusters at the end of short stemlets, from which they detach easily. The bottom of each berry has a small crown—a scalloped edge with 5 points. Blueberries contain many tiny seeds that are so soft you'll never notice they're there. All the guide books I've consulted say that huckleberries contain exactly 10 seeds, which is supposed to help distinguish the species from blueberries. Like the seeds of blueberries, huckleberry seeds are soft and don't need to be removed.

There are no dangerous lookalikes; if you've got a ¼-inch-wide purple-to-black fruit with a raised crown on the bottom that is growing on a shrub with small, woody twigs and alternate leaves, you've got a blueberry or huckleberry of some sort. Eat away.

HARVESTING TIPS

Blueberries and huckleberries grow in sunny areas, often at the top of a ridgeline; you will probably have to hike and climb a bit to get to them. Once you're in the berry patch, you'll probably be in full sun, and it can get mighty warm in midsummer when the berries are ripe. Be sure to carry a water bottle or canteen on your berrying expeditions.

If you're planning to make jam, harvest a few half-ripe berries; they'll be pink or red. These add tartness and flavor to your jam.

MORE ABOUT BLUEBERRIES & HUCKLEBERRIES: Wild blueberries and huckleberries were a prime food source for indigenous peoples, who ate them fresh, stewed them, dried them and even made tea from the leaves. Blueberries have been cultivated and harvested commercially since the Civil War era; modern highbush cultivars were developed at the turn of the century. Michigan is the number-one state in commercial highbush blueberry production, with 17,000 acres in cultivation according to data from Michigan State University Extension Services.

As our society becomes more health-conscious, articles are appearing even in the mainstream press about phytonutrients, the current darlings of the nutrition scene. According to *Fit for Life* (part of the Health & Wellness Reference Library), these trace chemicals occur naturally in foods and appear to promote health by reducing harmful levels of free radicals or eliminating cancer-causing substances. Blueberries (and presumably huckleberries, although they are not listed in any of the studies I've seen cited) are a rich source of anthocyanin, an antioxidant* phytonutrient that is believed to reduce the risk of cancer, high blood pressure, diabetes, heart disease and age-related memory loss. Blueberries also provide fair amounts of vitamin C, potassium and phosphorus, and a 1-cup serving provides 5 grams of fiber.

But best of all, wild blueberries and huckleberries taste great—even better than store-bought blueberries. Wild blueberries are much smaller than the store-bought kind; it takes about 400 wild berries to fill a 1-cup measure, while it takes just 50 of the domesticated variety. Because they're so small, wild blueberries have more skin in proportion to the pulp, but I think that the skin is more flavorful than the pulp. Huckleberries seem a bit more complex in flavor, although they are somewhat more mealy than blueberries.

Wild vs. domestic blueberries

If there have been forest fires in the area, look for blueberries and huckleberries starting the following year. They are among the first plants to re-grow in a burned area, and it's said that burning to produce blueberries was one of the first forms of crop manipulation to take place in America. Commercial blueberry growers still burn their fields every few years to increase the concentration of blueberry plants and improve the harvest. In the summer of 2003, I saw areas of the Boundary Waters Canoe Area Wilderness that had burned the previous year; already, lowbush blueberry shrubs were growing on the high ridges.

Blueberries and huckleberries can be stored in the refrigerator for up to a week, but don't wash them until you're ready to use them or they may begin to spoil. They also may be frozen with no preparation other than a quick picking over to remove leaves, twigs and other debris. To keep the frozen berries separated so you can pour out the amount you need, simply spread them on a baking sheet and freeze, then transfer to freezer containers or heavyweight plastic bags.

QUICK IDEAS FOR USING BLUEBERRIES OR HUCKLEBERRIES

- For the most attractive blueberry pancakes, don't mix the blueberries (or huckleberries) into the batter. Make pancake batter as usual and pour a portion onto the heated griddle, then immediately scatter 8 to 12 berries over the wet batter and cook as usual. This method prevents the entire pancake from turning purple.
- Top a bowl of fresh blueberries or huckleberries with a little cream and sugar for a quick and delicious dessert or snack.
- Use huckleberries (or wild blueberries) in any recipe that calls for domestic blueberries.
- Toss a few dried blueberries into hot cereal, or add to granola or trail mix.

OTHER RECIPES IN THIS BOOK FEATURING BLUEBERRIES OR HUCKLEBERRIES

- Golden Scones (page 88)
- As substitute in Currant Scones (page 164)
- As substitute in Gooseberry Crisp (page 173)
- Refrigerator Cookies with Dried Berries (page 235)
- Uncooked Blueberry Jam (chart, page 256)
- Wild Berry-Yogurt Popsicles or Soft-Serve Ice Cream (page 259)
- Wild Berry Parfait with Maypop or Lemon Mousse (page 262)
- Acorn and Wild Berry Porridge (page 272)
- Homemade Granola (page 293)
- Dried blueberries (page 421)

*Antioxidants work to neutralize harmful levels of free radicals, which are by-products of metabolism and are also found in the environment, that scientists believe may encourage cancer growth. A study at Tufts University in Boston puts blueberries at the top of a long list of fruits and vegetables in antioxidant production. (Source: Total Antioxidant Capacity of Fruits; H. Wang, G. Cao and R.L. Prior; *Journal of Agriculture and Food Chemistry, Volume 44, Number 3*)

Old-Fashioned Blueberry Malt

2 servings   Preparation: Under 15 minutes

Here's the way to get the flavor of this malt-shop classic at home. The optional jam or preserves provides an additional flavor kick.

¾ cup fresh blueberries or huckleberries
2 to 3 heaping scoops rich vanilla ice
    cream
1½ cups whole milk, very cold
3 tablespoons malted milk powder

2 tablespoons blueberry jam or preserves,
    optional
4 sugar wafers, preferably 2 vanilla and
    2 strawberry, optional

Combine all ingredients except wafers in blender. Cover tightly and pulse on-and-off several times, until ingredients are beginning to mix and have filled the bottom of the blender. Blend on regular setting until desired consistency, 30 to 45 seconds. Divide between 2 chilled malt glasses; tuck 2 wafers into each malt and serve immediately.

Huckleberry or Wild Blueberry Pie

1 pie   Preparation: About an hour

If the only blueberry pie you've had was made from canned filling, this pie will knock your socks off.

3 cups fresh wild huckleberries or
    blueberries, divided
½ cup sugar
3 tablespoons cornstarch
1 tablespoon lemon juice
1 tablespoon butter

A pinch of salt
A pinch of nutmeg, optional
Pastry for double-crust pie, divided into
    2 equal portions
1 egg yolk, beaten with 1 tablespoon water

In medium saucepan, combine 1 cup of the berries with the sugar, cornstarch and lemon juice; stir to mix. Heat to boiling over medium heat, stirring constantly; cook, stirring constantly, until liquid clears and thickens. Remove from heat; stir in butter, salt and nutmeg. Let cool for about 5 minutes, then add remaining 2 cups berries and set aside until cool.

When berry mixture has cooled, heat oven to 400°F; position oven rack in bottom third of oven. On lightly floured worksurface, roll out 1 portion of pastry and fit into ungreased pie plate. Scrape cooled berry mixture into pie plate. Roll out remaining pastry. Moisten edges of pastry in pie plate, then top with rolled-out pastry (or, if you prefer, make a lattice top; see page 151). Seal, trim and flute edges. Cut inch-long slits in the crust in 6 to 8 places for ventilation. Place pie on baking sheet (to catch drips). Brush top with egg yolk mixture. Bake until crust is golden and filling bubbles through slits, about 30 minutes. Transfer to rack to cool; best served warm.

Tender Whole Wheat Muffins with Wild Berries

12 muffins   Preparation: 7- to 24-hour resting period, followed by about an hour

Baked goods made with 100% whole wheat flour are often heavy and dense. However, a friend told me about soaking the flour overnight in water with a little yogurt; this softens the fibers and produces light, tender muffins. Try it; I think you'll be surprised. Wild blueberries or huckleberries are absolutely perfect in these delicious muffins, but you can use any other wild berry that doesn't have a stone in the center.

2½ cups whole wheat flour
1⅔ cups water
2 tablespoons plain yogurt
2 eggs, or ½ cup liquid egg substitute
1 tablespoon vanilla extract
½ cup sugar
3 tablespoons butter, melted and cooled slightly

1 teaspoon salt
1 teaspoon baking powder
1 teaspoon baking soda
¾ cup chopped butternuts, mockernuts, hickory nuts or other nuts, optional
1 cup wild blueberries, huckleberries or other suitable wild berries

In large mixing bowl, stir together the flour, water and yogurt. Cover loosely with a towel and set aside at room temperature for 7 to 24 hours.

When you are ready to bake, heat oven to 325°F. Generously spray 12-cup muffin pan with nonstick spray; set aside. In small bowl, beat eggs and vanilla with fork. Add sugar, butter, salt, baking powder and baking soda; stir to mix well.

Stir the flour mixture with a large spoon, then add the egg mixture and fold together. Fold in the nuts if using. Add berries and fold in gently. Divide batter among prepared muffin cups. Bake for 40 minutes, or until toothpick inserted into center of muffin in the middle of the pan comes out clean. Remove from oven and let stand for 5 minutes, then turn muffins out onto wire cooling rack; loosen sides of muffins with knife if they are sticking. Serve warm or room temperature.

Blintzes with Blueberry Sauce

4 to 6 servings   Preparation: About an hour

This looks like a bit of work, but you can prepare the various parts ahead of time, then assemble the blintzes just before serving. For an easier version, substitute purchased crèpes (sometimes found in the freezer department at large grocery stores) for the homemade crèpes.

Blueberry sauce:
2 cups wild blueberries or huckleberries, fresh or previously frozen
⅔ cup orange juice
3 tablespoons sugar
2 tablespoons cornstarch blended with 2 tablespoons cold water

Filling:
1 cup small-curd cottage cheese
2 tablespoons sugar
1 teaspoon vanilla extract
¾ teaspoon salt
1 egg, lightly beaten

Crèpe Batter:
1 cup whole milk
1 egg
2 tablespoons vegetable oil
½ teaspoon salt
1 cup all-purpose flour

Unsalted butter, melted
Powdered sugar for serving

To prepare sauce: In small saucepan, combine berries, orange juice and sugar. Heat to boiling over medium heat. Cook, stirring occasionally, for 10 minutes. Stir cornstarch mixture and add to pan, stirring constantly. Cook until mixture is clear and thickened, about 5 minutes. Remove from heat; keep warm. (If sauce is made in advance, refrigerate until needed, then re-warm just before using.)

To prepare filling: Combine all filling ingredients in large mixing bowl; beat with wooden spoon until well blended. Set aside. (If filling is made in advance, cover and refrigerate until needed.)

To make crepes: In blender, combine milk, egg, oil and salt; process until smooth. Add flour; process until just combined, scraping sides once. Set aside for 10 minutes to let thicken slightly. Heat 8-inch nonstick skillet over medium heat until hot. Brush with melted butter. Add 3 tablespoons batter, tilting pan so batter coats evenly. Cook until center is set and edges are beginning to color, 2 to 3 minutes. Shake skillet to loosen crèpe, then invert onto paper towel-lined plate. Repeat with remaining batter, placing paper towel between each crèpe. Set aside. (If crèpes are made in advance, re-stack cooled crepes with waxed paper between layers; cover and refrigerate until needed.)

To assemble blintzes: Place crèpe on worksurface, browned side down. Spread about a tablespoon of the filling in the center. Fold crèpe in half, then in half the other direction to form a rounded triangle. Repeat with remaining crèpes and filling. Brush griddle or large skillet with melted butter. Add filled blintzes; cook until golden on both sides, turning just once. Arrange 2 cooked blintzes on each serving plate; top with blueberry sauce and sprinkle with powdered sugar.

Blueberry Gingerbread Cake

Serves 9   Preparation: About an hour

Nicely moist and not too sweet, this cake is perfect for snacking, dessert … even breakfast! If you like, dress it up with a dollop of whipped cream, or serve it warm with ice cream.

1 cup milk (skim, 2% or whole milk all work fine)
2 tablespoons lemon juice
½ cup (1 stick) butter, softened
1 cup sugar
1 egg
¼ cup molasses

2 cups all-purpose flour
2 teaspoons ginger
1 teaspoon cinnamon
½ teaspoon salt
¼ teaspoon nutmeg
1 cup wild blueberries or huckleberries, fresh or previously frozen

Heat oven to 350°F. Lightly grease and flour an 8- or 9-inch-square pan; set aside. In measuring cup or small bowl, stir together milk and lemon juice; set aside. In large mixing bowl, cream butter with electric mixer. Add sugar and cream together. Add egg and molasses, and beat well (mixture may become granular-looking, but this is OK). Place flour, ginger, cinnamon, salt and nutmeg in a sifter or wire-mesh strainer; sift into mixing bowl. Beat with mixer until just smooth. Add blueberries and fold together gently with rubber spatula. Scrape into prepared pan. Bake for 50 to 60 minutes, or until toothpick inserted in center comes out clean.

Blueberry or Huckleberry Lemon Sauce

2 cups   Preparation: Under 15 minutes

Serve this over cake, ice cream, pancakes or hot cereal. It's best served warm, but is also good cold. It keeps for at least 10 days in the refrigerator.

2 cups wild blueberries or huckleberries, fresh or previously frozen
¼ cup honey

2 tablespoons freshly squeezed lemon juice
¼ teaspoon rum extract, optional
1 tablespoon unsalted butter

In medium saucepan, combine all ingredients except butter. Heat to boiling over medium heat, stirring constantly. Reduce heat; simmer for 5 minutes, stirring occasionally. Remove from heat; add butter, stirring until melted.

Cream Cheese Pie with Blueberry Topping

6 servings   Preparation: About an hour, plus cooling time

Similar to a cheesecake, this easy pie keeps well for several days in the refrigerator. To keep fat and calories down, use the lower-fat alternatives listed in the ingredients; you'll never know the difference.

12 ounces cream cheese (reduced-fat works fine), softened
½ cup sugar
2 tablespoons freshly squeezed lemon juice
2 eggs, or ½ cup liquid egg substitute
½ cup sour cream (reduced-fat works fine)

Topping:
3 cups wild blueberries or huckleberries, fresh or previously frozen
⅓ cup sugar
1 tablespoon cornstarch dissolved in 1 tablespoon cold water

Heat oven to 350°F. Spray pie plate with nonstick spray; set aside (use a standard pie plate, not a shallow one). In large mixing bowl, beat cream cheese with electric mixer for about 3 minutes, or until light and very smooth. Continue beating while adding sugar in small amounts, beating each addition well. Add lemon juice and beat in. Add eggs and sour cream and beat until well mixed. Scrape mixture into prepared pie plate. Place on center rack and bake until filling is set and wooden pick inserted in center comes out clean, 30 to 40 minutes. Set pie on rack and cool to room temperature; the center will sink in somewhat, creating a hollow for the topping.

While pie is baking, prepare topping: In saucepan, combine blueberries and sugar. Cook over medium heat, stirring constantly, until sugar dissolves and juices released by berries come to a boil. Boil for 1 minute. Stir cornstarch mixture, then add to blueberry mixture, stirring constantly. Cook until juices thicken and become glossy, stirring constantly. Set topping mixture aside to cool to room temperature.

When pie and topping have both cooled, pour topping over pie. Cover and refrigerate until well chilled, at least 2 hours.

Blueberry or Huckleberry Syrup

2 half-pints   Preparation: Under 30 minutes (plus optional canning time)

2 half-pint canning jars, with bands and
   new lids
2 cups wild blueberries or huckleberries,
   fresh or previously frozen

1 cup water
1½ cups sugar
¼ cup white corn syrup
1 tablespoon lemon juice

Prepare jars, bands and lids as directed on page 418 (even if you won't be canning the syrup, it's still a good idea to sterilize the jars and lids as directed). In saucepan, combine blueberries and water. Mash berries thoroughly with potato masher. Heat to boiling over high heat, mashing berries several times with potato masher. Cover and reduce heat; simmer for 10 minutes. Strain through 4 layers of dampened cheesecloth. You should have about 1¼ cups juice; add water if necessary to make the measure (if you have significantly more than this, reduce to 1¼ cups by boiling). Discard solids, or refrigerate and use later to add flavor to hot cereal and other dishes.

In 3-quart saucepan, combine 1¼ cups blueberry juice with sugar, corn syrup and lemon juice. Heat to boiling over medium-high heat, stirring until sugar dissolves. Increase heat if necessary and cook, stirring constantly, until liquid comes to a full, rolling boil that can't be stirred down. Boil for 2 minutes, stirring constantly. Remove from heat and let settle for a minute; skim any foam with metal spoon. Pour hot into hot, sterilized jars; seal with new lids and clean bands. To can, process in boiling-water bath for 10 minutes (if you are unfamiliar with canning procedures, read the canning information on pages 418-419).

Variation: Chokeberry Syrup
Follow instructions above, substituting chokeberries for the blueberries. Increase sugar to 1¾ cups. Proceed as directed.

Blueberries with Cinnamon Croutons and Custard

4 servings   Preparation: Under 30 minutes

If you're looking for "something different" to do with blueberries you've picked, try this. It's a delightful textural experience, and quite soothing. You could substitute any pit-free sweet wild berries such as strawberries, raspberries or blackberries for the blueberries.

4 cups day-old French bread cubes, crusts
   removed before cubing (½-inch cubes)
3 tablespoons butter, melted
2 tablespoons sugar
1 teaspoon cinnamon

<u>Custard:</u>
2 egg yolks
¼ cup sugar
1 tablespoon cornstarch
½ teaspoon vanilla extract
2 cups whole milk

2 cups fresh wild blueberries or huckleberries

Heat oven to 375°F. In large mixing bowl, toss together bread cubes, melted butter, sugar and cinnamon. Spread on rimmed baking sheet. Bake until golden brown, about 15 minutes, stirring occasionally. Remove from oven; return croutons to mixing bowl and set aside. (This can be done earlier in the day, or just before serving.)

To prepare custard: In mixing bowl, combine egg yolks, sugar, cornstarch and vanilla; whisk until smooth. In heavy-bottomed saucepan, heat milk over medium heat until small bubbles form around edges. Slowly pour hot milk into egg yolk mixture, whisking constantly. Return mixture to pan; cook over medium heat, whisking constantly, until mixture boils. Adjust heat so mixture boils gently, and cook for about 2 minutes longer, whisking frequently. Remove from heat.

Add blueberries to croutons in mixing bowl; stir gently. Add custard, stirring to combine. Serve immediately, garnishing each serving with a small scoop of ice cream or a dollop of whipped cream if you like.

North Shore Summer Salad

Per serving; make as many as you wish Preparation: Under 15 minutes

This recipe is from my book, The Seasonal Cabin Cookbook. *It's so delicious that it is worth repeating here.*

1½ to 2 cups mixed tender salad greens

3 ounces chunked smoked whitefish, herring, cisco or other light-colored fish (about 1 cup; skin and bones discarded, and fish broken into bite-sized pieces before measuring)

1 slice bacon, cooked crisp, drained and crumbled

⅓ cup fresh wild blueberries or huckleberries

1 thin slice red onion, quartered after slicing

2 tablespoons pecan or hickory-nut pieces*

2 tablespoons blue cheese crumbles, optional

Honey-Mustard Dressing (recipe below)

Place washed, dried greens on individual serving plate(s). Top with smoked fish, bacon and blueberries; scatter red onion, nuts and blue cheese crumbles on top. Serve Honey-Mustard Dressing on the side.

*The nuts are best if lightly toasted: Place the total amount you will need for all salads in a small cast-iron skillet, and toast over medium-high heat, stirring constantly, until fragrant and lightly browned. Transfer immediately to a cool dish after toasting to prevent overcooking; let cool before scattering over salad.

Honey-Mustard Dressing

1½ cups   Preparation: 5 minutes

½ cup extra-virgin olive oil

⅓ cup apple cider vinegar

¼ cup honey

¼ cup Dijon mustard

2 tablespoons dry white wine

¼ teaspoon salt

⅛ teaspoon white pepper

Combine all ingredients in 1-pint glass jar. Cover tightly and shake well to blend. Refrigerate up to 2 weeks.

Prunus Species—Overview

The *Prunus* family is large, and contains some of the best wild fruits: cherries, plums, peaches and apricots. In our region, only cherries and plums thrive. (A cultivated peach, *Prunus persica,* is occasionally found as an escapee in our area with the exception of Minnesota and the Dakotas.) Following is a summary of the USDA data on these categories.

CHERRIES

Within the cherry category, we find the following native wild cherries in our region:
Chokecherry (*P. virginiana*)—reddish or purplish black fruit, grows in hanging clusters (racemes)
Black or rum cherry (*P. serotina*)—purplish black fruit, grows in hanging clusters (racemes)
Pin or fire cherry (*P. pensylvanica*)—bright red fruit, grows singly or in small bunches
Sand cherry (*P. pumila*)—purplish black fruit, grows singly or in small bunches

In addition, the following cultivated cherries are occasionally are seen in the wild as escapees:
Amur chokecherry (*P. maackii*)—black fruit, grows in hanging clusters (racemes)
Common bird cherry (*P. padus*)—black fruit, grows in hanging clusters (racemes)
Mahaleb or St. Lucie cherry (*P. mahaleb*)—black fruit, grows singly or in small bunches
Nanking cherry (*P. tomentosa*)—red fruit, grows in small bunches close to stem
Sour cherry (*P. cerasus*)—bright red fruit, typically grows in pairs
Sweet cherry (*P. avium*)—bright red to purplish black fruit, typically grows in pairs

PLUMS

The following plums are native to our area:
American wild plum (*P. americana*)—red fruit, can be eaten raw
Allegheny plum (*P. alleghaniensis*)—dark purple fruit
Beach plum (*P. maritima*)—purplish black fruit; considered the best of the wild plums
Canadian plum (*P. nigra*; some listed as a variant of *P. americana*)—yellowish to red fruit
Chickasaw plum (*P. angustifolia*)—red fruit
Hortulan plum (*P. hortulana*)—yellow to red fruit
Mexican plum (*P. mexicana*)—reddish purple fruit
Wild goose plum (*P. munsoniana*)—reddish fruit

The European plum (*P. domestica*) is a cultivated variety that occasionally appears in the wild. It has blueish to reddish purple fruit, and can be eaten raw as well as cooked.

All of the fruits listed above are edible; some are tastier than others. Some can be eaten raw; most are better when cooked, and are frequently juiced to make jelly, syrup and other products.

Determining exactly which cherry or which plum you've found is often a matter of research. Check with your local University Extension office, or a knowledgeable local forager, to identify exactly which species you've found. Cherries, in particular, can be confusing. Here are steps you can take to determine if the plant you've found is, indeed, a *Prunus* species.

First, look at the leaves. *Prunus* species have simple, alternate leaves that are roughly oval with small teeth; some are broad, while others are narrowly oval, and all end in a noticeable point. They resemble serviceberry leaves (*Amelanchier* spp., page 232), which also grow alternately. However, serviceberry fruits are *pomes*, containing many seeds, while cherries and plums are *drupes*, containing a single seed (called a stone or pit). Serviceberry fruits (which are edible) also bear a *crown*, a remnant of the blossom at the bottom of the fruit, and the fruit has a dusty finish. Cherries are smooth and shiny, with no crown. Plums have a dusty finish but no crown; plums are also larger than serviceberries, and have a noticeable vertical cleft in the fruit.

As noted, all members of the *Prunus* family have leaves that grow in alternate arrangement on the stem. This immediately eliminates buckthorn (*Rhamnus* spp.), a plant with similar leaves and cherry-like fruits, since buckthorn leaves grow oppositely. (Buckthorns also usually have 3 or 4 seeds in each fruit, in contrast to the single stone found in a cherry or plum. Buckthorn is generally listed as toxic.) Viburnums also produce cherry-like fruits, and some have leaves that resemble those of the *Prunus* species, but like buckthorns, viburnum leaves grow oppositely so it is easy to distinguish them from the *Prunus* family.

Chokeberries (*Aronia* spp., page 147) have cherry-like fruits and alternate leaves that are similar to those of cherries and plums. Indeed, some sources list chokecherries among the *Prunus* family. Unlike cherries, however, chokeberries are *pomes*, containing multiple seeds; the seeds are quite soft, giving the impression of a fruit with no seeds. In addition, the bottom of the chokeberry fruit has a 5-pointed indentation that is easy to spot. Chokeberries are edible but quite astringent, so you would not want to confuse them with cherries while collecting.

KEY POINTS TO REMEMBER
- Leaves of the *Prunus* species are simple, alternate, finely toothed, and oval with pointed tips
- All fruits of the *Prunus* species contain a single large seed or stone
- All fruits of the *Prunus* species are smooth on the bottom (no crown or blossom remnant)
- Cherries are round, smooth and featureless, while plums have a vertical notch
- Cherries are smooth and shiny; plums have a waxy bloom on the skin
- Plums are larger than cherries; the pit is more flattened than the round pit of cherries

Now that we've got some basic species information out of the way, let's examine the groups separately. I've kept chokecherries separate from the other wild cherries, followed by plums.

Chokecherries (Prunus virginiana)

Here's a wild fruit that is easy to harvest in quantity. With their tart-sweet flavor, chokecherries make excellent jelly; the juice can also be used for delicious syrup, as well as pies and other desserts.

HABITAT, RANGE

Common or red chokecherries *(P. virginiana)* grow throughout our range, with the exception of the southern portions of Illinois and Indiana and a portion of southern Ohio; the black chokecherry *(P. virginiana* var. *melanocarpa)* grows in the Dakotas and western Minnesota but does not extend much farther east of there. Chokecherry shrubs grow—often in thickets—along sunny edges of cultivated fields and pastures, along trails and fences, and in disturbed areas.

Common chokecherry range

Black chokecherry range

PARTS USED

Ripe fruits, cooked (usually juiced)

SEASONS

Mid- to late summer

IDENTIFICATION TIPS, DANGEROUS LOOKALIKES

Chokecherry shrubs may reach heights of 25 feet, but are usually much shorter. The bark is gray to reddish brown and generally smooth, with visible breathing pores called *lenticels*;

Fruit

Leaf

Bark

the lenticels don't extend horizontally as they do on other *Prunus* species. Stems often have a reddish hue. The finely toothed leaves, 2 to 4 inches long, are dark green above with paler undersides, and grow alternately along the stem; they're widest near the base, tapering at or beyond the middle of the leaf to a broad point. Fragrant white 5-petalled flowers give way to green fruits that turn shiny red; the common chokecherry is red when ripe, while black chokecherries ripen to shiny purple or black. Mature fruits are about ⅜ inch across, and each contains a single egg-shaped pit which is fairly large in proportion to the amount of flesh.

Chokecherries can be distinguished from the other members of the cherry family by the leaves and fruits, as well as the growth patterns of the plants. Chokecherry leaves are broader and more egg-shaped than those of pin cherries (*P. pensylvanica*) or black cherries (*P. serotina*). Fruits of both chokecherries and black cherries grow in *racemes*, which are clusters along a hanging stem; pin cherries grow in small clumps that emanate from one central point (think of the twin fruits commonly seen in domestic cherries). Common chokecherries and pin cherries are red when ripe. Black chokecherries and black cherries also have red berries when underripe, but they turn purplish black when ripe. The cherries grow much taller, and are really small trees; chokecherries are more shrub-like. All of these fruits are edible and can be prepared in the same ways, so identification is more a matter of curiosity than anything else.

Please see the general *Prunus* introduction on page 102 for information on other plants that might be confused with chokecherries.

HARVESTING TIPS

The flowers and fruits are borne in hanging clusters, making harvesting easy. I like to hold an ice-cream pail underneath a cluster of fruits, then pull the cluster inside the bucket and strip off the fruits; a 1-gallon pail holds about 5 pounds.

SPECIAL CONSIDERATIONS

Like other members of the *Prunus* family, chokecherry and wild cherry pits, bark and leaves contain hydrocyanic acid, a cyanide-producing compound. Care should be taken to avoid crushing the pits when juicing the fruits. Drying, freezing or cooking eliminates the acid.

MORE ABOUT CHOKECHERRIES: Go to any county fair in the Upper Midwest, and you're sure to see jars of homemade chokecherry jelly; it's a staple in the pantries of most farm families, and often a favorite of those who taste it. Chokecherries may be the most commonly harvested wild fruit in our region; in fact, they were an important food for the Native American groups that inhabited this area before the coming of the pioneers. Native Americans living on the plains pounded chokecherries, fresh or dried, with fat and dried meat to make pemmican, a staple food for winter use as well as one of the original trail foods.

Native Americans also used chokecherry as a medicinal plant. Blackfeet tribes drank the juice to treat diarrhea, while Sioux, Crow and other tribes used a decoction of the bark to treat intestinal disorders. A strong tea made from the bark, particularly the root bark, was used by many tribes to treat cough. Decades later, chokecherries became one of the original ingredients in Smith Brothers Cough Drops (an ad from 1943 that gives a price of 5 cents for a box of Smith Brothers Cough Drops says, "Yes, a nickel checks that tickle").

Chokecherries have a deliciously sweet-tart flavor; fully ripe berries can be eaten out of hand as a trail nibble, although a few go a long way due to their tartness. Because the fruits are quite tart and have a large pit, they are most commonly juiced to make jelly, syrup, wine or desserts. Some industrious—and patient—cooks actually pit enough chokecherries to turn into a pie.

Like plums and other wild cherries, chokecherries are subject to infestations of black knot disease. This appears on the branches as a clump of black fungus anywhere from an inch to a foot in length. Eventually, the shrub may succumb to this disease, but in the meantime, the fruits are safe to harvest. To avoid spreading the disease, infected branches should never be moved out of the area.

How to make wild cherry or chokecherry juice: Please see detailed instructions on page 252.

JUST FOR FUN
Chokecherry pit-spitting contest
Planning a late-summer family reunion or picnic? Kids of all ages will enjoy an old-fashioned chokecherry pit-spitting contest; in fact, such an event has been a staple of the Montana Chokecherry Festival, held in Lewiston, Montana for many years. Simply line the contestants up and give each a cup with a half-dozen ripe chokecherries. Each contestant chews the fruit, then spits the pit as forcefully as possible. (Remember not to break the pit of the chokecherry, since it contains hydrocyanic acid.) A jar of homemade jelly would make a suitable prize for the winner.

QUICK IDEAS AND OTHER RECIPES IN THIS BOOK FEATURING CHOKECHERRIES
Please see the information under wild cherries on page 109.

Wild Cherries (various mambers of the *Prunus* family)

Wild cherries are more tart than their domesticated relatives, and are excellent in jams, jellies, syrup, cordials and sweetened desserts.

HABITAT, RANGE

Black cherries *(P. serotina)*, also called rum cherries, grow in the eastern half of the United States, all the way down to the Gulf of Mexico; in our region, only North and South Dakota and northwestern Minnesota do not have black cherries. Pin cherries *(P. pensylvanica)*, which are also called fire or bird cherries, are a more northern species that flourishes in Minnesota, Wisconsin, Michigan and the Upper Peninsula; their range continues far into Canada. Look for both of these cherries in areas with cool, moist soil. They grow on field borders and the sunny edges of woods, as well as in small woodlots. Pin cherries often appear in an area that has experienced a forest fire (hence its common name of fire cherry), and are also one of the species that flourishes after clearcutting.

Black cherry range

Pin cherry range

Sand cherry range

Sand cherries *(P. pumila)* are somewhat different from the other wild native cherries. As the name suggests, they grow in sandy areas, including beaches, dunes, gravel bars and shorelines of the Great Lakes and other large bodies of water. Where this type of habitat is found they are abundant throughout the northern two-thirds

Black cherries

Pin cherry

Immature black cherries

Pin cherry bark

of the U.S., from the East Coast to the Rocky Mountains. They are sometimes called beach plums, although that name is also used for *P. maritima,* a shrub that bears much larger fruit.

The introduced varieties listed on page 102 are scattered throughout our range, with some species being more locally common (probably depending on what farmers in the area are growing). All are more common in the southern part of our region than in the northern part, largely because of agricultural practices.

PARTS USED
Ripe fruits, generally cooked or juiced

SEASONS
Mid- to late summer

IDENTIFICATION TIPS, DANGEROUS LOOKALIKES
Black cherry and pin cherry are actually trees, although small specimens may appear to be shrubs. Young cherry trees, and the stems of older trees, have dark, smooth bark with prominent horizontal streaks; the bark of older trees becomes scaly. Sand cherries are sprawling shrubs rather than trees, but have similar bark.

Leaves of all the native cherries are simple, with finely serrated margins and elongated tips; they are narrower than those of chokecherries, and this is one of the ways to distinguish the plants (note that the introduced cherries, with the exception of the Amur and sour cherries, have shorter, wider leaves, similar to those of chokecherries). Black cherry leaves are lustrous on top, and the midrib on the underside is covered with fine brownish hairs. The fruit of black cherries and sand cherries turns purplish black when ripe, while that of pin cherries remains bright red even when ripe. Black cherries fruit in hanging clusters (*racemes*), while pin and sand cherries grow singly or in clumps with the stems emanating from a single point on the branch. The fruits of sand cherries are larger than the other cherries noted. All of these fruits can be prepared in the same fashion.

The Amur cherry is a striking tree, with richly copper-colored bark that is smooth and shiny. Like all cherries, it features prominent breathing pores (lenticels) on the trunk. Leaves of the Amur cherry are very similar in shape to those of the black cherry. Leaves of the other introduced cherries are rounder and generally shorter than those of native cherries; Mahaleb cherry leaves are stubby-looking, almost as wide as they are long.

Please see the general *Prunus* introduction on page 102 for information on other plants that might be confused with wild cherries.

HARVESTING TIPS

Black cherry trees grow to great heights, so the fruits on mature trees may be out of reach. When you find a large tree, look around the area for a smaller upstart that might be easier to pick from; birds disperse cherry seeds, so you probably won't have too far to look.

SPECIAL CONSIDERATIONS

Please see the information under chokecherries on page 105.

MORE ABOUT WILD CHERRIES: Cherries are handsome trees, and it's easy to understand why we've cultivated varieties for both beauty and fruit. Wild cherries grace the springtime woods with their lovely flowers, and in late summer or fall, the fruits provide touches of color to the landscape long before the maple leaves begin to turn. It's interesting to note that cultivated cherries flower before their leaves appear, but wild native cherries develop leaves before flowers.

Most wild cherries are a bit tart to eat raw, although a few make a refreshing nibble on a hot summer's walk. I've found that the introduced cherries, particularly sweet and Mahaleb cherries, tend to have fruit that tastes better raw than that of the true native cherries.

Black cherries and pin cherries are ¼ to ⅜ inch across and have a relatively small amount of fruit in proportion to the stone, so pitting them is an arduous task. If you do decide to try, hold the cherries over a bowl to catch the juice and any pulp that is pushed out by the cherry pitter. A pint of black cherries weighs a bit less than ¾ pound.

How to make wild cherry or chokecherry juice: Please see detailed instructions on page 252.

QUICK IDEAS FOR USING CHOKECHERRIES AND WILD CHERRIES
- Freeze in heavy plastic bags, then thaw and prepare juice as you would with fresh fruit.
- Pit wild cherries or chokecherries and use the fruit to make a pie, following any recipe for domestic (sour) pie cherries.

OTHER RECIPES IN THIS BOOK FEATURING CHOKECHERRIES AND WILD CHERRIES
- As substitute in Plum Chutney (page 117)
- Chokecherry and Wild Cherry Jelly (chart, page 254)
- Uncooked Wild Cherry Jam (chart, page 256)
- Chokecherry Gels or Gumdrops (page 260)
- As substitute in Chokeberry Barbecue Sauce (page 152)
- As substitute in Gooseberry Crisp (page 173)
- As substitute in Pumpkin Tart with Currant Glaze (page 163)

Layered Chokecherry-Cream Cheese Pie

8 servings   Preparation: About an hour, plus chilling time

Filling:
1 package (8 ounces) cream cheese,
    softened (reduced-fat works fine)
½ cup sugar
2 eggs, beaten
A few drops almond extract, optional
Purchased Oreo or graham cracker crust

Topping:
1¼ cups chokecherry juice (thick juice
    works well for this recipe), divided
½ cup plus 2 tablespoons sugar, divided
2 tablespoons cornstarch
¾ cup heavy cream
½ teaspoon vanilla extract

Heat oven to 350°F. To prepare filling: In mixing bowl, beat together cream cheese, sugar, eggs and almond extract until smooth. Pour into prepared crust. Bake for 30 minutes, or until just set. Remove from oven; set aside until cooled completely.

While pie is baking, prepare topping: In medium saucepan, combine 1 cup chokecherry juice with ½ cup of the sugar in medium saucepan. Heat to boiling over medium-high heat, stirring to dissolve sugar. Add cornstarch to remaining ¼ cup chokecherry juice in measuring cup, stirring to blend. Add to saucepan and cook, stirring constantly, until mixture thickens, bubbles and becomes translucent, about 2 minutes. Remove from heat; set aside until cool. Pour cooled chokecherry mixture over cooled pie filling, spreading evenly. Refrigerate for at least 1 hour, or until almost ready to serve.

When ready to serve, beat cream in mixing bowl (preferably chilled) until thickened. Add remaining 2 tablespoons sugar and the vanilla to cream and beat to combine. Spread over pie; for a decorative touch, pipe whipped cream onto pie with piping bag. Serve immediately.

Chokecherry or Elderberry Sorbet

About 3 cups   Preparation: Involved (requires ice-cream maker)

Everyone I've served this to has had the same reaction: "Wow!" This intensely flavored—and brilliantly colored—sorbet is quite soft immediately after churning; overnight freezing firms it up. It remains scoopable even after being frozen for days. For a lovely presentation, arrange a scoop of this with a scoop of rich vanilla ice cream and a third scoop of another sorbet; garnish with a mint leaf.

1¾ cups chokecherry or elderberry juice
    (preferably thick juice; see page 252)
1 cup Simple Sugar Syrup for Sorbet
    (page 427)

A pinch of salt
1 egg white (from commercially pasteur-
    ized egg if concerned about salmonella)

In 1-quart jar, combine fruit juice, sugar syrup and salt. Cover and refrigerate overnight (or longer); it must be very cold before churning. If using ice-cream maker that requires pre-freezing, place it in the freezer as directed by manufacturer, generally 12 to 24 hours.

Churn cold juice mixture until slushy and beginning to hold a soft shape, 7 to 10 minutes. In small bowl, beat cold egg white with a fork for about 45 seconds, then add to ice-cream maker with the slush. Continue to churn until mixture freezes to a soft ice-cream consistency, 12 to 15 minutes longer. The sorbet will be very soft at this point. For best consistency, pack sorbet into plastic container; cover and freeze for at least 3 hours, and as long as a week.

Wild Cherry or Other Wild Berry Syrup

1½ cups syrup per 1 cup of juice   Preparation: Under 15 minutes (plus optional canning time)

Use this as you would maple syrup: on pancakes, over ice cream, on hot cereal etc. For a refreshing beverage, pour a few tablespoons of syrup into a glass of sparkling water with ice cubes, or add a bit of syrup to a glass of chilled white wine.

Canning jar(s), with band(s) and new lid(s)
1 cup juice from wild cherries or other
    wild berries

1 cup sugar, or a bit more if the juice is
    particularly tart
3 tablespoons corn syrup

Note: The instructions are for 1 cup of prepared juice; however, you can proportionally increase the ingredients for any amount of juice. Prepare jars, bands and lids as directed on page 418 (even if you won't be canning the syrup, it's a good idea to sterilize jars and lids as directed). In medium nonreactive saucepan, combine juice and sugar. Heat over medium-high heat, stirring constantly, until sugar dissolves and mixture just begins to boil. Adjust heat so mixture boils gently. Add corn syrup and cook, stirring almost constantly, for 5 minutes; watch for boilover and adjust the heat to prevent a too-vigorous boil. After 5 minutes, pour hot into hot, sterilized jars; seal with new lids and clean bands. To can, process in boiling-water bath for 10 minutes (see page 419 for canning instructions). Or, cool and pour into a bottle for refrigerator storage.

Chokecherry Vinaigrette

About 2½ cups   Preparation: Under 15 minutes, plus 2 hours chilling time

Try this tangy-sweet vinaigrette on mixed greens topped with blue cheese crumbles. Store the vinaigrette in the refrigerator, and shake well before serving; it will keep for several weeks.

¾ cup cold chokecherry juice
1½ teaspoons unflavored gelatin
1 cup water
1 clove garlic
½ cup white wine vinegar

3 tablespoons honey
¾ teaspoon salt
¼ teaspoon white pepper
¼ teaspoon dry mustard powder, optional

Pour chokecherry juice into blender container. Sprinkle gelatin over juice; set aside for 5 minutes to soften. Meanwhile, heat water to boiling. When gelatin has softened, add gelatin, boiling water and garlic to blender. Process on the lowest speed for a minute or two; the gelatin should be completely dissolved. Add remaining ingredients and process on the highest speed for about a minute longer. Pour into serving bottle and refrigerate for at least 2 hours before serving.

Chokecherry or Wild Berry Gelatin

2 or 4 servings   Preparation: Under 15 minutes, plus several hours chilling time

You can make a simple gelatin dessert with the juice from any wild berries, such as elderberries, mulberries, blackberries etc.; chokecherry makes a particularly delicious gelatin (although the color is somewhat unusual!). If you like, you can fold in cut-up bananas or other fruit as you would when preparing store-bought gelatin desserts.

Ingredient:	For 2 servings:	For 4 servings:
Chokecherry or other juice	1 cup	2 cups
Sugar, to taste	½ to ¾ cup	1¼ to 1½ cups
Cold water	2 tablespoons	¼ cup
Unflavored gelatin	1½ teaspoons	1 tablespoon

In nonreactive saucepan, combine juice and the smaller amount of sugar. Stir to dissolve sugar, and taste for sweetness. Add additional sugar as needed until the sweetness is as you like it. (If you can't get the sugar to dissolve, heat the mixture, stirring constantly, until the sugar dissolves.)

Pour cold water into small bowl. Sprinkle gelatin evenly over water; set aside for 5 minutes to soften gelatin. Meanwhile, heat sweetened juice over medium heat until it comes to a boil. When gelatin has softened and juice is boiling gently, scrape gelatin the juice; quickly stir gelatin in. Boil gently for about a minute, then remove from heat and pour into individual dessert dishes (or into a single larger dish, if you prefer). Cool to warm room temperature, then refrigerate for several hours, until set. Cover if you'll be storing in the refrigerator longer than a few hours. Note: A dollop of lightly sweetened whipped cream is delicious on this tangy gelatin.

Homemade Cherry Cordial

About 1 quart   Preparation: Lengthy but easy

The black cherry, Prunus serotina, *is sometimes called rum or whiskey cherry because it was often used in the past to make a flavored liqueur. Here is a cordial you can make with any of the wild cherries.*

2 cups wild cherries
1-quart canning jar, with band and clean lid
1½ cups vodka
1½ cups brandy
2 strips of orange zest, each ½ x 1 inch long

4 whole cloves
⅔ cup sugar
⅓ cup water
½ teaspoon glycerin (from the drugstore)

In large bowl, crush cherries lightly with potato masher; pick out and discard pits, squeezing over the bowl to extract any flesh or juice. Sterilize canning jar as directed on page 418; drain and cool jar. Transfer cherries and juice to jar. Add vodka, brandy, orange zest and cloves. Seal jar with clean lid and shake to combine well. Set jar in a cool, dark spot for 4 weeks, shaking occasionally.

At the end of 4 weeks, strain mixture through wire-mesh strainer into a clean bowl; press on the cherries to extract the juice. Discard the solids from the strainer. Line a funnel with a damp paper coffee filter. Strain liquid into clean, sterilized bottle or 1-quart canning jar. In small saucepan, combine sugar and water. Heat over medium-low heat, stirring frequently, until sugar dissolves and syrup is clear. Remove from heat; set aside until completely cool. Strain syrup into bottle with cordial. Add glycerin; seal bottle and shake to blend. Let stand, tightly sealed, for 2 or 3 days before serving; store in a cool, dark place for up to 3 months.

Blackberry or Raspberry Cordial
Follow recipe above, substituting blackberries or raspberries for the cherries (since there are no pits, simply crush the fruit lightly and proceed as directed). Omit the cloves.

Chokecherry-Wild Grape Wine (recipe courtesy of Charlie Gutwasser)

9 or 10 bottles (750ml each)   Preparation: Involved

We "misplaced" several bottles of this wine in our basement cellar, and found them when they were 12 years old. Normally, that is too old for a homemade wine, but when we looked at the wine from one of the bottles, it was perfectly clear and looked very nice, so we gave it a try. It is the best home-made wine I have ever had, without question. You don't have to wait that long to drink it, though; it was excellent earlier in its life also.

3 pounds chokecherries	2 campden tablets, finely crushed
2 pounds wild grapes	2 teaspoons yeast nutrient
5 pounds sugar	1 teaspoon pectic enzyme
1½ gallons hot water	Simple Sugar Syrup (page 427) as needed
5-gram packet of Montrachet wine yeast	

Please read General Winemaking Notes on pages 423-427 before proceeding.

Day 1: Place fruit in sterilized 5-gallon ceramic crock. Crush fruit with your hands. Add sugar and hot water; stir well. When water cools to 70°F or less, add yeast, campden tablets, yeast nutrient and pectic enzyme. Cover loosely with muslin and let stand for 10 days, stirring occasionally with a sterilized spoon.

Day 10: Strain liquid into sterilized jugs (Charlie's notes at this point say, "beautiful burgundy color"). Cap with airlock. Ferment for 3 to 4 weeks.

Day 35 (approximate): Rack the wine, adding simple sugar syrup to top as necessary. (Charlie's notes on this day: "I think this wine will be very good!") After this, rack wine as necessary. Bottle when fermentation has ceased and wine has cleared (Charlie's notes for this particular batch of wine indicate that he bottled it about 15 months after starting; it could have been bottled sooner, but was not harmed by the delay). Charlie's notes on the day of bottling say "Savor this one!" It was an accurate observation, as it turns out.

Plums (American wild plum, *Prunus americana*, and others)

Wild plums vary quite a bit; some are sweet enough to eat out of hand, while others are best cooked in desserts, jams and other sweetened dishes. Try a sample from the tree you've found before harvesting a large quantity; individual trees produce fruit of varying sweetness.

HABITAT, RANGE

Wild plums grow throughout our range except in the northern parts of Wisconsin and Michigan, with the American wild plum being the most widespread. Canadian plums (*P. nigra*) grow in northeastern Minnesota, in a line from the far northwest corner of the state down to the southeast corner; they are also found in Wisconsin with the exception of the far north. Mexican

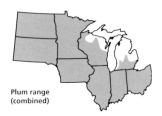

Plum range
(combined)

plums (*P. mexicana*) have a more southerly distribution, and do not appear in Minnesota, Michigan or North Dakota, although they're scattered in other states of our region; the Chickasaw plum (*P. angustifolia*) is even more southerly, and is found in southern Illinois and Indiana, as well as states further south. Beach plums and Allegheny plums (*P. maritima* and *P. alleghaniensis*) are eastern species, but both appear in Ohio and Michigan. The Hortulan plum (*P. hortulana*) grows in the mideastern regions of the country, and in our region is found in Iowa, Illinois, Indiana and Ohio. Finally, the wild goose plum (*P. munsoniana*) is found in our region only in southern Illinois and Ohio. Most wild plums grow in thickets on the edges of cultivated areas, along streams and other moist areas, and in pastures. Beach plums prefer sandy coastal areas.

PARTS USED

Ripe fruits, raw or cooked

American plums

Canadian plum leaves

Canadian plum bark

SEASONS

Mid- to late summer through early fall

IDENTIFICATION TIPS, DANGEROUS LOOKALIKES

Plums are easy to recognize because the fruit looks like the familiar specimens we find in the grocery store, although wild plums come in a variety of sizes and in colors ranging from yellow to rose to red to purple (see page 102 for a breakdown of the various species' colors). The fruit usually has a dusty bloom on the surface, like that found on grapes, and there is a slight vertical cleft or notch bisecting the fruit. Inside the fruit is a single stone, which tends to be flat rather than rounded like that of a cherry. The flesh is soft when the plum is ripe.

The fruit grows from a small tree that has dark bark with horizontal breathing pores (lenticels) like those on cherry trees. The oblong leaves are dark green with serrated edges and a pointy tip; they grow alternately on branches that have dull spines (note: beach plums have no spines). The 5-petalled flowers are an inch or less across and grow in clusters; they're usually white, but can be pinkish. All wild plums are edible; there are no dangerous lookalikes.

HARVESTING TIPS

It's best to wait to harvest plums until they are ripe, as plums that are picked underripe don't ever attain the sweetness of tree-ripened fruit.

SPECIAL CONSIDERATIONS

Like other members of the *Prunus* family, plum pits, bark and leaves contain hydrocyanic acid, a cyanide-producing compound. Avoid crushing the pits when juicing the fruits. Also note that unripe plums can cause serious digestive problems, and should not be eaten.

MORE ABOUT WILD PLUMS: Plum trees in bloom are a joy to the senses; their intensely fragrant blossoms scent the air for quite some distance. The gnarly, dark trees look particularly lovely with their burden of deep green leaves and bright white flowers; it's easy to see why plum trees have inspired Japanese brush artists for centuries.

As far as eating quality, wild plums vary quite a bit from species to species, and even from tree to tree. Some are sweet enough to eat ripe, while others have enough pucker power to require sweetening and cooking. Some seem to be all pit, with little flesh; others are juicy and plump. Many say that the beach plum is the best and sweetest; I've also enjoyed munching on fat, just-from-the-tree Canadian plums, as well as the smaller and less-fleshy American wild plums.

All wild plums are edible, and if you come upon a tree that is bearing heavily, you can pick your fill in that one spot. But before you load your basket up, taste one of the plums; if they are too tart, or the flesh is too thin, you may want to pass that tree up and search for another that has better fruit. It's interesting to note that wild birds don't eat plums, although they relish other members of the *Prunus* family such as cherries.

How to make plum juice: Cut plums in half; the pits can be added to the kettle when cooking juice, but care should be taken not to split or break the pit. Place fruit in heavy-bottomed pot; add enough water to come about a third of the way up the plums (use less if the plums are very juicy). Heat to boiling; reduce heat and simmer for 10 minutes, stirring frequently. Strain through a double layer of cheesecloth. Since plums vary so widely, it's difficult to predict how much juice you will get from a measure of fruit.

After the juice has been extracted, run the fruit through a conical strainer or food mill to get plum purée (you may need to add a little water first). Sweeten to taste and spread on drying trays, then dry to make a delicious leather (see page 263 for information on making leathers). Or, add 3 parts sugar to 4 parts of plum purée and cook down to make a smooth jam.

QUICK IDEAS FOR USING PLUMS
- Substitute cut-up plums for sweet cherries in recipes for baked goods.
- Add some cut-up plums to the kettle when cooking cherries, chokecherries, grapes or elderberries for juice. Or, make plain plum juice, then mix it with other fruit juices.

OTHER RECIPES IN THIS BOOK FEATURING PLUMS
- Plum Jelly (pectin-added jelly, page 255; no-pectin jelly, page 257)
- Dried plums (page 422)

Plum-Merlot Jam

4 half-pints   Preparation: About an hour

2½ pounds ripe plums	2 tablespoons freshly squeezed lemon juice
¾ cup merlot or other hearty red wine	4 half-pint canning jars, with bands and new lids
1 cinnamon stick, optional	
2½ cups sugar	

Prepare jars, bands and lids as directed on page 418. Pit plums and cut into ½-inch pieces. Combine with merlot and cinnamon in heavy-bottomed nonreactive saucepan. Heat to boiling over medium-high heat; reduce heat and simmer for 20 minutes, or until plums are tender, stirring occasionally. Add sugar and lemon juice. Cook over medium heat until thickened to a jam-like consistency (mixture should read 210°F on a candy thermometer); stir frequently to prevent sticking. Remove and discard cinnamon stick. Pour jam into prepared jars, leaving ½ inch head-space. Seal with prepared lids and bands. Process in boiling-water bath for 5 minutes.

Plum Chutney

About 1½ cups   Preparation: About an hour

Substitute any wild cherry for the plums in this recipe. Serve this with grilled meats and fish, and with curry dishes.

4 whole cardamom pods, or ½ teaspoon ground cardamom
4 whole spicebush berries, 2 whole allspice berries, or ¼ teaspoon ground allspice
3 cups cut-up plum pieces (pitted and cut into ½-inch pieces before measuring)
1 cup diced red bell pepper (¼-inch dice)
¾ cup diced onion (¼-inch dice)

¼ cup dried currants
¼ cup (packed) brown sugar
¼ cup balsamic vinegar or red wine vinegar
1 tablespoon minced candied ginger (found in the spice aisle)
½ teaspoon mustard seeds
½ teaspoon salt
¼ teaspoon hot red pepper flakes

Split cardamom pods and transfer seeds to mortar; add spicebush or allspice and crush until coarse. Combine spice mixture with all remaining ingredients in heavy-bottomed nonreactive saucepan. Heat to boiling over high heat. Reduce heat so mixture simmers steadily and cook until thick-ened and syrupy, about 45 minutes; stir frequently, especially near the end of the cooking time, to prevent sticking. Cool and transfer to clean pint jar; store in refrigerator for up to 3 weeks.

Pork Tenderloin with Plum Sauce

3 servings   Preparation: Under 30 minutes

1 pound wild plums
1 pork tenderloin (about 1¼ pounds)
Salt and pepper
1 tablespoon vegetable oil
1 teaspoon minced garlic

¼ cup sherry, white wine or chicken broth
3 tablespoons soy sauce
2 tablespoons rice vinegar or sherry vinegar
2 tablespoons (packed) brown sugar
1 tablespoon chopped candied ginger

Pit plums and cut into 1-inch pieces; set aside. Season pork with salt and pepper. Heat oil in large skillet over medium-high heat. Add pork; brown on all sides. Transfer pork to plate; tent with foil and set aside. Pour off excess oil from skillet. Add garlic to skillet. Cook over medium heat, stirring constantly, for about a minute. Add sherry; cook until reduced to about a table-spoon, stirring to loosen any browned bits. Add plum pieces, soy sauce, vinegar, sugar and ginger. Simmer for 15 minutes, stirring occasionally; if mixture becomes too thick, add a little water or chicken broth. Return pork to skillet along with any accumulated juices. Cook, spooning sauce over pork occasionally, until pork is just cooked through, about 5 minutes. Slice pork and serve with sauce.

Puffballs (giant puffball, *Calvatia gigantea*, and others)

Giant puffballs are easy to identify, and a single specimen may provide several meals. They can be sliced and cooked like steaks, or diced and used in sautés, soups or casseroles. Smaller puffballs can be used in place of domestic mushrooms in most recipes.

HABITAT, RANGE

Puffball range (combined)

Puffballs are common throughout our region. They are found in hardwood forests and prairies, along streams and creeks, in woodlots and shelterbelts, at the edges of pastures, and on stumps and woody debris such as sawdust piles. I have found many puffballs in the urban forests and stream corridors of the Minneapolis-St. Paul metro area. Giant puffballs (*Calvatia gigantea*) often thrive in relatively arid habitat, while the common puffball (*Lycoperdon perlatum*) and pear-shaped puffball (*L. pyriforme*) are often found on rotting wood.

PARTS USED

Entire fruiting body

SEASONS

Late summer through fall

IDENTIFICATION TIPS, DANGEROUS LOOKALIKES

With their pale, globular bodies ranging from marble- to basketball-sized, puffballs are easy to identify. Giant puffballs appear singly or in scattered clusters, growing right out of the ground with no appreciable neck or stem; they may be slightly flattened rather than

Giant puffball

Pear-shaped puffballs

Common puffballs

fully round. The smaller puffballs listed have short necks or stems, but never any gills or shelf; they develop a nipple-like bump at the top as they mature, and this will eventually open to release spores. Common puffballs and pear-shaped puffballs often grow in masses or colonies, at times covering a whole tree stump.

When cut open, all edible puffballs reveal a solid interior that is white throughout, with a consistency like firm cream cheese; in the smaller puffballs, the interior is continuous from the globe through the stem, with no visible break or difference between the two areas. To test puffballs, cut each specimen in half from top to bottom and examine it carefully before eating. If the skin and/or flesh is hard; if it is slimy inside; or if there is any yellowing, darkening or trace of a shadow inside the puffball, *discard it without tasting.* There are several reasons to discard any specimen that does not pass this test. First, puffballs become darker inside as they age, so a puffball with a yellowish or brownish interior is past its prime and will likely be bitter. Second, if the skin or interior is hard, you may have a young specimen of one of the earthballs (*Scleroderma* spp.), which can cause stomach upset. A slimy interior indicates a young stinkhorn (*Phallaceae* family), whose edibility is the subject of some debate. Finally, and most importantly, the early stages of the poisonous *Amanita* mushrooms resemble a small puffball on first glance, but reveal a ghostly outline of the developing stalk, cap and gills when cut open. Make it a firm and unyielding rule: Cut all puffballs in half from top to bottom and check the interior before eating! If you follow this rule, you will avoid an unpleasant and possibly dangerous meal.

HARVESTING TIPS

Since giant puffballs grow directly out of the ground, there is no neck to cut when harvesting one. Grab onto the puffball and gently twist it; you can also work a pocketknife under the puffball and make small cuts as close to the ground as possible. All puffballs mature rapidly when picked, so be sure to refrigerate your harvest as soon as possible to prevent the puffballs from becoming inedible.

SPECIAL CONSIDERATIONS

According to David Arora in *Mushrooms Demystified*, puffballs can have laxative effects on some people. As with all wild foods, it is prudent to sample only a small portion the first time to make sure that you won't have an adverse reaction.

MORE ABOUT PUFFBALLS: If you're rambling through the fall woods and see something that looks like a soccer ball in the distance, you may not give it a second thought other than to wonder where the playing field is. Check it out, however, as you've likely discovered a giant puffball; if you have, you're in for a treat. Giant puffballs are my favorite of the puffball family, because they lend themselves to some novel cooking treatments. They can be cut into steaks that are excellent fried or grilled. Bill Gregoire, who has been chef at several of Minneapolis' finer restaurants, reports that giant puffballs can be sliced very thinly and rolled around stuffing. Puffballs can also be diced and used in virtually any recipe calling for store-bought mushrooms. Giant puffballs are considered choice and highly edible, with a mild yet mushroomy flavor. Pear-shaped puffballs are also generally quite good, while common puffballs are often less flavorful (but still worth harvesting, as long as they are young and show no trace of yellow inside).

Puffballs are a member of the "foolproof four"—a quartet of wild mushrooms that are recommended for beginners because they are easy to identify (others include morels, chicken of the woods—also called sulfur shelf—and shaggy manes or chanterelles, depending on which list you look at). Puffballs get their name from their puffy appearance, and from the way that mature specimens disperse their spores in a cloud that resembles a puff of smoke. David Arora, in *Mushrooms Demystified,* reports that an average giant puffball specimen contains up to 7 trillion spores, each of which is capable of reproducing.

The skin of a puffball can be somewhat scaly, and sometimes is tough, so you may want to peel it; this is easily done during washing just prior to cooking. If the interior has worm holes, simply cut away and discard the affected portion; the remainder is fine for eating. Puffballs can be stored in the refrigerator, loosely wrapped, for a week or longer; don't wash them until you're ready to cook. I've read that giant puffballs can be frozen whole (uncooked); they'll apparently keep for a month or more. I've never tried this.

As an interesting side note, puffballs can be used to stop bleeding. This information is included in the U.S. Army's Survival Use of Plants website (as well as in other sources): "Antihemorrhagics. Make medications to stop bleeding from a poultice of the puffball mushroom, from plantain leaves, or most effectively from the leaves of the common yarrow or woundwort (*Achillea millefolium*)."

QUICK IDEAS FOR USING PUFFBALLS
- Substitute puffballs, sliced or diced as appropriate, for domestic mushrooms in any recipe.
- Simmer a handful of diced puffballs in a clear broth; top with snipped chives for a light and easy first course.

OTHER RECIPES IN THIS BOOK FEATURING PUFFBALLS
- Many recipes in the Wild Mushrooms chaper (beginning on page 350)

PLT Sandwiches (Puffball, Lettuce and Tomato)

Per serving; make as many as you wish   Preparation: Under 15 minutes

Great for a special lunch, these also pair well with a hearty soup for a lighter supper.

For each serving:

1 teaspoon butter or margarine

A small bit of minced garlic

1 bread-sized puffball slice, about ¾ inch thick

Seasoned salt, or plain salt and pepper

2 slices sandwich bread

1 teaspoon mayonnaise (reduced-fat works fine)

1 sandwich-sized piece of Romaine lettuce

2 very thin tomato slices

In skillet that will hold all the puffball slices you'll be cooking, melt the butter over medium heat. Add garlic and sauté for a minute or so. Add puffball slice(s), turning after a few seconds to coat both sides with melted butter. Cook until puffball is lightly golden on both sides, about 5 minutes, turning once. Sprinkle puffball slice(s) with seasoned salt.

While puffball slices are cooking, toast bread. Spread with mayonnaise. Top one slice with lettuce, and arrange tomato slices over lettuce. Top with cooked puffball slice, then with second slice of bread. Serve immediately.

Variation: PBLT Sandwiches
Add 1 or 2 strips crisp bacon to the sandwich, on top of the puffball slice.

Flying Saucers (Puffballs and Eggs)

Per serving; make as many as you wish   Preparation: Under 15 minutes

Kids who enjoy mushrooms will love this dish, which is pretty wacky looking (but delicious!). A large skillet should hold 3 or 4 of these at one time; a stovetop griddle that is oven-safe also works well.

For each serving:

½-inch-thick slice of puffball that is 4 to 5 inches across

1 tablespoon butter or margarine, divided

1 egg

Salt and pepper

1 tablespoon shredded Parmesan cheese

Heat oven to 400°F. Cut a 1½-inch-wide hole in center of puffball slice. In oven-safe skillet or on griddle, melt 1½ teaspoons of the butter over medium heat. When butter just stops foaming, add puffball slice and circle, sliding around a bit to ensure that all parts get coated with butter. Cook until puffball slice is golden, about 5 minutes. Transfer temporarily to small plate. Melt remaining 1½ teaspoons butter. Return puffball slice and circle to skillet browned-side up, sliding around again. Carefully break egg into hole in center of puffball slice. Season with salt and pepper to taste; sprinkle Parmesan cheese over egg. Place skillet in oven. Cook until egg white is no longer clear but yolk is still runny, about 5 minutes, or to desired doneness. Place puffball hole on top of egg yolk; serve immediately.

Grilled Giant Puffball Steaks

Per serving; prepare as many as you wish   Preparation: 10 to 45 minutes marinating time plus
10 minutes cooking time

The best puffballs for this recipe are about 6 inches across. If your puffballs are smaller, you may need more than one slice per serving; if the puffball is 8 inches across or larger, and you are using a center slice, cut it in half so each serving is a half-moon shape. Whatever size you use, the slices should be an inch thick.

For each serving:
1½ teaspoons extra-virgin olive oil
1½ teaspoons soy sauce
⅛ teaspoon dried basil
⅛ teaspoon dried marjoram

A pinch of salt and a few grindings of
    black pepper
1 puffball slice or as needed for each serving
    (see notes above), 1 inch thick

Prepare charcoal grill for medium heat (I find that this is best when cooked over genuine charcoal; gas grills seem to impart a slightly off-flavor). Combine oil, soy sauce, basil, marjoram, salt and pepper in small bowl. Use pastry brush to brush mixture over both sides of puffball slice; also brush edges. Place on a plate and let stand for 10 to 45 minutes. Place puffball slice(s) on grate over prepared coals; after about a minute, rotate the slice 90 degrees to mark the mushroom with diamond-shaped grill marks. Cook until puffball is tender and golden brown, 3 to 5 minutes per side. Serve immediately.

Creamy Mushroom-Turkey Skillet

3 or 4 servings   Preparation: Under 30 minutes

Use any mushrooms you have for this easy skillet dish, which is reminiscent of Turkey Tetrazzini. Puffballs are particularly well-suited; their mild flavor is highlighted by the herbs and Romano cheese.

¾ pound ground turkey breast

¾ cup diced onion

2 teaspoons vegetable oil

2½ cups cut-up puffballs or other mushrooms (about ⅜-inch cubes or pieces)

¾ cup light cream or 1 can (12 ounces) nonfat evaporated milk

½ cup chicken broth

½ teaspoon salt

1 tablespoon minced fresh parsley, or 1 teaspoon dehydrated parsley flakes*

1 tablespoon snipped fresh chives*

¼ teaspoon dried basil*

⅛ teaspoon dried chervil*

⅛ teaspoon dried tarragon*

A good pinch of white pepper

2 teaspoons cornstarch mixed with 2 tablespoons cold water

⅓ cup finely shredded Romano or Parmesan cheese

Hot cooked noodles or rice

In large skillet, cook turkey breast and onion in oil over medium heat until turkey is no longer pink, stirring to break up turkey. Add puffballs and cook for 5 minutes, stirring occasionally. Add cream, broth and salt. Increase heat and cook until mixture comes to a very gentle boil. Adjust heat to maintain gentle boil, and cook for about 10 minutes, stirring occasionally and adjusting heat as necessary to prevent boil-over. Add parsley, chives, basil, chervil, tarragon and white pepper, and cook for a few minutes longer. Add cornstarch mixture and cook, stirring frequently, until mixture thickens, 2 to 3 minutes. Stir in cheese and cook just until cheese melts. Serve over noodles or rice.

*For an easier dish, substitute 2 teaspoons dried Bonnes Herbes blend (sometimes called Parisian Blend) or other herb blend for the parsley, chives, basil, chervil and tarragon.

Two-Mushroom Lasagna

6 servings   Preparation: Over an hour

This recipe uses uncooked lasagna noodles for easier preparation. You don't have to buy special "no boil" noodles; regular noodles will work just fine.

¾ pound chanterelles or other sturdy mushrooms
½ pound puffballs or other mild, fleshy mushrooms
1 medium onion, chopped
3 garlic cloves, minced
1 tablespoon olive oil
2 medium tomatoes, peeled, seeded and and chopped (or ½ cup canned diced tomatoes, drained)

10 fresh rosemary leaves, minced (or ¼ teaspoon crumbled dried)
¼ teaspoon freshly ground pepper
1 cup mushroom broth or chicken broth
2 teaspoons cornstarch
½ teaspoon salt
6 uncooked lasagna noodles
8 ounces (2 cups) shredded mozzarella cheese, divided
½ cup grated Parmesan cheese, divided

Heat oven to 350°F. Lightly grease 9 x 9 x 2-inch baking dish; set aside. Slice chanterelles into lengthwise quarters, or eighths if large; cut puffballs into ½-inch cubes. Set aside. In Dutch oven, sauté onion and garlic in oil over medium heat until onion is just tender. Add mushrooms and cook, stirring frequently, until juices released by mushrooms have cooked away, about 10 minutes; the mushrooms will reduce in volume considerably.

When mushroom mixture has no more liquid, add tomatoes, rosemary leaves and pepper. Cook for 2 or 3 minutes, stirring occasionally. Blend together broth, cornstarch and salt; add to Dutch oven. Increase heat to high and cook, stirring frequently, until mixture thickens somewhat, about 5 minutes.

Layer one-third of the mushroom mixture into prepared baking dish. Top with 3 of the uncooked noodles, breaking off ends to fit pan and placing noodles side-by-side or overlapping slightly. Spread half of the remaining mushroom mixture over noodles. Sprinkle with half of the mozzarella cheese, then with half of the Parmesan cheese. Top with remaining noodles, trimmed to fit. Spread remaining mushrooms over noodles, and top with remaining mozzarella and Parmesan cheeses. Pour any leftover mushroom juice around edges of uncooked noodles. Cover dish with foil and bake for 30 minutes. Remove foil and bake for 15 minutes longer. Let stand for 10 minutes before cutting into squares.

Barley Soup with Small Puffballs

3 or 4 servings   Preparation: Over an hour

1 onion, minced	½ cup pearl barley
2 teaspoons minced garlic	3 carrots, sliced (½-inch slices)
2 tablespoons butter or olive oil	1 tablespoon soy sauce
1 pound small puffballs (about an inch in diameter), halved	½ teaspoon dried thyme
	½ teaspoon dried rosemary
⅓ cup dry sherry	Salt and pepper
1 quart chicken broth or vegetable broth	Chopped fresh parsley for garnish

In small stockpot, sauté onion and garlic in butter over medium heat until onion is golden brown, about 7 minutes. Add puffballs. Sauté until juices released by puffballs have mostly cooked away. Add sherry; increase heat to medium-high and cook until liquid is reduced to about a tablespoon. Add broth, barley, carrots, soy sauce, thyme and rosemary. Cover stockpot; adjust heat so liquid simmers and cook for 1 hour, stirring occasionally. Add salt and pepper to taste. Just before serving, garnish with parsley.

Puffball "French Toast"

2 servings; easily increased   Preparation: Under 15 minutes

Sliced puffballs get dipped in an egg batter and pan-fried, just like French toast. The result is an eggy, light dish with mushroom overtones ... perfect for brunch or a light supper. If you have a soccerball-sized puffball, cut two thick slices from the center, then cut each in half. If your puffballs are smaller (or larger), adjust the number of slices accordingly so each person gets the equivalent of two bread-sized slices.

1 egg	Butter or nonstick spray as needed
¼ cup milk	4 bread-sized slices of puffball (1 inch thick)
¾ cup all-purpose flour	
½ teaspoon mixed dried herb blend of your choice	Garlic salt, seasoned salt, or salt and pepper

In wide, shallow bowl, beat together egg and milk with a fork. Combine flour and herbs in another wide, shallow bowl or baking dish and mix well. Heat a large skillet or griddle over medium heat. Add about 2 teaspoons butter to the skillet, or spray with nonstick spray; if using griddle, spray with nonstick spray. Quickly dip a puffball slice into the egg mixture, turning to coat both sides. Dip in flour and shake off excess. Add to skillet; repeat with remaining puffball slices (if necessary, cook puffball slices in 2 or more batches). Cook until golden brown and lightly crusty on both sides, turning once. Transfer to serving platter and sprinkle with salt.

Cream of Puffball Soup

4 servings   Preparation: Under an hour

Substitute any wild mushroom for the puffballs in this classic cream soup. It's very rich; keep servings small.

¼ cup (half of a stick) unsalted butter,
    divided
2 shallots, chopped
¾ pound puffballs or other mushrooms,
    diced, divided

¼ teaspoon salt
1 quart beef broth
1 cup heavy cream
2 teaspoons olive oil
Fresh snipped chives and paprika for garnish

In large saucepan, melt half of the butter over medium heat. Add shallots; sauté for about 3 minutes. Add all but ⅓ cup of the diced mushrooms. Sprinkle with salt and sauté until juices released by mushrooms have cooked away and mushrooms are beginning to brown. Add broth. Cover and adjust heat so broth is simmering; cook for 20 minutes. Remove from heat; set aside to cool slightly. Working in batches, carefully purée mixture in blender or food processor; as each batch is puréed, transfer to wire-mesh strainer set over a clean saucepan. Strain purée, pressing on solids with a spoon to extract as much liquid as possible. Discard solids.

Add cream to purée in saucepan. Heat over medium heat until simmering. Add remaining butter, a teaspoon at a time and whisking well between additions until butter melts. Taste for seasoning, and adjust if necessary. Keep soup warm while you prepare garnish.

In small skillet, sauté reserved mushrooms in oil over medium heat until golden brown. Divide soup between 4 warm serving bowls. Top with sautéed mushrooms; sprinkle with chives and paprika. Serve immediately.

Surprise Stuffing

4 servings   Preparation: Under an hour

The "surprise" in this dish is that it is stuffed with a layer of mushrooms.

¾ cup diced celery
¾ cup diced onion
2 tablespoons butter, divided
4 cups unseasoned ½-inch croutons
¾ cup diced apple

¾ cup chicken broth or vegetable broth
1½ teaspoons mixed dried herb blend
½ teaspoon salt
2 cups diced puffballs, morels or other
    wild mushrooms

Heat oven to 350°F. Lightly grease 2-quart casserole with nonstick spray; set aside. In skillet, sauté celery and onion in half the butter over medium heat until tender, about 5 minutes. Transfer to large mixing bowl. Add croutons, apple, broth, herbs and salt; mix very well. Transfer half of the mixture to prepared casserole. Top evenly with cut-up mushrooms. Cover with remaining crouton mixture. Cut up remaining butter and scatter over croutons. Bake, uncovered, for 35 to 40 minutes, or until top is crispy.

Veggie Burgers

1 cup chopped onion
¾ cup coarsely chopped carrot
¼ cup minced celery
½ teaspoon minced garlic
2 tablespoons olive oil or vegetable oil, divided
2 cups coarsely chopped puffballs or other mushrooms (6 to 7 ounces)
2 tablespoons minced fresh parsley
½ teaspoon ground cumin
½ teaspoon salt
¼ teaspoon pepper
⅓ cup all-purpose flour
1¼ cups coarsely chopped cooked potato (about 1 medium baking potato, boiled)
¼ cup roasted sunflower nuts, optional
2 eggs, lightly beaten
1 cup fresh breadcrumbs*
Hamburger buns, condiments as desired (chutney is particularly good with these)

In large skillet, sauté onion, carrot, celery and garlic in 1 tablespoon of the oil over medium heat until tender. Add mushrooms, parsley, cumin, salt and pepper. Cook, stirring frequently, until mushrooms are tender, about 5 minutes. Add flour and cook for 3 minutes longer, stirring constantly. Remove from heat; transfer to mixing bowl and let cool until just warm to the touch, about 10 minutes.

Add potato, sunflower nuts, eggs and breadcrumbs to cooled mushroom mixture; mix well. Shape into 4 patties, about ¾ inch thick. Heat remaining 1 tablespoon oil in a clean skillet (preferably nonstick). Add mushroom burgers and cook until golden brown on both sides, turning just once. Serve in buns, with condiments as desired.

*To make fresh breadcrumbs, remove the crusts from sliced bread. Tear bread into 1-inch chunks. Turn on food processor or blender; add a handful of bread chunks through processor feed tube or open blender top and process until reduced to crumbs (be ready to put the lid on immediately after adding the bread to a blender, as it may jump high out of the blender jar). Day-old French or Italian bread works particularly well for this recipe.

Hickory Nuts (Carya spp.)

Although hickory nuts are often thought of as a southern species, they do grow in the warmer parts of our range, and some even extend into southern Minnesota, Wisconsin and Michigan. Hickory nuts have a wonderful flavor that is unlike any grocery-store nuts, and are well worth seeking out.

HABITAT, RANGE

Shagbark hickories *(C. ovata)* are found in the southeastern part of our range, with good populations in southeastern Iowa, throughout Illinois, Indiana and Ohio, and in central and southern Michigan. Shellbark hickories *(C. laciniosa)*, also called kingnuts, are much less common; they are found in scattered stands in southeastern Iowa and southern Illinois, as well as in Indiana, lower Michigan and Ohio. Mockernuts *(C. alba*; also called *C. tomentosa)*, a member of the hickory family, appear in our region primarily in central and southern Illinois and Indiana.

Shagbark hickory range

Shellbark hickory range

Mockernut range

Hickories grow in hardwood forests alongside elms, ash, basswood and oak. You may find shagbark, shellbark and mockernut in the same general area; hickories typically grow as single specimens among other trees, but are sometimes found in small groupings with several others of their species. In the northern part of their range (which is generally the southern portion of our area), hickories tend to be found on ridges and south-facing hillsides.

Shagbark hickory nuts

Shagbark hickory blade

Shellbark hickory nuts

Bark of shellbark tree

PARTS USED
Shelled nutmeats

SEASONS
Fall

IDENTIFICATION TIPS, DANGEROUS LOOKALIKES

Hickories are medium to large hardwood trees, typically growing 60 to 80 feet tall; according to *Trees, Shrubs, and Woody Vines of the Southwest,* shagbark can grow as tall as 130 feet and attain a diameter of over 9 feet. Shagbark and shellbark both develop shaggy bark as the tree matures, particularly farther up the tree (bark at the base of the tree does not get as shaggy). Bark of the mockernut and bitternut is smoother; these trees have shallow furrows with interlacing ridges.

Leaves help distinguish the hickories from one another. All hickories have pinnately compound leaves (or blades) that grow alternately on the branch; each blade has paired individual leaflets that grow along the axis, and each axis ends in a single leaflet. Individual leaflets have toothed margins. Note that on all hickories, the leaflets nearest the stem are smaller than the leaflets at the end of the blade; the terminal leaflet is often the largest. The blades of shellbark are the largest of all hickories discussed here, frequently a foot long and as long as 18 inches; each blade has 7 or 9 individual leaflets—3 or 4 pairs plus the terminal leaflet. This helps distinguish shellbarks from shagbarks, which have 5- to 8-inch-long blades with 5 individual leaves (occasionally 7). Mockernut blades have 5 to 9 leaves, but are smaller than those of shellbarks or shagbarks. Keep in mind that mockernuts have relatively smooth bark, that helps distinguish them from the other hickories; also, mockernut leaves are particularly fragrant when crushed. Bitternuts *(C. cordiformis),* a member of the hickory family which you don't want to harvest, have 5 to 11 leaflets, which are more slender than any of the other hickories (except pecans, another member of the hickory family, which have very long blades with 9 to 17 leaflets and so are easy to distinguish, should you be fortunate enough to encounter any).

On all hickories, the nut is encased in a thick, yellowish green husk that turns brownish or blackish when the nut is mature; the darkened husk splits into 4 parts to reveal a hard tan nutshell with pointed ends. The nutshells of shagbarks, shellbarks, mockernuts and bitternuts are ridged, unlike pecans which are smooth-shelled. Shellbark nuts are the largest of the hickories, generally an inch across (in the shell, but with husk removed) or better, while mockernuts are the smallest.

HARVESTING TIPS

Gather hickory nuts on the ground under the trees, discarding the outer husk as you go. Hickories are best when the nutmeats have dried a bit and become crisp. Check a few nuts when you get home; if the nutmeats are rubbery, spread the unshelled nuts on a screen or in an open box (in an area that is protected from critters) to cure for a few weeks before using or storing.

MORE ABOUT HICKORY NUTS: With many wild foods, harvesting is the easy part; the real work begins once you've got your harvest home. This is certainly the case with hickory nuts, which are protected by one of the hardest shells in the business. A normal nutcracker won't touch them; you need to use a hammer. The shells are brittle and often shatter if you're not careful (or lucky), so you need to examine your shelled nuts very carefully to pick out small bits of shell.

Hickory trees have been considered a valuable species in the Unites States for a very long time. The trees produce a beautiful, heavyweight wood that is hard yet resilient; it's been used for products as varied as hammer handles, wagon-wheel and automobile-wheel spokes, furniture, gun stocks and flooring. Hickory is a favored wood for smoking ribs and other barbecued foods, and is also used to make a natural-lump charcoal that purists feel gives superior flavor to grilled meats. The trees are spectacular to look at as well, especially in fall when the leaves turn a lovely golden yellow.

Considered by many to be the finest of the wild nuts, hickories are great eaten out of hand, and add a sweet, mellow flavor to baked goods and other dishes. You'll often see hickory trees with no nuts, however; according to information in *Silvics of North America*, shagbarks and shellbarks don't begin producing nuts until they are 40 years old; maximum production occurs between 60 and 200 years of age. Even when a tree does start producing, it goes in cycles, sometimes going 2 or 3 years with little or no nut production.

Hickory nuts are important food for wildlife, especially squirrels and black bears. They're also eaten by red and gray foxes and rodents, as well as wild turkeys, mallard and wood ducks, pheasants, Northern bobwhites and woodpeckers. When you're gathering fallen nuts, be sure to leave some for the wild critters who depend on them. After you've shelled a batch of hickory nuts, toss the shells in the yard or on a platform feeder, where birds such as chickadees, titmice and woodpeckers can peck out any bits of nutmeat that remain.

As noted above, shelling hickory nuts is a bit of a chore. A nutcracker won't break the shell, so you need to use a hammer. Don't try it on a wooden cutting board, either; the nutshell will dent even hard maple. Place each nut on cement, flat side up, holding it so the natural seam is between your fingers (see photo). Rap the nut with a hammer until the shell breaks into at least 4 pieces; the trick is to break the shell without shattering it.

Cracking a hickory nut

Once you've got the shell broken, pick out meats with nut pick; sit at table and do this over a large cutting board so you can sort through the small bits to pick out shell fragments. The nutmeat is soft and oily, and it is very difficult to remove it from the convoluted folds of the shell. Place larger pieces of nutmeat into a measuring cup, then place the smaller ones on a white plate and sort through to remove shell bits. A pound of shagbark or shellbark hickories yields 1½ to 1¾ cups broken nutmeats; because the nuts are smaller and have proportionately more shell, a pound of mockernuts yields 1 to 1¼ cups. I've noticed that mockernuts are a bit easier to shell, for some reason; they tend to come out of the shell better. Hit mockernuts more gently; their shells are more brittle in my experience, and shatter more easily than their larger cousins.

If you have a pressure cooker, you can make your hickory shelling go a lot more smoothly. I first read about this trick in Billy Joe Tatum's *Wild Foods Cookbook & Field Guide,* and it really helps. Put unshelled nuts in a pressure cooker, then add some water. Billy Joe says to fill the pot three-quarters full with nuts and add water to one-quarter the depth of the nuts, but that is more nuts than I care to shell in one sitting, so I do about a pound at a time in my pressure saucepan, adding just over an inch of water. Set for 5 pounds pressure, and put on the heat; when the control starts jiggling, adjust the heat so it jiggles 2 or 3 times per minute and cook for 10 minutes. Let the pressure drop naturally before opening the cooker, then begin shelling the nuts. You'll find that the shells are a bit softer and the nutmeats are more pliable, so it's easier to work the nutmeats from the shell. If the nutmeats are rubbery after this treatment, bake them at 350°F for a few minutes to crisp them up.

If you have more nuts than you care to shell at the time, store them in a cool place away from rodents, or in the freezer. They'll keep for a year or more, but should be checked periodically for worm holes (this is unnecessary if they're frozen). Once the nuts have been shelled, the nutmeats go rancid quickly, so you should refrigerate shelled nutmeats and use fairly quickly or freeze for longer storage.

JUST FOR FUN

Parrot Treats

If you have a parrot (or know someone who does), make a batch of these treats from your empty hickory-nut shells. Choose shell fragments that are fairly large and cupped. Shred a small sweet potato finely. Mix well with ¾ cup 7-grain breakfast cereal (uncooked), ½ cup whole wheat flour, ¼ cup cornmeal, ½ cup chunky peanut butter, an egg, a tablespoon of minced garlic, and 2 teaspoons each of sesame seeds, poppy seeds and dried hot pepper flakes. Pack this mixture into the nut shells, mounding the top and patting smooth; if you have leftover filling, roll out and cut into strips. Place on a baking sheet, and bake at 350°F for 20 minutes, then reduce oven to 200°F and bake for 30 minutes longer. Because there are no preservatives, I store the bulk of these in the freezer, taking out a week's worth at a time and keeping them in a small jar to use as treats.

QUICK IDEAS FOR USING HICKORY NUTS

- Use hickory nuts in any recipe calling for pecans.
- Save the shells and toss onto the coals when grilling, to add a delicious smoked flavor to your food.

OTHER RECIPES IN THIS BOOK FEATURING HICKORY NUTS

Browned-Butter Hickory Nut Pie

6 to 8 servings   Preparation: About an hour

Similar to a pecan pie, this rich dessert can be also made with mockernuts, butternuts or even hazelnuts. Pick through the broken nutmeats carefully and remove any stray bits of nutshell; this is especially important when working with shagbark hickory, which is particularly difficult to shell cleanly.

Pastry for single-crust pie
¼ cup (half of a stick) unsalted butter (no substitutes)
½ cup sugar

⅛ teaspoon salt
1 cup light corn syrup
3 eggs
1½ cups broken hickory nut meats

Heat oven to 350°F. On lightly floured worksurface, roll out pastry and fit into ungreased pie plate; trim and flute edges. Place in refrigerator while you prepare filling. Melt butter in a small heavy-bottomed pan over low heat. Increase heat slightly and cook until the butter is rich golden brown; be careful not to burn the butter. As soon as the butter is nicely colored, pour it into a glass or ceramic mixing bowl. Add the sugar and salt, and stir well. Add the corn syrup gradually, beating with an electric mixer. Beat in eggs, one at a time. Add nuts and stir in with a spoon. Pour mixture into pie shell. Bake until filling is set, about 45 minutes; a knife inserted about 1½ inches from the edge should come out clean. Cool pie on wire rack and serve warm or room temperature.

Quick Nut Bread

1 loaf   Preparation: Over an hour

Use hickory nuts, mockernuts, black walnuts or my personal favorite—butternuts—for this easy and not-too-sweet bread.

2½ cups all-purpose flour
¾ to 1 cup sugar, depending on preference
2½ teaspoons baking powder
½ teaspoon salt
½ teaspoon baking soda
1 egg

1½ cups milk
3 tablespoons butter, melted
½ teaspoon vanilla extract
1 cup chopped or broken hickory nuts or other nutmeats

Heat oven to 350°F. Grease an 8 x 4-inch loaf pan; set aside. In large mixing bowl, stir together flour, sugar, baking powder, salt and baking soda. In smaller mixing bowl, combine egg, milk, butter and vanilla extract; blend together with fork. Add egg mixture to flour mixture and stir with rubber spatula until just combined. Fold in nuts. Scrape mixture into prepared loaf pan. Bake until a tester inserted into the center comes out clean, 1 to 1¼ hours. Cool in pan for about 15 minutes, then turn out onto wire rack for final cooling. The bread can be served at warm room temperature, or cooled completely before serving.

Hickory-Honey Ice Cream

4 servings   Preparation: Involved (requires ice-cream maker)

Honey-roasted hickory nuts add delicious taste and crunch to this rich honey-sweetened ice cream.

2 cups heavy cream
1 tablespoon vanilla extract
4 egg yolks

½ cup plus 1 tablespoon wildflower honey,
   divided
½ cup chopped hickory nuts or other nuts

If using ice-cream maker that requires pre-freezing, place it in freezer as directed by manufacturer, generally 12 to 24 hours.

Combine cream and vanilla in top part of double boiler; place directly over medium-low heat. Add water to bottom part of double boiler, and begin heating water over medium heat. In mixing bowl, beat egg yolks with hand mixer until pale and thick enough to hold the shape of a ribbon when beaters are lifted (turn mixer off before lifting beaters!); this will take about 5 minutes. Keep an eye on the cream during this time; if it threatens to boil, remove from heat.

When yolks are thick, adjust heat under cream so it is just below the boiling point, then add to yolks in thin stream while beating with mixer on low speed. Pour cream mixture back into top part of double boiler; place over simmering water in double boiler. Cook, stirring frequently, until cream mixture reaches 185°F on instant-read thermometer. While cream mixture is cooking, add 2 inches of very cold water to sink. When cream mixture reaches proper temperature, immediately place pan into cold water in sink. Stir in ½ cup of the honey. Let cream mixture stand, stirring occasionally, until completely cool. Pour into bowl or plastic container; cover and refrigerate for at least 2 hours, or as long as overnight.

To prepare honey-roasted nuts, heat oven to 375°F. Line baking sheet with foil; spray generously with nonstick spray. In small bowl, combine remaining 1 tablespoon of honey with nuts; stir to coat. Scrape nuts out onto foil, spreading out with spoon as much as possible. Bake for 10 minutes or until nicely browned, stirring and spreading out nuts every few minutes. (Watch carefully, as nuts may burn very quickly near the end of baking time.) As soon as nuts have browned, remove from oven; pull foil off baking sheet and set aside until nuts have cooled completely. If preparing more than an hour before churning ice cream, transfer cooled nuts to jar; seal tightly until needed (this prevents the nuts from getting soft).

When you're ready to churn, start ice-cream maker (if using electric machine); pour chilled cream mixture into container. Churn until ice cream holds a soft shape, 15 to 20 minutes. Pour cooled nuts into mixture and churn until well mixed. Transfer ice cream to plastic container; cover and freeze for an hour or two before serving.

Hickory Fudge

36 pieces (about 3 pounds) Preparation: Under 15 minutes, plus cooling time

½ cup (1 stick) butter or stick margarine,
   plus additional for greasing foil
12 ounces semisweet chocolate chips
2½ cups sugar
⅔ cup evaporated milk (not sweetened
   condensed)

7 ounces marshmallow creme
¾ cup chopped hickory nuts
1 teaspoon vanilla extract
½ teaspoon salt

Line 9-inch-square pan with foil, extending the foil over the sides of the pan; butter foil generously. In microwave or double boiler, melt chocolate chips; keep warm while you prepare milk mixture. In saucepan, combine remaining ½ cup butter, sugar and milk. Heat to boiling over medium heat, stirring constantly. Boil for 5 minutes, stirring constantly. Remove from heat. Add marshmallow creme and melted chocolate; stir until smooth. Stir in hickory nuts, vanilla and salt; scrape into prepared pan, smoothing top. Cool to room temperature before cutting into squares.

Hickory-Honey Cream Cheese Spread

About 1¼ cups Preparation: Under 15 minutes

Serve this with apple slices and crackers. It's also wonderful spread on warm toast.

8 ounces cream cheese, softened
   (reduced-fat works fine)
1 tablespoon orange juice

1 tablespoon honey
A pinch of ground ginger
¼ cup chopped hickory nuts

In mixing bowl, combine cream cheese, orange juice, honey and ginger. Beat with electric hand mixer (or wooden spoon) until smooth and fluffy. Add nuts; stir in with wooden spoon.

Hickory Brittle

About 1¾ pounds   Preparation: Under an hour

½ cup (1 stick) unsalted butter, plus
    additional for greasing baking sheet
1 teaspoon vanilla extract
½ teaspoon baking soda
1½ cups sugar

¾ cup corn syrup
⅔ cup water
¼ teaspoon salt
1½ cups chopped hickory nuts

Grease rimmed baking sheet generously with butter, being sure to also butter the inside rim of the sheet; set aside. In small bowl, stir together vanilla and baking soda; set aside.

In heavy-bottomed 3-quart saucepan, combine sugar, corn syrup, water and salt. Heat to boiling over high heat; cook, stirring constantly, until sugar dissolves. Add remaining ½ cup butter, cut into 4 pieces, and the hickory nuts. Continue to cook, stirring constantly, until mixture reaches the hard-crack stage,* or 300°F on candy thermometer (mixture will be very foamy). Stir in baking soda mixture. Stir vigorously until light and smooth, about 1 minute, then pour onto prepared baking sheet. Quickly spread mixture out as evenly as possible; ¼ inch thick is ideal (you can pick up the baking sheet with potholders and tilt it to help the mixture flow evenly). Place baking sheet on cake-cooling rack (better yet, if it is cold outside, place baking sheet outdoors so it cools more quickly); cool as quickly as possible. When completely cool, break into pieces. Store in tightly sealed container.

*To test mixture for hard-crack stage, drop a bit of the boiling syrup into a bowl of cold water. When it is at the right stage, the syrup will form hard, brittle threads than can be broken. Don't rush this, or pull the syrup from the heat too soon; it takes me about 15 minutes to reach hard-crack stage.

Crescent Cookies

About 2 dozen cookies   Preparation: Under an hour

1 cup (2 sticks) butter, softened
1¼ cups confectioners' sugar, divided
1 cup finely chopped hickory nuts

2 cups all-purpose flour
1 teaspoon rum extract, optional

Heat oven to 300°F. In mixing bowl, combine butter and ¼ cup of the sugar. Cream with electric mixer. Add nuts, flour and extract; mix well. Form into small balls, using about 1 tablespoon of dough; shape into crescents. Place ½ inch apart on ungreased baking sheets. Bake until just set, 20 to 25 minutes; don't allow cookies to brown. Roll warm cookies in the remaining powdered sugar; place on rack to cool completely.

Hickory-Maple Caramel Corn

About 10 cups

The combination of hickory and maple is particularly delicious in this caramel corn.

1 tablespoon vegetable oil
⅓ cup uncooked popcorn
¾ cup coarsely chopped hickory nuts,
    toasted if you like

6 tablespoons (¾ of a stick) unsalted butter
1½ cups pure maple syrup (do not use
    substitutes for this recipe)
½ teaspoon salt

Spray a very large mixing bowl with nonstick spray, or grease with butter; set aside. In 3-quart saucepan, combine oil with several popcorn kernels. Heat over medium heat until kernels begin to pop. Add remaining popcorn; cover and cook, shaking pan constantly, until all popcorn has popped. Transfer popped corn to prepared mixing bowl. Add nuts; set aside.

In heavy-bottomed medium saucepan, melt butter over medium heat. Add syrup and salt; stir briefly. Boil without stirring until syrup reaches the hard-crack stage,* or 300°F on candy thermometer; this will take 15 to 20 minutes (don't try to rush it). Near the end of cooking time, spray a large wooden spoon and a baking sheet with nonstick spray, or rub lightly with vegetable oil.

When syrup reaches the hard-crack stage, pour over popcorn and nuts, stirring with oiled wooden spoon until well mixed. Immediately pour popcorn onto prepared baking sheet, spreading out with spoon. Cool before breaking into smaller clusters. Store in tightly covered container.

*To test mixture for hard-crack stage, drop a bit of the boiling syrup into a bowl of cold water. When it is at the right stage, the syrup will form hard, brittle threads than can be broken.

Hickory-Crusted Fish

4 servings   Preparation: Under 30 minutes

Use this easy recipe with any firm white fish such as walleye, halibut, sea bass or cod. The fillets should be at least ½ inch thick, but no thicker than 1 inch.

1¼ to 1½ pounds walleye fillets or substitute (see above), cut into 4 pieces
¼ cup finely chopped hickory nuts
¼ cup finely crushed cracker crumbs
¾ cup all-purpose flour
1 egg, lightly beaten with 1 tablespoon water

2 tablespoons butter, divided
1 tablespoon minced shallot, or 2 tablespoons minced onion
½ cup dry white wine
Half of a fish bouillon cube, dissolved in 1 cup water (or 1 cup fish stock)
1 tablespoon chopped fresh parsley

Heat oven to 375°F if fish fillets are ½ inch thick; if fillets are 1 inch thick, heat oven to 425°F. Spray baking dish large enough to hold fillets in single layer with nonstick spray; set aside. Rinse fish and blot dry with paper towels. In small bowl, stir together nuts and cracker crumbs. Dip fish in flour, shaking off excess. Dip floured fish in egg mixture, allowing excess to drip off. Dredge fish on both sides in crumb mixture, pressing crumbs into fish. Reserve 1 tablespoon of the flour; discard any remaining flour, egg mix and crumb mixture. Mix reserved flour with ¼ cup water in small bowl; set aside.

Melt 1 tablespoon of the butter in medium skillet over medium heat. When butter stops foaming, add fish. Cook until golden brown. Add another tablespoon of butter; turn fish and cook until second side is golden. Transfer fish to prepared baking dish; place in oven.

Add shallot to same skillet and cook for about a minute, stirring constantly. Add wine, scraping to loosen any browned bits. Increase heat to medium-high and cook until most of the wine has cooked away. Add bouillon mixture; cook for about 5 minutes, stirring occasionally. In the mean time, check the fish; it is done when the inside is just opaque. Remove fish from oven as soon as it is done, and keep it warm; it probably won't be ready until the sauce is finished, but it might be done sooner so keep an eye on it.

When sauce has cooked for 5 minutes, add flour-water mixture, stirring constantly to prevent lumps. Cook until sauce thickens somewhat and becomes bubbly, 3 to 5 minutes. By now, the fish should be cooked through; if not, simply keep sauce warm until fish is ready. Transfer fish to individual serving plates. Pour sauce over fish (strain through wire-mesh strainer if you like, to remove solids). Sprinkle with parsley; serve immediately.

Cheese and Hickory Crisps

About 70 crackers   Preparation: 15 minutes initial prep, followed by 1 hour freezing or overnight chilling; 15 minutes final prep

½ cup (1 stick) butter, softened
8 ounces (2 cups) shredded cheddar cheese
1 cup all-purpose flour
1 tablespoon dry sherry

½ teaspoon salt (use smoked salt or garlic salt if you like)
¼ teaspoon Tabasco sauce
¾ cup coarsely chopped hickory nuts

In food processor fitted with metal blade, cream butter until smooth and fluffy. Add cheese, flour, sherry, salt and Tabasco sauce; process until mixture is beginning to form a dough, stopping several times to scrape sides. Add nuts; process until mixture begins to form a ball. Divide into 2 portions. Squeeze each portion into a rough cylinder, then roll on worksurface to form a log that is about 9 inches long and 2 inches thick. Wrap in waxed paper. Freeze for 1 hour, or refrigerate overnight.

When you're ready to bake, heat oven to 375°F. Using very sharp knife, slice rolls ¼ inch thick or slightly thinner; arrange ½ inch apart on ungreased baking sheets. Bake until golden brown, about 15 minutes. Cool for a minute, then transfer to wire rack to cool. Store in airtight container.

FRUITS & BERRIES

I'D GUESS that the average forager picks more fruits and berries than any other class of wild food. Many are familiar because we can buy domesticated versions at the grocery store: blueberries, raspberries, strawberries, blackberries and grapes. Others, such as prickly pear fruit, gooseberries, currants, crabapples and persimmons, may appear in high-end or specialty markets for a short time each year. But there are others that are simply not available for purchase (except perhaps at a farmer's market, where some enterprising foragers are selling foods they have gathered): elderberries, service-berries, chokeberries, ground cherries, maypops, mountain ash berries, mulberries, nannyberries, pawpaws and rose hips.

Here is a collection of wild fruits and berries that can be safely foraged. The species are listed alphabetically in this section. Each includes a general description of the fruit, including habitat and range information as well as harvesting tips and any special cautions or concerns. Several recipes follow each species, along with quick ideas for using the fruit.

To finish this chapter, there is a section with recipes that apply to a wide variety of fruits. The highlight of this section is information on making small batches of jelly and jam from wild fruits. I've always been frustrated when I try to use standard recipes for jelly and jam with wild fruits, because they make such large batches (and require so much fruit). With the charts in this book, you can make 2, 4 or 6 pints of jelly or jam; hopefully, this will leave you enough fruit from your harvest to try some of the other delicious recipes in this chapter.

Blackberries (common or highbush, *Rubus allegheniensis,* and others)

Picking blackberries is a thorny job, so be sure to wear a heavy, long-sleeved shirt and long pants. The sweet, dark berries are worth the trouble.

HABITAT, RANGE

Blackberries are native shrubs that grow throughout our range in areas such as waste fields, along roadsides and trails, in forest clearings and in thickets. They like sunlight, but often grow in areas with dappled shade.

PARTS USED

Ripe berries, raw, cooked or juiced; young shoots, as a trail nibble; leaves for tea

SEASONS

Shoots in spring, berries in mid- to late summer, leaves from summer through fall

IDENTIFICATION TIPS, DANGEROUS LOOKALIKES

Blackberries grow as sprawling shrubs with arching, prickly canes; a similar, related fruit called the dewberry (*R. villosus* and *R. canadensis*) tends to sprawl along the ground. Blackberries

Ripe and underripe berries

ripen later than raspberries, and underripe blackberries do resemble red raspberries— except that the underripe blackberry will be hard and dry, not soft and juicy like a ready-to-pick raspberry. Once the blackberry ripens to purple-black perfection, it resembles its cousin, the black raspberry. It's easy to determine which you've got, however, simply by picking a ripe berry. Both are compound fruits; each berry is a cluster of many globular drupes growing from a core (often called a receptacle). When picked, the core remains inside blackberries and dewberries, giving the berry a solid appearance. Raspberries release cleanly from the core; the compound fruit is hollow and the core remains on the plant.

The canes of blackberries are reddish and sometimes appear ribbed or angular. First-year canes are unbranched and don't bear fruit; in the second year, canes become branched, developing flowers that turn to fruit in the summer. After 2 years, the canes die off, but the root produces new canes the following spring. Blackberries have alternate, compound leaves; generally there will be 5 toothed, grayish green leaflets that are lighter underneath.

A number of related species grow in our area. The USDA Plants Distribution database lists 68 species under the "blackberry" heading. However, this number includes dewberries, cloudberries and a host of regional blackberry subspecies, many of which don't grow in our area. For the forager, the distinctions are not so important; all species of blackberries are edible, although some are less sweet, or are smaller or less juicy. There are no dangerous lookalikes that could be confused with ripe blackberries, as the fruit is quite distinct. Some varieties of mulberries have similar-looking blackish fruit, but mulberries grow as a small to medium-sized thornless tree, so are easy to distinguish (they're also edible and delicious).

HARVESTING TIPS

Blackberries generally grow in thick patches; getting to the berries in the middle can be a real challenge. I wear a long-sleeved canvas shirt, even though it is generally quite warm when blackberries are ripe. If you're thinking about wearing a cap to protect your head, forget it; the cap will end up on the ground or tangled in a bristly cane. The best container for picking blackberries is a plastic ice-cream pail; a plastic bag will become shredded in a matter of minutes, and a canvas tote will get stained with the dark juices.

Because the fruits have so many nooks and crannies, they trap dust and grit rather easily. Don't pick blackberries in dusty areas such as along gravel roads; you'll never get them clean (and the fruit may have been contaminated by automobile fumes as well).

SPECIAL CONSIDERATIONS

If you're picking blackberry leaves to use as tea, harvest only fresh, sound specimens. Wilted leaves may contain an undesirable fungus. Blackberry leaf tea may cause a bit of stomach upset in sensitive individuals, especially if taken on an empty stomach, so you may want to have a snack with your tea.

MORE ABOUT BLACKBERRIES: Each spring, as I am headed to the woods in search of new places to pick morels, ramps, nettles and the other early wild foods, I also keep my eye out for the tangled remnants of last year's blackberry patch. Blackberry canes send up new shoots each spring, and I like to pick one, peel it, and munch on it as a delightful forest nibble. Very young and tender shoots can be sliced up and added to salads for a subtle, sweet, wholesome taste. (Don't cut more than a few shoots, however, especially if the thicket isn't large.)

Later in the season, I may return to the same area to pick gooseberries, currants and raspberries. The blackberry patches look hopeful, with lots of hard green fruits that promise a good harvest to come. Soon, many of the other fruits are done; but the blackberries are still hard and unyielding. I check the blackberries throughout midsummer, and finally, about the time I am looking for ripe elderberries, the blackberries begin to ripen. They will continue to ripen over the next week or two, so I will have plenty of opportunities to get my fill.

Blackberries have more vitamin A than an equal amount of cantaloupe or canned apricots, as well as plenty of vitamin C. They're rich in potassium and other trace minerals, and have good amounts of carotene and lutein. Blackberry-leaf tea is said to be good for sore throats; the leaves are often used in tea blends, where they contribute a good bit of tannin. If you would like to make tea from blackberry leaves alone, simply pour a cup of boiling water over a generous teaspoon of dried blackberry leaves; steep for 5 minutes, then strain and sweeten to taste.

Blackberries can be frozen for later use in jam, pies and other cooked desserts. Simply lay them on a baking sheet in a single layer and freeze; when the berries are solid, pack them into plastic bags or freezer containers for storage. The seeds of blackberries are more noticeable to me than those of other berries, so I often strain the fruit before using; frozen fruit is perfect for this, as the berries will be soft when thawed.

How to make blackberry juice: Place blackberries in a heavy-bottomed saucepan. Add a small amount of water, about ½ cup per quart of berries. Crush the fruit with a potato masher to start the juices flowing. Heat over medium heat until simmering, stirring constantly. Reduce heat to low; cover the saucepan and simmer for 10 minutes. Remove from heat and set aside until cool enough to handle, then strain through several layers of dampened cheesecloth. A quart of blackberries will yield just under 2 cups of juice.

JUST FOR FUN
Blackberry Festival in Bremerton, Washington
If you happen to be the Seattle area in late August, check out the blackberry festival held in Bremerton (adjacent to the ferry stop, so it's very easy to get to). In 2003, more than 70,000 people came to the 14th annual festival to enjoy blackberry treats (including Blackberry Slugs, a maple bar filled with blackberries), look at displays of sidewalk chalk art, and participate in the Berry Fun Run. For more information and specific dates, visit their website: http://www.blackberryfestival.org/

QUICK IDEAS FOR USING WILD BLACKBERRIES
- Add a few blackberries to a mixed-fruit salad; the seediness of the blackberries is less noticeable when they're mixed with other fruits.
- Use wild blackberries in any recipe calling for domestic blackberries.

OTHER RECIPES IN THIS BOOK FEATURING WILD BLACKBERRIES

- As substitute in Blueberries with Cinnamon Croutons and Custard (page 100)
- Wild Berry Syrup (page 111)
- Elderberry or Blackberry Coulis (page 169)
- As substitute in Gooseberry Crisp (page 173)
- Berry Pie with Soda-Cracker Crust (page 230)
- Wild Berry Vinegar (page 231)
- Blackberry Jelly (chart, page 254)
- Uncooked Blackberry Jam (chart, page 256)
- Wild Berry-Yogurt Popsicles or Soft-Serve Ice Cream (page 259)
- Wild Berry Parfait with Maypop or Lemon Mousse (page 262)

Blackberry Buckle

9 servings   Preparation: Over an hour

Substitute raspberries or blueberries for the blackberries in this rich coffeecake.

Topping:
½ cup sugar
⅓ cup all-purpose flour
¼ cup (half of a stick) cold unsalted butter,
    cut into ¼-inch slices
½ teaspoon cinnamon

Batter:
1⅓ cups all-purpose flour
½ teaspoon salt
¼ teaspoon baking powder
¾ cup (1½ sticks) unsalted butter, softened
¾ cup sugar
1 teaspoon vanilla
3 eggs
2 cups wild blackberries

Heat oven to 350°F. Spray 9-inch-square baking dish with nonstick spray; set aside. Prepare the topping: In small mixing bowl, combine sugar, flour, butter and cinnamon. Cut together with 2 knives or a pastry blender until mixture is coarse and crumbly. Refrigerate until batter is ready.

Prepare the batter: Combine flour, salt and baking powder in sifter or wire-mesh strainer; sift into large bowl and set aside. In another mixing bowl, cream butter and sugar with electric mixer until light and fluffy. Add vanilla and beat until mixed. Add one-third of the flour mixture and 1 egg to butter and beat well. Add half of remaining flour and another egg; beat well. Add remaining flour and egg; beat well. Fold in blackberries with rubber spatula. Scrape batter into prepared dish, spreading evenly. Sprinkle prepared topping evenly over batter. Bake until topping is golden and tester inserted in the center comes out clean, about 45 minutes. Best served warm.

Blackberries and Dumplings

4 to 6 servings

What a wonderful breakfast!

1 quart wild blackberries
¾ cup water
¾ cup sugar
2 tablespoons butter

Dumplings:
1¼ cups all-purpose flour
¼ cup cornmeal
3 tablespoons sugar
2 teaspoons baking powder
½ teaspoon salt
⅔ cup milk
3 tablespoons butter, melted

In small soup pot or large saucepan, combine blackberries, water, sugar and butter. Heat to boiling over high heat; reduce heat so mixture boils very gently and cook for 15 minutes, stirring frequently. Near the end of cooking time, prepare dumplings: Combine flour, cornmeal, sugar, baking powder and salt in sifter or wire-mesh strainer; sift into large mixing bowl. Add milk and melted butter; stir until flour is moistened. Drop dumpling mixture in heaping tablespoons onto boiling blackberry mixture. Cook for 5 minutes, then cover and cook until dumplings are firm, about 10 minutes longer. Cool slightly before serving.

Apple Pie with Blackberries

1 pie

The combination of blackberries and tart apples is exquisite in this simple pie.

1 pound Granny Smith apples, peeled,
    cored and sliced
8 ounces wild blackberries (about 1 cup)
3 tablespoons sugar, plus additional for
    sprinkling crust

2 teaspoons cornstarch
¼ teaspoon nutmeg
Pastry for double-crust pie, divided into
    2 equal portions
A little milk for brushing pie crust

Heat oven to 400°F; position oven rack in bottom third of oven. In mixing bowl, combine apples, blackberries, 3 tablespoons sugar, the cornstarch and nutmeg; stir to combine. Let stand for 10 minutes. Meanwhile, roll out 1 portion of pastry and fit into ungreased pie plate. Scrape apple mixture into pie plate, mounding slightly. Roll out remaining crust. Moisten edges of crust in pie plate, then top with rolled-out crust (or, if you prefer, make a lattice top; see page 151). Seal, trim and flute edges. Cut 6 slits about an inch long in top crust for ventilation. Place pie on baking sheet (to catch drips). Brush top with milk; sprinkle with a little sugar. Bake until crust is golden and filling bubbles through slits, 30 to 40 minutes. Transfer to rack to cool; best served warm.

Chokeberries (black chokeberry, *Aronia melanocarpa*, and others)

*This lesser-known fruit is a bit acrid, but can be used to make an extraordinary mincemeat.
It also works well in chutneys and savory sauces.*

HABITAT, RANGE, OTHER SUBSPECIES

Chokeberries can tolerate a wide range of growing conditions, and are typically found in
thickets and woods. Black chokeberries grow in almost every state east of the Mississippi
River, as well as Minnesota and Iowa. Purple chokeberries *(A. prunifola)* are found only
east of the Mississippi. Red chokeberries *(A. arbutifolia)* have a more south- to south-
easterly distribution, and do not grow in the upper midwest. (Note that some sources list
chokeberries as *Pyrus* spp. or *Photinia* spp.)

PARTS USED

Ripe berries

SEASONS

Early fall through early winter

IDENTIFICATION TIPS, DANGEROUS LOOKALIKES

Chokeberry shrubs are often leggy, and are usually 3 to 5 feet
tall but occasionally up to 10 feet tall. They are easy to identify
when they are fruiting, and there are no toxic lookalikes that
would be mistaken for chokeberries if you follow good
identification practices.

Black chokeberries

The dark green leaves are alternate and elliptical, with finely toothed margins; the leaves
become broader above the midpoint. In fall, the leaves turn a lovely crimson, which makes
them easier to spot in the woods. Leaves of the black chokeberry are smooth beneath,
while those of the red chokeberry are fuzzy underneath; both are lighter underneath than
on top. If you examine the top sides of the leaves with a magnifying lens, you will spot a
row of black hair-like glands along the midrib. This seems to be a reliable indicator for
positive identification of the species.

The fruits are actually pomes, and have 5 easy-to-spot depressions on the end of each
fruit (rather like an indented, rounded 5-point star). Fruits are ¼" to ⁵⁄₁₆" across, and
grow in clusters on branchlets that are often pinkish in hue. Black chokeberries ripen to
a rich purplish black; purple chokeberries are purple when ripe; and not surprisingly, red
chokeberries are red when ripe.

The berries somewhat resemble those of the common buckthorn (*Rhamnus* spp.), but chokeberry fruits grow in clusters at the ends of branches, while buckthorn fruits are clustered along the length of the branches, often in the crotch. Another distinction between the two species is that buckthorns have opposite leaves, rather than the alternate leaves found on chokeberries. (Buckthorn is generally listed as toxic because the fruits have strong cathartic properties.)

HARVESTING TIPS

Chokeberry shrubs bear large amounts of fruit, so it's easy to gather the quantity you need. Harvest fruit from several plants rather than stripping all the fruits from one plant, as some animals use chokeberries for winter food. The fruit remains sound even after several frosts. When the fruits eventually do dry up on the shrubs, they make a decent trail nibble.

MORE ABOUT CHOKEBERRIES: Here's a fruit that is almost completely neglected in common American wild-foods literature. Unlike chokecherries and many other fall berry-like fruits, chokeberries contain no inedible stone or large, annoying seeds. Chokeberries have a sweet flavor, but the flesh has an acrid quality that will leave your mouth feeling dry, similar to the effect of eating an underripe apple or a raw cranberry. Yet they make a delicious, rich juice; and in fact, I've come up with several recipes that use the whole fruit in which the dry feeling is diminished considerably or eliminated entirely. The Pear and Chokeberry Mincemeat (page 150) is a stellar example of this, and I highly recommend a pie made from this for your next holiday gathering.

Also called chokepears, chokeberries are from the *Rosacea* family, which also contains apples, pears, cherries and many other highly edible fruits. Chokeberries are apparently more popular in Europe and the Soviet countries, where the juice is used in combination with apple juice to make wine. The juice makes an excellent jelly or syrup, with no acrid feeling at all. The fruit contains a good bit of natural pectin as well, and combines well with other fruit juices in jellies and jams; even a small amount contributes a rich, blue-purple hue and nice body. They are rich in anthocyanins, a phytonutrient that may lower blood pressure and protect against circulatory problems caused by diabetes.

How to make chokeberry juice: I have worked with black chokeberries. The juice produced by these fruits is the darkest, most-staining juice I have ever encountered. It turns wooden spoons a rich, deep purple, and will readily stain laminate and Corian countertops (quick action with bleach usually takes care of the stain). If you chop chokeberries in a food processor, the white part of the blade will become spotted with blue. Finally, the juice will permanently stain most plastic containers, so glass jars are best.

I start with a quart of whole fruits (about 1¼ pounds), which I chop coarsely in the food processor; this seems to speed the process and slightly increase the yield. Combine 1¼ pounds fruit, chopped or whole as you prefer, with 2½ cups water in a stainless-steel pan (aluminum or enameled pans will be stained by the dark juices). Heat to boiling, then adjust heat and let the mixture boil gently for 20 minutes. If you've used whole fruits rather than chopped, use a potato masher to break up the fruits after about 10 minutes of cooking. After cooking for 20 minutes, pour the mixture into a wire-mesh strainer that has been lined with a double layer of cheesecloth. Rinse the pot with 1 cup of water, and pour that through the fruit in the cheesecloth. Let the fruit drip for 30 minutes or so, then tighten the cheesecloth around the fruit and squeeze gently to extract more juice. Measure the juice, and if there is less than 3 cups, pour additional water through the fruit, squeezing lightly after each addition, until you have a total of 3 cups juice.

QUICK IDEAS FOR USING CHOKEBERRIES

- Chokeberry juice can be used in any recipe calling for chokecherry, elderberry or wild cherry juice.
- I've never had the chance to try this, but I am sure that chokeberries, with their high tannin content and rich color, would make an outstanding wine.

OTHER RECIPES IN THIS BOOK FEATURING CHOKEBERRIES

- Chokeberry Syrup (page 99)
- Chokeberry Jelly (chart, page 254)

Pear and Chokeberry Mincemeat

1 quart   Preparation: About 1¼ hours, plus optional canning time

Because chokeberries have no noticeable seeds or pits, they can be used "as is" for cooking, although the flesh has a dry, acrid quality that makes them unsuitable for many uses. The mixture of fruits and flavors in this recipe eliminates that dryness. Use this filling to make a delicious mincemeat pie (recipe follows); warm the filling up and serve over ice cream or pound cake; or use in any recipe calling for mincemeat. It will keep for a week in the refrigerator, and the flavor actually improves after a day or two. For longer term storage, freeze in plastic freezer bags, or can following the instructions below.

2 pounds ripe but firm D'Anjou, Bartlett or other pears (about 4 D'Anjou)
⅔ cup chokeberries, fresh or frozen (thawed if frozen)
2 tablespoons freshly squeezed lemon juice
⅔ cup sugar
¾ cup water, divided
2 teaspoons corn syrup
½ cup golden raisins
¼ cup dried cranberries

½ teaspoon cinnamon
½ teaspoon allspice
¼ teaspoon nutmeg
¼ teaspoon salt
¾ cup chopped butternuts, hickory nuts or pecans (medium-fine)
2 tablespoons rum or brandy, or ½ teaspoon rum extract or brandy extract
2 tablespoons unsalted butter

Peel, quarter and core pears and place in food processor workbowl, cutting each piece into thirds as you add to the workbowl. Add chokeberries and lemon juice, and chop until pears are coarse, with pieces no larger than ½ inch (or, chop fruits by hand, sprinkling afterwards with lemon juice). Set aside.

In heavy-bottomed nonreactive 4-quart saucepan, stir together sugar, ¼ cup water and the corn syrup. Cook over medium heat, stirring constantly with a wooden spoon, until sugar dissolves and mixture comes to a boil. Continue to cook, stirring occasionally, until mixture turns golden, about 7 minutes; watch carefully, as the syrup colors quite rapidly when it is ready and it's easy to over-brown the syrup. Remove pan from heat and carefully add the remaining ½ cup water, avoiding the steam that will come up from the hot syrup. The syrup will harden when the water is added. Return the pan to medium heat and cook, stirring constantly, until the hardened syrup dissolves. Add pear mixture, raisins, cranberries, cinnamon, allspice, nutmeg and salt. Adjust heat so mixture boils gently and cook, stirring frequently, until thickened, 45 to 50 minutes.

Add nuts, rum and butter and cook, stirring frequently, for about 5 minutes. If canning, process immediately as described below; otherwise, cool completely before storing in refrigerator or freezing.

To can Pear and Chokeberry Mincemeat: Follow general canning instructions on pages 418-419. Pack hot mincemeat into hot pint jars. Process in boiling-water bath for 20 minutes.

Pear and Chokeberry Mincemeat Pie

1 pie   Preparation: Over an hour

For a holiday treat, serve this pie warm with a scoop of vanilla ice cream, or a dollop of lightly sweetened whipped cream.

Pastry for double-crust pie, divided into 2 equal portions

3½ to 4 cups Pear and Chokeberry Mincemeat

1½ teaspoons unsalted butter, cut into small pieces

1 egg yolk, beaten with 1 tablespoon cold water

On lightly floured worksurface, roll out 1 portion of pastry and fit into ungreased pie plate. Trim edges, leaving ¾ inch overhang. Cover and chill pie crust and remaining pastry dough for 30 minutes.

When pastry has chilled, heat oven to 425°F (400°F for glass pan); position oven rack in bottom third of oven. Spoon mincemeat into prepared pie plate, smoothing the top; the crust should be comfortably full but not over the edge. Dot top with butter. Roll out remaining pastry. Moisten edges of pastry in pie plate, then top with rolled-out pastry; if you like, you can make a lattice crust.* Seal, trim and flute edges. Brush top crust with egg yolk mixture; if you've used a plain top crust rather than a lattice, cut 6 to 8 slits about an inch long the crust for ventilation. Place pie on baking sheet (to catch drips) and bake in center of oven until crust is golden and filling bubbles through vents or lattices, about 25 minutes. Cool to warm room temperature before serving; best served on the day it is made.

*If you've never made a lattice crust, here is the general technique. Roll out the second half of the pastry about ⅛ inch thick. Cut into ½-inch-wide strips. Position a row of strips, running vertically across the top of the pie and separated by ½ inch. Now begin to weave a row of strips horizontally across the top of the pie, lifting the vertical strips over the horizontal strips in an alternating pattern. Trim all strips even with the edge of the overhanging crust, and pinch all edges very well to seal. Consult a good baking cookbook for more specific instructions.

Chokeberry Barbecue Sauce

About 1 cup

Chokeberry juice gives this tangy barbecue sauce a rich color as well as a wonderful taste. The recipe would work equally well with juice from chokecherries, wild cherries, nannyberries, blackhaws or even elderberries.

1 cup chicken broth
¾ cup chokeberry juice (page 148) or
    substitute as noted above
½ cup orange juice
3 tablespoons (packed) brown sugar
2 tablespoons seasoned rice vinegar
½ teaspoon cinnamon
¼ teaspoon cayenne pepper
2 bay leaves

½ teaspoon whole cloves
½ teaspoon whole peppercorns
½ teaspoon whole spicebush berries or
    allspice berries
½ cup ruby Port
2 teaspoons cornstarch
3 tablespoons catsup
½ teaspoon salt

In heavy-bottomed nonreactive saucepan, stir together chicken broth, chokeberry juice, orange juice, brown sugar, vinegar, cinnamon and cayenne. Tie up bay leaves, cloves, peppercorns and spicebush or allspice berries in a square of cheesecloth; add to saucepan. Heat to boiling over medium-high heat; cook until reduced by about one-third,* about 10 minutes.

Meanwhile, in measuring cup, stir together Port and cornstarch. When chokeberry mixture has reduced, remove and discard spice bag. Stir Port mixture again, and add to chokeberry mixture with catsup and salt, stirring well. Reduce heat so mixture boils gently and cook, stirring occasionally, until sauce has thickened and reduced to about 1 cup (pour into measuring cup to check the volume, if you like). Cool to room temperature before serving alongside grilled or broiled meats; you may also use in place of regular barbecue sauce in any recipe. The sauce will keep in a covered jar in the refrigerator for several weeks.

*A wooden chopstick offers an easy way to check the volume. Stick the chopstick, straight up, into the liquid in the saucepan before you start cooking. The juice is so dark that it will leave an easy-to-see mark on the light-colored chopstick. As the mixture cooks down, you can stick the chopstick back into the saucepan occasionally to check the level

Pork Tenderloin with Chokeberry Sauce

2 or 3 servings

The spicy pepper rub contrasts nicely with the sweet and tangy berry sauce in this easy main dish. Serve with rice pilaf and a bright green vegetable.

1 teaspoon whole black peppercorns
1 teaspoon fennel seeds
½ teaspoon salt, preferably coarse
1 boneless pork tenderloin, about 1 pound
1 tablespoon olive oil
1 medium onion, coarsely chopped
2 cloves garlic, minced

1 cup white Port or tawny Port
1 cup chokeberries, fresh or frozen
   (thawed if frozen)
¼ cup orange juice, preferably freshly
   squeezed
1 tablespoon honey
2 teaspoons red wine vinegar

Heat oven to 400°F. With mortar and pestle, crush together peppercorns, fennel seeds and salt until the texture of coarse sand. Cut tenderloin into 2 shorter halves to fit skillet and sprinkle with pepper mixture, pressing in with your fingertips. In ovenproof medium skillet, heat oil over medium-high heat until hot but not smoking. Add pork and brown on all sides. Transfer pork to plate; set aside.

Add onion and garlic to oil remaining in skillet and cook until golden, stirring frequently. Add Port, stirring to loosen any browned bits in skillet. Increase heat to high and cook until reduced to about half. Add chokeberries, orange juice, honey and vinegar. Heat to boiling, stirring frequently. Add pork and any accumulated juices to skillet, turning to coat with sauce. Transfer skillet to oven and cook, uncovered, until temperature of pork reaches 150°F, 20 to 30 minutes, turning pork in sauce several times during cooking; if sauce dries out and is threatening to burn, stir in a little water or additional orange juice. To serve, cut pork into ½-inch slices; spoon sauce over pork.

Crabapples (numerous members of the *Malus* or *Pyrus* genus)

Look for crabapples in city and suburban greenways and office parks, as well as in country lanes and byways. Crabapples make delightful pink jelly, as well as tasty sauce, jam and fruit leather.

HABITAT, RANGE, SUBSPECIES

The crabapple family is referred to variously as *Malus* or *Pyrus*, depending on which texts one consults. Some crabapples from our area include the southern crabapple, *M. or P. angustifolia*; the sweet crabapple, *M. or P. coronaria*; and the prairie crabapple, *M. or P. ioensis*. Native wild crabapples grow throughout the United States; in addition, many domesticated varieties such as the Hopa crabapple are often seen as escapees or abandoned trees. Crabapples grow in a wide variety of habitats, ranging from field edges and shelter-belts, to ditches and roadsides, to hilltops, old fields, thickets and abandoned farms. They need a fair amount of sunlight to produce ripe fruit.

PARTS USED

Ripe fruit, cooked or juiced

SEASONS

Late summer through fall

IDENTIFICATION TIPS, DANGEROUS LOOKALIKES

Crabapples

Crabapple trees vary widely, yet anyone would know one when they saw one with ripe fruit. The trees are similar in appearance to domestic apples, but usually smaller. Fruits are smaller as well, ranging from ⅜ inch to 2 inches across, and ripening in a variety of hues including red, reddish pink, reddish orange and yellowish with a blush. Like the familiar domestic apple, crabapples are *pomes*—fleshy fruits containing several seeds in a papery-covered core; at the bottom of each fruit, you can see the calyx, which is the dried remnant of the blossom. Crabapple leaves are sharply toothed and alternate on grayish to brownish stems.

Crabapples might be confused with hawthorns (*Crataegus* spp.), which produce similar fruits. The leaves of crabapples are more sharply toothed than those of hawthorns, and hawthorn fruits tend to be more oval in shape rather than round. Hawthorns have sharp thorns, while most crabapple trees are unarmed or have blunt thorns at best. Since hawthorns are edible as well and can be prepared in the same ways as crabs, don't worry overmuch about distinguishing between the two. There are no dangerous lookalikes.

HARVESTING TIPS

Crabapples are easy to harvest, as the trees are low enough to reach the fruits. Simply pull on a ripe fruit; the stem will usually come along and you'll have to remove it later. You can often grab several fruits at once, so harvesting goes quickly. Crabapples can withstand a light frost, providing a long harvesting season.

MORE ABOUT CRABAPPLES: Crabapples provide something for everyone, because they can be found in both rural and urban areas. Ornamental Hopa crabs are planted frequently at office parks and other developments, and generally the building owners don't mind if you harvest a few. Crabapples aren't generally bothered by the insects that feed on domestic apples, and they don't seem to get blight and other apple diseases either. They are too tart to eat raw, but make outstanding jellies and jams, often with a lovely rosy color. Like domestic apples, crabapples are rich in natural pectin, so it is possible to make jelly with no added pectin. Crabapples combine well with other fruits in jellies and jams.

The seeds of the crabapple are a bit of a bother if you want to dehydrate the fruit or use it whole (as in Spiced Whole Crabapples). If you're making juice or purée, however, the seeds will get strained out, so you don't need to be concerned with them.

How to make crabapple juice: Cut crabapples in half and place in nonreactive pot. Add water to just barely cover the crabapples. Heat to boiling over high heat, then reduce heat somewhat and boil gently for 15 to 20 minutes, or until fruit is very soft. Strain through 4 layers of dampened cheesecloth; for the clearest jelly, don't press or squeeze the pulp.

QUICK IDEAS FOR USING CRABAPPLES
- Use crabapple juice in place of apple juice in any jelly recipe.

OTHER RECIPES IN THIS BOOK FEATURING CRABAPPLES
- Crabapple Jelly (no-pectin jelly, page 257)
- "Many Things Wild" Casserole with Wild Rice (page 410)
- Dried crabapple wedges (page 421)

Spiced Whole Crabapples

2 pints (easily doubled or tripled) Preparation: About an hour, plus 2 weeks curing

Serve these tart-sweet crabapples as a garnish with meat, fish, poultry or cheese.

2 pint-sized canning jars, with bands and
  new lids
2 pints whole crabapples (1 inch in diameter)
1½ cups sugar
1¼ cups red wine vinegar
¾ cup water
2 slices peeled fresh gingerroot, each about
  the size of two stacked quarters

8 whole cloves
2 cinnamon sticks
6 whole allspice berries or spicebush
  berries
4 whole green, pink or white peppercorns,
  optional

Prepare jars, bands and lids as described on page 418; if you are unfamiliar with canning procedures, also read the canning information on that page. Remove blossom ends of crabapples; leave stems if desired (but remove any leaves). Poke each crabapple on 2 sides with a fork. Set aside.

In nonreactive saucepan, combine remaining ingredients. Heat to boiling over high heat, stirring frequently. Add crabapples and heat until mixture just comes to a boil. Reduce heat so mixture continues to boil very gently, and cook for 5 minutes, stirring gently a few times. Remove from heat.

Pack crabapples hot, into hot prepared jars, distributing spices evenly between jars. Pour hot syrup mixture over apples, leaving ½ inch headspace. Seal with prepared lids and bands. Process in boiling-water bath for 15 minutes. Store sealed jars in a cool, dark location for at least 2 weeks before serving. Refrigerate after opening.

Crabapple Sorbet

About 1 quart   Preparation: Involved (requires ice-cream maker)

For a stunning presentation, place a small scoop of this lovely pink Crabapple Sorbet in a dish with a small scoop of lemon sherbet and another of vanilla ice cream; stand a shortbread finger or sugar wafer upright in the dish.

> 2 cups Simple Sugar Syrup for Sorbet   1 cup crabapple juice, well chilled
>   (page 427)

(page 427)

If using ice-cream maker that requires pre-freezing, place it in freezer as directed by manufacturer, generally 12 to 24 hours.

Stir syrup and crabapple juice together in measuring cup or bowl; chill overnight. Transfer mixture to ice-cream maker and process as directed by manufacturer. It should be thick, smooth, and creamy; in my ice-cream maker this takes 15 to 20 minutes. Scoop sorbet into freezer-safe container and store in freezer until ready to serve.

Crabapple-Ginger-Cardamom Jam

5 half-pints   Preparation: Over an hour

Sparkling, bright red and tangy, this jam is a favorite of all who try it.

> 5 half-pint canning jars, with bands and   3⅓ cups sugar
>   new lids   2 cups water
> 2 pounds crabapples   2 tablespoons freshly squeezed lemon juice
> 1 piece peeled fresh gingerroot, about   ¾ teaspoon cardamom seeds (from about
>   1 x 3 inches or slightly larger   15 cardamom pods)

Prepare jars, bands and lids as directed on page 418; if you are unfamiliar with canning procedures, also read the canning information on that page. Cut crabapples into quarters; remove and discard cores. If crabapples are ½ inch in diameter or smaller, no further preparation is necessary; if crabapples are larger, cut each quarter in half from top to bottom so you have narrower wedges. Place crabapple wedges in nonreactive heavy-bottomed pan. Grate gingerroot and add to pan along with remaining ingredients.

Heat to boiling over medium-high heat, stirring frequently. Reduce heat so mixture is bubbling at a moderate pace and cook, stirring frequently, until thickened, 45 minutes to 1 hour; a small scoop of jam should jell as described in the jelly tests on page 258. Ladle into prepared jars, leaving ½ inch headspace. Seal with prepared lids and bands. Process in boiling-water bath for 10 minutes.

Crabapple Jelly and Leather

3 half-pints jelly and 1 sheet apple leather
(from 2 pounds fruit)

Preliminary preparation: Under an hour
Final jelly preparation: Under 30 minutes
Final leather preparation: 6 to 10 hours drying time

This recipe really takes advantage of your crabapple harvest: you get beautiful rose-colored jelly and fruit leather–also known as roll-ups–from one batch of crabapples! You can use any quantity of crabapples you have on hand, but don't try to make a batch of jelly with more than 4 cups of juice at a time; if you have more juice, make more than one batch of jelly.

For the juice and pulp:

2 pounds crabapples, or any quantity you have (see notes in recipe)

5 cups water, or as needed

Cut crabapples in half and place in nonreactive pot that is deep enough to hold the crabapples with several inches above them. Add water (if using a different quantity of crabapples, add enough water to just cover the crabapples). Heat to boiling over high heat, then reduce heat somewhat and boil gently for 15 to 20 minutes; fruit should be very soft. Line a 1-quart-capacity wire-mesh strainer with 4 layers of cheesecloth, and place over a pot large enough to hold the juice. Carefully pour the crabapples and all liquid into the cheesecloth-lined strainer, and let drain for about 5 minutes (do not press down on the crabapples to extract more juice, or the jelly will be cloudy).

Make the pulp for the leather: Set the strainer over a large mixing bowl (set the pot of juice aside for now). Dump the cooked crabapple mixture into the strainer by lifting and flipping the cheesecloth so the crabapples fall into the strainer. Stir with a wooden spoon, pressing down fairly hard, until the pulp has been pressed through the strainer. Scrape the pulp from the outside of the strainer, adding it to the bowl. Discard the leftover skins, seeds and any spices you may have added. 2 pounds of crabapples will yield about 2 cups of pulp.

Finish straining the juice for the jelly: Rinse the wire-mesh strainer very well to remove all traces of pulp (or, use a 1-pint-capacity strainer instead of the larger one). Line the strainer with a paper coffee filter, and place over a clean pot or 1-quart measuring cup. Pour about a cup of juice into the coffee filter and let stand until it has dripped through. Repeat with remaining juice; you may want to use a fresh coffee filter when you've strained about half of the juice. 2 pounds of crabapples will yield about 3 cups of juice.

At this point, you may refrigerate the pulp and juice separately, or proceed immediately with the final steps.

For the jelly:

3 half-pint canning jars, with bands and new lids

The juice from the crabapples

1 teaspoon lemon juice for each cup of juice

²/₃ cup sugar for each cup of juice

Prepare jars, bands and lids as described on page 418; if you are unfamiliar with canning procedures, also read the canning information on that page. In nonreactive heavy-bottomed saucepan, combine measured juice with the amount of sugar and lemon juice indicated. Heat to boiling over high heat, stirring frequently. Boil until the juice passes the jelly test, page 258; this will take 10 to 15 minutes. Pour into prepared jars, leaving ¼ inch headspace. Seal with prepared lids and bands. Process in boiling-water bath for 10 minutes.

FRUITS & BERRIES

For the crabapple leather:

The strained pulp from the crabapples

¼ cup sugar for each cup of pulp, or to taste

Combine pulp and sugar in heavy-bottomed pot. Heat just to boiling; reduce heat and simmer for 5 about minutes, stirring frequently to prevent scorching. Remove from heat and allow to cool to warm room temperature.

To dry in food dehydrator: Please read about food dehydrators on page 420. Spray solid liner sheets with nonstick spray. Spread cooled, sweetened pulp evenly on prepared sheets to about ¼ inch thickness. Dry at 130-140°F until leathery with no sticky spots, usually 6 to 8 hours but as long as 10 hours; peel from the sheets and flip once during drying if bottom is not drying properly. Peel from liner sheets while still warm; roll up and wrap in plastic wrap.

To dry in oven: Heat oven to lowest possible setting. Line a rimmed baking sheet with plastic wrap, taping the edges of the wrap to the rims of the sheet to keep it in place. One standard-sized sheet will hold about 2 cups pulp. Spread cooled, sweetened pulp evenly over prepared sheet to about ¼ inch thickness. Place filled sheet(s) in the oven and prop the oven door open a few inches with a ball of foil. Dry until leathery with no sticky spots, usually 6 to 8 hours but as long as 10 hours, rotating the tray(s) occasionally. Roll up the leather while it is still on the plastic sheets.

Variation: Spiced Crabapple Jelly and Leather

Add 1 cinnamon stick, and 15 whole allspice berries or 20 spicebush berries, to the cut crabapples and water before boiling. Proceed as directed.

Variation: Minty Crabapple Jelly and Leather

Add 4 sprigs fresh mint (wild or domesticated) to the cut crabapples and water before boiling. Proceed as directed.

Variation: Crabapple Sauce

The crabapple pulp makes an excellent sauce. Simply sweeten to taste, and serve warm or cold.

Currants (numerous members of the *Ribes* genus)

Sweet-tart and delicious, currants can be used for wonderful desserts, and also pair well with pork and other meats in savory sauces. Some are sweet enough to eat raw with cream and sugar.

FRUITS & BERRIES

HABITAT, RANGE, SUBSPECIES
Currants found in our area include the golden currant, *Ribes aureum* or *R. odoratum* (also called buffalo currant or clove currant); the American black currant, *R. americanum*; the red or swamp currant, *R. triste*; the wax currant, *R. cereum*; the northern black currant, *R. hudsonianum*; and the European black currant, *R. nigrum*.

Currants can be found in thickets, along fencerows and sunny field edges, near stream edges, and where woods meet grassy areas. They prefer somewhat moist habitats, with rich soil. The golden currant and American black currant are found throughout our area; the red current is less common but still present in much of our area, although it is particularly scarce in Iowa and Indiana. The wax currant is a western species found in North and South Dakota. The northern black currant grows in small numbers in Minnesota, Wisconsin, Michigan and the Upper Peninsula, and Iowa. The European black currant inhabits Minnesota, Wisconsin, Illinois, Michigan and the Upper Peninsula, and Ohio.

PARTS USED
Ripe berries, cooked or uncooked

SEASONS
Early to late summer, depending on location and subspecies

Red or swamp currant

IDENTIFICATION TIPS, DANGEROUS LOOKALIKES
Currant shrubs generally are chest high or shorter, and often grow in a tangle of other plants, giving them the appearance of vines. Their characteristic scalloped leaves, rather like maple leaves, are the first clue to identification. The leaves are alternate on the stem, as are those of gooseberries (page 170), which have similarly shaped but generally larger leaves. Currant leaves generally have shallower notches between the lobes than those of gooseberries, and the lobes of most currants give a more

Currant (left) and gooseberry leaves

pointed, maple-leaf-like appearance. Mapleleaf viburnum (*Viburnum acerifolium*) and highbush cranberries (*V. trilobum*) have leaves with a similar maple-like shape (although they have fewer teeth on the edges), but the leaves grow opposite each other on the stem rather than alternately. Berries from both of these viburnums are edible.

The fruits of both currants and gooseberries grow in clusters along branches or on the ends of the branches. Currants often grow in larger clusters that hang well away from the main branch, but both species also grow in 2- or 3-fruit clusters as well. Both species have a remnant of the dried flower at the bottom that is often called a "pigtail." Gooseberries are often prickly and are difficult to detach from the stems; currants are smooth-skinned and pull away easily from the stems. All gooseberries have thorns on the branches, while currants other than the bristly currant (*R. lacustre*) are smooth-branched. The only dangerous member of the currant family is the sticky currant, *R. viscosissimum*, which is reported to cause strong digestive upsets; fortunately, this is a Western species rarely found on the edge of our range that is easily identified by the sticky substance on the leaves, twigs and fruits. Other plants that may be confused with currants have been discussed above; none have fruits that are dangerous.

HARVESTING TIPS

Look underneath the leaves to find fruits that may be hidden from above. Currants ripen over a period of weeks, and an individual plant can have both ripe and underripe berries on it. Harvest the ripe berries for pies and other dishes where the berries will be used whole; underripe berries are too sour to eat, although a few added to the pot when making juice for jelly will provide more pectin. The fruit should detach easily from its individual stem; if it doesn't, you may have a smooth-skinned gooseberry on your hands rather than a currant.

MORE ABOUT CURRANTS: Like their cousins the gooseberries, wild currants have been the target of eradication efforts because the plant is an integral part of the life cycle of white pine blister rust. A number of currant species grow wild in our region; some are native, while others are escapees from cultivation. The golden currant is often considered to be the tastiest. Golden currant—also called clove currant because of its spicy aroma—gets its name from the cheery yellow flowers it sports in spring; the fruit is red to black when ripe. American black currant also has berries that turn black when ripe, but the fruit is not as sweet. Red currants are cardinal-red to a purplish black when ripe. Other wild currants come in shades of black, purple or red; some are dry, while others are juicy but of poor flavor. The best advice is to pick a few berries from a plant you've positively identified as a currant and taste them. If they're good, harvest a reasonable amount; if not, leave them for the wildlife. Currants ripen a bit later in the season than gooseberries.

Most currants are somewhat tart when raw; some are pleasantly sweet-tart, while others are downright inedible until cooked with sugar. But like rhubarb, lemons and other tart fruit, currants have a delightful flavor when properly prepared. They make delicious jelly, pies and sauces; as a bonus for jellymakers, they are rich in natural pectin and require little or no added pectin. If you're juicing the currants, don't bother removing the flower remnant (pigtail); if you're making pie, sauce or a dish in which the currants will be used whole, pinch off the pigtail as part of the cleaning process.

Currants freeze well. Simply wash them and remove the flower remnant, then freeze in heavyweight plastic food-storage bags or tightly lidded plastic storage containers. Currants are also a good choice for dehydrating (page 421).

How to make currant juice: Place currants in small soup pot. Crush gently with potato masher to start flow of juice. Add ¼ cup water per quart of currants. Heat over medium heat until boiling gently; cook for 10 minutes without stirring. Cool somewhat and strain through cheesecloth-lined strainer; for clear jelly, don't press down or squeeze the fruit (see page 252 for more information on making fruit juices). One quart of currants yields about 2 cups of juice.

QUICK IDEAS FOR USING CURRANTS
- Some people like raw currants in a bowl topped with cream and lots of sugar.
- If you have a recipe calling for dried currants in a standard cookbook, be aware that the dried "currants" sold in supermarkets are actually a small species of grape that is unrelated to wild currants. You can dry your own currants and use them like commercial "currants" in any recipe; however, the taste will be different (probably better!).

OTHER RECIPES IN THIS BOOK FEATURING CURRANTS
- Curried Cattail Hearts (page 87)
- Wild Berry Syrup (page 111)
- Plum Chutney (page 117)
- As substitute in Gooseberry Crisp (page 173)
- Two-Layer Pie with Gooseberries or Currants (page 175)
- As substitute in Ground Cherry-Cranberry Chutney (page 185)
- Currant Jelly (pectin-added jelly, page 255; no-pectin jelly, page 257)
- Acorn and Wild Berry Porridge (page 272)
- Dried currants (chart, page 421)

Pumpkin Tart with Currant Glaze

1 pie (6 to 8 servings)   Preparation: Over an hour

Currant juice is particularly good with pumpkin pie; the tartness seems to cut through the richness of the pie filling very well. You could substitute elderberry juice, chokecherry or other wild cherry juice, or almost any other wild juice that you like for the currant juice; darker juices like these mentioned look best with the tart.

FRUITS & BERRIES

Pastry for single-crust pie
Dried beans or pie weights for pre-baking crust
1 can (15 ounces) pumpkin
8 ounces cream cheese, softened
2 large eggs
¾ cup sugar
1 teaspoon rum extract or vanilla extract, optional

1 teaspoon cinnamon
½ teaspoon ground ginger
¼ teaspoon allspice

Currant glaze:
3 cups currant juice or other dark juice
2 tablespoons cornstarch mixed with 2 tablespoons cold water

Heat oven to 375°F; position oven rack in bottom third of oven. On lightly floured surface, roll out pastry and fit into 11-inch quiche or tart pan; trim edges just slightly higher than rim of pan. Line crust with foil, pressing well into corners; fill with dried beans or pie weights. Bake for 10 minutes. Remove foil and beans carefully, then return crust to oven and bake for 5 to 10 minutes longer, until beginning to crisp and color. Remove from oven and set aside while you prepare filling.

Reduce oven temperature to 350°F. To prepare filling, combine pumpkin and cream cheese in large mixing bowl. Beat with hand mixer until smooth. Add eggs, sugar, extract, cinnamon, ginger and allspice; beat until smooth. Scrape into pre-baked crust, smoothing top. Bake at 350°F until set, 45 to 60 minutes. Remove from oven and set aside until cool.

While tart is cooling, prepare glaze. Boil currant juice until reduced to 2 cups. Stir in cornstarch mixture. Cook, stirring constantly, until thickened and bubbly. Remove from heat; set aside to cool slightly. Pour cooled mixture over tart, spreading and smoothing with back of spoon. Serve at room temperature; refrigerate leftovers.

Currant Scones

6 scones   Preparation: Under an hour

You can substitute blueberries, huckleberries or mulberries for the currants.

1¼ cups all-purpose flour, plus additional
for kneading
2 tablespoons sugar
1½ teaspoons baking powder
¼ teaspoon salt

¼ cup (half of a stick) chilled unsalted
butter, cut into ¼-inch-thick slices
¾ cup cleaned* fresh currants, or rehydrated
dried currants (about ½ cup dried)
⅓ cup plus 1 tablespoon half-and-half

Heat oven to 400°F. Spray baking sheet with nonstick spray; set aside. Sift together flour, sugar, baking powder and salt into large mixing bowl. Add cut-up butter and rub together with finger-tips until mixture resembles coarse meal with a few pea-sized chunks. Add currants and half-and-half, and mix gently with a spoon just until blended; take care not to break up the currants. Turn out dough onto floured worksurface and knead a few times. Pat into 6-inch disk. Transfer to prepared baking sheet. Use table knife to score disk into 6 wedges; the scores should go about halfway through the disk. Bake in center of oven for 20 to 25 minutes, until golden brown and cooked through. Break into 6 pieces, and serve warm or at room temperature.

Currant-Cornmeal Tea Cake

9 servings   Preparation: Over an hour

¼ cup (half of a stick) butter, softened
1 cup sugar
1 egg
½ cup milk
1 teaspoon vanilla extract
1½ cups all-purpose flour
¼ cup yellow cornmeal
2 teaspoons baking powder

½ teaspoon salt
1 cup cleaned* fresh currants, or rehydrated
dried currants (about ⅔ cup dried)

Crumble Topping:
⅓ cup sugar
⅓ cup all-purpose flour
¼ cup (half of a stick) cold butter, cut up

Heat oven to 350°F. Spray 8 x 8-inch baking dish with nonstick spray; set aside. In large mixing bowl, combine softened butter, sugar and egg; beat with electric mixer until light and fluffy. In measuring cup, combine milk and vanilla. Add to butter mixture in thin stream, beating constantly until smooth. Combine flour, cornmeal, baking powder and salt in sifter or wire-mesh strainer; sift into butter mixture. Stir with wooden spoon until dry ingredients are just moistened. Add currants; stir gently to combine. Do not overmix batter, or cake will be tough. Scrape batter into prepared dish, smoothing top. In food processor, combine topping ingredients. Pulse just until coarse and crumbly. Sprinkle over batter. Bake until golden brown and center tests done with toothpick, 45 to 50 minutes. Cool slightly before serving; best served warm.

*Flower ends removed before measuring

Elderberries, Common (Sambucus canadensis)

Flowers and berries are often used for wine; the berries also make wonderful jelly, especially when the juice is combined with other fruit juices.

HABITAT, RANGE

The common elderberry grows throughout our region in sunny spots that have rich, moist soil. Look for them along the edges of farm fields and woodlots, in ditches, along fencerows, and alongside streams and ponds.

PARTS USED

Ripe fruit, cooked (usually juiced) or dried; flowers

SEASONS

Flowers are harvested in late spring to early summer; berries are ripe and ready for harvest in late summer.

IDENTIFICATION TIPS, DANGEROUS LOOKALIKES

Elderberries grow as a shrub or short, shrubby tree; they often grow in clusters, with several leggy plants combining in one area to form a dense mat of elderberries. Leaves are toothed and pinnately compound, similar to sumac or walnuts; each com-

Ripe elderberries

pound leaf, or *blade*, has 2 to 5 pairs of opposite leaflets and a terminal leaf at the end of the blade. The blades grow opposite one another on the main branches of the plant. Flowering heads, which later give way to fruiting clusters, grow on a separate branchlet with no leaves. The main branches are grayish to light brown; the leaves and flowers occur near the top of the branches, so the base of the shrub is somewhat barren looking.

Elderberry flowers

The delightfully fragrant flowers appear in late spring or early summer, and are creamy white with 5 petals. When the flowers drop their petals a week or so later, the buds develop into hard, light green berries, which ripen in late summer to deep purplish black. Each berry has several small seeds.

Elderberry plants are very easy to spot. In the early summer bloom season, look for the distinctive flat-topped flower clusters atop the tall, leafy shrub. When the petals drop and the fruits begin to develop, you can spot elderberries from a distance because the stemlets on each flowering head are burgundy in color; the plant appears to be crowned with lacy burgundy heads.

The red elderberry (*S. racemosa*; sometimes named *S. pubens* or *S. callicarpa*) is sometimes seen in our region; the fruits are not edible. Identification is easy when the plant is fruiting, because the berries are scarlet rather than blue-black.

Poisonous water hemlock (*Cicuta maculata*) has leaves and flowers that resemble those of elderberries. Although water hemlock is generally shorter than elderberry shrubs, it may be safest to harvest elderflowers only from plants from which you have harvested elderberry fruits the previous summer; the fruits of elderberries don't resemble those of water hemlock at all, making late-summer identification easy.

Poisonous water hemlock

HARVESTING TIPS

It's easiest to snip whole clusters of ripe elderberries from the plant, then wash and clean them at home. The elderberry stemlets are bitter, and become brittle the longer the picked cluster sits, so it's best to pull the berries off the clusters the same day you harvest them.

If you want to try using elderblow (the fresh petals of the elderberry flower), remember that any flower clusters you cut from the plant won't produce berries later in the year. Unless you're making fritters from the whole cluster (see below), it's best to harvest just the petals by shaking a flowering cluster inside a collection bucket. This way, the buds will remain on the plant and will produce fruits in a month or so.

As with all wild fruits, be sure to leave some berries for the birds and other wild creatures that depend on them for fall and winter food.

SPECIAL CONSIDERATIONS

Roots, stems and leaves of elderberry plants contain compounds that can cause nausea, diarrhea and vomiting. Many people have an adverse reaction to raw elderberries, and in any case the raw fruit doesn't taste very good so it should not be eaten. Some people will also have digestive problems from eating the seeds; if you make an elderberry pie from whole berries, try just a small piece at first to be sure you won't have a problem.

MORE ABOUT ELDERBERRIES: As I write this, my fingers are still stained purple from a day of picking elderberries and wild grapes. I have come to think of late summer as the Purple Time, because it seems that so many of the wild fruits I harvest in this season have a similar deep-purple hue—blackberries, chokecherries, chokeberries, black cherries, grapes, and of course, elderberries.

Elderberry juice makes an outstanding jelly, particularly when combined with juice from another fruit such as grapes or apples. Euell Gibbons was probably the first writer to note that elderberry juice is particularly good when combined with sumac juice for jelly; see below for my method of making elderberry-sumac juice. Elderberry juice makes a wonderful syrup or an intense and beautiful sorbet; it can also be used for fruit gels and other candies.

If you have an abundance of elderberries, freeze cleaned fruit in a plastic container or freezer-weight food storage bag, then thaw and juice them when you have a bit of spare time. Elderberries are also easy to dry, and can sometimes be found in this form at winemaking supply stores. In addition to being used in winemaking, dried elderberries are used in baked goods, although if you want to try this, keep in mind that the seeds will still be in the dried fruit. To reconstitute dried elderberries, simply cover them generously with warm water and let stand until plumped up. A few reconstituted elderberries added to a batch of muffins, or to an apple pie, will make a delicious and different dessert. The soaking liquid can be added to other fruit juice for an interesting beverage.

Since pioneer times, elderflowers have been used as a tea to cure headache. Dried petals work best for this; simply steep a tablespoon or two of petals in a cup of boiling water and sweeten to taste. Fresh or dried petals are also added to baked goods, and dried petals are sold at winemaking stores to make elderblow wine, a straw-colored drink with a subtle fragrance.

I see recipes in many wild-foods cookbooks for elderflower fritters. I've never tried this; I prefer to let the flower heads develop into fruits. If you'd like to try it, simply dip a whole flowering head into thin pancake batter, and fry in hot oil; sprinkle with powdered sugar and serve hot.

How to make elderberry juice: Place measured elderberries in small soup pot. For each quart of elderberries (about 18 ounces), add 1 cup water. Heat to a gentle boil; adjust heat and boil gently for 10 minutes. Crush gently with potato masher; cook for 10 minutes longer. Cool somewhat and strain through cheesecloth-lined strainer (see page 252 for more information on making fruit juices). One quart of elderberries yields about 2 cups of juice.

For a delightful variation, make Elderberry-Sumac Juice: Place 3 cups elderberries in a small soup pot with 2 cups sumac juice (see page 250; reduced sumac juice works particularly well). Heat to a gentle boil; adjust heat and boil gently for 10 minutes. Crush gently with potato masher; cook for 10 minutes longer. Strain as directed above. This makes a wonderful jelly that is even better (I think) than plain elderberry jelly.

Note: I've heard some people say that they get a sticky, gooey greenish mess in the strainer after running a batch of cooked elderberries through, and that the saucepan they used to cook the berries was also gummed up. I've never had this experience, but since more than one person reported this phenomenon I wanted to mention it. The juice is still fine to use; one theory is that the green substance is a covering of the seeds.

QUICK IDEAS FOR USING ELDERBERRIES
- Use the whole berries to make a pie, following any recipe you've got for blueberry pie; reconstituted dried berries are particularly good for pie. As noted above, eat only a very small portion of this pie until you know you're not going to have a reaction to the seeds.
- For a refreshing drink, combine elderberry juice with some apple or grape juice, and sweeten to taste; chill before serving.
- Use elderberry juice in any recipe calling for chokecherry juice, such as the Wild Fruit Gels on page 260 or the Purple Dream Pie on page 261.
- Add 1 cup of elderberry petals to a standard recipe for pancakes or muffins; fresh petals are best for this use rather than dried. Use a bit more water in the batter than normal.

OTHER RECIPES IN THIS BOOK FEATURING ELDERBERRIES
- Elderberry Sorbet (page 110)
- Wild Berry Syrup (page 111)
- Wild Berry Gelatin (page 112)
- As substitute in Chokeberry Barbecue Sauce (page 152)
- As substitute in Pumpkin Tart with Currant Glaze (page 163)
- Wild Berry Vinegar (page 231)
- Elderberry Jelly (chart, page 255)
- Dried elderberries (page 421)

Elderblow Mead *(recipe courtesy of Joel Anderson)*

5 bottles (750 ml each)   Preparation: Involved

"Mead" refers to wine made with honey. This elderblow mead is typical of wildflower meads, with a light fragrance and straw color.

¾ pound raisins	½ ounce acid blend
1 ounce dried elderflowers	¼ ounce malic acid
1 pound sugar	¼ teaspoon tannin (1 gram)
1 pound honey	2 teaspoons yeast nutrient
½ gallon water	5-gram packet of Montrachet wine yeast

Please read General Winemaking Notes on pages 423-427 before proceeding.

Day 1: Place raisins in colander. Rinse very well with hot water, stirring raisins around so each raisin is rinsed. (This removes sulphites from the raisins.) Drain raisins and chop coarsely; place chopped raisins and elderflowers in sterilized 2-gallon crock. In stainless steel pot, combine sugar, honey and water; heat to boiling. Remove from heat and set aside until cool. Pour cooled honey mixture over elderflowers and raisins. Add acid blend, malic acid, tannin, nutrient and yeast. Cover loosely and let stand for 7 days, stirring once a day with sterilized spoon.

Day 7: Strain liquid into sterilized 1-gallon jug. Cap with airlock. Ferment for 3 to 4 weeks.

Day 35 (approximate): Rack the mead, adding spring water (blended with a little sulphite, preferably) to top as necessary. After this, rack mead as necessary. Bottle when fermentation has ceased and mead has cleared, generally 2 or 3 months.

Elderberry or Blackberry Coulis

1 cup   Preparation: Under 15 minutes

Coulis is a French term for a smooth, puréed sauce. For an elegant presentation, spoon this rich, dark sauce onto individual serving plates, then top the puddle of sauce with a poached pear or a piece of cake (cheesecake is especially nice when served this way). Or, simply pour the sauce on top of ice cream, cake, French toast, yogurt or hot cereal.

2 cups fresh elderberries or blackberries	2 teaspoons freshly squeezed lemon juice
⅔ cup apple juice	¼ to ⅓ cup sugar

In nonreactive saucepan, combine berries, apple juice and lemon juice. Heat to boiling over medium-high heat; reduce heat and simmer for 15 minutes, stirring occasionally. Strain through fine wire-mesh strainer, pressing to force the cooked berries through the mesh (leaving the seeds behind); or, use a conical strainer. Stir in sugar while purée is warm; start with the lesser amount, taste, and add additional until purée is as sweet as you like. Set aside until completely cooled; the purée will thicken as it cools. Store in tightly covered container in refrigerator for up to 2 weeks.

Gooseberries (numerous members of the *Ribes* genus)

Very common throughout our region, but often overlooked. Gooseberries are tart when raw, but make excellent desserts and sauces.

HABITAT, RANGE, SUBSPECIES

Gooseberries, in one form or another, are found throughout our region. They inhabit thickets and tangles, ravines, scrubby shelterbelts and moist woods, especially those along rivers and streams. They prefer shady spots rather than sunny areas.

The prickly gooseberry (*Ribes cynosbati*), which is also called the Eastern prickly or pasture gooseberry as well as dogberry, is probably the most common species that is found throughout our region; it grows in most states in the eastern half of the U.S. as well as the Dakotas. The smooth or hairystem gooseberry (*R. hirtellum*) inhabits the northern half of the U.S. from Montana to the East coast. The Missouri gooseberry (*R. missouriense*) has distribution similar to the smooth gooseberry, although it extends further south; it is scarce in Michigan. The Canadian or northern gooseberry (*R. oxyacanthoides*) is a more northwestern species that is found in northern states from Michigan and the Upper Peninsula all the way to the West coast; its range extends to the Arctic Circle (it is scarce to nonexistent in Iowa, Illinois and Indiana). The black or swamp gooseberry (*R. lacustre*), which is sometimes referred to as the prickly or bristly black currant, is also a northern species, appearing in our region primarily in the northern parts of Minnesota, Wisconsin, and Michigan (including the Upper Peninsula).

PARTS USED

Ripe berries, cooked (often juiced for jelly)

SEASONS

Mid- to late summer

IDENTIFICATION TIPS, DANGEROUS LOOKALIKES

Prickly gooseberries

Gooseberries grow as an arching shrub that is generally about 3 feet in height. All gooseberries have prickly stems and branches, in contrast to the related currants (page 160), which are smooth-stemmed. Both gooseberries and currants have leaves that are shaped like maple leaves; gooseberry leaves tend to be more rounded, and are often more deeply divided between the lobes than currant leaves. (See page 160 for photos of gooseberry and currant leaves.) Gooseberry flowers range from white to greenish to yellow.

The fruits have subtle stripes running from the stem to the blossom end. Prickly gooseberries produce fruits that are covered with spines; when ripe, they are pinkish to reddish brown (not all will turn reddish when ripe). Smooth, Missouri and Canadian gooseberries have smooth-skinned fruits, and range in color from deep purple (smooth) to brownish purple (Missouri) to reddish (Canadian). Black gooseberries are purplish black when ripe. Gooseberry fruits grow in small clusters, generally 2 or 3 berries.

For a discussion of lookalikes, please see the currant text on page 160.

HARVESTING TIPS

Look underneath the arching branches of the gooseberry shrub to find fruit that may be hidden from above. Gooseberries don't pull off the stemlet readily (as do currants); to harvest them, pull the fruits, with attached stemlets, away from the main stem. Since the shrubs are very prickly—and on some varieties of gooseberries, the fruit itself is prickly—you may want to wear canvas gloves when harvesting the fruit. Like currants, not all gooseberries are equal as far as eating quality; you may want to taste a few before harvesting a large amount (don't sample uncooked prickly gooseberries … ouch!).

MORE ABOUT GOOSEBERRIES: Gooseberries are a large and confusing species of the *Ribes* family, closely related to currants (page 160). In fact, one member of the clan, *R. lacustre*, is variously called bristly black currant or black gooseberry. Does it really matter if this plant is a currant or a gooseberry? To the cook, probably not, as both can be used interchangeably in recipes.

Like currants, gooseberries retain a dried remnant of the flower at the bottom of the fruit; this "pigtail" should be removed before using the fruit for pies, cobblers or jam, although it can be left in place if you're juicing the fruit for jelly, wine or syrup. I find that I can use my fingernails to pinch off the pigtail and the stem on the other end as I am washing the fruit; a small scissors or very sharp knife also works well. This is tedious work; allow plenty of time to get gooseberries ready for cooking.

Prickly gooseberries, which are covered with small spines, are rather unfriendly looking to the cook. Fortunately, the spines soften during cooking, so the fruit is fine for baked desserts, cooked jam and the like (prickly gooseberries are not eaten uncooked, due to the spines). Don't worry about getting pricked by the spines while harvesting; they look fiercer than they feel. (The spines on the stems, however, are another matter; these will prick you if you're not careful.)

With their somewhat sour flavor, gooseberries are not to everyone's liking. I find the taste of the cooked fruit similar to rhubarb, and in fact, baked gooseberry desserts even look like similarly prepared rhubarb desserts.

Gooseberries freeze well. Simply wash them and remove the stems and flower remnants, then freeze in heavyweight plastic food-storage bags or tightly lidded plastic storage containers.

How to make gooseberry juice: Place gooseberries in small soup pot (you don't need to remove the stems or flower remnants first). Crush gently with potato masher to start flow of juice. Add ½ cup water per quart of gooseberries. Heat over medium heat until boiling gently; cook for 10 minutes without stirring. Cool somewhat and strain through cheesecloth-lined strainer; for clear jelly, don't press down or squeeze the fruit (see page 252 for more information on making fruit juices). One quart of gooseberries yields about 2 cups of juice.

QUICK IDEAS FOR USING GOOSEBERRIES
- Try substituting gooseberries in any rhubarb recipe.
- Some dead-ripe gooseberries are sweet enough to eat raw, topped with sugar and cream (don't eat prickly gooseberries raw, however).

OTHER RECIPES IN THIS BOOK FEATURING GOOSEBERRIES
- Gooseberry Jelly (pectin-added jelly, page 255; no-pectin jelly, page 257)
- Dried gooseberries (page 421)

Gooseberry Crisp

6 to 8 servings Preparation: Over an hour

Currants, ground cherries, blueberries, raspberries, blackberries or pitted wild cherries can be substituted for the gooseberries in this easy recipe. This is best served warm; however, leftovers are good topped with a little milk or cream for a delicious breakfast.

<u>Filling:</u>
4 to 5 cups cleaned* fresh gooseberries or
    other fruit (see above for suggestions)
½ cup white sugar
¼ cup (packed) golden brown sugar
1 tablespoon cornstarch
2 teaspoons lemon juice, optional

<u>Topping:</u>
½ cup (1 stick) cold butter, cut into
    ½-inch pieces
⅔ cup (packed) brown sugar
½ cup all-purpose flour
¼ teaspoon salt
½ cup rolled oats

Heat oven to 400°F (375°F for glass dish). Spray 8 x 8-inch or 9 x 9-inch baking dish with nonstick spray; set aside. Combine filling ingredients in mixing bowl; stir gently to combine. Set aside while you prepare topping.

To prepare topping: In large mixing bowl, combine all topping ingredients except rolled oats. Toss together with your hands,† rubbing butter to break into smaller pieces and coat them with flour and sugar. When mixture is the size of peas, add rolled oats; mix gently. Transfer gooseberry mixture to prepared baking dish, evening top with spoon. Sprinkle topping mixture over gooseberries. Bake for 35 to 45 minutes, or until topping is golden brown and fruit is bubbling. Refrigerate any leftovers.

*Stems and flower ends removed before measuring
†If you have a food processor, combine all topping ingredients except rolled oats in work bowl. Pulse on-and-off until mixture is the size of peas. Add rolled oats; pulse a few times to mix.

Strawberry-Gooseberry Dessert Sauce

About 2 cups   Preparation: Under 15 minutes

Serve warm or cold. Use it to top pound cake, shortcake, ice cream or waffles, or stir into oatmeal for a flavor booster. You may also enjoy it served simply in a dish, perhaps with a dollop of whipped cream.

2 cups cleaned* fresh gooseberries, or
    thawed frozen
¾ cup sugar
⅓ cup orange juice or water
1 teaspoon minced fresh gingerroot, optional

A pinch of ground cloves
1 cup sliced strawberries, wild or domestic
1 tablespoon cornstarch, blended with
    2 tablespoons water

In saucepan, combine gooseberries, sugar, orange juice, gingerroot and cloves. Heat to boiling; reduce heat and simmer for 10 minutes, stirring occasionally. Add strawberries; cook for about 3 minutes longer. Stir in cornstarch slurry; increase heat to medium-high and cook, stirring constantly, until mixture boils and thickens. Cool slightly before serving or refrigerating.

*Stems and flower ends removed before measuring

Gooseberry Wine (recipe courtesy of Charlie Gutwasser)

5 bottles (750ml each)   Preparation: Involved

2½ pounds gooseberries
2 pounds sugar
1 campden tablet
½ teaspoon pectic enzyme
½ teaspoon acid blend

¼ teaspoon grape tannin
½ teaspoon yeast nutrient
Half of a 5-gram packet of white wine
    yeast
Simple Sugar Syrup (page 427) as needed

Please read General Winemaking Notes on pages 423-427 before proceeding.

Day 1: Place gooseberries in sterilized 1-gallon plastic ice-cream pail. Crush berries with your hands. Add sugar, campden tablet and pectic enzyme. Cover loosely and let stand overnight.

Day 2: Add enough warm water to fill pail. Stir in acid blend, tannin and yeast nutrient. When liquid cools to 70°F, add yeast. Stir well; cover and let stand for 4 days, stirring once a day with sterilized spoon.

Day 5: Strain liquid into sterilized gallon jug. Cap with airlock. Ferment for 3 weeks.

Day 36 (approximate): Rack the wine, adding sugar syrup to top as necessary. After this, rack wine as necessary, topping with spring water each time. Bottle when fermentation has ceased and wine has cleared (Charlie's notes for this particular batch of wine indicate that he bottled it 16 months after starting; it could have been bottled sooner, but was not harmed by the delay).

Two-Layer Pie with Gooseberries or Currants

1 pie   Preparation: Over an hour

The filling mixture in this pie separates during baking into 2 layers: a custard-like layer and a topping. It's really easy to make, though, and it looks like you worked harder than you did.

Pastry for single-crust pie
3 eggs
1 cup sugar
¼ cup (half of a stick) butter, softened
¼ cup all-purpose flour
2 tablespoons frozen orange juice
    concentrate, thawed

¼ teaspoon baking soda
¼ teaspoon salt
2 cups cleaned* fresh gooseberries
    or currants

Heat oven to 375°F position oven rack in bottom third of oven. On lightly floured worksurface, roll out pastry and fit into ungreased pie plate; trim and flute edges. Refrigerate crust while you prepare filling.

For filling, separate eggs, putting whites into large mixing bowl and yolks in another large mixing bowl. Add sugar, butter, flour, orange juice concentrate, baking soda and salt to yolks. Beat with electric mixer until light in color. Fold in gooseberries or currants with wooden spoon or rubber spatula.

Clean beaters very well and dry them, or switch to whisk. Beat egg whites until soft peaks form. Fold gently into yolk mixture. Scrape into pie crust. Bake for 15 minutes, then reduce heat to 325°F and bake for 45 minutes longer; filling will be puffy and deep golden brown. Transfer pie to rack; cool before serving. Refrigerate leftovers.

*Stems and flower ends removed before measuring

Grapes (Vitis spp.)

Easy to harvest in quantity, grapes often sprawl along fencelines in suburban areas and country lanes. Wild grapes have more flavor than domestic grapes, but are less sweet and also contain seeds.

HABITAT, RANGE
Wild grapes, in one variety or another, grow throughout our region. Most prefer moist soil and full sun. Look for them climbing trees and fences along rivers and streams, at the edges of woodlands and thickets, and in abandoned fields and forest clearings.

PARTS USED
Ripe fruit, generally juiced but also raw; leaves, cooked

SEASONS
Fruit, late summer through early fall; leaves are best in spring

IDENTIFICATION TIPS, DANGEROUS LOOKALIKES

Tendrils on wild grape plant

According to the USDA Plants Database, over 50 varieties of wild native grapes are found in various parts of the country; however, only 7 species inhabit our area. It can be hard to know exactly which grape you have in hand. All wild grapes are edible, so once you've properly identified the fruit as a grape, it doesn't matter that much which grape you have—as long as it is sweet, juicy and tasty. Some wild grapes are too sour to be of much interest, and I think this has as much to do with habitat and weather as with the specific variety. My advice is to sample a few grapes from the plants you've found, and determine if they meet your standards before harvesting.

All grapes grow in clusters from a trailing, winding vine that has large, sharply lobed, alternate leaves with an overall heart shape. The vines have tendrils that wrap themselves around whatever they're climbing on, and the plants often completely cover a fence or shrub. The fruits are hard and green at first, ripening to some shade of purple, usually with a noticeable bloom. Each fruit contains several rounded seeds in the pulpy interior; this is an important point, as it helps distinguish the grape from the poisonous moonseed (*Menispermum canadense*). There are several distinct characteristics that separate the moonseed from a grape. First, the moonseed contains just a single seed that is shaped like a flat crescent. Second, the stem of the moonseed leaf is attached to the lower part of the leaf, slightly away from the base of the leaf (so the base of the leaf flares away from the stem slightly); by contrast, a grape leaf grows directly on the stem's axis. Third, moonseed vines don't have tendrils; the vine itself wraps around the supporting plant, while grapes have tendrils that wrap around the support (see photo on facing page). Leaf tips are also slightly more rounded on moonseeds than on grapes, but the other characteristics are more definite and easy to confirm. Whenever you find a new patch of plants you believe to be grape vines, always split a fruit open and check to be sure there are numerous seeds in each fruit; this is the quickest test.

The Virginia creeper or 5-leaved ivy (*Parthenocissus quinquefolia*) is a plant that I encounter on a regular basis, and the fruits look a lot like grapes; each fruit from the Virginia creeper has multiple seeds, just like a grape. Most references report that the fruits of Virginia creeper are toxic (*Poisonous Plants of North Carolina* says it is "highly toxic; may be fatal if eaten"). If you see Virginia creeper growing by itself, it's easy to distinguish from grapes, because each leaf consists of 5 leaflets that are roughly oval and toothed. These 5-part leaves look entirely unlike grape leaves, so are easy to tell apart from that standpoint. I've also noticed that the leaves of Virginia creeper tend to turn reddish in late summer, which helps distinguish them from the still-green grape leaves. Frequently the stems of Virginia creeper are a bright pink color, a phenomenon I've never seen on grapes.

Unfortunately for the unwary forager, Virginia creeper often grows right among the grapes, twining itself around the grape vines (see photo at right). When you begin working a patch of grapes, examine it first to determine if any Virginia creeper is also growing there. If it is, take the time to follow the stem down from each cluster of grapes you plan to pick, to ensure that it is growing from the grape vine rather than from the Virginia creeper vine.

Virginia creeper growing among grapes

Finally, porcelainberry (*Ampelopsis brevipedunculata*) is another grape lookalike that you should watch out for. The fruits are smaller than grapes, about ¼ inch across. Fruits are in a variety of colors, including white, yellow, lavender, turquoise, brilliant blue, red or light purple—all on the same plant, at the same time. Leaves may be very deeply lobed, almost like a rounded, deeply lobed maple leaf; however, in many cases the leaves of porcelainberry look quite like grape leaves. The stems and trunk of the vine are much smoother than those of grapes, which have long, stringy or "shreddy" bark on the trunk; the pith in the stems of porcelainberries is white, while that of grape vines is brown. Grapes are larger and stouter overall, while porcelainberries are more delicate. Porcelainberries aren't as common in our area as grapes, and grow in Wisconsin, Illinois, Michigan and Ohio; they are considered an invasive nuisance plant, as they are quite aggressive in their growth habits where they do appear. Fruits are inedible and may be toxic, according to Steve Brill in *Identifying and Harvesting Edible and Medicinal Plants in Wild (and Not So Wild) Places.*

HARVESTING TIPS

Snip off whole clusters of grapes and add them to your collection bucket, then pull off the individual grapes at home after washing. This is much more efficient than trying to pull off individual grapes in the field, and the clusters are easier to wash when they're whole; you'll lose too much juice if you try to pick individual grapes in the field because much of it will be squeezed out or washed off. Grape juice is very potent in color, and stains fingers even more than elderberries.

MORE ABOUT GRAPES: When I was a kid, I remember that almost all the grapes we bought in the store had seeds; the fine art of seed-spitting was one of the things we enjoyed in the back yard during the summer as we slowly savored each grape. These days, most commercial grape varieties have been tinkered with to produce seedless grapes, so we have forgotten what to do with grapes that still have seeds. Wild grapes will help you remember!

Many wild grapes are too tart to eat raw, although if you get a handful of sweet wild grapes, there are few things better on a hot summer day than sitting in the shade and enjoying this most excellent wild fruit. Most wild grapes are destined to be turned into juice, however; the juice can be sweetened and used as a beverage on its own or blended with other fruit juices, and of course, it makes excellent jelly and desserts.

Stuffed grape leaves are a traditional dish in Greece; variations are made in Lebanese and Persian cooking as well. Harvest fully developed leaves in the spring or very early summer, choosing the largest leaves you can find. Par-boil them in heavily salted water. Drain and rinse with very cold water to set the color, and proceed with any recipe calling for commercially prepared grape leaves. If you would like to preserve some grape leaves for use later in the season, par-boil and drain as described above; blot dry, roll into a tight bundle, pack in freezer-weight plastic bags and freeze until you are ready to use them.

How to make grape juice: Place washed grapes (stems removed) in nonreactive saucepan. Add ½ cup of water per pound of grapes (1 pound is about 3 cups). Crush grapes with potato masher. Heat for 5 minutes at medium heat (do not boil). Crush again, and cook for 5 to 10 minutes longer, or until skins lose much of their color. Strain through several layers of dampened cheesecloth. You should get about 1½ cups of juice from each pound of grapes.

Grape juice often contains tartaric acid, which causes crystallization in jelly. To remove the tartrate crystals, let the juice stand in the refrigerator overnight, then pour the juice through a paper coffee filter or 3 layers of dampened cheesecloth, leaving any sediment behind.

OTHER RECIPES IN THIS BOOK FEATURING GRAPES
- Chokecherry-Wild Grape Wine (page 113)
- Grape Jelly (no-pectin jelly, page 257)

Stuffed Grape Leaves

4 to 6 servings (appetizer or light meal)   Preparation: Over an hour

25 to 30 grape leaves, as large as possible	**A good pinch of allspice**
½ cup uncooked long-grain rice	**½ pound ground lamb**
½ teaspoon salt	**1 tablespoon butter, melted**
¼ teaspoon pepper	**1 lemon, thinly sliced**
¼ teaspoon cinnamon	

Heat a large pot of salted water to boiling over high heat. Add grape leaves; return to boiling and cook until leaves are limp, about 3 minutes. Drain and rinse with plenty of cold water, then let drain thoroughly. (If you're working with grape leaves that you've previously blanched and frozen, simply thaw and they're ready to go.)

Place rice in colander and rinse under cold running water for a minute or so, stirring the rice with your fingertips. Let drain thoroughly, then transfer to mixing bowl. Sprinkle rice with salt, pepper, cinnamon and allspice; stir to mix well. Add lamb and butter; mix well with your hands. Cover bottom of a nonreactive Dutch oven or small soup put with a layer of lemon slices.

To stuff leaves, place a drained leaf on worksurface. Pinch off a generous teaspoon of the rice mixture and form into a small log. Place at the base (stem end) of the leaf. Roll leaf over filling once, then fold sides over filling and continue rolling until you have a nice, compact bundle. Arrange rolls on lemon slices in pot as you go, packing together neatly. When all rolls have been made, place a heavy, heat-proof plate on top of the rolls. Add water to cover the plate by an inch. Heat to boiling over high heat, then reduce heat so mixture simmers gently. Cook for 40 minutes, or until rice is tender. Drain and serve hot, warm or cold.

No-Cook Grape Jelly

3 half-pints   Preparation: Under 30 minutes, plus overnight setting time

This uncooked jelly has a wonderful grape flavor, and comes out sparkling clear. Jelly making doesn't get much easier than this.

3 half-pint canning jars, with bands and clean lids; or plastic freezer containers
1½ cups grape juice from wild grapes*
2½ cups sugar

Half of a 1.75-ounce box powdered pectin†
⅓ cup plus 1 tablespoon water

Sterilize jars and lids as directed on page 418. Combine juice and sugar in glass or Pyrex mixing bowl, stirring to dissolve sugar. Let stand for 10 minutes, stirring occasionally.

In small saucepan, combine pectin and water; stir well (mixture may be lumpy). Heat to a full, rolling boil over high heat, stirring constantly. Cook at a rolling boil for 1 minute, stirring constantly. Pour pectin mixture into juice in bowl. Stir constantly with wooden spoon until sugar is completely dissolved and no longer grainy, about 3 minutes; a few grains may remain, but the mixture should no longer look cloudy (or the jelly will be cloudy).

Pour mixture into prepared jars or containers, leaving ½ inch headspace; cover with clean lids. Let stand at room temperature for 24 hours; the jelly should be set. If it is not set, refrigerate for several days until set before using or freezing; grape jelly may take as long as a week to set. The jelly will keep for 3 weeks in the refrigerator, or it may be frozen for up to a year.

*Let juice stand overnight in refrigerator and strain before using; see page 179.
†See 254 for information on dividing powdered pectin.

Ground Cherries *(Physalis* spp.)

Here's a fruit that old-time country grandmothers knew and loved, yet is largely unknown by younger folks today. It's related to the trendy tomatillo, but is sweet and sunny yellow-orange in color.

HABITAT, RANGE

Ground cherries, in one form or another, grow throughout the United States; they are fairly common in our region. Look for ground cherries in abandoned fields and along field margins, in clearings or open woods, or sprawling on fences in the countryside; they also favor burned areas, so often grow at the crowns of ditches that have been burned. Many farmers consider the ground cherry a pest in their cultivated fields, and would be glad to let you pick your fill.

PARTS USED

Ripe fruit, raw or cooked

SEASONS

Late summer to early fall, before frost

IDENTIFICATION TIPS, DANGEROUS LOOKALIKES

Ripe ground cherries

Unripe ground cherries in husks

Here's another plant that has a big family, with lots of relatives. Ground cherries grow in a variety of forms—some are perennial, but most that grow in our region are annual. Some tumble across the ground, while others grow as a climbing vine and still others take the form of an erect shrub up to 3 feet tall. On some varieties, the leaves are fuzzy, while on others they are smooth; sizes range from ½ inch to 3½ inches long. Leaves are alternate and generally toothed, but some species have leaves with smooth edges. Colors of the ripe fruit vary as well; the only wild ground cherries I've seen are golden yellow when ripe, but they can also be red, orange or even purple. Fruits are round and generally about ½ inch across, but can be as large as an inch.

The one thing that all ground cherries have in common is that the fruit grows inside a loose, ribbed, papery husk that looks like a tiny Chinese lantern; the husk becomes dry and turns tan or straw-colored as the fruit ripens. If you know what a tomatillo looks like in the husk, you know what to look for when looking for ground cherries.

Ground cherries tinged with green should not be eaten. Although it is possible to encounter an escaped tomatillo in the wilds, odds are better that any green ground cherry you have found is underripe or inedible. If you've found some ground cherries that are tinged with green, let them ripen until they are soft and the fruit has turned yellow, orange or brownish; if it remains green, it should not be eaten.

Naturalist Steve Brill, in his book *Identifying and Harvesting Edible and Medicinal Plants in Wild (and Not So Wild) Places,* discusses several dangerous lookalikes. If you find a fruit that resembles a ground cherry but the papery husk is tight to the fruit, or if the husk is unribbed, don't pick these; they are not edible, according to Brill. Also, if you find fruits that have husks smaller than ½ inch, do not pick these either; they are nightshades (which are related to ground cherries), and should not be eaten.

HARVESTING TIPS

Ground cherries often sprawl along the ground in grassy areas, and so may be hard to see; even when the plant is growing as a vine or upright, the fruit falls to the ground when it is ripe. Look for the leaves and vines, then dig into the grass to look for the fallen fruits. The plants are generally prolific, so it is easy to gather a good amount; as a bonus, you generally don't have to worry about overharvesting ground cherries.

SPECIAL CONSIDERATIONS

The only part of the ground cherry that can be eaten is the ripe fruit. Stems, leaves and husks should be considered toxic. Eating too many ground cherries may cause diarrhea, so eat them in moderation. Finally, although it is rare, there are people who are allergic to members of the nightshade family such as tomatoes; such persons should not eat ground cherries.

MORE ABOUT GROUND CHERRIES: Mention ground cherries to someone who grew up in a small town or rural area, and you will probably trigger nostalgic memories of the treats that Mom or Grandma used to make from the fruits. Like the pioneer women before them, these countrywomen knew the value of this delightful fruit, which grew in abundance and provided an excellent source of jams, jellies, pies and other desserts. Today, the ground cherry is little known except to foragers and a few country folk who still remember it.

Ground cherries really are delightful fruits. They resemble tiny tomatoes, complete with tiny seed-filled compartments; however, the seeds are so soft that they do not need to be strained or removed. The fruit has a sweet taste that reminds me of strawberries, with overtones of something green (honeydew, perhaps); they are quite unlike anything else I've eaten. I enjoy using them raw in mixed fruit salads, as well as the cooked uses noted above.

Ground cherries that are slightly underripe can be stored at room temperature, where they will ripen in a week or two; the husks will dry out and become papery, and the fruit will turn golden (or whatever color the particular species should be; all I've ever seen is the golden variety). Like their relatives the tomatillos, ground cherries need to be husked before using. Simply pull off the papery husk and wash the fruit, which tends to be a bit sticky. Husked ripe fruits can be stored in the refrigerator, where they will keep for several weeks. If you have an overabundance of ground cherries, simply pop the husked fruits in a freezer container or heavyweight plastic bag and freeze them, whole; no other preparation is necessary. The frozen fruits will be soft when thawed, but they are fine for cooked desserts or jam.

QUICK IDEAS FOR USING GROUND CHERRIES

- Cut ground cherries in half and add to fruit salads. They're also good in mixed green salads, especially if you're using a slightly sweet dressing such as honey-mustard or poppyseed.
- Use ground cherries in uncooked mixed-fruit tarts. These sorts of tarts are often called composed or arranged tarts, and consist of a crust filled with custard that is topped with raw fruit; the fruit is usually glazed with a jelly mixture.
- Try ground cherries in recipes that call for tomatillos.
- Cook ground cherries, alone or in combination with apples, as you would when making applesauce.
- Use dried ground cherries like raisins; they're great in trail mixes, adding a unique flavor with strawberry overtones.

OTHER RECIPES IN THIS BOOK FEATURING GROUND CHERRIES

- As substitute in Gooseberry Crisp (page 173)
- Autumn Sunshine Jam (page 243)
- Dried ground cherries (page 421)

Dutch Crumble Ground Cherry Pie

1 pie

Pastry for single-crust pie
½ cup sugar
¼ cup quick-cooking tapioca
½ teaspoon vanilla extract
3 cups husked, washed ripe ground cherries

Crumb topping:
¼ cup all-purpose flour
2 tablespoons (packed) brown sugar
2 tablespoons quick-cooking oatmeal
  (not instant)
2 tablespoons room-temperature butter,*
  cut into smaller chunks

Heat oven to 425°F; position oven rack in bottom third of oven. Roll out pastry and fit into ungreased pie plate; trim and flute edges. In mixing bowl, stir together sugar, tapioca and vanilla; mix well. Add ground cherries, stirring to combine. Crush a few of the ground cherries with the spoon to start the juices flowing. Let mixture stand for 15 minutes, stirring occasionally. Pour into prepared pie pan. Place pie pan on a baking sheet, and bake for 15 minutes.

Meanwhile, make crumb topping: In small bowl, combine flour, brown sugar and oatmeal. Stir to mix well, then add butter. Rub butter into the dry ingredients with your fingers until mixture is evenly crumbly.

When pie has baked for 15 minutes, remove from oven by lifting out baking sheet. Sprinkle oatmeal mixture evenly over top of pie. Return pie, still on baking sheet, to the oven and reduce temperature to 350°F. Bake for 30 minutes longer; filling should be bubbly, and crust edges and crumb topping should be golden. Remove from oven and let stand until pie is just slightly warm before cutting, or cool completely and serve at room temperature.

*If using unsalted butter, also add a pinch of salt to the crumb topping.

Ground Cherry-Cranberry Chutney

3 half-pints   Preparation: About an hour

This sweet and tangy condiment is excellent served with roast or grilled meat, and pairs naturally with Indian food. I also love it alongside red beans and rice … non-traditional, but very good.

3 half-pint canning jars, with bands and
  new lids

3 cloves garlic, peeled

1 piece peeled fresh gingerroot, about
  1 inch square

Strip of lemon zest (yellow part only),
  about ½ inch wide and 1 inch long

⅔ cup (packed) brown sugar

3½ cups husked, washed ripe ground
  cherries

2 fresh hot red peppers, thinly sliced

1¼ cups diced red onion

½ cup dried cranberries, currants or raisins

¼ cup balsamic vinegar or red wine vinegar

¼ cup sherry vinegar

1 tablespoon mustard seed

½ teaspoon whole allspice berries or
  spicebush berries

½ teaspoon salt

Prepare jars, bands and lids as directed on page 418; if you are unfamiliar with canning procedures, also read the canning information on that page. In food processor fitted with metal blade, combine garlic, gingerroot and lemon zest. Pulse on-and-off until chopped to medium consistency. Add brown sugar and process until mixture is the consistency of coarse sand. Combine with remaining ingredients in nonreactive heavy-bottomed pot.

Heat to boiling over medium heat, stirring occasionally. Reduce heat to medium-low and simmer, stirring occasionally, until most of the liquid has evaporated and the mixture is thick, about 45 minutes. Spoon into prepared jars, leaving ½ inch headspace. Seal with prepared lids and bands. Process in boiling-water bath for 10 minutes.

Ground Cherry Jam

FRUITS & BERRIES

5 pint-sized canning jars, with bands and
new lids

1¼ pounds husked, washed ripe ground
cherries (about 3 pints before husking)

1 unblemished medium-sized lemon,
well washed

⅛ teaspoon nutmeg

Half of a 1.75-ounce box powdered pectin*

3½ cups sugar

Prepare jars, bands and lids as directed on page 418; if you are unfamiliar with canning procedures, also read the canning information on that page. Chop ground cherries to medium consistency with food processor or by hand; you should have 3 cups. Place in heavy-bottomed nonreactive pot. Holding fine grater over pot, grate all the yellow zest from lemon into pot (do not grate white part, just yellow surface). Squeeze lemon juice into measuring cup, and add ¼ cup juice to the pot (reserve any remaining juice for another use; if you have less than ¼ cup juice, add additional juice from another lemon, or a bit of cold water, to make up the difference). Add nutmeg to pot. Heat to boiling over medium-high and cook for about 10 minutes, stirring frequently.

Add pectin to pot. Heat to a full rolling boil, stirring constantly. Immediately add sugar, stirring constantly. When boil can't be stirred down, begin timing; cook for 1 minute, stirring constantly. Remove from heat, then stir for about a minute to settle the foam. Ladle into prepared jars, leaving ½ inch headspace. Seal with prepared lids and bands. Process in boiling-water bath for 10 minutes.

Note: I find that the seeds float in this jam. To make a more attractive and consistent-looking product, you can wait until the canned jars have cooled for an hour or so (they should be warm room temperature, not hot), then turn the jars over several times to re-distribute the seeds. Or, wait until you open the jar of jam to use it, and stir well.

*See page 254 for information on dividing powdered pectin.

Sweet and Snappy Ground Cherry Salsa

About 1 cup

Ground cherries are not something you might expect in a salsa, but the fruity, sweet taste makes a wonderful foil to the bite of hot peppers and the tang of fresh cilantro. Enjoy this salsa with chicken fajitas, bean burritos or tostadas, or warm tortilla chips. It is a very juicy salsa, so you may want to place a fork rather than a spoon into the serving dish. Use any leftover liquid to add spice to a pot of beans or a stir-fry.

1 clove garlic	1 cup husked, washed ripe ground cherries
1 or 2 fresh jalapeño peppers, depending on heat level desired	One-quarter of a medium red onion
	1 tablespoon seasoned rice vinegar*
About ¼ cup fresh cilantro leaves	¼ teaspoon salt, or to taste

To prepare in food processor: Chop garlic finely with metal blade. Add pepper(s) and pulse on and off a few times. Add cilantro and process until everything is finely chopped. Transfer mixture to small mixing bowl. Add ground cherries to food processor and chop to medium consistency; the texture doesn't have to be completely even so don't worry if there are a few larger chunks of fruit in the mix. Transfer ground cherries to mixing bowl. Cut onion into ¼-inch dice; add to mixing bowl. Add vinegar and salt. Stir well to mix. Let stand for 15 minutes, then taste for seasoning and adjust salt if necessary. Serve at room temperature; refrigerate leftovers.

To prepare without food processor: Chop garlic, peppers and cilantro together with chef's knife until fine. Transfer mixture to small mixing bowl. Cut ground cherries into eighths and add to mixing bowl. Cut onions into ¼-inch dice; add to mixing bowl. Add vinegar and salt. Stir well to mix. Let stand for 15 minutes, then taste for seasoning and adjust salt if necessary. Serve at room temperature; refrigerate leftovers.

*If you prefer, substitute white wine vinegar and a pinch of sugar for the seasoned rice vinegar.

FRUITS & BERRIES

Maypops (Passiflora incarnata)

Found in the southern part of our range, this fruit of the wild passionflower has a surprising tropical-punch taste. It's great eaten out of hand, and adds its unique taste to jam, curd and numerous desserts.

HABITAT, RANGE

Maypops are the fruit of the purple passionflower, which thrives in southeastern states as a roadside "weed". It is found in the southern part of our range, primarily in southern Illinois, Indiana and Ohio. It thrives in sunny locations such as field edges, fencerows, railroad embankments and ditches; it prefers sandy soil.

PARTS USED

Ripe fruit, raw or cooked (frequently juiced)

SEASONS

Late summer to early fall

IDENTIFICATION TIPS, DANGEROUS LOOKALIKES

Maypop fruits and vine

The purple passionflower is hard to miss, and its fruits—called maypops—are equally distinctive. This fast-growing vine uses its tendrils to twine itself around other plants, fences and even buildings to reach heights of 8 to 12 feet; it also crawls along the ground. The large leaves—often hand-sized—grow alternately on the vine, and generally have 3 rounded lobes (sometimes 5); the edges are finely toothed. The 2- to 3-inch-wide flowers, which grow from the leaf axil, have purple petals with a wild-looking fringe of purple "threads" that almost look like the end of a frayed rope; the center of the flower is creamy white with purple accents, and has an odd arrangement of criss-crossing sepals and stamen in the center of the flower.

The fruit of the passionflower looks like a small, green hen's egg hanging from the vine. The outer shell is a spongy material, almost like a soft styrofoam. When the fruit is under-ripe, the shell is medium-dark green and smooth. As the fruit ripens, the shell becomes lighter in color, eventually turning yellow-green or even yellow. It also becomes wrinkled and looks partially caved in, and this is the best indicator of ripeness as it is less subjective than color. Many people prefer to wait until the vines start to wilt and the fruits turn wrinkled and yellow before harvesting.

The flowers and fruit are so distinctive that it would be difficult to confuse them with anything else. The yellow passionflower, *P. lutea,* grows in the same areas as the purple passionflower, but the flowers are yellow rather than purple so are easy to distinguish. No other passionflowers grow in our region.

HARVESTING TIPS

Underripe maypops can be left at cool room temperature and most will ripen in a week or so, but for best flavor, let the fruit ripen on the vine.

SPECIAL CONSIDERATIONS

Passionflower vines and leaves are widely used in herbal medicine as a sedative; even the jam seems to have a mild sedative effect, and a spoonful may help ease muscular aches and aid in sleep. If you are sensitive to sedatives, be aware of the possible effects of maypop products. (Note that passionflower is on the USDA's "GRAS—Generally Regarded as Safe" list.)

MORE ABOUT MAYPOPS: The wild passionflower is the official state wildflower of Tennessee. Wild maypops are related to commercially raised passion fruit, which sell at high-end supermarkets for as much as $2 each. Commercially raised passion fruit is maroon in color, while the fruit of wild passionflowers is yellowish green; the pulp of the commercial variety is also darker and more intensely flavored than the wild kind. Maypops have a sweet-tart flavor, which is somewhat reminiscent of kiwifruit but with a more "tropical" taste. The smell of the ripe fruit is very similar to pawpaws (page 212); both have a tropical, almost banana-like scent. Maypops are rich in potassium, iron and vitamins A and C.

Inside the shell is a mass of seeds surrounded with pulp, rather like oversized pomegranate seeds. Underripe maypops are quite tart, and the pulpy seeds are reluctant to release from the inner shell. The pulp of ripe maypops scrapes cleanly out of the shell, and is quite sweet. Ripe maypops can be eaten raw, straight out of the shells; the fruit is good served with a little sweetened cream (whipped or not, as you prefer). The seeds are edible but crunchy in a brittle sort of way, and take a bit of getting used to. The seeds are a bit difficult to remove, as there isn't much pulp in proportion to the seeds.

To prepare maypops, cut the fruit in half. Use a spoon to scoop out the pulpy seed mass, discarding the shell. There are three spongy ribs that the seeds are attached to. If you're using the pulp with the seeds intact (as in the Rice Pudding with Maypops, page 192, or the Pavlova, page 193), remove these ribs; if you'll be cooking the pulp and discarding the seeds as in the nectar instructions below, you can leave the ribs in with the pulp. A pound of may-pops (15 to 20 average maypops) will produce just under 2 cups of pulpy seeds.

How to make maypop nectar: Cooking the pulp briefly with a bit of water is the best way to remove the seeds. The resulting juice is somewhat thickened and milky; I refer to it as maypop nectar. To prepare maypop nectar, measure the pulp and transfer it to a saucepan; add 1 cup of water for each 2 cups of pulp. Heat to boiling over medium-high heat, then cover, reduce heat and simmer for about 15 minutes, stirring occasionally. Pour the mixture into a wire-mesh strainer that has been set over a bowl. Stir with a wooden spoon until most of the pulp has passed through the strainer. (If you have a cone-shaped colander as discussed on page 253, it would work very well for this job.) Two cups of pulp, prepared in this way, will yield about 1½ cups of milky nectar.

QUICK IDEAS FOR USING MAYPOPS
- Combine maypop nectar with sugar and lemon juice to taste; chill and serve as a delightfully different beverage.
- Eat out-of-hand in the field as a refreshing snack.
- Leaves and flowers are used by herbal medicinalists to make a tea with lightly sedative properties.

OTHER RECIPES IN THIS BOOK FEATURING MAYPOPS
- Maypop Jelly (chart, page 255)
- Wild Berry Parfait with Maypop Mousse (page 262)

Maypop Scones

12 scones   Preparation: Under 30 minutes

Fluffy and light, with a subtle maypop flavor, these scones are great for breakfast or snacking. For a really delicious maypop treat, serve these with Maypop Curd, page 193.

1 egg
½ cup maypop nectar (page 190), plus a little additional if needed
2 cups all-purpose flour, plus additional for rolling out dough
3 tablespoons sugar

2 tablespoons nonfat dry milk powder
½ teaspoon baking powder
½ teaspoon baking soda
¼ teaspoon salt
5 tablespoons cold butter, cut into 6 or 7 pieces

Heat oven to 425°F. Lightly grease baking sheet; set aside. Break egg into measuring cup with maypop nectar, and beat with fork; set aside.

Combine flour, sugar, dry milk powder, baking powder, baking soda and salt in workbowl of food processor fitted with metal blade. Pulse on-and-off a few times to mix well. Add butter to workbowl. Pulse on-and-off until butter has been cut in and mixture is crumbly.

With processor running, pour egg mixture through feed tube into workbowl in steady stream, and process just until mixed; don't over-process or scones will be tough. If the mixture is too crumbly to hold its shape when pressed together, add up to 1 tablespoon additional maypop nectar, processing very briefly.

Turn mixture out onto lightly floured board and knead about a dozen times. Divide dough into 2 even pieces, shaping each into a smooth ball. Roll each into a circle that is about ½ inch thick and 6 inches across. Cut each circle into 6 wedges, as though cutting a pie. Transfer wedges to prepared baking sheet. Bake until puffed and golden, 12 to 15 minutes. Transfer to wire rack to cool. These are best served warm, but can also be eaten at room temperature.

Rice Pudding with Maypops

6 servings Preparation: Over an hour

In this interesting dessert, creamy rice pudding gets an unexpected twist with the addition of maypops —including the seeds. The subtle tropical tang of the maypops comes through nicely, and the crispy maypop seeds add an interesting texture to the pudding. For a more traditional version without the seeds, see the variation below.

5 maypops
1½ cups cooked, cooled rice (leftover refrigerated rice works fine)
1 cup heavy cream or half-and-half
½ cup milk

¼ cup sugar
2 eggs
1 teaspoon vanilla extract
A pinch of salt

Heat oven to 350°F. Lightly grease 1½-quart casserole; set aside. Scoop pulpy seed mass from maypops into mixing bowl. Add rice, breaking up any clumps with your hands if it has been refrigerated. Stir maypops and rice to combine them well and break up seed clusters. In 2-cup measure or a separate mixing bowl, combine remaining ingredients, beating lightly with fork to mix. Add cream mixture to rice and stir well. Transfer to prepared casserole. Bake until center is just set, about 1¼ hours; a knife inserted into the center should come out clean (no liquid on the knife blade, just softly set custard). Cool slightly or completely before serving; serve warm or chilled.

Variation: Rice Pudding with Maypops, seeds removed

Scoop maypop seed mass into a small saucepan. Increase milk to ⅔ cup, and add milk to saucepan. Heat over medium heat to simmering, and cook at a gentle simmer, without boiling, for 15 minutes, stirring occasionally. Pour mixture into wire-mesh strainer set over a bowl, and stir with a wooden spoon to separate the pulp from the seeds. Discard the seeds. Add pulp mixture to rice and proceed as directed.

Maypop Sangria

About 2 quarts Preparation: 5 minutes

Maypop juice has a delightful tropical taste that makes a refreshingly different sort of sangria.

1 bottle (750ml) berry-flavored white wine
2 cups maypop nectar (page 190)
1 cup pineapple juice

1 cup white grape juice
¼ cup freshly squeezed lime juice
1 can (12 ounces) lemon-lime soda

Combine all ingredients in pitcher or punch bowl. Serve over ice; garnish individual glasses with fresh fruit or orange slices.

Maypop Pavlova

6 servings   Preparation: Over an hour

Pavlova is a classic Australian dessert that is often prepared with passionfruit, the domesticated version of maypops.

Meringue:
4 egg whites
1¼ cups sugar
1 teaspoon white vinegar
1 teaspoon vanilla extract
1 tablespoon cornstarch

2 cups heavy cream
⅓ cup sugar
¼ teaspoon orange or vanilla extract
Pulpy seeds from 4 or 5 maypops, broken
    into small clusters
1 cup sliced fresh strawberries

Heat oven to 350°F. Draw 9-inch circle on a sheet of baking parchment; place on baking sheet. In mixing bowl, beat egg whites until soft peaks form. Add sugar gradually, beating constantly; beat until thick and glossy. In small bowl, stir together vinegar, vanilla and cornstarch. Add to egg white mixture; beat for about 2 minutes. Spread mixture on parchment, spooning to edge of circle. Smooth top, making shallow depression in center; edges should be slightly thicker. Place in oven; immediately reduce temperature to 225°F. Bake for 1 hour. Turn oven off and prop oven door open an inch or two (a ball of foil works well for this); leave meringue in oven until cold. Transfer cooled meringue to serving plate. In cold mixing bowl, combine cream, sugar and extract; beat until soft peaks form. Spoon or pipe whipped cream over meringue shell. Scatter maypop seeds over whipped cream; arrange strawberries decoratively. Serve immediately.

Maypop Curd

1½ cups   Preparation: 15 minutes

Lemon curd is a British dessert sauce; maypop nectar makes a delightful variation. Use as filling between cake layers; top with fresh berries for a simple dessert; dollop onto biscuits or scones (try it with the Maypop Scones, page 191). For a quick frosting, mix chilled Maypop Curd with stiffly whipped cream.

½ cup maypop nectar (page 190)
3 eggs
½ cup sugar

1 unblemished lemon, well washed
5 tablespoons unsalted butter, cut into 7 or
    8 chunks

Combine maypop nectar, eggs and sugar in a heavy-bottomed nonreactive medium saucepan. Holding a fine grater over the pot, grate about a third of the yellow zest from the lemon into the saucepan (do not grate the white part, just the yellow surface). Whisk ingredients well. Place over medium-low heat and add the butter. Cook, whisking frequently, until the mixture develops body and a few bubbles begin to pop on the surface of the curd in the center of the pan, 10 to 12 minutes; don't overcook or the sauce will curdle. Transfer curd to a bowl and let cool slightly. Cover with plastic wrap, pressing wrap directly onto the surface of the curd. Chill for at least 1 hour before serving; the flavor seems to mellow and improve after a day in the refrigerator. The curd will keep for 2 weeks in the refrigerator.

Mountain Ash (American mountain ash, *Sorbus americana*, and others)

The bright orange-red berries cheer the autumn and winter landscape in the northern part of our range. Juice from the fruit makes interesting jelly or savory sauces. Easy to harvest.

HABITAT, RANGE
American mountain ash (*Sorbus americana,* also listed as *Pyrus americana*) is a native tree that grows in the colder areas of our region, chiefly the northern parts of Minnesota, Wisconsin and Michigan's Upper Peninsula. The showy mountain ash (*S. decora*) is another native that has an even smaller range, mostly confined to northern Minnesota and scattered spots in Wisconsin. European mountain ash (*S. aucuparia*) is an introduced tree that can tolerate a broader range of conditions; it grows as an escaped or introduced plant in all states of our region except South Dakota.

The trees are a common sight on rocky shorelines of the Great Lakes, and also grow in cool, moist, sun-dappled woods. They prefer higher elevations, and can be found along ridges and at the edges of forested patches in the hills.

PARTS USED
Ripe berries, generally cooked or juiced for jelly

SEASONS
Fall through winter

American mountain ash

IDENTIFICATION TIPS, DANGEROUS LOOKALIKES
Mountain ash is small tree (up to 30 feet tall) that is easy to identify in the fall, when the bright orange to red berries grow in clusters at the ends of branches. Bark is smooth and greenish brown, turning gray with age. The leaves grow alternately in compound sets with a dozen or more narrow, toothy, opposite-growing leaves per set (similar to leaves of sumac, walnuts and locusts). Leaves are slightly more pointed on the American mountain ash, and its berries are smaller than those of showy or European mountain ash.

Showy mountain ash has red berries, while the berries of American mountain ash are more orange-red. Although the berries of the showy mountain ash are said to have a slightly better taste than the others, the berries of all mountain ash can be used in the same way, so identification of the exact subspecies is not important to the cook. There are no toxic lookalikes.

HARVESTING TIPS

When picking, have a helper hold the branch down so you have easy access to the berries. Cup a fruit cluster in your hand, wrapping your fingers loosely around the berries, and pull it down toward your collection bag; the clusters should pull off easily without damaging the branch.

Mountain ash berries are more acrid earlier in the season, before they have been touched by frost. They can be harvested throughout winter if you can get to the trees through the snow (and if hungry birds such as cedar waxwings, ruffed grouse and pine grosbeak have not beaten you to the trees).

SPECIAL CONSIDERATIONS

Raw mountain ash berries can cause stomach pain and nausea if eaten in large quantities; cooked or dried fruit does not have this effect. Since the fruits are not very good when raw, it is unlikely to be an issue with the forager.

MORE ABOUT MOUNTAIN ASH: The European mountain ash, also called rowan in Europe, was of major symbolic importance to the early Celts and Druids. A necklace of rowan berries was said to ward off evil. Rowan switches were used to drive cattle, and a hoop of rowan wood around the churn was said to ensure better butter. Rowan trees were planted near the barn and at the entrance to the farmyard with the branches trained to grow as an arch over the entrance; this was believed to protect the livestock. A branch from the rowan tree, which was also called witch-wand, was used for dowsing or divining metal. The green bark was used to fashion a garter, which was worn to ward off witches and evil spirits. Closer to home, Native Americans used the wood from the mountain ash to make bows and arrows.

Early peoples also used the fruit for culinary purposes. Rowan berries were used to make jelly; dried berries were ground into flour. The Welsh fermented the berries to make a strong ale. Decoctions of the bark and fruits were also used medicinally, to treat a variety of ailments from diarrhea to sore throat.

The center of the berries can be quite bitter—almost acrid—but this effect lessens later in the season. If the berries you've gathered are too bitter to use whole, they still make a fine jelly, and work especially well in a tart jelly to be used as a condiment with meats and cheeses (see Tart Mountain Ash Jelly, page 198).

Harvested mountain ash berries keep very well in the refrigerator, and also can be dried for later use. To store them in the refrigerator, simply place the unwashed berry clusters—still on the stems—in a plastic bag. Twist the top just lightly to allow some air to enter the bag, and refrigerate for as long as 3 weeks, checking the berries occasionally.

If you prefer to dry mountain ash for storage, wash the berry clusters in cold water, then place into a large paper bag. Close the bag loosely to exclude dust, and hang in a cool, dry location; let them dry for about 2 weeks, then pull dried berries from stems and place into jars for storage. Also see the information on page 421 for drying mountain ash berries in the oven or a food dehydrator.

How to make mountain ash juice: Pull individual berries off the stems. Some of the berries will be partially discolored or withered, and it's OK to use some of these as long as you also have a good amount of unblemished fruit. Discard any berries that have turned black or are very hard. Two cups of fresh berries weighs about 9 ounces.

Rinse the berries well, then measure them and place into a nonreactive saucepan. Add an equal amount of water if using fresh berries; if using dried berries, increase the water by half (so for 2 cups of berries, you'd use 2 cups of water for fresh berries, or 3 cups of water for dried berries). Heat to boiling, then reduce heat and simmer for 20 minutes if using fresh berries; dried berries need to cook for about 30 minutes. Mash the berries lightly with a potato masher, and cook for 5 minutes longer. Strain through a double thickness of cheesecloth, pressing lightly on the berries to extract more juice. Two cups of berries should yield about 1 cup of juice; add a bit of water or apple juice as needed to equal 1 cup for each 2 cups of berries you started with.

QUICK IDEAS FOR USING MOUNTAIN ASH BERRIES
- Mountain ash berries can be eaten raw, as a trail nibble; I find them too mealy and bitter to be of much interest, but individual trees may yield better-tasting fruit.
- A number of sources say that mountain ash berries can be used to make a pie, although I've never done this. If you wish to try, stew and sweeten the fruits as though making cranberry sauce, then bake in a lattice-top pie crust.
- Some people make wine from mountain ash berries; see *Wines from the Wilds* by Steven A. Krause for a recipe.

OTHER RECIPES IN THIS BOOK FEATURING MOUNTAIN ASH BERRIES
- Sweet Mountain Ash Jelly (chart, page 255)
- Dried mountain ash berries (page 421)

Pork Chops Glazed with Mountain Ash

2 servings; easily increased   Preparation: Under 30 minutes

It's worth it to make a batch of Tart Mountain Ash Jelly (page 198) just so you can enjoy these delicious chops. The tangy cranberry-like flavor of the jelly is a perfect complement to seared chops or steaks.

2 boneless pork loin chops, about
    1 inch thick
Salt and pepper
1 tablespoon olive oil
½ cup diced onion

3 tablespoons dry sherry
1 cup chicken broth
2 tablespoons Tart Mountain Ash Jelly
    (page 198)

Heat oven to 375°F. Sprinkle chops on both sides with salt and pepper to taste. Heat oil in medium skillet over medium-high heat. Add chops and brown well on both sides. Transfer chops to oven-proof dish and place in oven.

Pour off all but a thin film of oil from skillet. Add onion and cook over medium heat for about 3 minutes, stirring frequently. Add sherry to skillet, stirring to loosen browned bits. Cook until sherry has evaporated almost completely. Add chicken broth and jelly to skillet. Stir to dissolve jelly. Increase heat to high, and cook until liquid has reduced to just a few tablespoons, stirring frequently.

Return chops and any accumulated juices to skillet, turning to coat with pan juices. Cook until heated through and just done.

Variation: Venison Chops or Steaks Glazed with Mountain Ash

Substitute boneless tender venison steaks or chops for the pork; the venison should be 1 inch thick, and trimmed of all fat and connective tissue. Use an oven temperature of 300°F rather than 375°F. Proceed as directed, remembering that venison is best when served rare to medium-rare (the lower oven temperature keeps the steaks warm without further cooking while you make the sauce).

Rice Pilaf with Mountain Ash Berries

4 servings   Preparation: Under 45 minutes

½ cup minced onion
1 clove garlic, minced
1 tablespoon butter
1 cup long-grain white rice
2 cups chicken broth

3 tablespoons dried mountain ash berries,
   or ¼ cup fresh
A pinch of powdered saffron
¼ cup toasted slivered almonds or pine nuts
1 tablespoon chopped fresh parsley

In saucepan, sauté onion and garlic in butter over medium heat for 5 minutes. Add rice, stirring to coat; cook for about 1 minute longer. Stir in broth, mountain ash berries and saffron. Heat to boiling, stirring several times. Cover pan, reduce heat to medium-low and cook until liquid is absorbed and rice is just tender, about 20 minutes. The cooked rice can stand, covered, for 10 to 15 minutes before serving. When ready to serve, fluff rice with fork; stir in almonds and parsley.

Tart Mountain Ash Jelly

2 half-pints   Preparation: Over an hour

This is good with chops and steaks, especially venison; it's also very good with cheese and crackers. (For a recipe that uses Tart Mountain Ash Jelly, see Pork Chops Glazed with Mountain Ash, page 197).

2 cups fresh mountain ash berries, or
   1¾ cups dried
1½ cups water
½ cup red wine vinegar
10 to 12 juniper berries
10 spicebush berries or whole allspice

½ teaspoon Szechuan peppercorns or
   whole regular peppercorns, optional
One-quarter of a 1.75-ounce box powdered
   pectin*
½ cup sugar

Prepare jars, bands and lids as described on page 418. In saucepan, combine mountain ash berries, water, vinegar, juniper berries, spicebush berries and peppercorns. Heat to boiling, then reduce heat and simmer for 20 minutes if using fresh berries; dried berries need to cook for about 30 minutes. Mash berries lightly with a potato masher, and cook for 5 minutes longer. Strain through double thickness of cheesecloth, pressing lightly on berries to extract more juice.

Combine mountain ash juice and pectin in nonreactive saucepan (use one that is at least 4 times as deep as the juice, to allow room for foaming). Heat to boiling over high heat, stirring frequently. When mixture comes to a full rolling boil that can't be stirred down, add sugar. Cook, stirring constantly, until mixture again comes to a full, foaming boil. Cook for 2 minutes, stirring constantly. Remove from heat, and stir for a minute or two to settle the foam (if there is still foam on top, skim and discard with a clean metal spoon). Pour into prepared jars, leaving ¼ inch headspace; seal with prepared lids and bands. Process in boiling-water bath for 5 minutes.

*See page 254 for information on dividing powdered pectin.

Mulberries (red mulberry, *Morus rubra;* white mulberry, *M. alba*)

This shrub is a familiar sight in both rural and urban areas. The sweet berries have a flavor that's unlike any other fruit; they work well as a substitute for blackberries or raspberries.

HABITAT, RANGE

Red mulberry is a native tree that grows primarily in the southeastern region of the Unites States; it extends north to the middle of Minnesota, Wisconsin and Michigan, and as far west as Iowa (it is not found in the Dakotas). Red mulberries grow in rich valleys and floodplains, along roadsides, in moist fields and meadows, particularly along the edges, and on streambanks that are not too shaded. White mulberries are an introduced species that has become naturalized throughout our entire region and, indeed, throughout most of the United States. They inhabit much of the same areas as the red mulberry, but can tolerate a wider range of climates and moisture levels. Mulberries are quite common in urban areas including parks and backyards.

PARTS USED

Ripe fruit, raw or cooked

SEASONS

Early to mid-summer

Mulberry fruit and leaves

IDENTIFICATION TIPS, DANGEROUS LOOKALIKES

Although red mulberry trees can reach heights of 75 feet, most red or white mulberry trees are generally under 25 feet tall, and often appear to be little more than a large shrub. They are messy trees, throwing a profusion of fruit on the ground; in urban settings, you can spot a mulberry by looking for the tell-tale purple splotches on the sidewalk. Red mulberry trees have bark that is brown to reddish brown, becoming rough and scaly as the tree matures; white mulberry trees have thinner bark that is grayish brown and sometimes flakes from the trunk. Both trees develop vertical ridges or fissures in the bark as they mature. Branches exude milky sap when broken.

The leaves are alternate and bright green, rough on top with prominent veins and hairy undersides. They take a variety of shapes; some are heart-shaped with a pointy tip, while others are scalloped like a rounded oak leaf; frequently, leaves are irregularly lobed or notched, giving them a shape that looks a lot like a mitten.

The fruits are compound, resembling an elongated blackberry or raspberry; like the blackberry, the core of the mulberry remains inside the fruit when it is picked (the core of a raspberry remains on the plant when it is picked, so the fruit is hollow). Mulberries are quite easy to distinguish from blackberries or raspberries because mulberries are trees, while blackberries and raspberries are brambles. The fruit of red mulberries is dark purple or black when ripe, while white mulberries have white or pinkish ripe fruit. There are no dangerous lookalikes.

HARVESTING TIPS

Mulberry trees can grow so tall that it is hard to reach the fruits; a stepladder makes the job easier. Another method is to put a drop cloth under the tree and shake the branches with a pole (or by climbing, if the tree is climbable) to dislodge the fruits.

Mulberry fruits vary quite a bit from tree to tree, even if they're the same species, so before you fill your bucket, you should taste a few to see if they meet your standards.

SPECIAL CONSIDERATIONS

Unripe berries, as well as raw leaves of the mulberry plant, are toxic and may cause hallucinations. The milky sap exuded by broken mulberry branches may cause skin irritation in sensitive individuals.

MORE ABOUT MULBERRIES: Mulberries are common throughout both urban and rural areas, but not many people gather the fruit. Mulberries are delicious and sweet, with a flavor all their own; to me, it seems almost perfumey, but in a nice, edible way. The fruits are compound, like blackberries and raspberries; the seeds are less annoying than those of blackberries. The green stemlet remains attached to the fruit, however, and you may want to pull this off when preparing the fruits for pie or fresh use. If you'll be making juice, don't bother about these stemlets; and many cooks leave the stemlet on even when using the fruit for pies.

Red mulberries are native to the United States, and were extensively used by indigenous peoples in fresh, cooked and dry forms. White mulberries were introduced to America in 1603 by King James I of England, who sent mulberry seeds and silkworm eggs to Virginia with hopes of starting a silk industry there (the white mulberry leaf is the sole food of the silk-producing caterpillar named *Bombyx mori*). However, the young colonies did not have a viable textile processing infrastructure, and the industry died out. The trees, however, continued to thrive, soon spreading across much of the country. Both red and white mulberries are a favored food of numerous birds, as well as small mammals such as opossum, raccoon and squirrels (I've seen raccoons sitting under mulberry trees at night, happily munching away). Old-time farmers used mulberries to fatten hogs and to feed the chickens.

Once you've harvested mulberries, use them within a day or two, as they will spoil quickly. They freeze beautifully; simply pack them into containers or heavyweight plastic bags and freeze. They can be dried successfully; the texture of a dried mulberry is similar to that of a dried fig. Dried mulberries can be eaten out of hand as a nibble, or rehydrated in warm water and used like fresh berries.

How to make mulberry juice: Place a quart of ripe mulberries in a small soup pot with 1 cup of water; if you have more mulberries, follow this same ratio. Mash the fruits thoroughly with a potato masher. Heat until the mixture is simmering, then cover and adjust heat so mixture simmers gently; cook for 20 minutes, stirring occasionally. Remove from heat and set aside until cool enough to handle safely, then strain through 3 layers of dampened cheesecloth. You should get about 2 cups of juice per quart of mulberries, although this can vary with the juiciness of the berries.

QUICK IDEAS FOR USING MULBERRIES
- Use mulberries in any recipe you have for blackberries or raspberries.
- Sweeten mulberry juice to taste with honey or sugar; it probably won't need much, especially if you've made juice from white mulberries which are sweeter than red mulberries. Serve the juice cold. It's also delicious mixed with apple or cranberry juice.
- If you are an amateur winemaker, use mulberries in any recipe you have for blackberry wine.

- Add ½ to ¾ cup of mulberries to any apple pie recipe you prefer.

OTHER RECIPES IN THIS BOOK FEATURING MULBERRIES
- Wild Berry Syrup (page 111)
- Wild Berry Gelatin (page 112)
- As substitute in Currant Scones (page 164)
- Mulberry Jelly (chart, page 254; included with Blackberry listing)
- Dried mulberries (page 422)

Mulberry Fool

4 servings   Preparation: Under 30 minutes, plus chilling time

A "fool" is a British dessert that consists of sweetened fruit with whipped cream. Sometimes the two are folded together; other times, the fruit is layered parfait-style in a glass, as it is here.

3 cups fresh or previously frozen mulberries   A pinch of salt
⅓ cup plus 2 tablespoons sugar, divided   1 cup heavy cream
¼ cup orange juice, preferably freshly   1 teaspoon vanilla extract
   squeezed

In medium nonreactive saucepan, combine mulberries, ⅓ cup of the sugar, the orange juice and salt. Heat to boiling, then reduce heat and simmer, stirring occasionally, until fruit is very tender, 15 to 20 minutes. Transfer to glass or Pyrex mixing bowl and cool to room temperature, then cover and refrigerate until cold, at least 1 hour (you may prepare the fruit as much as a day in advance; simply store in the refrigerator until you're ready to assemble the fools).

When you're ready to assemble the fools, beat cream with vanilla and remaining 2 tablespoons of sugar in chilled large bowl until soft peaks form and cream has doubled in volume. Divide half of the chilled mulberry mixture between 4 parfait glasses. Divide half of the whipped cream between the 4 glasses. Divide remaining mulberry mixture and remaining whipped cream between the glasses. Serve immediately, or cover and chill for an hour or two before serving.

Mulberry-Yogurt Muffins

8 muffins   Preparation: Under an hour

Baking mix makes these muffins quick and easy to prepare.

1 cup fresh or previously frozen mulberries
1 tablespoon lemon juice
1 egg
1 cup plain or vanilla yogurt (reduced-fat works fine)

3 tablespoons butter, melted
2½ cups buttermilk baking mix such as Bisquick

Heat oven to 375°F. Spray 8-cup muffin pan with nonstick spray; set aside. In small mixing bowl, toss mulberries with lemon juice; set aside for 5 minutes. In large mixing bowl, beat egg with fork or electric hand mixer. Add yogurt and melted butter; beat until smooth. Add baking mix; stir with wooden spoon until just moistened. Fold in mulberries. Spoon batter into prepared muffin cups. Bake until springy to the touch, about 25 minutes; a toothpick inserted in center of a muffin should come out clean. Cool in muffin pan for 5 minutes, then turn out and finish cooling on wire rack.

Mulberry Barbecue Sauce

About 1 cup   Preparation: About an hour

3 cups fresh or previously frozen mulberries
⅓ cup orange juice
¼ cup chopped shallot
2 tablespoons freshly squeezed lemon juice
1 tablespoon minced fresh gingerroot
½ teaspoon ground cumin

1 small fresh hot pepper, minced (remove seeds for milder sauce)
½ teaspoon freshly ground black pepper
⅓ cup (packed) brown sugar
2 tablespoons tomato paste
2 tablespoons white wine vinegar
1 teaspoon salt, or to taste

In heavy saucepan, combine mulberries, orange juice, shallot, lemon juice, gingerroot, cumin, hot pepper and black pepper. Heat to gentle boil over medium heat; cook until most of the liquid has cooked away, about 20 minutes, stirring occasionally. Remove from heat and cool slightly, then purée with food mill (or process until smooth in food processor; sauce will not be as smooth). Return purée to saucepan. Add remaining ingredients. Simmer over low heat for 20 minutes; if sauce is too thin, simmer until thickened to desired consistency.

Nannyberries, Blackhaws *(Viburnum lentago, V. prunifolium)*

Nannyberries and blackhaws are less well known than many other wild fruits, but are delicious. They make a delightful field snack, and can be cooked to produce a thick nectar for making jam or desserts.

HABITAT, RANGE

Nannyberries are found throughout Minnesota, Wisconsin and Michigan including the Upper Peninsula; their range extends slightly into the Dakotas, as well as scattered portions of Iowa, Illinois and Ohio. Blackhaws are less common; in our region, they're found in southern Wisconsin and southern Michigan. Both plants inhabit low, moist woods; they're also found along streams and marshes, and occasionally in swampy areas. They will grow in both sunny and shady areas.

PARTS USED

Ripe berries

SEASONS

Late summer through early fall; some fruits persist through winter

IDENTIFICATION TIPS, DANGEROUS LOOKALIKES

Nannyberries and blackhaws are both members of the large *Viburnum* family, which also includes the highbush cranberry (*V. trilobum*). Highbush cranberries, however, belong to a sub-class often called the maple-leaf group, as their leaves are lobed like those of a maple tree. Nannyberries and blackhaws have opposite, oval leaves with

Nannyberries

finely toothed edges. Nannyberry leaves are larger and wider than those of blackhaws—usually 3 or even 4 inches long, in contrast to the 1- to 2-inch-long leaves of the blackhaw. Nannyberry leaves are pointed at the tip, while those of blackhaw are rounded. The leaf stems of the nannyberry are winged—they have flattened margins, similar to the garden shrub called winged euonymus (*Euonymus alatus*). The stems of both species have a "dragon's beak"—a sharply pointed bud at the end of the branch (see photo). Leaves of both species turn a lovely red in the fall.

Nannyberry leaves and dragon's beak

Both plants grow as shrubs or as small trees that can get up to 30 feet tall; they have short trunks with dark brown bark, and the branches are reddish brown. Bark on the main trunk becomes scaly or alligatored as the plants mature.

The fruits of nannyberries and blackhaws are quite similar, and can be used in the same ways; that, and their limited range, is the reason they are being discussed together. Nannyberry fruits start out as light green, developing a reddish blush (like an apple) and finally turning black when ripe. Blackhaw fruits are pinkish white when immature, turning bright red and finally ripening to blueish black. Both fruits usually have a light bloom, and each contains a single, flat seed; the fruits are about ½ inch long and somewhat oblong, with a small bit of blossom remnant at the bottom. The flesh is a bit sticky, rather like a raisin.

Nannyberries and blackhaws are easy to identify because of the leaf shape and distinctive fruits. Fruits resemble some of the hawthorns, although hawthorn fruits have a pronounced blossom remnant at the bottom and are usually more round than oval; hawthorn leaves, however, are quite dissimilar. Many hawthorns are edible, and none are toxic. Winged euonymus has opposite leaves and stems that are similar to nannyberries, and also produces oval fruits, but the fruits are much smaller—generally about ¼ inch long and dark red rather than black.

If you're in Michigan, Indiana or Ohio, you may also encounter the edible northern wild raisin or withe rod (*V. cassinoides*, also called *V. nudum var. cassinoides*). The fruit is white or pink when underripe, turning blueish black when ripe. Fruits tend to grow in large clusters, and the shrub is generally 5 to 8 feet tall. Treat the fruit from this plant the same as nannyberries (which are also occasionally called wild raisins, lending to the confusion).

Finally, please read about buckthorn on page 103. It's quite easy to distinguish buckthorn, which is generally considered toxic, from nannyberries; however, the two plants often grow side by side and both have rounded, blackish fruits.

HARVESTING TIPS

Nannyberries and blackhaws ripen over a period of several weeks, so you may find ripe and underripe fruits on the same plant. Harvest the ripe fruits, then return a few days or a week later to get additional ripe fruits.

A few fruits may persist on individual plants into the winter. You can identify the plant at this time by looking for the distinctive bark and the dragon's beak at the ends of the stems. Although the fruits will be shrivelled and dried out, they make an excellent, sweet trail nibble.

MORE ABOUT NANNYBERRIES: Nannyberries were an accidental discovery for me. One day in early fall, I was walking on a path that runs behind an office complex in Plymouth, a northwestern suburb of Minneapolis that still retains some of its rural character. I had seen several wild edibles on my walk that day, including wild grapes, elderberries and staghorn sumac; earlier in the season, I'd found wild currants and raspberries along the same path. As a result, I was keeping my eyes open for anything else that looked interesting. Shortly, I noticed a tall, spreading shrub that had what appeared to be hanging berries (actually, they looked like flattened, half-ripe miniature apples). I knew what they weren't: buckthorn, highbush cranberry, or any of the wild cherries. I snipped off a branch tip with a few fruits (see photo at right), then consulted with a few other foragers as well as several identification guides. Turns out my mystery fruit was, indeed, edible and choice; I had found a nannyberry shrub with underripe fruits.

Mystery fruit that turned out to be underripe nannyberries

After positively identifying my "new" fruit and sampling some after it ripened, I came to appreciate the short description in *Field Guide to North American Edible Wild Plants*: "flavor excellent, seeds a nuisance." The seeds, which are shaped like watermelon seeds, are probably the biggest reason that nannyberries are not more popular; they're relatively large in proportion to the amount of flesh. But the fruit is excellent, with a flavor that seems to me like dates crossed with oranges. They make an excellent trail nibble. Blackhaws are similar in taste, and have the same type of large seed.

If you gather enough nannyberries or blackhaws, you can cook them to extract the pulp, then use it to make jam, fruit leather or butter. I've also had some excellent nannyberry mustard; it was made by Sam Thayer, who is director of Forager's Harvest (previously called the Wild Foods Institute) based in Bruce, Wisconsin. Sam is a premier forager who largely lives off the land, and he makes some delightful things from wild foods. He didn't part with the recipe, but mentioned that it contained cloves, turmeric, sugar, vinegar, salt and mustard seeds. If you're the tinkering sort, it would be fun to experiment with this to see what you can come up with; the nannyberries gave the mustard a sweet, wonderful flavor.

How to make nannyberry or blackhaw nectar: I call this nectar rather than juice, because it is thicker than most fruit juices. Place nannyberries or blackhaws in heavy-bottomed saucepan or small soup pot. Add water (or fruit juice if you prefer) to almost cover fruit. Heat just to boiling, then reduce heat and simmer, uncovered, for 20 minutes. Cool slightly, then strain through a conical strainer or food mill to remove the seeds (you can also put the cooked fruit in a wire-mesh strainer and press the pulp through with a wooden spoon, but this is really tedious because of all the seeds). For a slightly better yield, mix the seeds and skin remaining in the strainer with a little more water, then strain again. You will need roughly 2¾ cups of fruit (about 8½ ounces) to yield about 2 cups of nectar.

QUICK IDEAS FOR USING NANNYBERRIES OR BLACKHAWS
- Add a handful of nannyberries or blackhaws to cut-up apples when making applesauce; this works only with recipes that call for cooking and then straining the apples to remove seeds.

OTHER RECIPES IN THIS BOOK FEATURING NANNYBERRIES OR BLACKHAWS
- As substitute in Chokeberry Barbecue Sauce (page 152)

Nannyberry Carrot Cake

12 servings   Preparation: Over an hour

Nannyberry or blackhaw nectar gives a rich, deep color and delightful sweetness to this cake. It's great just as it is, but if you like, you can top it with your favorite cream-cheese frosting or serve it with lightly sweetened whipped cream.

2 cups all-purpose flour
1 teaspoon baking soda
¾ teaspoon cinnamon
1/2 teaspoon salt
3 eggs
1⅓ cups sugar
½ cup vegetable oil

¾ cup nannyberry or blackhaw nectar
   (page 207)
1 teaspoon vanilla
2¼ cups grated raw carrots
1 cup chopped walnuts, hickory nuts or
   pecans

Heat oven to 350°F. Grease and flour 13 x 9-inch baking dish; set aside. Sift together flour, baking soda, cinnamon and salt. In mixing bowl, combine eggs, sugar, oil, nectar and vanilla. Beat with hand mixer until smooth. Add flour mixture; stir just until combined. Add carrots and nuts; stir just until combined. Scrape into prepared dish. Bake until center tests done with wooden pick, 40 to 50 minutes. Serve warm or at room temperature.

Nannyberry or Blackhaw Butter

About 1 cup   Preparation: Over an hour

Serve this on hot buttered toast for an exceptional breakfast treat. It's also delicious spooned on top of hot oatmeal.

4 cups (about 12 ounces) nannyberries or
   blackhaws
1½ cups apple juice

1 cinnamon stick, optional
½ cup (packed) brown sugar

In saucepan, combine fruit, apple juice and cinnamon stick. Heat to boiling. Cover and adjust heat so mixture just simmers; cook for 25 minutes, stirring several times. Remove from heat; remove and discard cinnamon stick. Cool slightly, then strain through a conical strainer or food mill to remove the seeds. Transfer pulp to small, heavy-bottomed saucepan; stir in brown sugar. Cook over medium-low heat, stirring occasionally, until mixture is thick enough to hold a mounded shape in a spoon. Another way to determine if the butter is adequately cooked is to spoon a small amount onto a plate; if the mixture does not seep liquid around the edges, it is done. Store in a glass jar in the refrigerator, where it will keep for several weeks.

Abandoned Orchards

These fruits won't be as pretty as the ones you buy in the store, but you might find a variety that is unavailable commercially. Harvest more than you need, to allow for cutting away insect spots.

A number of years ago, I worked at an office building that had been built in what was then a remote suburb of Minneapolis. When I first started working there, this building was one of the few in the area. There was a beautiful pond next to it, and it was surrounded by trees and rolling hills. I'd often see deer and pheasants in the parking lot in the morning. Soon, of course, the area was subjected to increasing development; and one year we learned that a new hotel was going to be put on the hill across from our building.

I had often walked on this hill during my lunch hour; there was an abandoned apple orchard there, with small but sweet fruits of an unfamiliar variety. When I learned that the site was slated for development, I was genuinely sad to know that these fruit trees, which had survived for so long, were to be destroyed. To make a long story short, a co-worker who was as concerned as I called the University of Minnesota's horticultural department, and I understand that they came out to take cuttings from these trees which were then grafted onto some of their nursery stock. In that way, this piece of living history was preserved. Every time I read about a new apple variety that has been developed, I think fondly of those trees and wonder if they contributed anything to any new cultivars.

It's fairly common to find the remnants of an old farmstead orchard in the countryside, or occasionally even the leftovers of an abandoned commercial orchard. Although the only abandoned orchards I've seen are apple orchards, I understand that abandoned pears are also occasionally found in the southern portion of our region.

Domesticated apples and pears have been hybridized and improved to produce larger fruit that is easier to transport. In addition, most commercial fruit operations, and a fair number of small-time and individual orchard operators, use fertilizers to ensure larger fruits and better yields, as well as pesticides to keep insects from damaging their fruit. Once the fertilizer and pesticide application stops, however, the trees begin to revert to their native forms, producing fruits that are smaller and more misshapen each season. If you find an abandoned orchard, you're likely to see fruits that are small or have odd shapes, and may have insect damage as well.

These fruits are still worth picking; usually, all you need do is cut away any portions that have been affected by insects. The odd shapes and small size are of no concern if you're going to cook the fruit. You may find that the fruits are less sweet than their domestic cousins; this is just something you'll have to adjust for in processing and cooking. On the other hand, you might just get lucky and discover an abandoned tree with fruit that is far superior to the types you buy in the store. Many old-time varieties have all but died out, yet you can occasionally find a specimen of them in the wild.

Apples and pears from abandoned orchards can be used in any recipe that calls for cooked domestic fruit, and of course, they often make delicious out-of-hand snacks. On the next few pages are a few ideas to get you started in working with these fruits.

How to make apple juice: Follow instructions for crabapple juice on page 155, cutting apples int 1- to 2-inch chunks.

OTHER RECIPES IN THIS BOOK FEATURING APPLES OR PEARS
- Pear and Chokeberry Mincemeat (page 150)
- Rosy Applesauce (page 245)
- Apple Jelly (chart, page 257)

Pear Muffins

12 muffins   Preparation: Under an hour

Pears make these muffins moist and add a unique flavor.

2 cups all-purpose flour
½ cup sugar
1 tablespoon baking powder
½ teaspoon salt
½ teaspoon nutmeg
1 cup whole milk
1 egg, lightly beaten

¼ cup (half of a stick) butter, melted and cooled
1 cup finely diced pears (peeled, cored and diced before measuring)
½ cup chopped hickory nuts, walnuts or pecans

Heat oven to 425°F. Spray 12-cup muffin pan with nonstick spray; set aside. Combine flour, sugar, baking powder, salt and nutmeg in sifter or wire-mesh strainer; sift into large mixing bowl. In another bowl, stir together milk, egg and butter. Add milk mixture to dry ingredients; stir until just moistened (batter should still be lumpy). Add pears and nuts; mix together gently.

Spoon batter into prepared muffin cups, filling ⅔ full. Bake until tops are browned and center springs back, 20 to 25 minutes. Remove from pan immediately; cool to warm room temperature before serving. Best served warm.

Easy Applesauce (Microwave)

About 2½ cups   Preparation: Under 30 minutes

Here's an easy applesauce that is ideal for using less-perfect fruits from abandoned orchards. Cut away and discard any soft or insect-infested spots before measuring the fruit. Serve this warm over French toast, or chill and enjoy as an accompaniment to poultry or meat.

3 cups sliced wild apples (peeled, cored
  and sliced before measuring)
½ cup sugar, or additional as needed
⅓ cup water

½ teaspoon cinnamon
¼ teaspoon nutmeg
A good pinch of ground cardamom,
  optional but recommended

Combine all ingredients in large microwave-safe mixing bowl. Cover with waxed paper. Microwave on high/100% power for 10 minutes or until apples are soft, stirring once halfway through. Cool apple mixture slightly, then mash to desired consistency with potato masher. Taste, and add additional sugar if necessary (stir the sugar into the warm sauce, and heat briefly in the microwave to incorporate the sugar). Serve warm or chilled.

Pear-Apple Jam

3 half-pints   Preparation: Over an hour

Actually, you can make this with just pears, just apples, or a mix of the two.

3 half-pint canning jars, with bands and
  new lids
1 cup finely chopped pears (peeled, cored
  and chopped before measuring)
1 cup finely chopped apples (peeled, cored
  and chopped before measuring)

Half of a 1.75-ounce box powdered pectin*
2 tablespoons lemon juice
¼ teaspoon cinnamon
3 cups sugar

Prepare jars, bands and lids as directed on page 418; if you are unfamiliar with canning procedures, also read the canning information on that page. In heavy-bottomed nonreactive saucepan, combine pears, apples, pectin, lemon juice and cinnamon. Heat to full, rolling boil that can't be stirred down, stirring constantly. Add sugar. Return to a full, rolling boil; cook for 1 minute. Remove from heat; stir for about a minute. Ladle into prepared jars, leaving ¼ inch headspace. Seal with prepared lids and bands. Process in boiling-water bath for 10 minutes.

*See page 253 for information on dividing powdered pectin.

Pawpaws (Asimina triloba)

This homely fruit has a delightful banana-pineapple taste, quite unlike anything you'd expect to find in our region. It makes excellent cake, pudding and quick breads.

HABITAT, RANGE

Pawpaw trees prefer open woods with dappled sunlight, and are often found along streams and in ravines. In our region, they are scattered throughout Wisconsin (primarily in the southeastern area), southern Michigan (rarely in the Upper Peninsula), Iowa, Illinois, Indiana and Ohio. Other names include papaw, Indiana banana, Hoosier banana, Michigan banana and custard apple.

PARTS USED

Ripe fruit, raw and cooked

SEASONS

Mid- to late fall, before the first frost

Pawpaws

IDENTIFICATION TIPS, DANGEROUS LOOKALIKES

Pawpaw trees tend to grow in thickets. They can reach heights up to 30 feet; trunks are clad in smooth brown bark that is sometimes splotched with gray. Leaves are 4 to 10 inches long, alternate on the stems, with a narrow base that becomes broadest well above the midpoint, tapering again to a narrow bristle-like point. Crushed leaves give off a distinctive odor that has been likened to green peppers. Should you be lucky enough to see them, the flowers are a real treat; they're deep red, about 1½ inches across with 3 large outer petals and 3 smaller, darker inner petals. Flowers give way to fruit in midsummer; by early fall, the rounded, oblong, slightly flattened fruits are 3 to 6 inches long, and go from pale green to brown-spotted yellow when ripe. There are no lookalikes that could be mistaken for pawpaw fruit; and if somehow one did become confused, the tropical aroma of ready-to-pick pawpaws would clear up any confusion.

HARVESTING TIPS

Pawpaws are best when allowed to ripen on the tree, although picked fruit will ripen when allowed to sit at room temperature for a few days. As with most fruits, pawpaws that are picked green will never develop the full taste and sweetness of a fruit that was picked when ripe. Ripe pawpaws bruise easily; don't pack too many into your collecting basket. Judge ripeness of pawpaws by squeezing the fruit gently; ripe fruit also has a pleasant tropical aroma and the skin may be flecked with brown spots.

SPECIAL CONSIDERATIONS

Pawpaws cause digestive difficulties for some people, so start with just a small amount. Underripe and overripe pawpaws are particularly problematical, and should not be used. Kay Young, in *Wild Seasons,* reports that handling pawpaws causes a rash in some people.

MORE ABOUT PAWPAWS: With their tropical taste, pawpaws seem almost out of place growing in, say, the Indiana woods. Yet the pawpaw is a native plant; it's the only member of the tropical custard apple family that grows in North America. Its taste is reminiscent of a banana, with pineapple and apricot overtones. The overall effect is one of mixed tropical fruit, and is quite stunning in this wild fruit from the heartland of America.

Pawpaws have a high caloric content and are relatively rich in unsaturated oils (for a fruit, that is), and so make a good survival food. A serving of pawpaw has about the same amount of vitamin C as a serving of cantaloupe; they are very rich in potassium and niacin, and provide good amounts of vitamin A as well. It's the largest native fruit in North America, and was extensively used by Native Americans and early settlers. In September of 1806, the explorer William Clark, while on the homeward journey after crossing America with Meriwether Lewis, noted that the group had been eating pawpaws and biscuits, and wrote in his journal, "the party appear perfectly contented and tell us that they can live very well on pappaws."

Humans are not the only critters in the woods that relish pawpaws, however. You may need luck to beat the raccoons to the pawpaw harvest; opossum, fox, squirrels and many birds also eagerly consume the ripe fruit. As another note of interest, pawpaw leaves are the favored food of larval zebra swallowtail butterfly.

Each pawpaw has 8 to 13 large, flat oval seeds, which should never be eaten. Cut the pawpaw in half gently, avoiding the seeds; if you can't cut all the way through, cut as deeply as possible and pry the two halves apart like an avocado. Pull out the seeds by hand. Scoop the flesh from the half-skin with spoon; if the pawpaw is very ripe, you can peel the skin away. You could also use a paring knife, but you may lose more flesh.

The ripe fruit can be eaten raw, but is more commonly mashed or puréed for use in breads, cakes and other baked goods. The puréed or mashed fruit freezes well; simply pack into appropriate containers and freeze. It takes about 2 pounds of pawpaws to make 1½ cups of purée (pawpaws weigh 5 to 12 ounces each, with the occasional bruiser that tips the scales at a pound). Overripe pawpaws often have reddish blotchy coloration in the flesh, and should not be used. To keep picked fruit from spoiling, store it in the refrigerator once it's ripe; it will keep for a week or possibly two. Mash and freeze for longer storage. A word to the uninitiated: ripe pawpaws have a powerful tropical scent, and the scent of overripe pawpaws can take over the house.

JUST FOR FUN

Pawpaw Festival

Albany, Ohio holds an annual pawpaw festival in September. Featured activities include a pawpaw judging contest, pawpaw cookoff, and pawpaw eating contest (contestants have their hands tied behind their backs and must eat a pound of pawpaw pulp; the first contestant who spits out all their cleaned seeds is the winner). For more information, visit www.ohiopawpaw.org/pawpawfest.html.

QUICK IDEAS FOR USING PAWPAWS

- Use pawpaw in almost any recipe calling for bananas.
- Blend pawpaw with yogurt, spices and a bit of orange juice to make a delightful smoothie.

OTHER RECIPES IN THIS BOOK FEATURING PAWPAWS

- Dried pawpaw slices (page 422)

Pawpaw Cheesecake

9 to 12 servings   Preparation: Over an hour, plus overnight chilling

The pawpaw flavor really comes through in this dense, rich cheesecake.

Graham-cracker crust:
1½ cups graham cracker crumbs*
⅓ cup sugar
6 tablespoons (¾ of a stick) butter or
    margarine, melted

Filling:
1½ pounds cream cheese (reduced-fat
    works fine), room temperature
1¼ cups sugar
1 teaspoon vanilla extract
3 large eggs
1½ cups well-mashed pawpaw pulp (from
    about 2 pounds fresh, whole pawpaws)

Prepare the crust: Heat oven to 350°F. Lightly grease 9-inch springform pan; set aside. In mixing bowl, stir together graham cracker crumbs and sugar. Add melted butter in thin stream, stirring constantly to mix evenly. Press mixture into bottom (not sides) of prepared pan. Bake until crust is firm and beginning to brown, about 12 minutes. Remove from oven and set aside to cool completely. This may be prepared earlier in the day, or just before you assemble the cheesecake.

For the cheesecake: Heat oven to 325°F (or reduce the heat if you've just prepared the crust). In large mixing bowl, beat cream cheese with electric mixer until smooth. Add sugar and vanilla, and beat until mixed, scraping bowl occasionally. Add eggs 1 at a time, beating well after each addition. Add mashed pawpaw and beat well, scraping bowl to mix evenly. Pour filling into crust-lined pan. Bake until cheesecake is golden and just set, about 1½ hours; the center will still be slightly loose. Cool at room temperature for an hour or two, then cover loosely with waxed paper and refrigerate for 8 hours or overnight.

To serve, run a table knife between the cake and the edges of the pan and remove the outside band. Cut cake into serving-sized pieces and remove with spatula.

*You may use whole graham crackers instead if you have a food processor. Place 13 standard graham crackers and the sugar in workbowl fitted with the steel blade. Pulse on-and-off until the crackers are fine crumbs. With machine running, pour the melted butter through the feed tube and let run until well combined, scraping the sides of the workbowl with a rubber spatula once. Pour crumb mixture directly into prepared pan and press into bottom as directed.

Pawpaw-Sour Cream Coffee Cake

10 to 12 servings   Preparation: Over an hour

This is a moist, dense coffeecake that makes a substantial breakfast or brunch dish; servings can be small.

Nut topping:
1 cup chopped pecans, walnuts or
    pistachios
¼ cup sugar
½ teaspoon cinnamon

Cake:
2 cups all-purpose flour
1 teaspoon baking powder
¼ teaspoon nutmeg
¼ teaspoon salt
½ cup (1 stick) butter or margarine,
    softened
1 cup plus 2 tablespoons sugar
2 eggs
1 cup well-mashed pawpaw pulp
⅔ cup sour cream
1 teaspoon vanilla extract

Heat oven to 350°F. Grease and flour a 9- or 10-inch bundt or tube pan; set aside. In small bowl, mix nut-topping ingredients thoroughly; set aside. Sift flour, baking powder, nutmeg and salt together; set aside.

In large mixing bowl, cream butter with electric mixer. Add sugar and beat until mixture is light and fluffy, scraping bowl occasionally. Add eggs, 1 at a time, beating well after each addition. Add mashed pawpaws, sour cream and vanilla, and beat until well combined. Add dry ingredients and stir with wooden spoon or spatula until just moistened.

Sprinkle half of the nut mixture into prepared pan. Spoon half of the batter into the pan. Sprinkle with remaining nut mixture, then spoon remaining batter into pan, smoothing the top. Bake for 55 minutes to 1 hour, or until toothpick inserted in center comes out clean. Cook cake on rack for 10 minutes. Loosen edges if necessary and invert onto serving plate. Serve warm or at room temperature.

Pawpaw-Pecan Bread

1 loaf Preparation: Over an hour

Similar to banana bread, but even more delicious, with an intriguing tropical flavor.

1¾ cups all-purpose flour	½ cup (1 stick) butter, softened
1¼ teaspoons baking powder	1 cup sugar
¼ teaspoon ground allspice or ground	2 eggs
dried spicebush berries	2 teaspoons lemon juice
¼ teaspoon salt	1½ teaspoons vanilla extract
1 cup chopped pecans	1 cup well-mashed pawpaw pulp

Heat oven to 350°F. Grease and flour a 9 x 5 x 3-inch loaf pan; set aside. In small mixing bowl, combine flour, baking powder, allspice and salt; mix well. Add pecans and stir to coat; set aside.

In large mixing bowl, beat butter with electric mixer until fluffy. Gradually add sugar, beating until well blended. Add eggs 1 at a time, beating after each addition and scraping bowl occasionally. Stir lemon juice and vanilla extract into pawpaw pulp in measuring cup. Add pulp mixture to butter mixture, and beat to combine, scraping bowl to mix evenly. Add flour-pecan mixture and stir in with a wooden spoon or rubber spatula just until moistened and combined. Scrape mixture into prepared pan. Bake until tester inserted into center of bread comes out clean, about 1 hour 15 minutes. Cool in pan for 5 minutes, then turn out onto rack and cool completely before slicing.

Fruit and Turkey Salad Plate with Curry Dressing

2 servings; easily increased Preparation: Under 15 minutes

<u>Curry dressing</u>:	1 cup cubed honeydew melon or
½ cup salad dressing such as Miracle Whip	cantaloupe
(reduced-fat works fine)	1 cup cubed fresh pineapple, or drained
2 tablespoons orange juice	canned pineapple chunks
1 tablespoon honey	10 to 12 whole ripe strawberries
¼ teaspoon curry powder blend	(depending on size), halved
	10 to 12 whole red or green grapes, halved
<u>Salad</u>:	4 to 6 ounces smoked turkey breast, cut
3 cups cut-up Romaine lettuce	into julienne strips or ½-inch cubes
1 ripe pawpaw	¼ cup slivered almonds

In small bowl, combine all dressing ingredients, stirring to blend. Line individual plates with lettuce. Peel pawpaw and remove seeds. Cut fruit into ½-inch cubes; arrange over lettuce in a wedge shape (as though the lettuce is a pie that you have cut into wedges). Arrange remaining fruit and turkey in similar wedges; each wedge should take up about one-sixth of the lettuce area. Sprinkle almonds over all. Serve with dressing on the side.

Persimmons (Diospyros virginiana)

Cheerful orange globes liven autumn and winter landscapes, and the sweet, soft fruit is unforgettable. A warm-weather species, persimmons are found only in the southern portion of our range.

FRUITS & BERRIES

HABITAT, RANGE

Persimmons thrive in areas with moderate summers and mild winters. In our region, they are found in the southern parts of Iowa, Indiana, Illinois and Ohio. An ornamental version, the Japanese persimmon (*D. kaki*), is also occasionally seen in the wild. Persimmons prefer rich soil, and often grow in bottomlands along major rivers. They are also seen along edges of forests and woodlots, on hillsides, and near clearings in large forests. If you're taking a fall drive in the country in persimmon territory, watch along the roadsides for this distinctive tree.

PARTS USED

Ripe fruit, raw or cooked; leaves, fresh or dried, for tea

SEASONS

Late fall (typically after a frost) through early winter

IDENTIFICATION TIPS, DANGEROUS LOOKALIKES

Native persimmon (also called American persimmon) is a tree that can grow up to 50 feet tall. The bark of the mature persimmon tree is unusual; it's broken into small squares or blocks (somewhat reminiscent of dried, cracked, flaky mud). The trees have glossy, oval deep-green toothless leaves that grow alternately and average 4½ inches long, but they can be as long as 6 inches. The plum-shaped fruit is green at first, ripening to orange or reddish orange; the fruit has a cap of greenish leaves at the top, similar to a strawberry but with a much wider center. Leaves may also change color in the fall, turning yellow, orange or red.

Unripe persimmmons

Ripe persimmmons

Native persimmon trees are generally 20 feet or taller before they bear fruit; if you see a short, stocky tree with fruit on it, you've found an escaped Japanese persimmon. Fruit from both persimmon trees is edible, so don't let the "ornamental" moniker scare you away. Persimmons are quite distinctive, and there are no poisonous lookalikes.

HARVESTING TIPS

Persimmons that are a bit underripe are easy to pick if you can find a tree with fruits that are low enough to reach with a pole. Spread a tarp underneath the tree, then use a broomstick to shake the branches, dislodging the fruit. If you are picking persimmons that are fully ripe, you'll want to pick each fruit by hand rather than shaking the tree, as the ripe fruit would bruise and possibly break open if forced to drop from the tree. A ladder will be needed, as the fruits are generally out of reach.

You can also look at the base of the tree to find fruits that have fallen of their own accord. Fully ripe fruits may have split open upon impact, but if their fall was cushioned by leaves, the fruits may be intact. Underripe fruits will be whole; you can bring them home and let them ripen on the countertop, although the taste will not be as good as a tree-ripened fruit. Persimmon leaves also make a delicious tea, so save a few to use fresh or to dry for later use.

MORE ABOUT PERSIMMONS: In fall and winter, you may find domesticated persimmons in the grocery store. Two varieties are commonly sold: the rounded, flattened Fuyu and the acorn-shaped Hachiya. Wild persimmons look like a small crossbreed of the two; they're pretty close to round with a pointed end like a plum, and are much smaller than either of the domestic varieties you'll find in the store. The wild variety also has a richer, sweeter taste, so is worth seeking out if you are in the right area of the country. Persimmons are high in vitamin C; tea made from the leaves also has a good amount of this vitamin. The fruits also provide potassium, phosphorus and calcium.

Underripe wild persimmons are quite astringent; many describe them as "puckery." When fully ripe, the fruit is very soft and sweet; the skin may appear slightly wrinkled, and is usually brownish in spots, particularly near the stem. The flesh reminds me of a tomato without all the small seeds, but more jelly-like. Persimmons usually have several flat, brownish seeds, although occasional specimens are seedless.

When you're sorting your harvest, plan on eating or processing the ripe fruits immediately. I use a food mill to process persimmon pulp, simply cutting out the leafy core and putting the rest of the fruit in the mill; the skins and seeds will be left behind. A cone-shaped colander (page 253) works as well as a food mill. You should get about 2 cups of purée from each 2 pounds of fruit. The purée can be frozen with no further treatment, and can also be canned in a water-bath canner; process half-pints for 30 minutes (see pages 418-419 for information on canning).

Ripe persimmons are excellent raw, eaten out of hand; any hiker or hunter in persimmon country will appreciate coming upon a persimmon tree with ripe fruit. Euell Gibbons talks about finding a tree with lingering persimmons on a January hike, and of stuffing his pockets with the fruit after eating his fill.

QUICK IDEAS FOR USING PERSIMMONS
- Steep a handful of persimmon leaves, dried or fresh, in hot water as you would use bulk tea leaves. Strain and sweeten to taste.

Soft Persimmon Cookies

About 3 dozen cookies   Preparation: Under an hour

Big, soft cookies with a wonderful persimmon taste.

1 cup persimmon pulp	1 egg
1 teaspoon baking soda	1 teaspoon vanilla extract
½ teaspoon nutmeg	½ teaspoon finely grated orange peel, optional
¼ teaspoon ground spicebush berries or allspice	1¾ cups all-purpose flour
½ cup (1 stick) butter or stick margarine, softened	¾ cup chopped hickory nuts, mockernuts or black walnuts
½ cup white sugar	½ cup golden raisins
½ cup (packed) brown sugar	

Heat oven to 350°F. Lightly grease 3 baking sheets; set aside. In small bowl, stir together persimmon pulp, baking soda, nutmeg and ground spicebush; set aside for 10 minutes. The pulp will thicken to a custard-like texture during this time, and that is normal.

While pulp is resting, cream butter with electric mixer in mixing bowl. Add white sugar and beat until fluffy. Add brown sugar and beat until fluffy. Add egg, vanilla and orange peel; beat until light in color. Add persimmon pulp and beat until well mixed. Add flour and beat until just mixed. Stir in nuts and raisins with a spatula or large spoon.

Drop dough by spoonsful (each about 2 tablespoons) onto prepared baking sheets, keeping 2 inches between cookies. Bake until golden, 16 to 18 minutes. Transfer to wire racks to cool.

Chicken with Persimmon Sauce

2 servings; easily increased

Serve the chicken with a dish of rice to sop up the delicious sauce.

2 boneless, skinless chicken breast halves
Salt and pepper
2 slices Brie cheese, each about
   1 x 3 x 3/16 inch thick
Flour for dredging (about 1/4 cup)

2 tablespoons vegetable oil
1/4 cup diced onion
1/2 cup cut-up persimmon (no need to
   remove seeds or peel)
1 cup chicken broth

Heat oven to 375°F. Butterfly each chicken breast by holding a knife parallel to the cutting board and cutting into two thinner portions; stop cutting before the edge so you can open the meat up like a book. Pound gently with the flat side of a meat mallet to even the thickness. Sprinkle with salt and pepper. Place a slice of Brie on one opened half of each portion. Fold the top and bottom edges over the cheese, then roll the meat up as neatly as possible, tucking in loose edges. You should have a roll that is about 3½ inches long and 2½ inches thick.

Dust each roll with flour, shaking off the excess. Heat the oil over medium-high heat in medium skillet. Add chicken rolls, and brown on all sides (be careful to keep rolls from unraveling when turning). Transfer browned rolls to baking dish and place in oven; set timer for 25 minutes, and begin timing.

As soon as you put rolls in oven, pour off all but a thin film of oil from skillet. Add onion and cook over medium heat, stirring frequently, for about 3 minutes. Add cut-up persimmon and continue cooking and stirring for about 3 minutes longer. Add chicken broth. Increase heat to high, and cook until mixture has reduced to sauce-like consistency; this will take 7 to 10 minutes. Pour mixture into wire-mesh strainer set over a bowl, and stir with wooden spoon; most of the onion will remain in the strainer, along with the persimmon skins, but the persimmon pulp should press through the mesh. Scrape pulp from outside of strainer into bowl as well. Discard solids in strainer. Stir sauce, and pour it over and around chicken rolls in baking dish. Continue baking until rolls have been in the oven for 25 minutes. Serve immediately.

Persimmon Ice Cream

1½ quarts   Preparation: Involved (requires ice-cream maker)

Pale orange and luscious, this rich ice cream is great with gingersnaps. The superfine sugar gives a smoother texture, but you may substitute regular granulated sugar if you like. If you are concerned about the raw egg, use ¼ cup egg substitute in place of the whole egg.

1 very fresh egg   2 cups heavy cream
¾ cup superfine sugar   ½ cup whole milk
1 cup persimmon pulp (refrigerated until
    cold before using)

If using ice-cream maker that requires pre-freezing, place it in freezer as directed by manufacturer, generally 12 to 24 hours. In large mixing bowl, beat egg with electric mixer or whisk until foamy and light. Add sugar gradually, beating after each addition, and beat until mixture is very smooth, light and thick, 1 to 2 minutes. Add persimmon pulp, cream and milk, and beat well. Cover and refrigerate for at least 2 hours, or as long as overnight.

When ready to churn, transfer mixture to ice-cream maker and process as directed by manufacturer. It should be thick, smooth, and creamy; in my ice-cream maker this takes 15 to 20 minutes. Scoop ice cream into freezer-safe container and store in freezer until ready to serve.

Persimmon Muffins

12 muffins   Preparation: Under an hour

Hickory nuts are traditional with baked goods featuring persimmons; however, you may substitute any nuts you like. The persimmon flavor comes through nicely in this not-too-sweet muffin.

2 cups all-purpose flour   ¾ cup (packed) brown sugar
1 teaspoon baking soda   ¼ cup vegetable oil
1 teaspoon baking powder   2 eggs
½ teaspoon salt   ½ cup chopped hickory nuts, slivered
¼ teaspoon ground nutmeg   almonds or other nuts
1 cup persimmon pulp

Heat oven to 350°F. Lightly grease 12-cup muffin pan; set aside. Sift together flour, baking soda, baking powder, salt and nutmeg; set aside. In large mixing bowl, combine persimmon pulp, sugar and oil. Beat well with electric mixer. Add eggs, 1 at a time, beating well after each addition; mixture should be somewhat fluffy after second egg has been beaten in. Add nuts and flour mixture to mixing bowl; stir gently with rubber spatula just until dry ingredients have been moistened (if you over-mix the batter, the muffins will be tough). Spoon batter evenly into prepared muffin cups. Bake until lightly browned and tops spring back when touched lightly, about 25 minutes.

FRUITS &
BERRIES

Persimmon "Pudding" Cake

9 servings   Preparation: Over an hour

When I started researching recipes for this book, I soon discovered that Persimmon Pudding was one of the most popular uses for this sweet fruit. Here's my version of this moist, dense cake. It's truly fabulous served warm with a dollop of Maypop Curd (page 193).

1¼ cups persimmon pulp
⅔ cup (packed) brown sugar
2 eggs
½ cup buttermilk
¼ cup (half of a stick) butter, melted
1½ cups all-purpose flour

¾ teaspoon baking soda
½ teaspoon baking powder
¼ teaspoon salt
½ cup chopped black walnuts, hickory
    nuts or other nuts

Heat oven to 325°F. Lightly grease 8-inch-square baking dish; set aside. In mixing bowl, beat together persimmon pulp, brown sugar and eggs with an electric mixer until smooth and creamy, about 1 minute. Beat in buttermilk and melted butter. Combine flour, baking soda, baking powder and salt in sifter or wire-mesh strainer; sift into persimmon mixture and beat on low speed until just mixed. Stir in walnuts. Scrape batter into prepared pan. Bake until a toothpick inserted in the center comes out clean, 50 to 55 minutes. Serve warm or at room temperature.

Quick Persimmon Loaf

10 to 12 servings   Preparation: Over an hour

Prepared buttermilk baking mix makes this recipe quick and easy to prepare. I use Reduced Fat Bisquick, but the regular version works just as well.

3 eggs
¼ cup skim or regular milk
3 tablespoons vegetable oil
1 cup persimmon pulp
⅔ cup granulated sugar

2½ cups buttermilk baking mix
½ cup (packed) brown sugar
½ cup chopped walnuts, hickory nuts or
    other nuts
¼ teaspoon nutmeg

Heat oven to 350°F. Lightly spray 9 x 5 x 3-inch loaf pan with nonstick spray; set aside. In mixing bowl, use fork to beat eggs with milk and oil. Add persimmon pulp and sugar, and beat together. Add baking mix, and stir with fork until mix is completely moistened; there may still be a few small lumps in the batter.

In small bowl, combine brown sugar, nuts and nutmeg, mixing well with your fingers or a clean fork. Sprinkle half of the brown sugar mixture evenly into prepared loaf pan. Top with half of the batter, spreading evenly. Sprinkle remaining brown sugar mixture evenly over batter; top with remaining batter. Bake for 50 to 60 minutes, or until toothpick inserted in center comes out clean. Remove from oven and let stand 10 minutes, then turn out onto plate. Let cool for at least 1 hour before slicing.

Persimmon-Poppy Seed Dressing

About 1¼ cups   Preparation: 5 minutes

Serve this slightly sweet salad dressing on mixed greens. It goes especially well on a salad that includes a a few nuts and pieces of fruit such as apples, orange sections, pears or grapes.

½ cup cut-up persimmon (peeled, seeds removed)
½ cup vegetable oil
3 tablespoons white wine vinegar
2 tablespoons honey

1 tablespoon diced onion
½ teaspoon dry mustard powder
½ teaspoon salt
¾ teaspoon poppy seeds

Combine all ingredients except poppy seeds in blender. Purée on high speed. Add poppy seeds. Pulse on-and-off a few times to mix in seeds. This keeps well in the refrigerator for several weeks.

Simlets

32 squares   Preparation: 30 minutes active prep, plus 8 hours standing time

When you look at candy at the store, you'll sometimes see Aplets, Cotlets or Grapelets: small, soft candy squares that are made from apples, apricots or grapes. This adaptation uses persimmon for a unique treat.

2 envelopes unflavored gelatin (.25 ounces per envelope)
1 tablespoon cornstarch
1 teaspoon lemon juice
1 teaspoon vanilla extract
1 cup persimmon pulp
1½ cups sugar

¾ cups chopped black walnuts, hickory nuts or other nuts

Dusting mixture:
⅓ cup powdered sugar
2 tablespoons cornstarch

Generously spray 9 × 5 × 3-inch loaf pan (preferably nonstick) with nonstick spray; set aside. Pour ¼ cup cold water into small bowl. Sprinkle gelatin over the water and stir well; set aside. In another small bowl, blend together cornstarch, lemon juice and vanilla. Combine persimmon pulp, sugar and cornstarch mixture in heavy-bottomed medium nonreactive saucepan. Heat over medium heat until bubbles form around the edge, stirring constantly. Whisk in gelatin mixture. Continue cooking, whisking constantly to dissolve gelatin, until mixture boils. Reduce heat to low and simmer for 15 minutes, stirring frequently. Stir in nuts. Pour mixture into prepared loaf pan. Cover loosely with waxed paper and let stand for 8 hours, or overnight.

When you're re ready to finish the Simlets, combine dusting-mixture ingredients in sifter or wire-mesh strainer; sift into a pie plate. Use wet spatula to gently pry persimmon mixture from loaf pan, working spatula along all the edges and finally under the mixture; turn out onto a piece of waxed paper. With wet knife, cut into 8 strips across the length; cut each strip into 4 squares. Roll each square in dusting mixture, shaking off excess. These can be kept in a loosely covered container for a week or two at room temperature, or frozen for longer storage.

Raspberries (Rubus species)

Smaller than domestic berries, but with more flavor, wild raspberries are found throughout our region. One of the best trail nibbles around, and very welcome in the kitchen as well.

HABITAT, RANGE

Raspberries thrive in disturbed areas, along fences and roadsides, on streambanks and floodplains, and in ravines, clearings and forest edges. You will often find them a year or two after an area has been logged or otherwise cut. They prefer sun, but will tolerate partial shade and are often found in sun-dappled woods.

The red raspberry (*Rubus idaeus* or *R. strigosus*) is most familiar, as it looks like a small version of the store-bought raspberry. Black raspberries (*R. occidentalis*), also called blackcaps, are smiliar, but are rich purplish black in hue. Red and black raspberries are found in every state of our region, although populations of each variety may be locally scarce. A related variety, the thimbleberry (*R. parviflorus*), is a more Western species but it is found occasionally in the northern part of our area (primarily in Michigan's Upper Peninsula, the northern part of the Lower Peninsula, parts of South Dakota and northern Minnesota). Note that black raspberries are called thimbleberries by some people, so you may want to make clear exactly which plant is being discussed when someone mentions thimbleberries. (See the identification information below to distinguish thimbleberries from raspberries.)

Domestic vs. wild raspberries

PARTS USED

Ripe berries; raw, cooked or juiced. Leaves can be collected for tea from summer through fall.

SEASONS

Early to mid-summer for black raspberries, mid-summer for red raspberries. Raspberries sometimes produce a second, smaller crop in fall.

Black raspberries

IDENTIFICATION TIPS, DANGEROUS LOOKALIKES

Raspberries grow as sprawling shrubs in thickets. The stems, which are called canes, grow in a tangle that can get up to 5 feet tall; they may be upright—particularly red raspberries—but are commonly arched. Black raspberry canes are well armed with sharp, curved prickles; red raspberries have smaller, less obtrusive prickles, and some canes are unarmed. Raspberry canes are woody on the outside, but have a pithy interior. First-year canes are unbranched and don't bear fruit; in the second year, canes become branched, developing flowers which turn to fruit in the summer. After 2 years, the canes die off, but the root produces new canes the following spring.

Raspberries have compound leaves, each with 3 to 5 toothed leaflets (occasionally you'll see a red raspberry with 7 leaflets); the compound leaves grow alternately on the canes. Undersides of individual leaves are covered with white down; leaves are oval in shape, broadest at the base with a narrow tip. Thimbleberry leaves are much larger, as big as a tea saucer, and they're shaped like maple leaves, so they are easy to distinguish from raspberries.

Like their kin the blackberry, raspberries are compound fruits. Each fruit is a cluster of many globular drupes growing from a small cone, or core (often called a receptacle); each drupe contains a small seed. Raspberries release cleanly from the cone; the compound fruit is hollow and the cone remains on the plant. Blackberries and dewberries, as well as mulberries (another similar compound fruit) retain the cone inside the fruit. This is the easiest way to distinguish black raspberries from blackberries.

All raspberries start out hard and green, eventually turning red. Red raspberries are, of course, red when ripe. Black raspberries ripen to a rich dark purplish black; if you find raspberries that are red but still hard, chances are good that you have underripe black raspberries. Come back in a week or 10 days to harvest the ripe berries. As a further point of distinction, the canes of black raspberries tend to be purplish with a light bloom, while those of red raspberries are more reddish or brownish.

In addition to raspberries, blackberries and thimbleberries, there are dozens of plants in the *Rubus* genus, including dewberries, cloudberries, mayberries and salmonberries; to further complicate the situation, the plants hybridize naturally, and there are dozens of raspberry subspecies listed in the USDA databank. All of these plants produce fruits that are edible; some are tastier than others, but none are dangerous. The only dangerous plant that you may confuse with raspberries is goldenseal (*Hydrastis canadensis*). Goldenseal has raspberry-like red fruits, but the leaves are quite large and have 3 to 5 lobes; the fruit grows from the center of the leaf on a short stem, and the plant grows simply from the ground rather than as a cane. Goldenseal fruits should not be eaten.

HARVESTING TIPS

Raspberries are fragile and crush easily, so don't overfill your collection container. Carry a stack of short plastic or paper drinking glasses in a bucket; as you pick, fill each glass partially, then place the filled glasses into your bucket. Separate layers of glasses with cardboard or newspaper.

For the plumpest raspberries, look for them in moist areas such as along streams, near woodland ponds, and in ravines that have a trickle of water in the bottom. Fruits picked from these areas will be larger than those taken from dry areas.

Even though it may be quite warm during raspberry season, you should wear a long-sleeved shirt and sturdy pants when picking raspberries; the thorns can be quite scratchy, and often you'll find nettles growing in among the raspberries.

SPECIAL CONSIDERATIONS

If you're picking raspberry leaves to use as tea, harvest only fresh, sound specimens. Wilted leaves may contain an undesirable fungus.

MORE ABOUT RASPBERRIES: Next time you're out walking in the woods in the summer, watch for a flash of red along the edges of the path; you may discover a small patch of raspberries where you had not expected them. I often find raspberries while I am out looking for a different plant; I've found them growing around the feet of an elderberry tree I stopped to inspect, as well as in a patch of nettles I was picking. I'm always glad to find them; few wild foods provide such a sweet treat to enjoy on the spot.

Like wild blueberries, wild raspberries are generally much smaller than their domestic counterparts. The best wild raspberries also have much more flavor than domestic berries, but this can vary from plant to plant. Black raspberries are considered by many to be among the most flavorful of the wild berries, and make outstanding jam or jelly as well as a variety of desserts. They do have more seeds than red raspberries, and are often less juicy.

Plan on using your raspberries within a day or so of picking, as they are quick to mold. If you've picked more than you can use, freeze them. I like to arrange them in a single layer on a baking sheet and let them freeze; then I pour them into plastic freezer containers for storage. Frozen raspberries get soft when they're thawed, but they work just fine for jam, jelly or baking.

Tea made from the leaves of the red raspberry plant has been used medicinally for generations.

It's said to help relieve morning sickness and nausea during pregnancy, to help in breast milk production, and to act as a general uterine toner. To prepare, heat 1 cup of water to boiling. Remove from the heat, then add 2 teaspoons crumbled dried leaves (or to taste). Stir and let stand for 10 minutes before straining.

How to make raspberry juice: Place raspberries in a heavy-bottomed saucepan. Add a small amount of water, about ½ cup per quart of berries. Crush the fruit with a potato masher to start the juices flowing. Heat over medium heat until simmering, stirring constantly. Reduce heat to low; cover the saucepan and simmer for 10 minutes. Remove from heat and set aside until cool enough to handle, then strain through several layers of dampened cheesecloth. A quart of red raspberries will yield just under 2 cups of juice; with black raspberries, expect about 1½ cups of juice per quart.

QUICK IDEAS FOR USING RASPBERRIES
- Purée raspberries in a food processor or blender; strain out seeds if you wish, sweeten to taste and serve the purée over ice cream or cake.
- Sprinkle raspberries over cold cereal; the combination is really special.
- Pile raspberries in a bowl and top with milk (or cream) and sugar, then devour. This is especially good with black raspberries.

OTHER RECIPES IN THIS BOOK FEATURING RASPBERRIES
- Dandelion Rosé Wine (page 53)
- As substitute in Blueberries with Cinnamon Croutons and Custard (page 100)
- Wild Berry Syrup (page 111)
- As substitute in Gooseberry Crisp (page 173)
- Refrigerator Cookies with Dried Berries (page 235)
- English Trifle Pudding (page 238)
- Raspberry Jelly (chart, page 255)
- Uncooked Raspberry Jam (chart, page 256)
- Wild Berry-Yogurt Popsicles or Soft-Serve Ice Cream (page 259)
- Wild Berry Parfait with Maypop or Lemon Mousse (page 262)

Raspberry Swirl Cheesecake

8 to 12 servings   Preparation: Over an hour, plus overnight refrigeration

Crust:

1¼ cups vanilla wafer cookie crumbs
    (about 40 wafers)
¼ cup (half of a stick) unsalted butter,
    melted

Raspberry purée:

3 cups red or black raspberries
¾ cup water
½ cup sugar
2 teaspoons lemon juice

Filling:

2 pounds cream cheese, room temperature
1¼ cups sugar
2 teaspoons vanilla extract
4 eggs, room temperature
1 pint sour cream, room temperature

Prepare the crust: Heat oven to 350°F. Lightly grease 9-inch springform pan; set aside. Place vanilla wafer crumbs in mixing bowl. Add melted butter in a thin stream, stirring constantly to mix evenly. Press mixture into bottom (not sides) of prepared pan. Bake until crust is firm and beginning to brown, about 12 minutes. Remove from oven and set aside to cool completely. This may be prepared earlier in the day, or just before you assemble the cheesecake.

Prepare the raspberry purée: In heavy-bottomed saucepan, combine raspberries, water and sugar. Heat to boiling, stirring constantly until sugar dissolves. Adjust heat so mixture boils gently; cook for 5 minutes. Remove from heat and let stand until mixture has cooled somewhat, about 10 minutes. Pour into wire-mesh strainer that has been set over a clean bowl. Stir with wooden spoon, pressing down to extract as much purée as possible. Add lemon juice to purée. This may be prepared in advance; cover and refrigerate if made more than an hour in advance.

For the cheesecake: Heat oven to 275°F (or reduce the heat if you've just prepared the crust). In large mixing bowl, beat cream cheese with electric mixer until smooth. Add sugar and vanilla, and beat until mixed, scraping bowl occasionally. Add eggs 1 at a time, beating well after each addition. Add sour cream and beat well, scraping bowl several times. Pour half of the filling into crust-lined pan. Spoon half of the raspberry purée over filling in a random arrangement of dollops. Top with half of the remaining filling; dot with remaining purée. Top with remaining filling mixture. With blunt knife, cut through batter in swirling motion to distribute filling; don't cut all the way to the bottom or you will disturb the crust.

Place pan on baking sheet; bake in lower third of oven for 1 hour. Without removing cheesecake, turn oven off; let cheesecake sit in oven for 1 hour longer. Transfer cake to rack and allow to cool to room temperature. Cover and refrigerate overnight before unmolding and serving.

Berry Pie with Soda-Cracker Crust

6 servings

With its easy-to-make soda-cracker crust and the crumbly cracker topping, this is something like a cross between a pie and a fruit crisp.

2½ cups red raspberries, black raspberries
  or wild blackberries, or a mix
⅔ cup sugar, approximate
¼ cup freshly squeezed lime or lemon
  juice
2 tablespoons cornstarch

Crust:
3 ounces soda crackers (saltines),
  approximate
1 cup all-purpose flour
⅔ cup sugar
¼ teaspoon baking soda
½ cup (1 stick) butter, melted

Heat oven to 375°F; position oven rack in bottom third of oven. In saucepan, stir together berries, sugar and lime juice (if berries are very sweet, use a bit less sugar; if somewhat tart, use a bit more). Heat to boiling over medium heat, stirring occasionally. Cook berries for about 5 minutes, stirring frequently. Meanwhile, blend cornstarch with 2 tablespoons cold water in small bowl. When berries have softened and released their juices, stir in cornstarch, a little at a time, and continue cooking until mixture thickens and becomes glossy. (Depending on the juiciness of the berries, you may not need all of the cornstarch.) Remove from heat.

To prepare crust: Crush soda crackers in food processor, blender, or in plastic bag with rolling pin until texture is like rolled oatmeal. Crush enough to measure 1 cup; transfer to mixing bowl. Add flour, sugar and baking soda; stir with fork to mix well. Pour butter into mixture in thin stream, stirring constantly with fork. Continue stirring until well incorporated. Pour about half—or a bit more—of the mixture into 9-inch pie plate. Press firmly with fingertips into bottom and up the sides, almost but not quite to the top.

Scrape berry mixture into crust. Sprinkle remaining crust mixture over the berries; do not press down. Bake until top is nicely browned and bits of filling bubble up in spots, about 30 minutes. Cool slightly or completely before serving.

Easy Raspberry Trifle Loaf

8 servings   Preparation: Under 30 minutes (custard must be made in advance)

1 quart fresh red or black raspberries
2 tablespoons sugar
¼ cup raspberry or other jam
¼ cup cream sherry

1 purchased (or homemade) sponge cake loaf
1 package custard mix, prepared and
    chilled according to package directions
Whipped cream for garnish, optional

In mixing bowl, combine raspberries and sugar, stirring gently to coat. Let stand while you prepare the other ingredients. In small saucepan, stir together jam and sherry. Heat over medium heat, stirring constantly, until just simmering; remove from heat. Slice sponge cake loaf into 3 horizontal layers (cutting parallel with worksurface).

To assemble trifle, place bottom layer of cake on serving platter. Spoon one-third of the jam mixture evenly over cake. Top with half of the custard, spreading evenly. Top custard with a third of the berries. Place middle layer of cake over berry layer. Spoon half of the remaining jam mixture over cake layer. Top with remaining custard. Top with half of the remaining berries. Place top layer of sponge cake over berry layer. Spoon remaining jam mixture evenly over cake. Spoon any juices from the berries over cake. Cover and refrigerate for 30 minutes to 1 hour; cover and refrigerate remaining berries as well. To serve, cut slices and place on individual serving plates. Top with remaining berries and any accumulated juices; garnish with whipped cream if you like.

Wild Berry Vinegar

1 quart   Preparation: Under 15 minutes, plus 1 week standing time

Use in salad dressings, or in marinades for poultry, meat or fish. This makes a lovely gift.

1 pint raspberries, blackberries, strawberries,   1 quart white wine vinegar
    elderberries or highbush cranberries

You'll need a jar that holds at least 2 quarts for this; a glass canister such as the type used for storing flour works well. Wash jar and lid very well. Fill with hot water and add a few drops of bleach; swish around, then let stand for a few minutes. Drain and rinse very thoroughly to remove any traces of bleach. Add berries to cleaned jar. In medium saucepan, heat vinegar over low heat until it just begins to steam; don't let vinegar boil. Pour warm vinegar over berries in jar. Let stand until cooled to room temperature, then seal jar and shake gently. Set jar in dark, cool place for 1 week, shaking jar occasionally. Strain through a sieve lined with a coffee filter into clean 1-quart measure; discard berries. Pour into clean pint jars, or a single quart jar. The vinegar will keep, at room temperature, for at least 6 months.

For a more decorative presentation, spear a few fresh raspberries and a curl of lemon zest on a wooden skewer; place skewer in storage jar before adding strained, finished vinegar to jar.

Serviceberries (Amelanchier spp.)

Found throughout out region, the serviceberry is versatile and delicious, and was very important to the diet of native peoples. Easy to harvest in quantity, but be sure to leave enough for the wildlife that depends on it for winter forage.

HABITAT, RANGE

Serviceberries—also called juneberries, shadberries or sarvisberries—are found throughout our region in thickets and open forests, on ridgetops and rocky slopes, along rivers and ponds, and in forest openings. Downy or common serviceberries (*Amelanchier arborea*) are the most common serviceberry found in our region. They grow in the eastern half of Minnesota and a narrow strip of eastern Iowa; from there, their range continues south and east all the way to the Atlantic. The Saskatoon serviceberry (*A. alnifolia*) is a more western species; it's often called Western serviceberry. Its range begins in the western half of Minnesota, and extends to the West coast. The roundleaf serviceberry (*A. sanguinea*) is fairly uncommon; in our region it appears only in northeastern Minnesota, far northern Wisconsin, and the upper part of Michigan (including the Upper Peninsula). The inland serviceberry (*A. interior*) is even less common, appearing primarily in northeastern Minnesota and a few spots on the Minnesota-Wisconsin border.

PARTS USED

Ripe fruit, raw or cooked

SEASONS

Early to late summer

IDENTIFICATION TIPS, DANGEROUS LOOKALIKES

Serviceberries are a large shrub or small tree, usually head-high or shorter but occasionally as tall as 35 feet. They resemble members of the *Prunus* family (cherries and plums; page 102); both have simple, oval leaves that are finely toothed and grow alternately on the branches. The bark is slightly different, however; serviceberries have grayish bark that is often blotchy with vertical striations, becoming cracked and scaly on older specimens; it lacks the breathing pores (lenticels) of the *Prunus* species. Serviceberry twigs are reddish brown and noticeably pointed; the leaves are about 2 inches long and may be slightly hairy, especially when young. See harvesting tips, below, for a description of serviceberry flowers.

Roundleaf serviceberry

Roundleaf serviceberry

The fruits of serviceberries are *pomes*, apple-like fruits containing many seeds, while cherries and plums are *drupes*, fruits that contain a single seed. Serviceberry fruits also bear a crown, a remnant of the blossom at the bottom of the berry, and the fruit usually has a dusty finish. Cherries are smooth and shiny, and have no crown. Plums have a dusty finish but no crown; plums are also larger than serviceberries, and have a noticeable vertical cleft in the fruit.

You may confuse serviceberries with crabapples; the plants and fruits are similar in general appearance, but serviceberry fruits are much smaller—usually ¼ to ⅜ inch across, while crabapples are ⅜ to 2 inches across. Crabapples tend to ripen a bit later, although there will probably still be ripe serviceberries on the plants when crabapples are ripe. Hawthorns (*Crataegus* spp.) have similar fruits as well, although they tend to be more oval than round like the serviceberry; also, hawthorns are armed with thorns, which are completely lacking on the serviceberry. Since all of these fruits are edible, it would not be a tragic mistake if you confused them with serviceberries. Note that occasionally, you might find a serviceberry shrub with fruits that don't taste very good; simply pass it by. No fruits that carry a crown on the bottom are toxic, so you don't have to worry about getting sick from sampling these fruits.

Serviceberry fruits are green when immature, turning red and finally purple when ripe; they persist on the shrubs through the winter if they're not eaten first by hungry birds and other woodland critters.

HARVESTING TIPS

I think the best time to locate stands of serviceberry is in the spring, when they are flowering. This takes place in late April or early May in our region. If you're out gathering fiddleheads or ramps in late spring, look for shrubs with clusters of white flowers having 5 white, strap-like petals. The flowers often appear on the shrubs before the leaves, and the forest is pretty sparse at this time, so the flowers are quite noticeable. These are likely to be serviceberry flowers, so make a note of the location and return in late June or July to look for ripe fruits. Serviceberries bear for a month or longer, although the fruit is often devoured by wildlife as soon as it is ripe.

MORE ABOUT SERVICEBERRIES: The Saskatoon serviceberry was collected and catalogued as a useful plant by explorers Meriwether Lewis and William Clark in Oregon in the spring of 1806. Lewis and Clark were merely discovering for themselves something the Native Americans had known about long before—that serviceberries produce an excellent fruit with a variety of uses. In the early days, serviceberries were apparently more common than they are today; the plants are subject to a variety of diseases and pests, the latter including increased encroachment by human habitation.

I seem to find most serviceberries when I am not looking for them. This is probably because they don't grow in the areas I forage the most; rather, I find them when I am up hiking or fishing on Minnesota's North Shore, scouting for asparagus in North and South Dakota, or rambling through the woods in Wisconsin. But if you are in the areas where serviceberries are found, you should be able to harvest a good quantity of this delicious fruit.

Serviceberry fruits are easy to process; just dump them into a sinkful of cold water, remove any lingering stems, and drain the fruit. Each fruit has several small seeds. They're soft enough to chew and have an agreeable enough flavor; however, you may want to cook the fruits and strain out the seeds for the best texture in sauces and baked goods.

Serviceberries are an important food for wildlife; they're eaten by birds including waxwings, robins, magpies and grosbeaks, and mammals such as bears, deer, raccoon and even coyotes. Be sure to harvest only a reasonable amount of fruits so you don't deprive these animals of an important source of winter forage. If you have more serviceberries than you can use, simply freeze on a baking sheet, then pack the frozen fruit into heavyweight plastic bags or freezer containers; the fruit will be soft when it is thawed but will work fine for baked goods or jam.

QUICK IDEAS FOR USING SERVICEBERRIES
- Add fresh or dried serviceberries to muffins or quick breads, in the same way that you would use blueberries.
- Cook a mixture of serviceberries and apples in a small amount of water, then strain through food mill to remove seeds and skins. Sweeten to taste, and cook down to make a sauce or butter as you would with just apples.
- Cook serviceberries as directed for crabapples (page 155); use the juice to make jelly, following the instructions for blackberries in the chart on page 254.
- Apparently a decent wine can be made from serviceberries. I've never made this, but you could substitute serviceberries for currants in a standard recipe.

OTHER RECIPES IN THIS BOOK FEATURING SERVICEBERRIES
- Dried serviceberries (page 422)

Serviceberry Crumble Pie

1 pie   Preparation: About an hour

Pastry for single-crust pie
3½ to 4 cups serviceberries
2 tablespoons freshly squeezed lemon juice
¾ cup all-purpose flour, divided

½ cup white sugar
¼ teaspoon salt
½ cup (packed) dark brown sugar
¼ cup butter, melted

Heat oven to 425°F; position oven rack in bottom third of oven. Roll out pastry and fit into ungreased pie plate; trim and flute edges. Refrigerate crust while you prepare filling and topping.

In mixing bowl, combine serviceberries and lemon juice, tossing to coat berries with juice. Combine ¼ cup of the flour with the white sugar and salt in sifter or wire-mesh strainer; sift over serviceberries. Stir to coat berries with flour mixture; set aside for 10 minutes.

In second mixing bowl, stir together brown sugar and remaining ½ cup flour. Pour melted butter into mixture, stirring with fork until crumbly. Stir berry mixture, then scrape into crust. Sprinkle brown sugar mixture over the top. Bake in center of oven for 40 minutes, or until crust and topping are golden brown.

Refrigerator Cookies with Dried Berries

About 24 cookies   Preparation: 30 minutes, plus several hours chilling; 20 minutes baking

1 cup (2 sticks) unsalted butter, softened
1½ cups sugar
2 eggs
2 tablespoons cognac or brandy, or
    ½ teaspoon brandy flavoring

1 teaspoon nutmeg
3½ cups all-purpose flour, plus additional
    for rolling out dough
½ cup dried serviceberries, blueberries,
    strawberries or raspberries

In large mixing bowl, cream butter with electric mixer until light and fluffy. Add sugar; beat until fluffy. Add eggs 1 at a time, beating well after each addition. Add cognac and nutmeg; beat until smooth.

In another mixing bowl, combine flour and dried berries; stir to blend. Add flour mixture to butter mixture; stir until soft dough forms (do not overmix). Cover and refrigerate for several hours or overnight.

When you're ready to bake, heat oven to 350°F. Lightly grease baking sheets; set aside. On lightly floured board, roll out dough to ¼-inch thickness. Cut with 3-inch round cookie cutter; transfer to prepared baking sheets. Bake until lightly browned around the edges, 15 to 20 minutes. Transfer to wire rack to cool.

Strawberries (Fragaria virginiana)

Wild strawberries are the premiere wild berry. It's hard to gather enough to bring to the kitchen; enlist the help of kids, whose small fingers are perfectly adapted to picking the tiny fruit.

HABITAT, RANGE

Native wild strawberries grow throughout our area (indeed, throughout much of the United States), in open woodlands and pastures, on field borders, and along roadsides and streams. They prefer dry, sunny locations but will tolerate partial shade; I think of them as plants that thrive in poor, sandy soil.

PARTS USED

Ripe berries, raw or cooked; leaves, dried for tea

SEASONS

Fruits, late spring to early summer; leaves can be harvested all year until they are covered with snow (they remain green all winter)

IDENTIFICATION TIPS, DANGEROUS LOOKALIKES

Wild strawberries are like miniature versions of the domestic fruit, and so are easy to recognize. The plants grow as low,

Wild strawberry

creeping vines, and have a 3-part leaf on a short, hairy stem. Each leaflet is narrow at the base and widens to a rounded tip; edges are jagged. Strawberries flower in mid- to late spring; the flower has 5 rounded white petals and a yellow center, and there are usually several flowers in a cluster. Ripe fruits are bright red and soft, with the heart shape of domestic strawberries, but wild strawberries are generally only ½ inch long. Nothing else resembles a strawberry, so you can pick in safety when (if!) you're lucky enough to find a patch.

HARVESTING TIPS

The hardest part about picking wild strawberries for pie or jam is refraining from devouring them all on the spot. Wild strawberries are tiny; it can take several hundred to fill a 1-cup measure, and they're so delicious when fresh-picked that the tendency is to eat several for each one that goes in the collecting pail. They don't keep particularly well in the refrigerator, either, so you can't just keep adding to your stash until you have enough for your recipe. If you've got your heart set on a pie or some jam, plan on a full day of berrying, and enlist the help of friends. Many hands make light work when it comes to gathering wild strawberries.

Strawberries reproduce primarily by underground runners; the seeds on the berries are an additional means of reproduction. Therefore, you don't need to worry about over-harvesting strawberries. If you're picking leaves for tea, take only a single leaflet from each plant, and don't pick from every plant in a patch. Wait to pick leaves until after the plants have fruited, so the leaves can help the plant draw energy from the sun to ripen the berries.

SPECIAL CONSIDERATIONS

I often see strawberry plants growing along dusty gravel roads. Remember that the plants will pick up fumes from passing cars, so if the road is heavily travelled, you might not want to pick the berries—and in particular, the leaves, which have a more lengthy exposure to the fumes—that grow there (especially right next to the road).

MORE ABOUT STRAWBERRIES: Strawberries are probably the wild fruit that is least likely to be used in jam or desserts, simply because it's difficult to pick enough of the tiny berries to do the job. They're also one of the best wild fruits to eat fresh and raw, and that is, perhaps, the best use for these delicate fruits.

If you do want to make jam, you'll appreciate my small-batch method for uncooked strawberry jam. A standard strawberry jam recipe calls for a quart of berries, which is a lot of wild strawberries. The Uncooked Strawberry Jam recipe on page 256 can be made with as little as 1 cup of strawberries; as a bonus, it's easy to make because no cooking or canning is required.

Strawberry-leaf tea has lots of vitamin C, and a pleasant flavor; the leaves are also good in tea blends. To make tea from strawberry leaves alone, pour a cup of boiling water over a generous teaspoon of dried strawberry leaves; steep for 5 minutes, then strain and sweeten to taste.

QUICK IDEAS FOR USING WILD STRAWBERRIES

- For a delightful variation on blueberry pancakes, use wild strawberries instead. A few go a long way, maximizing a small harvest. For the best-looking pancakes, don't mix the berries into the batter. Make pancake batter as usual and pour a portion onto the heated griddle, then immediately scatter 8 to 12 berries over the wet batter and cook as usual.
- Top a small bowl of wild strawberries with a dollop of yogurt and a sprinkle of granola.

OTHER RECIPES IN THIS BOOK FEATURING WILD STRAWBERRIES

- As substitute in Blueberries with Cinnamon Croutons and Custard (page 100)
- Strawberry-Gooseberry Dessert Sauce (page 174)
- Wild Berry Vinegar (page 231)
- Refrigerator Cookies with Dried Berries (page 235)
- Uncooked Strawberry Jam (chart, page 256)
- Wild Berry Parfait with Maypop or Lemon Mousse (page 262)
- Dried strawberries (page 422)

English Trifle Pudding

8 servings   Preparation: Under 30 minutes, followed by 6 to 12 hours chilling

A cross between the classic Italian dessert called trifle, and the English favorite called summer pudding, this easy dessert should be prepared early in the day and refrigerated until serving time. Use any fresh berries you like, although the dessert will be prettiest if you avoid blueberries, blackberries or other blue-black fruit.

5 cups fresh wild berries: strawberries, raspberries, cloudberries etc. (all of one kind, or a mix of fruits)

1 cup sugar

½ cup marsala (sweet Italian wine) or sweet sherry; or 1 tablespoon lemon juice

1 frozen pound-cake loaf (10.75 ounces), thawed, or homemade pound-cake loaf*

Sweetened whipped cream for serving, optional

In nonreactive saucepan, combine berries, sugar and wine or lemon juice. Heat to boiling over medium-high heat. Reduce heat slightly and cook at a gentle boil for about 3 minutes. Pour into wire-mesh strainer set over bowl. Return juice to saucepan. Cook over high heat until reduced to 1½ cups, about 5 minutes. Remove from heat and set aside to cool. Meanwhile, cut pound cake into 4 horizontal layers of equal thickness; it's easiest to lay it on its side and slice down with a long bread knife. Cut 2 pieces of corrugated cardboard that are just slightly smaller than the inside top of an 8½ x 4½ x 2½-inch loaf pan; tape edges together. Line loaf pan with plastic wrap.

When berry juice has cooled to warm room temperature, pour about ½ cup into the lined loaf pan. Top with the bottom layer of the pound cake, placing the cut side down in the juice. Top with one-third of the berries and one-third of the remaining juice. Continue layering, pressing each slightly, until all the berries, juice and pound cake have been used; the top layer will be pound cake. Press down gently but firmly on the top layer. Place a piece of plastic wrap over the top. Place the packed loaf pan into a baking dish (to catch any juices). Lay the corrugated cardboard over the top layer of pound cake. Place the baking dish with the loaf pan into the refrigerator, and weight the top with several large cans of vegetables or with a clean brick. Refrigerate for at least 6 hours, or as long as 12 hours. To serve, remove the top layer of plastic wrap, then place a serving plate upside-down on top of the loaf pan. Quickly but carefully invert the plate and loaf pan. Remove the loaf pan and plastic wrap. Slice the dessert into 8 pieces, and top each serving with whipped cream if you like.

*If you are using a homemade pound cake and it comes over the top of the pan, slice it into 5 layers rather than 4. Use the 5th layer for another purpose rather than using it in the dessert; otherwise, the loaf pan will be too full.

Strawberry-Rhubarb Pie

1 pie   Preparation: About an hour

Since this pie uses just 1 cup of strawberries, it allows you to turn a small harvest into something that will delight a few of your closest friends.

1½ cups sugar

3 tablespoons quick-cooking tapioca

¼ teaspoon nutmeg

¼ teaspoon salt

1 pound rhubarb, cut into ½-inch pieces
   (about 3 cups)

1 cup whole wild strawberries

Pastry for double-crust pie, divided into
   2 equal portions

1 tablespoon butter, cut into small pieces

Heat oven to 400°F; position oven rack in bottom third of oven. In mixing bowl, combine sugar, tapioca, nutmeg and salt; stir to combine. Add rhubarb and strawberries, stirring to coat. Let stand for 20 minutes. Meanwhile, roll out 1 portion of pastry and fit into ungreased pie plate. Scrape rhubarb mixture into pie plate, mounding slightly. Dot with butter. Roll out remaining crust. Moisten edges of crust in pie plate, then top with rolled-out crust (or, if you prefer, make a lattice top; see page 151). Seal, trim and flute edges. Cut 6 slits about an inch long in top crust for ventilation. Place pie on baking sheet (to catch drips). Bake until crust is golden and filling bubbles through slits, 35 to 45 minutes. Transfer to rack to cool.

Strawberry Dip

About 2 cups   Preparation: Under 15 minutes, plus 2 hours chilling

Serve this as part of a brunch buffet, or with cookies and tea for a mid-afternoon snack. Use any or all of the dippers; have a pretty jar filled with toothpicks on hand for the pineapples and pound cake, if using.

16 ounces cream cheese, softened
   (reduced-fat works fine)

½ cup wild strawberries

¼ cup sour cream (reduced-fat works fine)

2 tablespoons honey

1 teaspoon vanilla extract

A few drops of orange extract or ¼
   teaspoon grated orange zest, optional

Dippers for serving: Pineapple chunks,
   pound cake cubes, vanilla wafers, pieces
   of chocolate bars, or assorted cookies

In food processor, combine all ingredients except dippers; process until smooth. Scrape into serving bowl. Cover and refrigerate for at least 2 hours before serving.

Wild Roses (Rosa spp.)

Packed with vitamin C, rose hips have a tart flavor that is welcome in tea blends as well as jams and desserts.

HABITAT, RANGE

There are dozens of varieties of wild roses, and they are found in one form or another throughout our region. Wild roses prefer sunny areas, and are found in pastures, along fencelines and road ditches, near swamps and small ponds, on sand dunes and at the edges of shelterbelts.

PARTS USED

Petals, hips

SEASONS

Early summer (petals); early fall through winter (hips)

Pasture rose

IDENTIFICATION TIPS, DANGEROUS LOOKALIKES

Roses are so familiar that a brief description will suffice. Wild roses grow as small shrubs or rambling vines, often in tangles containing many plants. The stems are well-armed with thorns or bristles, and are often reddish. Leaves are toothed and pinnately compound, similar to sumac or walnuts; each compound branchlet has 3 or more pairs of opposite leaves and a terminal leaf at the end of the branchlet. The branchlets grow alternately

Wild rose hips

on the main branches of the plant. Flowers grow at the end of separate stemlets; there may be several flowers on each stemlet. Rose flowers have 5 petals, with colors ranging from white to yellow to pale pink to deep rose-pink; the center of the flower has numerous small, thin stamens and pistils. When the petals drop, the central bud begins to swell, developing into the fruit we call a hip. Ripe hips are deep orange or red, depending on the variety, and can range from pea-sized to an inch in diameter. Hips have a prominent blossom remnant at the bottom; the interior is somewhat mealy, with numerous bitter white seeds. All wild roses produce edible petals and hips, although the flavor varies quite a bit between the species and even from plant to plant. There are no similar-looking plants that could be confused with wild roses.

HARVESTING TIPS

Gather petals on a sunny morning, when the flowers are open and the morning dew has dried off; if you wait until the afternoon, the sun's heat may have dissipated much of the fragrance. Plants with the most fragrance will yield the best, most fragrant petals. Remember that if you pull off the entire flower, there will be no hip later in the season; you may want to pull off just the petals, leaving the central bud on the plant.

Rose hips are best harvested when deeply colored and slightly soft but not mushy; many harvesters wait until after the first frost. To harvest hips, simply pull them sharply from the plant; hold the stem steady with your other hand (but watch for the thorns). The hips persist on the plants through the winter, unless they are eaten first; snowshoers may be able to harvest hips if the plants aren't completely covered with snow.

SPECIAL CONSIDERATIONS

It may be tempting to try making edible products from your garden roses, but before you do, consider what chemicals might be in the plant. If you've sprayed your roses, don't use the petals or fruit. Even if you don't spray, be aware that the nursery from which you purchased the rose probably has used chemicals that linger in the plant's system for years.

MORE ABOUT WILD ROSES: Wild roses are one of nature's loveliest plants; they are so well-loved that the wild rose is the state flower in both Iowa and North Dakota. Although rose petals have their place in the kitchen, it is the hips that most foragers are interested in. Hips have so much vitamin C that they are used in the manufacture of some vitamin C capsules. Picking hips is an activity that the whole family will enjoy in the fall, whether this involves driving into the country or heading out the door of the cabin.

Rose hips have a tart flavor; many compare it to persimmons. The flavor of hips does vary from species to species; some foragers mix hips from several species when preparing tea, for a more complex taste.

Petals are used to make jams and syrups, or, more commonly, are used sparingly to decorate salads and other foods. The inner end of the petal is bitter; use a scissors to snip off this white area before cooking or serving the petals. Rose petals don't keep well, and should be used the same day they are gathered.

Hips are cooked to make sauce, jelly and jam, and are frequently dried to use as tea. The blossom remnants at the bottom should be removed; I use my thumbnail to pinch these off as I am washing the hips, but a small scissors does the job as well. The seeds inside the hips are bitter, and should be removed before making tea blends. If you're cooking the hips to turn into a sauce or jam, the seeds will be strained out during the preparation.

How to dry rose hips: Most people remove the seeds from rose hips before drying, although you may wish to try a batch with the seeds left in. To remove the seeds, cut one hip in half from top to bottom; if you can easily remove the seeds, go ahead and process all remaining hips in this fashion, also removing the blossom remnants at the bottom. If the pulp is too sticky to remove the seeds easily, let the whole hips dry at room temperature for a few days, then try again. Don't let them get too dry, or the seeds will be even more difficult to remove. Dry split hips at room temperature on a screen laid over a baking sheet, turning daily; or, dry in food dehydrator or 150°F oven for about 5 hours (see pages 420-422 for more information on dehydrating). Store dried hips in tightly sealed glass jars in a dark location.

How to dry rose petals: Please see pages 420-422 for more information on dehydrating. If you'll be eating the dried petals, snip off the white core of the petals; if you're using the petals for a potpourri or the Bath Bubble Bag at right, you needn't bother with this step. Spread petals on dehydrator screen, or on screen placed over a baking sheet. Dehydrate at lowest temperature possible; higher temperatures will cause the petals to lose their fragrance and turn brown. Drying time will be 1 to 2 hours.

JUST FOR FUN
Rose Petal Bath Bubble Bag
Make small bags (about 3 inches square) from muslin cloth. Use a box grater to grate a bar of Ivory or other simple soap. In a mixing bowl, combine 1 cup oatmeal, 1 cup dried rose petals, and ⅔ cup of the grated soap. Fill the muslin bags loosely with the mixture; sew the ends shut. Use as a washcloth in the shower.

QUICK IDEAS FOR USING ROSE PETALS
- Sprinkle a few over the top of a salad (be sure to cut away the bitter white base of the petals first).
- Make candied rose petals, following the instructions for Candied Violets (page 332). Use to garnish cakes, muffins, pudding and other desserts.
- Add a small handful of rose petals (white bases removed) to muffins or quick bread.

OTHER RECIPES IN THIS BOOK FEATURING WILD ROSES
- Salade Sauvage (page 54)
- Wild Fruit Gels (page 260)
- Wildflower Bath Tea (page 330)
- Substitute rose petals for the violets in Violet Syrup (page 331)
- Wild Potpourri (page 415)

Autumn Sunshine Jam

3 half-pints

This smoothly textured jam has an appealing, golden-rose color that will remind you of autumn leaves even in the middle of winter.

2 cups husked, washed ripe ground cherries
2 cups rose hips (measured after removing stems and blossom ends)
1 cup water
3 half-pint canning jars, with bands and new lids

About ¼ cup smooth applesauce
One-third of a 1.75-ounce box powdered pectin*
2 cups sugar

Combine ground cherries, rose hips and water in saucepan. Heat to boiling over high heat. Reduce heat so mixture bubbles gently; cover and cook for 25 minutes. Meanwhile, prepare jars, bands and lids as described on page 418; if you are unfamiliar with canning procedures, also read the canning information on that page.

Check fruits after they've cooked for 25 minutes; the rose hips should be soft (if not, continue cooking a bit longer). Place wire-mesh strainer over a bowl, and pour cooked fruit mixture into strainer. Stir with wooden spoon, pressing fairly hard, to push pulp through strainer. Scrape pulp from outside of strainer into bowl, then discard seeds and skin.

Measure pulp and juice, adding applesauce if needed to equal 2 cups. In heavy-bottomed saucepan, combine fruit mixture and pectin; stir with whisk to blend in the pectin. Heat to boiling over high heat, stirring frequently, until mixture comes to a hard boil that can't be stirred down. Add sugar in gradual stream, stirring constantly. Continue cooking until the mixture again comes to a hard boil, then begin timing. Boil for 2 minutes, stirring constantly. Remove from heat. Stir for about a minute to settle the foam, then skim off and discard any remaining foam. Ladle into prepared jars, leaving ½ inch headspace. Seal with prepared lids and bands. Process in boiling-water bath for 5 minutes. Remove from boiling water and set aside to cool for several hours. At this point, you can shake the jars to distribute the ground-cherry seeds throughout the jam (otherwise, they will float in a layer on top of the jam).

*See page 254 for information on dividing powdered pectin.

Rose Hip-Peach Tart with Cornmeal Crust

6 servings Preparation: Over an hour

Substitute pears or apples for the peaches, if you like. Although this recipe looks quite complicated, it really goes together easily, and the finished tart is gorgeous. For an easier version, substitute purchased pie crust for the version given here.

Rose hip mixture:
2 cups fresh rose hips (about 4½ ounces)
1 Granny Smith apple (about 8 ounces),
    cut into 1-inch pieces
½ cup water
1 tablespoon sugar

Cornmeal crust:
1 cup all-purpose flour, plus additional for
    rolling out pastry
2 tablespoons cornmeal

1 tablespoon sugar
½ teaspoon salt
½ cup (1 stick) unsalted butter, very cold,
    cut into ¼-inch slices
Ice water as needed (about 3 tablespoons)

Dried beans or pie weights for pre-baking
    crust
3 medium peaches (about 1¼ pounds)
1 tablespoon rum (substitute fruit juice or
    water if you prefer)

Remove and discard blossom remnants, and any stems, from the hips. Combine hips with apple, water and sugar in medium saucepan. Heat just to boiling over medium-high heat. Adjust heat to a strong simmer; cover and cook for 25 minutes, stirring occasionally.

While rose hip mixture is cooking, prepare crust: In food processor, combine flour, cornmeal, sugar and salt; pulse a few times to blend. Add butter; pulse until mixture resembles coarse cornmeal (but don't over-process, or the pastry will be tough). With machine running, add water through the feed tube until mixture begins to clump. Turn processor off immediately. Pinch a bit of the dough with your fingertips; if it holds together, you've added enough water. If the mixture won't hold together, turn machine back on and add a bit more water. Pour mixture into plastic bag (it will be crumbly); press from the outside to form a ball. Flatten into a disk. Place in freezer for 10 minutes, or refrigerate for at least 30 minutes.

When rose hip mixture has cooked for 25 minutes, remove from heat and set aside to cool a bit; meanwhile, heat oven to 375°F; position oven rack in bottom third of oven. Process cooled fruit with food mill or cone-shaped colander (page 253), or press through wire-mesh strainer with a wooden spoon; set aside.

Roll out pie crust and fit into 9-inch quiche pan. Line crust with foil, pressing well into corners; fill with dried beans or pie weights. Bake for 10 minutes. Remove foil and beans carefully, then return crust to oven and bake for 5 to 10 minutes longer, until beginning to crisp and color. Remove from oven and set aside to cool slightly.

Peel peaches by dipping in boiling water and then refreshing in cold water; the skins will slip off easily. Cut in half, removing pits. Slice peaches into ¼-inch-thick crescents. Reserve 3 tablespoons of the rose hip purée; spread remainder evenly in bottom of pre-baked crust. Arrange peaches in a fan around the outer edge of filled crust, laying them flat and overlapping slightly. Create a second fan of peaches inside the first. Bake for 45 minutes. Near the end of baking time, combine rum with reserved 3 tablespoons rose hip purée. Remove tart from oven; turn oven to broil and/or 550°F. Use soft pastry brush to brush rum-purée mixture over peaches. Return tart to oven (if using broiler, rack should be 6 to 8 inches from heat element) and bake for a few minutes longer, until topping colors a bit. Serve warm or at room temperature. This is best on the first day it is made, as the crust gets soggy quite quickly. If you do have leftovers, wrap them well and store in the refrigerator.

Spiced Rose Hip Tea

4 servings   Preparation: Under 30 minutes

1 quart plus ½ cup water
3 whole cloves
1 cardamom pod, split open
1 whole cinnamon stick

A piece of lemon zest, about 1 x ½ inch
3 tablespoons dried rose hips
Honey or sugar to taste

In saucepan, combine water, cloves, cardamom pod and seeds, cinnamon stick and lemon zest. Heat to boiling over high heat. Reduce heat and simmer for 10 minutes. Add rose hips; remove from heat and let steep for 5 to 10 minutes longer. Strain into individual cups, or into preheated teapot. Serve with honey or sugar so each person can sweeten their tea to taste.

Rosy Applesauce

About 2 cups   Preparation: Under an hour

Use apples from abandoned orchards, or store-bought Granny Smith apples, for this lovely sauce. Serve it as you would applesauce: with pork roasts, on top of pound cake, stirred into hot breakfast cereal, or as a side dish.

3 to 4 cups fresh rose hips (7 to 9 ounces)
1 pound Granny Smith or other apples,
   cut into 1-inch pieces

1 cup water
¼ cup sugar
1 whole cinnamon stick, optional

Remove and discard blossom remnants, and any stems, from the hips. Combine hips and remaining ingredients in heavy-bottomed saucepan. Heat just to boiling over medium-high heat. Adjust heat to a strong simmer; cover and cook for 25 minutes, stirring occasionally. Remove from heat and set aside to cool a bit. Remove cinnamon stick if used; process fruit mixture with food mill or cone-shaped colander (page 253), or press through wire-mesh strainer with a wooden spoon. Serve warm, room temperature or cold; refrigerate leftovers.

Minor Fruits

This section is sort of a catch-all for some of the fruits that grow only in small parts of our region, or are of limited use but still worth discussing. Each fruit has some basic information, followed by suggestions for use and a recipe.

Hackberries (Celtis occidentalis)

Hackberries grow throughout our range. This tall tree is a member of the elm family, and has distinctive, warty bark with prominent ridges. The leaves are 2 to 3 inches long, shiny green on top and lighter underneath; they come to a sharp point and have toothed margins. In late summer, the trees produce numerous small fruits, about the size of a coffee bean and orange to purplish brown. Look for the trees along streambanks and in valleys; it is commonly planted as a curbside tree in cities, and so is within reach of most urban foragers.

For such a common wild fruit, hackberries have surprisingly few references in the standard wild-foods texts. Perhaps it is because the berry—actually a drupe—has very little flesh in proportion to its pit, and the flesh that does cling to the pit is rather dry. But the flavor is outstanding and, unlike many stone fruits such as cherries, hackberries have a pit that is entirely edible with the proper preparation. I've seen a few references to hackberries that call them sugarberries, and it's an apt name; the fruit is quite sweet, with an almost date-like flavor.

Hackberry fruit and leaves

The few references I found while researching this humble fruit stated that it is used primarily as a trail nibble; I also found several mentions of native peoples drying the fruits whole and then crushing them to use as a seasoning for venison. One source stated that the fruit could be crushed, pits and all, to use in jam making, but gave no more specifics. It further stated that if one were to remove the covering of the pit, the center was tasty, with a date-like flavor. (Unfortunately, it gave no clue as to how to remove the covering!)

Because the trees can grow quite tall—as much as 100 feet in height—it can be difficult to reach the hanging fruits. If you're lucky, you may be able to find a tree growing at the foot of a hilly streambank, and you'll be able to get at the fruits by using the hill to your advantage.

Squirrels seem to love hackberries, and in fact, I sometimes first discover a hackberry tree after noticing squirrels' amusing antics as they work to get at the fruit hanging on light-weight branches. Because so many of the fruits are so high up, and because the tree usually has lots of fruit, over-harvesting is not a concern. Also, no one else is typically picking them, so your only competition will probably be the squirrels. The berries seem to me to get sweeter after a frost, and can be picked through late fall.

Pillow Cookies with Hackberry Filling

About 30 cookies   Preparation: Over an hour

The pits of hackberries are edible, but are very crunchy even when crushed. It is an odd sensation to encounter in a cookie—not unpleasant, just unexpected, rather like finding a piece of eggshell that got into the dough. But unlike the eggshell, the pieces of hackberry pit can be chewed and swallowed.

Filling:
⅔ cup hackberry fruits, stems removed
⅓ cup sugar
½ cup water
½ cup chopped pecans or other nuts

Dough:
½ cup (1 stick) butter, softened

½ cup (packed) brown sugar
½ cup white sugar
1 egg
1 teaspoon lemon extract, orange extract or vanilla extract
½ teaspoon baking soda
½ teaspoon salt
2 cups all-purpose flour

Prepare filling: Pound hackberries with mortar and pestle until pits are pulverized; for the least crunchy filling, pound until berries are a smooth paste. (Tip: It's easiest to work in small batches of a tablespoon or two at a time; this way, no large chunks of pit will escape your notice. Scrape pounded fruit into a small saucepan as you go, continuing until all fruit has been pounded.)

Combine pounded fruit with sugar and water in small saucepan. Heat over medium heat, stirring constantly, until boiling gently. Cook for 4 minutes or until thick, stirring constantly. Stir in pecans. Remove from heat and let cool completely before assembling the cookies.

To make dough: Cream butter in mixing bowl with electric mixer. Gradually add brown and white sugars, beating until smooth. Add egg, extract, baking soda and salt; beat well. Add flour and beat just until well mixed. If you prepare the dough right after cooking the filling, gather the dough into a ball, wrap it tightly and refrigerate until you're ready to bake. Or, simply prepare dough after the filling has cooled, and proceed immediately to baking.

When you're ready to bake, heat oven to 350°F. Spray baking sheets with nonstick spray; set aside. Roll out half of the dough about ⅛ inch thick, or just a bit thicker. Cut into 2-inch circles with a glass or cookie cutter. Place half of the circles on prepared baking sheet, allowing ½ inch between circles. Place 1 teaspoon filling mixture in center of each circle, keeping it away from edges. Place a second circle of dough over each mound of filling, forming it into a gentle dome shape over filling and gently pressing the edges together (they will seal together during baking, so don't worry about pressing too much). Repeat with remaining ingredients to fill the second baking sheet. Bake until golden brown, 13 to 15 minutes. Cool before serving.

Prickly Pear Fruits (Opuntia spp.)

I vividly remember the first time I encountered a prickly pear cactus in the wild. I was afield in Wyoming one fall, and suddenly came upon a herd of antelope. Not wanting to frighten them, I sat straight down, without even looking or turning for fear my movement would scatter the herd. Of course, I ended up directly on a prickly pear plant. Believe me, those antelope took off running as I leapt up yelling.

Although they do occasionally grow in Minnesota, Iowa and states east of there, prickly pear cactus is a species that prefers the arid regions of the West. They thrive on the Dakota plains, as well as states further west and south.

Prickly pear pads and fruit

Prickly pear is a low-growing cactus with thick oval-shaped pads. In late spring and early summer, each pad puts forth a brilliantly colored flower, which gives way to the barrel-shaped fruit that is sometimes called *tuna* (from the Latin name) or Indian fig. Both pads and fruits are well armed with sharp thorns that can penetrate even boot soles; some of the thorns are very fine and are virtually invisible, so it pays to treat these plants with respect.

The fleshy fruits range in color from yellow to rose-red to purple, with ruby red or golden interiors. Size ranges from an inch in length to several inches long; wild specimens are smaller than their domestic counterparts. The flesh is studded with many seeds; those in larger fruits are tough, like large blackberry seeds, and are best removed by straining before making jam, salsa etc. The fruit has a taste that reminds me of grenadine, or like cranberries without the tartness. The pads are edible, and domesticated prickly pear pads are used in Mexican and Southwest cooking, where they are called nopales (when whole) or nopalitos (when cut up).

Wear heavy leather gloves when picking the fruits or pads. I like to use tongs as an extra measure of protection when handling these prickly plants. To remove the thorns from the fruit, rub them briskly with a coarse, damp towel, then peel off the rind.

How to make prickly pear fruit juice: Peel fruits and cut in half. Place in saucepan. For each pound of fruit, add 1½ cups water. Heat to boiling, then cover and reduce heat; cook at a gentle boil until the fruit is tender, about 10 minutes. Mash fruit with a potato masher; re-cover and cook for 5 minutes longer. Line a strainer with 4 layers of cheesecloth; place over a pot that is large enough to hold the juice. Pour the pulp and juice into the strainer and allow to drip naturally; don't press on the fruit or the juice will become cloudy. The pulp will be pale and useless; discard it. A pound of fruit yields about 1½ cups of juice.

Use prickly pear fruit juice to make jelly by following the recipe for blackberry jelly on page 254. The juice can also be added to other fruit juices for a mixed-fruit beverage. It would also make an outstanding sorbet; follow the directions for Chokecherry Sorbet on page 110.

Rosy Cactus Chicken

4 servings · Preparation: Over an hour

Prepare this with small prickly pear fruits; the seeds in larger fruits can be tough. Check the seeds when you cut the fruits open, and if they seem tough, follow the alternate instructions below.

1 jalapeño pepper, stem and seeds removed	½ teaspoon dried thyme
8 ounces peeled prickly pear fruits, cut into ½-inch chunks	1 teaspoon oil
	⅓ cup diced onion
3 tablespoons seasoned rice vinegar	1 tablespoon honey
1 teaspoon salt, plus additional for seasoning chicken	⅛ teaspoon ground cumin
	4 boneless, skinless chicken breast halves

Cut pepper in half lengthwise, then cut into thin half-moon slices. Combine in medium saucepan with prickly pear, vinegar, salt and thyme. Heat to boiling over medium-high heat; reduce heat and simmer for 5 minutes. Remove from heat and cool slightly. Spoon off ¼ cup of the liquid, leaving the seeds and pulp in the pan. Set the liquid aside to cool.

Heat oil in small skillet over medium-high heat. Add onion and cook until golden brown, about 5 minutes, stirring occasionally. Transfer to pan with prickly pear; add honey and cumin. Cook over medium heat, stirring frequently, until the mixture has thickened, about 5 minutes. Transfer to serving dish and set aside to cool. This salsa can sit at room temperature for an hour or 2 before serving; for longer periods, cover and refrigerate, but bring to room temperature before serving. As soon as you're done cooking the salsa, brush cooled, reserved liquid over both sides of chicken breasts. Cover and refrigerate for at least an hour, and as long as 6 hours.

When you're ready to cook, prepare grill for medium heat. Sprinkle chicken with salt; place on grill and cook, turning several times, until just done, 10 to 15 minutes. A few minutes before chicken is done, spoon a small amount of the salsa on top of each piece, spreading salsa slightly. Serve chicken with remaining salsa.

Variation: Seed-Free Salsa

Do not add jalapeño peppers to prickly pear for initial cooking; simply cook fruit with vinegar, salt and thyme as directed. When fruit is tender, transfer to wire-mesh strainer and collect the ¼ cup juice as it drips out; set juice aside as directed. Press fruit with a spoon, forcing pulp through mesh. Discard solids in strainer. Add jalapeños to onion in skillet and cook until onion is golden brown. Combine fruit purée with onion mixture and proceed as directed.

Sumac Berries (various *Rhus* species)

Smooth sumac (*Rhus glabra*) is found throughout the United States; staghorn sumac (*R. hirta* or *R. typhina*) and winged sumac (*R. copallina*) are more eastern species, rarely

appearing west of Minnesota and Iowa. All of these sumacs are small native trees or large shrubs with long, pinnately compound leaves on soft stems; the trees spread by underground rhizomes and tend to grow in large colonies. The leaves turn brilliant red or orange in the fall, providing beautiful color to the autumn landscape. The stems and leafstalks of staghorn and winged sumac are hairy, while smooth sumac gets its name because the stems and leafstalks are free of hair. Winged sumac has wings, or flattened leafstalks, on the central rib of each compound leaf.

Staghorn sumac

Sumac can be found almost anywhere, but seem to prefer sunny fields and fencerows, disturbed areas, and waste ground. The trees produce upright fruit clusters consisting of sticky, hairy, reddish orange berries in a large cluster. On smooth sumac, the clusters are irregular and widely branching; on staghorn sumac, the clusters are neater, giving a triangular appearance; and on winged sumac, the clusters are broad and vase-shaped. Clusters of all species are roughly 3 or 4 inches long, in my experience. (**Caution:** Poisonous sumac, *R. vernix,* has drooping white berries, and sparser, more open leaves. All parts of this plant cause severe allergic reaction when touched; sensitive individuals can even be affected simply by being in proximity to the plant. Don't even go near any sumac-like plant with anything other than reddish orange berries.)

Sumac is rather a one-trick pony. The berries can be soaked to make a tart, lemony liquid that is used as a type of lemonade and is also excellent in jellies; see the chart on page 255 for Elderberry-Sumac Jelly.

It's best to harvest sumac berry clusters in late summer, while they are fully ripe but before too many autumn rains have washed away all the flavor. Check the clusters; if they are sticky and taste tart, they will have enough flavor. Use a pruning snippers to cut off the entire cluster of berries; you won't hurt the plant by doing this, as they reproduce by underground runners. You can let the clusters dry in a loosely closed paper bag, then use them in winter to make a soothing hot tea (see recipe at right). The berries have small hairs that are somewhat irritating to the throat, so whether you brew a hot or cold beverage, you should strain it through several layers of cheesecloth (or better yet, a paper coffee filter) to eliminate these hairs.

How to make sumac juice: Use fresh berry clusters that are still sticky; berries that are dry to the touch have likely had most of the flavor washed from them by rains. Place a good number of berry clusters—15 or 20, perhaps—in a soup pot or plastic bucket, then add cold water just to cover. Squeeze the berries with your hands, and rub them up and down along the sides of the pot as though scrubbing on a washboard. Do this for a few minutes, then let the mixture stand for a few minutes and repeat. I usually let them soak for 10 to 20 minutes after that; I want to extract as much flavor as possible. Strain the mixture through a wire-mesh strainer, then again through layers of cheesecloth or a paper coffee filter. Sweeten to taste, and serve cold as a lemonade-type beverage.

For stronger sumac juice, you can reduce it to approximately half-volume by cooking (however, you are eliminating much of the vitamin C by heating it). Or, add more sumac clusters to already-made sumac juice and repeat the juice-making process to get a stronger liquid.

Sumac Tea

3 servings; easily increased or decreased   Preparation: Under 30 minutes

Sumac makes a pleasant hot tea that is slightly tart with floral overtones. It's similar to chamomile tea, or to a mild version of the commercial herbal-tea blend called Red Zinger. If you want iced tea, chill the brewed tea for an hour before serving (the iced tea is best served the day it is made). I like hot sumac tea unsweetened, but you can add sugar or honey to taste if you prefer; iced tea tastes better if sweetened lightly.

4 good-sized sumac clusters	**Honey or sugar to taste, optional**
4 cups water	

Rinse the sumac clusters briefly, and set aside to drain. Heat water to boiling in saucepan; remove from heat and set aside to cool for about 5 minutes. While water is cooling, cut smaller clusters away from woody stems, discarding stems. Add clusters to hot water and let stand for 5 minutes. Use potato masher or large wooden spoon to bruise the sumac; you don't want to crack the seeds doing this, so don't use too much force. Let the stand for about 5 minutes longer, then strain through damp tea towel or several layers of cheesecloth. Serve warm or cold, adding sugar to taste if desired.

Variation: Sumac-Mint Tea
Add a few fresh mint leaves to the hot water with the sumac.

General Fruit Recipes

Information on juicing, jam- and jelly-making, and recipes that work for most fruits.

How to make juice from wild fruits

Chokecherries are used in these instructions because they are abundant and commonly juiced. Follow these instructions for any wild fruit; note that some fruits require less water or a different amount of cooking time (see the listing for each specific fruit). Instructions are given for 4 cups of chokecherries; for a larger batch, simply increase the amount of chokecherries and water proportionally. Chokecherry juice—and juice from any wild fruit—can be blended with other juices to produce interesting jellies, sorbets, syrups and the like.

For a delightful flavor variation, use champagne instead of water when cooking the fruit (use a bit more champagne than the amount of water called for, and cook the fruit uncovered to allow the alcohol to cook away). Another way to add flavor is to toss a cinnamon stick or a few whole cloves into the pot while the fruit is cooking. You could also add a few drops of a flavoring extract such as vanilla, almond or rum-butter to the juice at the same time you stir in the pectin. If you want to make jelly or jam from chokecherries, gooseberries, currants or grapes, pick a few underripe fruits. They will add not only flavor but natural pectin.

To make the juice: In heavy-bottomed nonreactive saucepan, combine 1 quart chokecherries (about 1¼ pounds) with enough water to come just below the surface of the chokecherries (about 1½ cups water). Heat to boiling. Cover and reduce heat; simmer for 30 minutes, stirring occasionally.* Remove from heat and set aside until cool enough to handle comfortably. Place a wire-mesh strainer, lined with 4 layers of dampened cheesecloth, over a bowl. Pour cooled chokecherries and juice into strainer and let drip for 20 minutes.

To make crystal-clear, sparkling jelly, simply use the juice that has dripped through. You should have about 1¼ cups juice; add a little water (or apple juice or cherry juice) if necessary to fill out the measure. For a slightly better yield of juice, squeeze the chokecherries to extract more juice. The resulting jelly will not be as clear, but the flavor will be slightly better because you probably won't have to add any water to make the measure.

For a thicker, more jam-like product, transfer the drained chokecherries to a large bowl. Add about 1 cup water, and squeeze the chokecherries well with your hands to extract more pulp. Press through a colander that has holes small enough to exclude the pits. Add the pulpy juice to the juice yielded by dripping. If you have less than 3 cups, return the chokecherries to the bowl and add a little more water. Squeeze and strain again to make the 3-cup measure.

Another option is to use a special cone-shaped colander. This old-fashioned device is similar to a food mill, but uses a wooden pestle rather than the metal paddles of a food mill. To use the cone-shaped colander, pour the cooked chokecherries and juice into a cone-shaped colander that has been set over a pot. Stir and mash with the pestle until you've extracted as much pulp as possible (you don't want to break the pits,* so don't be too vigorous). This will yield 1½ to 2 cups of thicker, richer chokecherry juice, which is perfect for jam or sorbet; it works for jelly also, but the jelly won't be as clear as that made from simple dripping.

*Don't crush chokecherries during cooking or straining. The pits of chokecherries (as well as those from apples, apricots, peaches and other cherries, wild or domestic) contain small amounts of a cyanide-forming compound that can cause illness if eaten in large quantities.

Wild Fruit Jelly and Jam

Jelly and jam are probably the most common foods made from wild fruit. They're easy to make, and the basic product is familiar to everyone. It's easy to become overrun with jelly and jam, however, especially if the recipes you have require you to make 8 jars—or more—of a specific flavor. Recipes are written this way because most require the use of commercial pectin to make the juices set. Commercial pectin is tricky to work with, and manufacturers spend a lot of time developing recipes using exact measurements to make their products work. The leaflet from a box of Sure-Jell powdered pectin shows yields ranging from 5 to 10 cups (half-pint jars)—and they're very specific in their cautions to follow the recipe exactly.

I decided to develop jelly and jam recipes that allowed me to use smaller amounts of juice. To do this, I had to measure and divide the pectin because I needed just a portion of a box for my smaller batches. The difficulty comes in trying to determine the amount of sugar and pectin to use for each type of fruit juice, because pectin-added jelly is not a one-size-fits-all formula. Some fruit juices require more sugar than others, some formulas use lemon juice, and some fruits have natural pectin, changing the ratio of juice needed for a specific amount of added pectin (less added pectin is needed per cup of juice that contains natural pectin).

In addition, smaller batches tend to lose proportionately more liquid due to evaporation than larger batches. After much experimentation, I've come up with the following charts to make small batches of jelly and jam. As with all jelly making, your results may vary slightly; even if you follow the full-batch recipe exactly as it is written in the leaflet that comes with the pectin, your results may vary because different-sized saucepans allow for more (or less) evaporation of juices, which affects final yield and firmness of the finished product.

There are two types of pectin-added products: cooked and uncooked. Most jellies and jams are cooked, but the few that can be made without cooking will have a fruitier, brighter flavor. Below is a chart for cooked jelly with pectin added, followed by a chart for uncooked jam with pectin added. Uncooked jam is sometimes known as freezer jam because it has to be stored in the refrigerator or freezer. This section finishes with information on jelly that you can make without added pectin. (Cooked-jam recipes are with each individual fruit.)

HOW TO DIVIDE POWDERED PECTIN

When you're dividing pectin, it's important to measure accurately. The best method is to weigh the contents of a full box of pectin on a gram scale (ounce scales are not detailed enough), then weigh out the portion you need. A typical 1.75-ounce box of Sure-Jell powdered pectin weighs 51 grams, so if the chart calls for ⅔ of a box, use 34 grams (51 divided by 3 is 17; multiply by 2 to get 34). If you don't have a gram scale, measure the powder very carefully with measuring spoons (scoop or spoon the powder into the measuring spoon until it is completely full and somewhat mounded, then level off the top with the back of a knife), then divide accordingly. The same box of pectin that weighs 51 grams measures 16½ teaspoons (5 tablespoons plus 1½ teaspoons), so ⅔ of a box would be 11 teaspoons (16.5 divided by 3 is 5.5; multiply by 2 to get 11).

Cooked Wild Fruit Jelly—Pectin Added

2, 4 or 6 half-pints

Fruit	Ingredient	2 half-pints (2-qt. pan)	4 half-pints (4-qt. pan)	6 half-pints (6-qt. pan)
Blackberry, Mulberry	Blackberry juice (page 144) or mulberry juice (page 201)	1½ cups	2¾ cups	4 cups
	Powdered fruit pectin	⅓ box	⅔ box	1 box
	Lemon juice	1 tablespoon	2 tablespoons	¼ cup
	Sugar	1¾ cups	3½ cups	5¼ cups
Cherry, Wild	Cherry juice (page 252)	1⅓ cups	2½ cups	3⅔ cups
	Powdered fruit pectin	⅓ box	⅔ box	1 box
	Lemon juice	1 tablespoon	2 tablespoons	3 tablespoons
	Sugar	1⅓ cups	2¾ cups	4¼ cups
Chokeberry	Chokeberry juice (page 148)	1⅓ cups	2⅓ cups	3½ cups
	Powdered fruit pectin	⅓ box	⅔ box	1 box
	Lemon juice	1 tablespoon	2 tablespoons	¼ cup
	Sugar	1¼ cups	2½ cups	4¼ cups
Chokecherry	Chokecherry juice (page 252)	1⅓ cups	2½ cups	3¾ cups
	Powdered fruit pectin	⅓ box	⅔ box	1 box
	Sugar	1⅓ cups	2¾ cups	4¼ cups

Fruit	Ingredient	2 half-pints (2-qt. pan)	4 half-pints (4-qt. pan)	6 half-pints (6-qt. pan)
Currant, Gooseberry	Currant juice (page 162) or gooseberry juice (page 172)	1⅓ cups	3 cups	4¼ cups
	Powdered fruit pectin	¼ box	⅓ box	⅔ box
	Sugar	1½ cups	3¼ cups	4⅔ cups

Juice prepared from ripe fruits. For spiced jelly, add 1 cinnamon stick and 8 cloves while cooking fruits for juice.

Fruit	Ingredient	2 half-pints (2-qt. pan)	4 half-pints (4-qt. pan)	6 half-pints (6-qt. pan)
Elderberry or Elderberry-Sumac	Elderberry or elderberry-sumac juice (page 167)	1⅓ cups	2½ cups	3¾ cups
	Powdered fruit pectin	⅓ box	⅔ box	1¼ boxes
	Lemon juice	1½ tablespoons	3 tablespoons	⅓ cup
	Sugar	1⅓ cups	2¾ cups	5½ cups
Maypop	Maypop nectar (page 190)	1½ cups	2⅔ cups	4¼ cups
	Powdered fruit pectin	⅓ box	⅔ box	1 box
	Lemon juice	1 tablespoon	2 tablespoons	¼ cup
	Sugar	1⅔ cups	3¼ cups	5 cups

For a slightly tart jelly, use a few underripe fruits when making nectar

Fruit	Ingredient	2 half-pints (2-qt. pan)	4 half-pints (4-qt. pan)	6 half-pints (6-qt. pan)
Plum	Plum juice (page 116)	1⅓ cups	2¾ cups	3¾ cups
	Powdered fruit pectin	⅓ box	½ box	¾ box
	Sugar	1⅜ cups	3¼ cups	4¼ cups
Raspberry, Black Raspberry	Raspberry juice (page 228)	1½ cups	2¾ cups	4 cups
	Powdered fruit pectin	⅓ box	⅔ box	1 box
	Sugar	1⅞ cups	3⅔ cups	5½ cups
Sweet Mountain Ash	Mountain ash juice (page 196)	1½ cups	3 cups	4 cups
	Powdered fruit pectin	⅓ box	⅔ box	1 box
	Sugar	2 cups	4½ cups	6¾ cups

See page 198 for Tart Mountain Ash Jelly

Instructions: Prepare jars, bands and lids as described on page 418. Combine juice, pectin, and lemon juice if used, in nonreactive saucepan. Heat to boiling over high heat, stirring frequently. When mixture comes to a *full rolling boil that can't be stirred down*, add the sugar. Cook, stirring constantly, until the mixture again comes to a full, foaming boil. Cook for 1 minute, stirring constantly. Remove from heat, and stir for a minute or 2 to settle the foam; if there is still foam on top, skim and discard with a clean spoon. Pour into prepared jars, leaving ¼ inch headspace; seal with prepared lids and bands. Process in boiling-water bath for 5 minutes (see page 419).

Uncooked Wild Fruit Jam—Pectin Added (Freezer Jam)

2, 4 or 6 half-pints

Fruit	Ingredient	2 half-pints	4 half-pints	6 half-pints
Blueberry	Crushed blueberries	1 cup	1¾ cups	3 cups
	Sugar	1⅓ cups	2¾ cups	5¼ cups
	Powdered fruit pectin	⅓ box	⅔ box	1 box
	Water	⅓ cup	⅔ cup	¾ cup
Blackberry,	Crushed blackberries	1 cup	1¾ cups	3 cups
Raspberry	Sugar	1⅓ cups	2¾ cups	5¼ cups
	Powdered fruit pectin	⅓ box	⅔ box	1 box
	Water	⅓ cup	⅔ cup	¾ cup
Cherry, Wild	Finely chopped pitted cherries	⅞ cup	1⅔ cups	2½ cups
	Sugar	1¾ cups	3¼ cups	5 cups
	Powdered fruit pectin	⅖ box	⅘ box	1⅕ boxes
	Water	½ cup	¾ cup	1⅓ cups
Strawberry	Crushed hulled strawberries	1 cup	2 cups	2⅔ cups
	Sugar	1¾ cups	3½ cups	5 cups
	Powdered fruit pectin	⅖ box	⅘ box	1⅕ boxes
	Water	½ cup	¾ cup	1⅓ cups

Uncooked jam is not processed in a water-bath canner, but the jars and lids should still be sterilized as described on page 418 (or, use clean plastic freezer containers). Prepare fruit as directed. Most fruits should be crushed with a potato masher or chopped to medium consistency in a food processor; don't purée the fruit, as jam should have small bits of fruit in it. As a general rule, the fruits listed here lose half their volume during crushing, so if you need, say, 2 cups of crushed strawberries, start with a quart. Place fruit in glass or other nonreactive mixing bowl. Add sugar; mix well with wooden spoon and let stand for 10 to 15 minutes, stirring occasionally.

In small saucepan, combine pectin and water; stir well (mixture may be lumpy). Heat to a full, rolling boil over high heat, stirring constantly. Cook at a rolling boil for 1 minute, stirring constantly. Pour pectin mixture into fruit in bowl. Stir constantly with wooden spoon until sugar is completely dissolved and no longer grainy, about 3 minutes; a few grains may remain, but the mixture should no longer look cloudy (or the jam will be cloudy).

Pour into prepared jars or containers, leaving ½ inch headspace; cover with clean lids. Let stand at room temperature for 24 hours; the jam should set. If it is not set, refrigerate for several days until set before using or freezing. Jam will keep for 3 weeks, refrigerated, or frozen for up to a year.

Cooked Wild Fruit Jelly—No Added Pectin

Some fruits have enough natural pectin that you do not need to add packaged pectin when making jelly. Apples are the most pectin-rich fruit (and in fact, commercial pectin is generally made from apples), but currants, gooseberries, grapes and plums also have good amounts of pectin. Fully ripened fruits have less pectin than less-ripe fruits, so one-quarter of the fruits used should be somewhat underripe when you're planning to make jelly with no added pectin. Another way to add pectin without using a commercial product is to combine juice from, for example, plums, with apple juice; you can also use apple juice instead of water when making juice from the fruit.

Acid is also critical to proper gelling; too little and the jelly won't set, while too much causes the jelly to weep. Commercial pectin has acid in the mix; for jelly made without commercial pectin, lemon juice adds the necessary acid as well as a nice flavor accent.

Because commercial pectin is not used, you're not confined to a specified formula that requires a certain amount of juice to work with the pectin, so it's easy to make smaller batches. Simply measure your juice, add sugar and lemon juice as noted below, and cook until the mixture passes one of the jelly tests on page 258. Process finished jelly the same way as instructed for pectin-added jelly, page 254; you'll need 2 half-pint jars for each cup of juice you started with (because the added sugar increases the volume).

Here are recommended ratios of fruit juice, sugar and lemon juice for wild fruits. Measurements are given per cup of juice; increase sugar and lemon juice proportionally to reflect the amount of juice you are using.

Apple: 1 cup apple juice (page 210), ¾ cup sugar, 1½ teaspoons lemon juice
Crabapple: 1 cup crabapple juice (page 155), 1 cup sugar, ½ teaspoon lemon juice
Currant (one-quarter underripe): 1 cup currant juice (page 162), ¾ cup sugar, 1 teaspoon
  lemon juice
Gooseberry (one-quarter underripe): 1 cup gooseberry juice (page 172), 1 cup sugar,
  ½ teaspoon lemon juice
Grape (one-quarter underripe): 1 cup grape juice (page 178), ¾ to 1 cup sugar depending on
  tartness of grapes (no lemon juice)
Plum (one-quarter underripe): 1 cup plum juice (page 116), ¾ to 1 cup sugar depending on
  tartness of plums,
  ¼ teaspoon lemon juice

Prepare jars, bands and lids as described on page 418. In nonreactive saucepan that holds at least 4 times as much liquid as the amount of juice you're using, heat juice to boiling over medium-high heat. Add sugar and lemon juice. Cook, stirring constantly, until sugar dissolves. Increase heat to high and cook, stirring occasionally, until liquid reaches 220°F/104°C (see page 258 for temperatures for high-altitude jelly-making) or passes one of the jelly tests on the following page.

Remove from heat, and stir for a minute or two to settle the foam; if there is still foam on top, skim and discard with a clean metal spoon. Pour into prepared jars, leaving ¼ inch headspace; seal with prepared lids and bands. Process in boiling-water bath for 5 minutes (see page 419). *The sheet test for jelly or jam:* Dip a clean, cool metal spoon (such as a tablespoon from your dinnerware set) into the boiling mixture. Holding the spoon well above the pot (out of the steam), turn it sideways. When the syrup forms 2 large drops that flow together and come off the spoon in a sheet, it is sufficiently cooked.

The cold saucer test for jelly or jam: Chill a saucer in the refrigerator. Place a small spoonful of the mixture on the chilled saucer. Place the saucer in the refrigerator for a minute, then remove and turn the plate sideways. If the mixture remains in place, with only a slight bit of running, it is sufficiently cooked. You can also poke the chilled mixture with your fingertip; if it wrinkles, the mixture is done.

High-altitude temperatures for jelly-making:

1,000 feet	218°F (103°C)	4,000 feet	212°F (100°C)
2,000 feet	216°F (102°C)	5,000 feet	211°F (99°C)
3,000 feet	214°F (101°C)		

Recipes Using Various Fruit Juices

The recipes in this section can be made with juice from a variety of fruits. Each recipe includes some suggestions for types of fruit juices that would work well; however, they'll probably work just as well with juices from almost any other fruit you care to try. Keep in mind that you may need to adjust the amount of sweetening, depending on how sweet—or tart—your fruit juice is.

Wild Berry-Yogurt Popsicles

8 to 12 popsicles, depending on mold size   Preparation: Involved (requires ice-cream maker)

Use raspberries, blueberries, blackberries or any other wild berry that doesn't have a pit for these creamy popsicles. The basic mixture is prepared in an ice-cream maker, then spooned into popsicle molds for final freezing. Process the berries in the blender until they are fairly smooth but not completely puréed. The small bits of fruit that remain will freeze into flavorful bits, adding texture to the popsicles or soft-serve ice cream.

> 1 container plain yogurt (8 ounces)   1 cup raspberries or other wild berries
> 1½ cups Simple Sugar Syrup for Sorbet
>   (page 427)

If using ice-cream maker that requires pre-freezing, place it in freezer as directed by the manufacturer, generally 12 to 24 hours.

Combine yogurt and syrup in blender, and process for a few seconds until well blended. Add berries and pulse on-and-off until the berries are partially, but not completely, puréed. Pour mixture into ice-cream maker and process until the consistency of soft ice cream, 20 to 25 minutes. Spoon mixture into popsicle molds, and freeze until solid, 8 hours or longer.

Wild Berry-Yogurt Soft Serve Ice Cream

Follow the directions above for preparing the mixture and processing it in the ice-cream maker. Serve immediately, or freeze for up to 1 hour before serving; the consistency will be like soft-serve ice cream. If you allow the mixture to freeze for a longer time, it will become very hard, like a block of ice. It's still good to eat, but you will need to let it stand at room temperature for 30 minutes or so before serving it.

Wild Fruit Gels (Gumdrops)

This works great with the juice from any wild fruit (prepare the juice as though you were making jelly). Juice from dark fruits like prickly-pear fruit, chokecherries, raspberries or blackberries makes attractive, richly colored gels; juice from ground cherries makes lusciously golden gels; and gels made from violet or rose-petal liquid add color to a plateful of mixed-fruit gels (add a few drops of rosewater to the violet or rose-petal liquid, for flavor).

Half of a 1.75-ounce box powdered pectin*
⅜ cup wild fruit juice
¼ teaspoon baking soda

½ cup sugar, plus additional for rolling the gels
½ cup white corn syrup

You'll need two medium saucepans (large, if you're doubling the recipe), two long-handled spoons and a standard-sized loaf pan (glass or nonstick metal work best). Combine the pectin, fruit juice and baking soda in one pan; combine the ½ cup sugar and the corn syrup in the other. Place a spoon in each pan, and keep those spoons separate from one another throughout the procedure.

Stir both mixtures well, and place both pans over medium-high heat. The pectin mixture will foam up at the beginning; stirring will prevent it from boiling over. Cook both mixtures, stirring alternately, until the foam subsides from the pectin mixture and the sugar mixture is boiling vigorously, about 5 minutes. Pour the pectin mixture in a thin, steady stream into the sugar mixture, stirring constantly. Boil the mixture, stirring constantly, for 1 minute longer. Pour the mixture immediately into the loaf pan. Let stand at room temperature, covered very loosely with a piece of cheesecloth to discourage flies, until completely cool; this will take about 2 hours. (Alternately, you can pour the mixture into tiny molds, if you have them.)

The cooled mixture is a bit tricky to remove from the pan. I've found the best way to do this is to put the pan into the refrigerator for an hour, then to place it into a larger pan that has been partially filled with very hot water. Let the loaf pan sit in the hot water for a minute or two, then use a knife dipped in warm water to cut the mixture into small pieces. Pry the pieces from the pan with a small spatula or a fork, and immediately roll each in sugar. Refrigerate or freeze for longer storage, keeping a little space between each gel and using waxed paper between layers.

*See page 254 for information on dividing powdered pectin.

Purple Dream Pie

1 pie   Preparation: Over an hour, plus several hours chilling

Use syrup or juice from any dark-colored wild berries for this pie: chokecherries, wild cherries, nanny-berries etc. It looks rather unusual, with its dusky purple-hued layer (rather like a purplish chocolate pie). It's very sweet and rich, so a little goes a long way.

1 purchased shortbread crust (6 ounces) or deep graham-cracker crust (9 ounces)

1 can (14 ounces) Eagle Brand sweetened condensed milk (reduced-fat works fine)

4 egg yolks

1 whole egg

¾ cup wild berry syrup, or ⅔ cup wild berry juice mixed with ⅔ cup sugar

2 packages (3 ounces each) cream cheese, softened

½ cup powdered sugar

½ cup sour cream (reduced-fat works fine)

1 teaspoon vanilla extract

Heat oven to 350°F; position oven rack in lower third of oven. Bake the crust for 5 minutes. Remove from oven and set aside to cool while you prepare the filling. Reduce oven to 325°F.

In large mixing bowl, combine sweetened condensed milk, egg yolks, whole egg and syrup (or juice/sugar mixture). Beat with electric mixer or sturdy whisk until smooth and completely combined. Place prepared crust onto a baking sheet, and pour in the condensed-milk mixture. Bake in center of oven for about 45 minutes, or until knife inserted in center of pie comes out clean.

While pie is baking, prepare cream cheese topping. In medium mixing bowl, combine cream cheese, powdered sugar, sour cream and vanilla. Beat with electric mixer or wooden spoon until smooth and uniform. When pie filling tests done, remove pie from oven and spread cream cheese mixture evenly over the top, spreading gently with rubber spatula. Return to oven and bake for 10 to 15 minutes longer, or until cream cheese mixture can be touched lightly without sticking. Remove pie from oven and cool completely before covering and placing in refrigerator to chill for several hours. Serve cold.

Wild Berry Parfait with Maypop Mousse

4 servings; easily increased   Preparation: Under 30 minutes

Wow your guests with this special yet easy-to-make dessert. It makes a small harvest of berries go a long way. Use any wild berries that are suitable for eating out-of-hand: raspberries, strawberries, blueberries, huckleberries, blackberries etc. For a really attractive presentation, use different berries for each layer.

½ cup sweetened flaked coconut

⅔ cup heavy cream

¾ cup chilled Maypop Curd, page 193
(about half the batch)

2 cups ready-to-eat wild berries

Heat oven to 350°F. Spread coconut on baking sheet. Bake until golden brown, about 10 minutes, stirring occasionally. Transfer to a bowl and allow to cool completely. Meanwhile, make mousse by beating whipping cream until stiff peaks form. Fold in the Maypop Curd.

Place about 2 tablespoons of the berries in the bottoms of 4 stemmed 10-ounce glasses. Top with about 2 tablespoons of the maypop mousse; sprinkle with a teaspoon of the coconut. Repeat layers until all ingredients are used up. Cover and chill if not serving immediately; the parfaits can be prepared up to 4 hours before serving.

Variation: Wild Berry Parfaits with Lemon Mousse

This is a good option if you don't have any maypops! Follow the recipe for Maypop Curd on page 193, substituting freshly squeezed lemon juice for the maypop juice. Proceed as directed. Use remaining lemon curd as suggested for Maypop Curd.

Lollipops

About 24   Preparation: Under an hour

2 cups sugar

⅔ cup light corn syrup

1 cup wild fruit juice

A few drops oil of lemon or other
flavoring, optional

Food coloring, optional

Wooden ice cream sticks or skewers

Spray baking sheets with nonstick spray; set aside. In heavy-bottomed large saucepan, combine sugar, syrup and fruit juice. Heat over medium-high heat, stirring constantly, until sugar dissolves. Boil without stirring until syrup registers 310°F on candy thermometer; this will take 15 to 20 minutes (don't try to rush it). Keep sides of saucepan clear of sugar crystals by brushing sides several times with a pastry brush dipped in water.

When mixture has reached 310°F, remove from heat; stir in flavoring and food coloring if using. Quickly spoon large dollops onto prepared baking sheets, immediately placing ice cream stick in position before candy sets. Allow to cool until set, then remove from baking sheet and wrap in clear plastic wrap.

*Fruit Leathers**

Almost any fruit can be dried into a leather; generally, all you need do is simply purée the fruit in a blender or food processor, sweeten to taste as needed, and dry in a food dehydrator or low oven. (Please see the section on dehydrating foods on pages 420-422 for more information about using food dehydrators and home ovens for drying foods.) Hard fruits, such as apples and pears, should be cooked in a little water with a few drops of lemon juice before puréeing; soft berries can be puréed and dried with no cooking.

The purée to be dried into a leather should be fairly thick—a consistency like applesauce works well. If you try to dry a purée that is too thin or watery, the leather will take forever to dry, and may be brittle once it's dry. If the fruit you're working with is watery, or the purée too runny, cook it down for a bit to thicken it before spreading on the drying sheets.

You can add spices to your purées to vary the flavor; for example, try cinnamon or nutmeg with apple or pear purée, or a bit of orange extract with berry purée. For additional interest, sprinkle the purée before drying with finely chopped nuts, shredded coconut or granola.

Commercial dryers come with solid liner sheets that work well, but I've found that some of them need to be sprayed with nonstick spray, especially if the fruit is extremely sticky. Experiment with a small batch of purée to see how your liner sheets perform. If you're drying in the oven or in a homemade dryer, line rimmed baking sheets with plastic wrap, then tape the wrap to the rims of the baking sheets to keep it in place during filling and drying. One standard-sized sheet will hold about 2 cups.

Pour the purée onto prepared baking sheets or dehydrator liners. Tilt the sheets to evenly distribute the purée; it should be about ¼ inch deep. Dry at 130°F-150°F until leathery with no sticky spots; peel from the sheets and flip once during drying if the bottom is not drying properly. Total drying time is generally 4 to 10 hours, but this may vary depending on your equipment, the purée and the weather. If you've used baking sheets lined with plastic wrap, the leather can be peeled off any time; if you've used solid liner sheets with a dehydrator, peel off the leather while it is still warm. Roll up all leathers, and wrap in plastic wrap. They keep well at cool room temperature if properly dried; for long-term storage, wrap the plastic-wrapped rolls in freezer wrap and store in the freezer.

*Note: This information is taken from my book, *The Back-Country Kitchen.*

NUTS

NUTS ARE one of the more familiar foods that can be foraged. Even though some of the varieties we forage might be unavailable commercially—butternuts and hickory nuts, in particular—they can be used in almost any recipe that calls for domestic nuts. The exception to this is the acorn; although it is a nut (from the oak tree), it is used in a completely different way than the walnuts, almonds and pecans we grew up with.

In this chapter, I'm going to talk about four of the nuts most commonly harvested by foragers in our area: black walnuts, butternuts, hazelnuts and, of course, our odd little friend the acorn. Another popular nut, the hickory nut, is one of the Top Ten species, and can be found starting on page 128. I'm also including sunflower seeds here, because their use is nut-like. All nuts are seeds, after all; we just don't always think of them that way.

There are other nuts out there in the wilds; most don't grow in our area, however, preferring gentler climates. If you happen to be in another region (particularly the South), ask local foragers or University Extension Services about the nuts that you might find.

Feel free to use your wild nuts in any of your favorite recipes, substituting them for domestic nuts as noted with each species. You'll discover new and exciting tastes that will have you looking forward to your next nutting expedition in the fall.

Acorns (Quercus spp.)

Easy to harvest even in urban areas; try an "acorn walk" with the kids in the fall. Acorns need special preparation to remove bitter tannin, but were an important food for many native tribes.

HABITAT, RANGE

Acorns are the nuts of oak trees. There are numerous oak species, and one or another grows throughout our region (and indeed, throughout most of the United States). They are sometimes the dominant species in hardwood forests, but also grow in companionship with elm, maple, beech, hickories and cherry. Oaks prefer warmer climates, and don't grow in the cold evergreen forests of the northern part of our region.

PARTS USED

Nutmeats, leached and cooked

SEASONS

Fall; some acorns can be harvested through early spring

IDENTIFICATION TIPS, DANGEROUS LOOKALIKES

Oaks are gnarly-looking, slow-growing trees that come in a variety of sizes and forms, with a variety of leaf shapes. One thing they all have in common is the acorn—a small nut that is attached to the branch by a scaled, bristly or furry cup-like cap. The shell of the acorn is smooth and rounded, with a pointed

Northern red oak (*Q. rubra*)

tip; it may be half-embedded in the cap, or only slightly covered by the cap. The nutmeat is rounded and generally easy to remove from the shell; it splits naturally into two halves. Acorns from the red-oak group have a hairy lining on the nutmeat, while those from the white-oak group are skinless once released from the shell.

Members of the red-oak group that are found in our area include the northern red oak (*Q. rubra*), as well as two pin oaks (*Q. palustris* and *Q. ellipsoidalis*), the black oak (*Q. velutina*) and the scarlet oak (*Q. coccinea*). Leaves of the red-oak group are lobed, and each lobe is sharply pointed at the tip; that's the quickest way to distinguish them from the white-oak group, whose lobed leaves have rounded tips. White-oak members found in our region include two white oaks (*Q. alba* and *Q. bicolor*), the bur oak (*Q. macrocarpa*), two chinquapins (*Q. muehlenbergii* and

White oak (*Q. alba*)

NUTS

Q. prinoides) and the post oak (*Q. stellata*). Oaks hybridize naturally, so exact identification is often a matter for botanists.

All acorns contain tannin, a bitter, water-soluble substance. Acorns from the white-oak group have whitish nutmeats that contain less tannin, and are generally considered the best for eating; however, the red-oak acorns, which have yellowish nutmeats, are completely edible. Indeed, there are no acorns (or acorn lookalikes) that are poisonous once they have been leached.

Bur oak and the two white oaks are often considered the prime acorns for eating. Bur oaks are easy to identify, because the scaly cap covers all but the tip of the acorn and has a hairy fringe where it abuts the nutshell; the nut is the largest of the North American acorns and can be as wide as 1½ inches. Bur oak leaves are very deeply lobed, and can be up to a foot long. White-oak acorns have a much smaller cap that cups about one-quarter of the nut; the leaves are similar to those of the bur oak. For exact identification, consult a tree identification book, or a local forester.

HARVESTING TIPS

Wait until a quantity of acorns falls from the trees to gather them; this is generally in early fall, and the nuts can be gathered any time after that. Red-oak acorns can be gathered all winter if they can be located, and even in the spring when the snow melts. Gather only acorns that have turned brown; if you find green-shelled acorns on the ground, pass them by as they will be more bitter.

The longer an acorn sits on the ground, the more the likelihood that it will be compromised by insects or rot, but even the first acorns of the season may have been attacked by insects while still on the tree. When you are gathering acorns, note the relative weight of each. Crack a few open, and you'll soon discover that heavier acorns are sound, while lightweight acorns are moldy, or hollow due to insects. You will quickly learn to reject lightweight acorns just by their feel. Another way to separate the good acorns from the bad before shelling them is to put them all in a bucket of water while they are still fresh (this does not work as well with dried acorns). Heavy, sound acorns sink, while hollow or compromised acorns float and should be discarded.

SPECIAL CONSIDERATIONS

All acorns have tannin in the nutmeat; acorns of the red-oak group have more tannin than those of the white-oak group. Tannin is quite bitter, and also causes stomach upset. Acorns must always be leached to remove the tannin; see the instructions below. Raw acorns can cause livestock poisoning, a good reminder of the value of proper processing.

MORE ABOUT ACORNS: The oak has been revered by people all over the world since history began recording such things. Druids considered the tree sacred, and it has been said that oak leaves whispered secrets of the Druids to those who knew how to listen. In long-ago Wales, maidens and young men would hold an Eastertime "round dance" around the oldest oak in the village; friendships were made and marriages were arranged during the dance. There are many other superstitions and legends attributed to the oak; it seems to have been an object of great respect wherever it grew.

Early Native Americans revered the oak as well, but for more practical reasons: it provided much-needed carbohydrates and fat to a diet that was heavy with fruits, greens and meat, but few grains. Acorns were stored in special acorn granaries for years, providing a sure food source in uncertain times. For additional reading, I highly recommend *It Will Live Forever*. This book, written by naturalist Beverly Ortiz, is the story of traditional Yosemite Native American acorn preparation as told by Julia Parker, a member of the Miwok/Paiute clan who began demonstrating acorn preparation at Yosemite National Park in the 1960s. Anyone who doubts the edibility of acorns—black-oak acorns in particular—will have their eyes opened by reading this book. It explains the historical and long-standing importance of acorn to her tribe, and details traditional ways of preparing acorns for food.

As noted, acorns contain bitter tannin that must be leached out by large amounts of water. Opinions vary widely as to the best technique, so a number of variations are discussed below. Feel free to experiment with these methods; I don't think there is any single "right way" to do it, and the method that fits your style best is the one you should use.

No matter which method you are using, the acorns must be shelled before leaching. To make this job easier, roast them at 250°F for an hour or two, or place them in a sunny location for a few days; this isn't essential, but if you're having a hard time getting the nutmeats out, you might try this. To crack the shell, stand the acorn on its tip and rap it with a hammer; or, place acorns between thick towels and strike lightly with a hammer. Remove the nutmeats from the cracked shells. If you're working with acorns from the red-oak group, the nutmeat will have a skin on it that should be removed before processing (don't worry about little bits of skin that remain inside the folds; just remove the major portion). You may prefer to dry red-oak acorns before shelling because the skin will come off more easily when the nut has been dried; it often adheres to the inside of the shell rather than coming out with the nutmeat.

Next, the acorns must be soaked to remove the tannin; this process is called *leaching*. Some foragers proceed directly to this step after shelling; others like to dry the acorn meats first.

As a general rule, if you're leaching large pieces of nutmeat, you don't need to dry them; if you prefer to leach ground nutmeats, you may want to dry them before grinding.

Leaching is quicker with hot water than with cold, but some people feel that hot water actually sets the bitter tannin in the nutmeats. It also changes the texture of ground acorns, making the final product less versatile for baked goods. Cold-water leaching is more traditional, and works well with ground acorns since the tannin will come out of the smaller particles more readily than out of larger pieces of nutmeats. I've tried both hot- and cold-water leaching; I prefer the hot-water method for large pieces, and the cold-water method for ground acorns.

For hot-water leaching of acorn pieces, heat 2 pots of water to boiling. Add the acorn pieces to one, and cook at a gentle boil until the water turns tea-colored with tannin. Drain the nutmeats and add them to the second pot of boiling water. Repeat until the water no longer becomes stained, always adding the drained nutmeats to a fresh pot of boiling water. Acorns from the white-oak group usually take 4 or 5 changes of water, while those of the red-oak group take a dozen or more. The nutmeats will be brown after leaching.

Once the acorn pieces are sweet, drain and use (or refrigerate) right away, or dry and store in a cool location for future use. I dry them in my food dehydrator, where it takes 2 to 3 hours; you can also spread them on a sheet and dry them in a 150°F–200°F oven for about the same amount of time. If you like, you can grind the leached but still wet acorns with a meat grinder or food processor, then use this meal as is or dry it for storage. Finally, you can process dried leached acorns in a flour mill to get acorn meal.

To leach acorn pieces in cold water, simply place them in a bucket of cold water and change the water several times a day until the acorns taste sweet. This may take anywhere from a week to 3 weeks; red-oak acorns take more time than white-oak acorns. Drain the leached acorns, and use immediately or dry as described above.

Ground acorns are best leached in cold water; if leached in hot water, the particles lose their ability to bind together. To grind acorns, first dry the shelled nutmeats in a food dehydrator or oven at low temperatures; it will take 2 to 5 hours to dry the nuts enough for grinding (red-oak acorns dry more quickly than white-oak acorns). You could also dry them naturally by spreading them on trays in a warm room. Once the nuts are dry enough to grind, process them in a coffee grinder (or flour mill, if you have one), or run several times through a meat grinder with a fine plate. Now you're ready for leaching.

It's easy to lose the finer particles when changing water during leaching; here are 2 methods that prevent you from washing all your acorn down the drain. For the first, put the ground acorns in a muslin bag or old pillowcase and hang it under the faucet. Let the cold water run slowly into the bag all night; the acorn meal should be sweet by the morning. This method isn't recommended for folks who have to pay for water by the gallon, however; it works best for those who have a well or who filter their own water from a lake or river.

The second method takes longer, but uses less water. Place the ground acorns in a jar that holds at least three times as much water as the quantity of ground acorns you have. Fill the jar with cold water, then fasten a double layer of cheesecloth to the top. Shake the jar gently and let it stand for a few hours, shaking it once or twice if you happen to walk by. Drain off the water several times a day by pouring off the liquid slowly; don't drain it all off, as you will lose the finer acorn particles. Re-fill the jar and continue the soak-and-drain cycle until the water no longer turns brown; this usually takes 3 to 10 days, depending on the size of the acorn meal and the type of acorn. The leached acorn meal can be used in the wet state, or dried in a food dehydrator or oven and stored for later use.

What, exactly, is the result of all this leaching and processing? If you've leached acorn halves or quarters and are using them without drying, you end up with a chewy nut that somewhat resembles boiled peanuts in texture. If you've dried these pieces, you have something that is rather like an unsalted peanut, but harder and less oily. Dried acorn meal is akin to coarse cornmeal, and can be used in similar ways; wet or fresh ground acorn is rather like cornmeal mush. Acorns don't have an extremely distinctive taste; they're rather bland and somewhat sweet (when properly blanched), and are useful primarily as an ingredient to be added to other dishes rather than one to be savored on its own.

JUST FOR FUN
Tanning with Acorn Tannin
Actually, I'm not sure that this could be called "fun," but it is a non-food use for acorns that you may enjoy trying if you are interested in such skills. Save the water that acorns have been leached in, and let it evaporate until all you are left with is a brown powder (you can hurry this along by boiling the water to reduce its volume before setting it aside to dry naturally). Mix this brown powder with kosher or canning salt, then rub this into fresh, de-haired hides. Proceed as you would with standard tanning methods, which is a bit of a procedure. I've experimented with tanning hides, but truthfully have never used the tannin from acorns; however, the method sounds valid to me and would be worth experimenting with if you are so inclined. (I read about this technique in the magazine *Mother Earth News*.)

QUICK IDEAS FOR USING LEACHED ACORNS

- Use quartered acorns in place of garbanzo beans in stews and soups. If they have been dried, add to boiling water, then remove from heat and soak for 30 minutes to soften before using; or use a recipe that calls for dried beans.
- Substitute dried acorn meal (ground acorns) for up to one-quarter of the flour in baked goods such as muffins, quick breads and pancakes.
- Add water to wet ground acorn, and cook like porridge or soup (note that if you've leached ground acorn with boiling water, it won't thicken when cooked, so use cold-water-leached acorn for this recipe). Season with salt and herbs to taste.
- Toss dried acorn pieces with a little oil; spread on a baking sheet and salt lightly. Roast at 350°F until browned, about 15 minutes.

Squash Stew with Acorns

3 or 4 servings   Preparation: Under an hour

This makes a nice autumn meal; all you need to accompany it is a green salad and some hearty bread.

1½ pounds butternut or acorn squash	½ to ⅔ cup freshly leached acorn pieces*
1 onion, diced	¼ teaspoon salt, or to taste
Half of a red bell pepper, diced	A few grindings of black pepper
2 cloves garlic, chopped	2 tomatoes, coarsely cut up
1 tablespoon olive oil or canola oil	1 tablespoon chopped fresh parsley
¾ cup chicken broth	Hot cooked brown rice or white rice

Peel squash and remove seeds. Cut squash into ½-inch cubes; set aside. In small Dutch oven or small soup pot, sauté onion, bell pepper and garlic in oil over medium heat until just tender, stirring frequently. Add squash cubes, broth, acorn pieces, salt and black pepper. Heat just to boiling. Reduce heat so mixture bubbles gently and cook for about 20 minutes, stirring occasionally. Add tomatoes; cook for 10 to 15 minutes longer. Mixture should be stew-like rather than soupy; add a little more chicken broth or water if it is becoming dry near the end of cooking. Stir in parsley. Serve with hot rice.

*The acorn pieces for this dish should still be wet, or freshly processed. If you're using acorn pieces that have been dried, add to boiling water, then remove from heat and soak for 30 minutes to soften before starting recipe.

Acorn-Apple Muffins

12 muffins

Preparation: Under an hour

⅔ cup milk
½ cup canola oil
1 egg
1 teaspoon vanilla
½ cup dry acorn meal
½ cup (packed) brown sugar
¼ cup white sugar
1½ cups all-purpose flour

1 tablespoon baking powder
½ teaspoon salt
¼ teaspoon nutmeg
1 cup finely chopped apple (about 1 large, or several smaller apples)
½ cup chopped black walnuts or other nuts

Heat oven to 400°F. Spray 12-cup muffin pan with nonstick spray; set aside. In large mixing bowl, combine milk, oil, egg and vanilla; beat with fork or wire whisk. Add acorn meal and sugars; stir with wooden spoon until well mixed. Combine flour, baking powder, salt and nutmeg in wire-mesh strainer or sifter; sift into mixing bowl with other ingredients. Stir until just moistened (batter should still be lumpy). Add apple and nuts; mix together gently.

Spoon batter into prepared muffin cups, filling ⅔ full. Bake until tops are browned and center springs back, 20 to 25 minutes. Remove from pan immediately; cool to warm room temperature before serving. Best served warm.

Acorn and Wild Berry Porridge

3 or 4 servings

Preparation: Under 15 minutes

1 cup wet ground acorn*
¾ cup apple juice
¾ cup water
¼ cup dried blueberries, currants or other dried berries†

2 tablespoons honey or maple syrup, or to taste
1 tablespoon butter
¼ teaspoon salt

In heavy-bottomed saucepan, combine all ingredients.† Heat to boiling over medium-high heat, then reduce heat and simmer for 15 minutes, or until porridge is thickened to desired consistency. Serve hot.

*The acorn for this recipe should be leached with cold water; if it's leached with boiling water, the porridge will not thicken properly. Make this from freshly leached ground acorns, not from dried ground acorns.

†If you prefer, use ½ cup fresh berries in place of the dried berries. Add the fresh berries during the last 5 minutes of cooking; or, if you prefer, use them uncooked to top the hot porridge.

Black Walnuts (Juglans nigra)

With a sharp, rich taste that is unlike that of commercial English walnuts, the black walnut is highly prized for desserts, breads and muffins.

HABITAT, RANGE

This handsome and valuable native tree is found in our region in the southern portions of Minnesota, Wisconsin and Michigan, and throughout Iowa, Illinois, Indiana and Ohio. Black walnuts are not prolific; they grow in small groupings in low deciduous forests that have rich, well-drained soil, as well as on floodplains and river bottoms and occasionally in pastures and meadows. They are often associated with sugar maple, poplar and red oak.

PARTS USED

Nutmeats, raw or cooked

SEASONS

Early fall

IDENTIFICATION TIPS, DANGEROUS LOOKALIKES

Black walnut in husk

Black walnut can attain large sizes, and is known for straight trunk growth. It has an open appearance and a gracefully rounded crown. The bark is deeply furrowed and grayish, turning almost black as the tree matures. Leaves are pinnately compound; each leaf has 13 to 23 leaflets (6 to 11 pairs plus sometimes, though not always, a terminal leaf; see diagram in the hickory section on page 129). The leaves I see are generally 12 to 18 inches long; I've read that they are sometimes as long as 24 inches. Individual leaflets are light green in color and have toothed margins; they're oblong, often to the point of appearing skinny, and end in a well-defined point.

Nuts are encased in a thick, round, green husk that is about 2 inches across; the husk is seamless (unlike the husk on nuts from the hickory family, which are naturally divided into 4 parts). Usually, nuts are clustered in groups of 2 or 3 at the ends of branches. As the nuts mature, the husk turns chocolate brown before turning black and crumbling away from the nut. There are no dangerous lookalikes; the only thing you may mistake for a walnut is another edible nut such as a butternut.

HARVESTING TIPS

Wait for a quantity of nuts to drop in the fall before harvesting. Sometimes, I see a few nuts on the ground in mid- to late summer; these always seem to be rotten inside, which is perhaps why they fell from the tree early. You will be able to dent the husk with your thumbnail when the nut is ripe, even though the husk will still be green. Also, the squirrels seem to know when the nuts are ready; when you see them gathering walnuts, you can begin harvesting as well. If you can reach any nuts that are still on the tree, you can pull them off before the squirrels get to them; just be sure that you can dent the husk with your thumbnail. Black walnuts ripen over a period of 4 to 6 weeks, so not all nuts on any given tree will be ready at once.

SPECIAL CONSIDERATIONS

Although it is uncommon, walnuts can trigger an allergic reaction in some individuals. People with known nut allergies should not harvest or eat walnuts.

MORE ABOUT BLACK WALNUTS: As I am writing this, it is late September, and the black walnut tree in my back yard is laden with nuts. I've been observing a little red squirrel gathering these for his winter cache, and it is pretty amusing to watch as he scrambles down a branch, pulls off a nut that is much larger than his head, and struggles to carry off the heavy nut. Although black walnut is used extensively by squirrels and chipmunks, it is not a major food source for larger wildlife, although deer will browse on the fallen nuts.

Black walnut trees have been valued for their wood for generations; it's smooth and hard, with a straight and lovely grain that is prized for furniture and gunstocks. A large walnut tree can fetch thousands of dollars on the timber market, which may help explain why they are less common in the wild than they used to be.

Although black walnuts make lovely specimens in the yard, people often avoid planting them because the trees are messy when they are throwing nuts. Also, the roots, as well as fallen leaves and husks, leach a substance called juglone into the soil; this may hinder the growth of other plants under the tree. Tomatoes are particularly sensitive; I've never been able to get one to grow near my own black walnut tree, and I've read that paper birch and many pines are likely to be affected by decomposed walnut litter as well. As a final strike against the tree, the husks will stain almost anything that their juices touch. This includes driveways, clothes, fences, wooden ladders and wicker baskets.

The flavor of black walnuts, however, is so extraordinary that it is worth any headache associated with all of these problems. Black walnuts have a rich, sharp taste that makes store-bought English walnuts seem pale and flat by comparison. It reminds me somewhat of the smell of rich black earth in the spring, as it has that same sort of clean, sharp quality. The flavor is excellent for baked goods, but also pairs well with savory foods such as salads, bread dressing and baked squash.

In the fall, when the nuts are ready to pick, it's fairly easy to gather a bucketful; then, the work begins. Although you can set the nuts aside until the husks turn black and crumble off, the flavor of the nuts is best if the husks are removed while they are still green. There's no real easy way to do this, unfortunately. Probably the most common way to shell walnuts is to put them on a driveway and drive over them repeatedly with a car; however, this can be dangerous because the nuts turn into projectiles (and there's that stained driveway). I've had good success rolling the nut under my foot on cement until the husk is broken away, but this method will stain your shoes (and your driveway). I've also read of putting walnuts in a cement mixer with water and a shovelful of gravel, then running the mixer to break up the husks; if you have access to one of these machines, it couldn't hurt to try this. You could rig up a smaller version of this in a bucket and agitate the nuts with a broom handle; I haven't tried this, preferring to stain my driveway. Once the bulk of the husk has been broken away, you can agitate the nuts in a bucket of water to clean off more of the clinging husk, or proceed directly to the next step. The husks contain juglone, the chemical which may stunt plant growth. Don't use them as garden mulch or add to the compost pile; it's best to discard them in the trash (see **Just for Fun**, below, for another use).

After the husks have been removed, set the nuts aside to cure for a few weeks. Place them in shallow boxes, no more than a few deep, in a spot where squirrels can't get them (an enclosed garage works well). If there are large bits of husk still on the nuts, place the boxes on heavy plastic tarps to catch any inky liquid that may ooze from the husks as they blacken. Eventually, any clinging bits of husk will turn dry and crumbly, and can be rubbed off easily. Crack open a few nuts after 2 or 3 weeks to check them. When the nuts are ready, the nutmeats will be crisp enough to break cleanly with a snap.

Once the nutmeats are dry and crisp, the nuts can be shelled or stored. Black walnuts keep very well in the shell—some people keep them for several years in a cool place (under 60°F is recommended). Be aware that the flavor will continue to change slightly; it's a good idea to sample a few nuts occasionally to see how they are doing. I store whole cured black walnuts in my chest freezer; this keeps the flavor from changing and also keeps the squirrels away! If you prefer to shell the nuts before storing, they'll take up less room; however, shelled nuts go rancid quickly and should be stored in the refrigerator or freezer.

Special crackers are sold for black walnuts, as they are harder to shell than English walnuts. A hammer also works well; hold the nut on a hard surface with the pointed end down and rap the base sharply. To make shelling easier, you can soak the nuts overnight in a bucket of hot water; drain and crack before the nuts have a chance to mold or to dry out again.

Once the shell is opened, pick out the nutmeats with a nut pick. The folds are more convoluted, and the nutmeats smaller and thinner, than those of English walnuts, so this can be a somewhat tedious job. (Black walnuts are much easier to shell than hickory nuts, however.) Expect to get just under a cup of nutmeats from each pound of walnuts in the husk.

The flavor of black walnuts is improved by a light roasting. Spread nutmeats on baking sheets, and bake at 225°F for 10 to 15 minutes, stirring occasionally. I guarantee that the rich aroma will put you in the mood for baking! Roasted nuts can be stored at room temperature for a several weeks without going rancid; nutmeats that have not been roasted should be stored in the refrigerator or freezer.

NUTS

JUST FOR FUN
Black Walnut Dye
The husks of black walnuts have been used for generations to make a strong, rich brown dye that is used for fabrics as well as basket-making materials. Place your husks in an old pillowcase, and tie the neck shut with rope. Hang the pillowcase inside a plastic bucket, with the end of the rope hanging outside the bucket so you can easily grab onto it later. Fill the bucket with hot water, then cover and let it steep for several days; agitate the pillowcase several times each day. When the dye is as strong as you like, strain out any solids and add a little vinegar; this helps prevent mold and also will help set the color of the dyed items. Use within a few days, or freeze for later use.

QUICK IDEAS FOR USING BLACK WALNUTS
- Use black walnuts in any recipe that calls for regular (English) walnuts. The flavor will be stronger, so you can reduce the amount of nuts slightly if you like.
- Sprinkle roasted black walnuts over green salads; this is especially delicious with salads that contain apples or other fruits.

OTHER RECIPES IN THIS BOOK FEATURING BLACK WALNUTS
- Waldorf Salad with Cattails (page 86)
- Quick Nut Bread (page 133)
- Nannyberry Carrot Cake (page 208)
- Pear Muffins (page 210)
- Pawpaw-Sour Cream Coffee Cake (page 216)
- Soft Persimmon Cookies (page 220)
- Persimmon "Pudding" Cake (page 223)
- Quick Persimmon Loaf (page 223)

Banana Cake with Black Walnuts

12 servings   Preparation: About an hour

Black walnuts go particularly well with ripe bananas. This cake has a wonderful flavor from the combination of the two.

3/4 cup (1 1/2 sticks) butter, softened
1 3/4 cups sugar
3 eggs
2 1/2 cups cake flour
1 1/4 teaspoons baking powder
1 1/4 teaspoons baking soda
1/2 teaspoon salt

2/3 cup buttermilk
1 1/2 cups mashed ripe banana (3 or 4 ripe bananas)
1 cup chopped black walnuts
Cream cheese frosting or other frosting, optional

Heat oven to 350°F. Spray 9 x 13-inch baking dish with nonstick spray; set aside. In large mixing bowl, cream butter with electric mixer until fluffy and light. Add sugar and beat well. Add eggs 1 at a time, beating after each egg. Combine flour, baking powder, baking soda and salt in wire-mesh strainer or sifter. Sift about a third of the flour mixture into the butter mixture; add a third of the buttermilk and beat together on low speed. Repeat with remaining flour and buttermilk, adding in 2 batches and beating after each. Add bananas and beat in until just mixed. Fold in walnuts with spatula. Scrape into prepared baking dish. Bake for 45 minutes, or until wooden pick inserted into the center of the cake comes out clean. Cool on wire rack. Frost if desired; the cake must be completely cool before frosting.

NUTS

Black Walnut-Molasses Pie

1 pie   Preparation: Over an hour

Pastry for single-crust pie, plus flour for
    rolling out
3 eggs
¾ cup light corn syrup
⅔ cup sugar

⅓ cup butter, melted and cooled slightly
¼ cup molasses
1 teaspoon rum extract or vanilla extract
¼ teaspoon salt
1½ cups coarsely chopped black walnuts

Heat oven to 350°F. On lightly floured surface, roll out pastry and fit into ungreased pie plate; trim and flute edges. Set aside. In large mixing bowl, beat eggs lightly with electric mixer or whisk. Add corn syrup, sugar, butter, molasses, rum extract and salt; beat until smooth and well mixed. Stir in walnuts with spatula or wooden spoon. Place prepared crust on baking sheet (to catch any drips). Scrape filling into crust. Cover edges of pastry with foil strips; this prevents over-browning. Bake for 25 minutes, then remove foil and bake for 20 to 25 minutes longer, or until knife inserted near the center comes out clean. Cool pie on wire rack. Refrigerate leftovers.

Wild Rice-Walnut Pilaf

4 to 6 servings   Preparation: Under 30 minutes

½ cup diced red onion
½ cup diced apple
¼ cup diced celery
1 tablespoon minced shallot
1 tablespoon butter

½ cup chopped black walnuts
3 cups cooked wild rice, or wild-and-
    brown-rice blend
¼ cup vegetable broth or chicken broth
½ teaspoon salt, or to taste

In large saucepan, sauté onion, apple, celery and shallot in butter over medium heat until vegetables are just tender, stirring occasionally. Add walnuts; cook for a few minutes longer, until walnuts become fragrant. Stir in rice, broth and salt. Reduce heat to low; cover and cook for about 10 minutes. Fluff before serving.

Butternuts (White Walnuts) *(Juglans cinerea)*

Rich and oily, the butternut has a mild flavor that works well in most nut recipes (it's my favorite nut). Like black walnuts, they're a bit of work to process—but are well worth the effort.

HABITAT, RANGE

Butternut is the most northern-hardy member of the walnut family, and was fairly common in the northeastern portion of the United States until a cankerworm infestation devastated many trees; it is still found, although not in its previous abundance. The butternut's range stretches in a jagged line from southeastern Minnesota down to Missouri, and from there to the Atlantic coast; the northern boundary of its range cuts through northern Wisconsin and central Michigan. Butternuts are found on streambanks, in bottomlands and floodplains, and in mixed deciduous forests, often in the company of basswood, black cherry, beech, elm and black walnut. They require rich, well-drained soil that is reasonably moist, and won't grow in the shadow of taller trees.

PARTS USED

Nutmeats, raw or cooked

SEASONS

Late summer through early fall

IDENTIFICATION TIPS, DANGEROUS LOOKALIKES

Immature butternuts

The butternut tree is shorter than the black walnut, attaining heights of 40 to 60 feet on average (although a long-lived tree can grow to 100 feet in good conditions). Like its cousin the black walnut, the butternut has pinnately compound leaves that are 12 to 24 inches long; butternut leaves have 11 to 17 oval leaflets (5 to 8 pairs, plus a terminal leaflet). The undersides of butternut leaves are densely covered with fine hairs, which are lacking on the black walnut. The quickest way to identify a butternut—other than by the nuts, of course—is by its distinctive bark, which is smooth when the tree is young but becomes very deeply furrowed as the tree matures. To me, the bark looks almost as though it has been carved with diamond-shaped fissures that make the broad ridges stand out in relief. Trunks are often crooked, and tend to be more forky than black walnut; the bark is slightly lighter on butternuts than on black walnuts.

Nuts grow in clusters of 2 to 10. Like black walnuts, butternuts are covered in a light green solid husk, but the butternut is football-shaped rather than round like the black walnut. The husk of the butternut is fragrant, and is covered with sticky hairs, which are lacking on the black walnut. Butternut husks are 2 to 3 inches long and about half as wide as they are long, making them quite distinctive. There are no dangerous lookalikes.

HARVESTING TIPS

Harvest nuts that have fallen to the ground; you can help this along by shaking low-bending branches with a pole to dislodge nuts that are ready to drop.

SPECIAL CONSIDERATIONS

Butternuts may cause an allergic reaction in people who are sensitive to walnuts; such persons should not handle or consume butternuts.

MORE ABOUT BUTTERNUTS: Butternut wood is highly prized for its *chatoiance*—a term for the shimmering quality of the fine-grained, lustrous wood. The word is taken from the French term for cat's eye, and describes the strange phenomenon by which the grain of the wood appears to shift as you look at it from different angles. (Mahogany is another wood that is noted for this unusual quality.) Unfortunately, overharvesting for this extraordinary timber, along with the butternut canker noted above, has cause once-abundant stands of butternut to diminish in our forests.

Like black walnuts, butternuts have an outer husk that must be removed to reveal the nutshell. I find that the butternut husks are easier to remove than those of black walnuts, but the same methods described for black walnuts on page 275 will also work for butternuts. Butternut husks seem to disintegrate more readily than black walnut husks. As I write this, I have a batch of butternuts ripening in my basement; they were harvested about a week ago, and already the husks are dark brown and soft enough to remove (I just roll them under my foot in the driveway, then peel them away). If you want to take a more leisurely approach, set the unhusked nuts in a protected location and let the husks blacken and shrivel up; they may ooze some staining liquid, so place them accordingly. Some people leave them all winter, then crumble off any clinging husks in the spring, and the butternuts don't seem the worse for it.

If you remove the husks immediately after harvesting the nuts, you'll have to cure them as described for black walnuts (page 275); if you let the hulls disintegrate naturally over the course of a month or more, the curing is already done.

The shell of the butternut is completely different from those of black walnuts; it's extremely

NUTS

wrinkled and convoluted, looking rather like a morel mushroom cap. Butternut shells are harder than black walnut shells, but once the shell is cracked the nutmeat itself seems easier to extract from the shell. I often get complete halves of butternuts (just like the fancy-grade English walnuts sold in the stores), which I seldom can manage with black walnuts. To shell the nuts, I like to place them in a heavyweight plastic bag on a cement floor, then rap each nut with a hammer; if you want to hit them individually, hold the nut with the pointed end up, but watch out for flying shell fragments. It takes a firm touch with the hammer to crack the tough butternut shell. For easier shelling, you can soak the nuts in a bucket of water for a few days, or even a week; the shells will be softer and you'll get more whole nutmeats.

Butternuts are rich and soft, with a mild but exceptional flavor. They are aptly named, as they seem very buttery to me; they're high in oil, and have a soothing feel in the mouth. Expect to get about a cup of nutmeats from each 2 pounds of unhusked nuts. Store them as described in the text for black walnuts on page 275.

QUICK IDEAS FOR USING BUTTERNUTS
- Substitute butternuts for pecans or English walnuts in any recipe.
- Stir chopped butternuts into hot breakfast cereal; the soft texture and mild flavor of these nuts makes them particularly good with the cereal.

OTHER RECIPES IN THIS BOOK FEATURING BUTTERNUTS
- Tender Whole Wheat Muffins with Wild Berries (page 95)
- Pear and Chokeberry Mincemeat (page 150)
- As substitute in Browned-Butter Hickory Nut Pie (page 133)
- Quick Nut Bread (page 133)
- Homemade Granola (page 293)

Double Butternut Squash

3 or 4 servings   Preparation: Under an hour

1 butternut squash (about 1 pound),
   peeled, seeds removed
1 tart green apple such as a Granny Smith,
   peeled and cored
½ cup chopped butternuts
3 tablespoons (packed) brown sugar

A pinch of ground cardamom
A pinch of ground ginger
Salt and pepper
3 tablespoons butter, melted
1 tablespoon freshly squeezed lemon juice

Heat oven to 350°F. Spray medium casserole dish with nonstick spray. Cut butternut squash into 1-inch pieces; add to casserole. Dice apple; add to casserole with squash, mixing lightly. Scatter butternuts over squash mixture. Sprinkle with brown sugar, cardamom, ginger, and salt and pepper to taste. Drizzle melted butter and lemon juice over all. Bake, uncovered, until squash is tender, 30 to 40 minutes.

Honey-Roasted Nut Clusters

About 1 cup   Preparation: Under 15 minutes

This is a perfect recipe for those small pieces of nutmeat that you get when shelling wild nuts. They make a great garnish for a tossed salad, ice cream, waffles or pudding, and are also a nice out-of-hand snack.

1 cup small nutmeat pieces from butternuts, hickory nuts, black walnuts or
   other nuts

2 tablespoons honey
A good pinch of salt

Heat oven to 425°F. Line baking sheet with foil; spray foil with nonstick spray. In a small bowl, gently stir together the nutmeats, honey and salt. Spread on the foil-lined baking sheet. Bake until light golden brown, stirring every 3 or 4 minutes. Remove from oven before the nuts are as dark as you'd like them, because they will continue to cook for a few minutes after you remove them from the oven. Let cool completely; store in an airtight container.

Variation: Seasoned Honey-Roasted Nut Clusters
Add a good pinch of curry powder, cinnamon, cumin or other spice to the mixture before stirring it all together.

Nut-Topped Toffee Crisps

25 to 30 cookies

Use any nuts you like to make these crisp-yet-chewy cookies. Because you need a relatively small amount of nuts, this is a good recipe to try when you want to stretch a small harvest—or when you don't feel like working the nut pick for several hours!

$\frac{1}{2}$ cup (1 stick) unsalted butter, softened
$\frac{3}{4}$ cup (packed) golden brown sugar
$\frac{1}{8}$ teaspoon salt
1 egg, separated

1 teaspoon vanilla extract
1 cup all-purpose flour
$\frac{1}{2}$ cup finely chopped butternut or other
   nutmeats, approximately

Heat oven to 350°F. Spray 2 baking sheets with nonstick spray; set aside. In mixing bowl, cream butter on low speed of electric mixer. Add brown sugar and salt, and beat until light. Add egg yolk and vanilla, and beat until fluffy, about 1 minute. (The mixture may look curdled; don't worry if it does.) Add flour and beat just until mixed; the mixture will be very crumbly. Use your hands to finish mixing the dough, working in all the small particles until the dough is relatively smooth (don't overmix, just enough to gather in all the small bits).

Pinch off a tablespoon of dough; it's a good idea to measure the first one, and then use it as a guide for the rest of the dough. Roll the tablespoon of dough into a smooth ball and place on prepared baking sheet. Continue until all the dough has been rolled, spacing the balls 2 inches apart. Press each ball with a smooth-bottomed glass that has been dipped in water, flattening the balls to about $\frac{1}{4}$ inch. Beat the egg white with a fork. Brush the tops of the cookies with the egg white. Sprinkle a heaping $\frac{1}{4}$ teaspoon nuts on each cookie; press the nuts lightly into the cookie with your fingertips. Bake until cookies are golden brown around the edges, 12 to 14 minutes. Let cookies rest on the baking sheets for 2 minutes, then transfer to a wire rack to cool completely.

NUTS

Hazelnuts (beaked hazelnut, *Corylus cornuta;* American hazelnut, *C. americana*)

Although hazelnuts are very common in the northern part of our range, you'll need good timing to beat the wild critters to the harvest when the nuts ripen. Wild hazelnuts are just like a slightly smaller version of the domestic hazelnut (or filbert) and can be used in the same ways.

HABITAT, RANGE

Beaked hazelnuts grow only in the northern part of our range. They're found in the northeastern portion of Minnesota, where their range can be defined by a line that runs from the northwest corner of the state to the southeast corner, extending slightly into northeastern Iowa. They are relatively common throughout Wisconsin, all of Michigan's Upper Peninsula, northern Michigan (especially the portion that abuts Lake Huron), and northern Ohio. Scattered populations also appear in North Dakota, and in the northern portions of South Dakota and Illinois. American hazelnuts have a wider range, and grow throughout our region. Both hazelnuts are found in woodlands and thickets, and can tolerate both dry and moist conditions. They can be locally quite common, often growing by the hundreds per acre.

PARTS USED

Nutmeat, raw or cooked

SEASONS

Late summer to early fall

IDENTIFICATION TIPS, DANGEROUS LOOKALIKES

Both of these native hazelnuts are easy to identify when they are bearing nuts; nothing else looks quite like either species at this time (during spring and summer, however, hazelnuts may be confused with young alder or paper birch). Hazelnuts grow as rather leggy shrubs; beaked hazelnuts are up to 9 feet tall, while American hazelnuts may be over 15 feet in height (but both are often quite short). Leaves of both species are alternate and simple, and range from 1½ to 4 inches in length; they're coarsely toothed and heart-shaped, broadest below the midpoint with a sharp tip at the end. The veins appear deeply graved in the leaf.

American hazelnuts

Beaked hazelnuts

Nuts of both species grow at the ends of the stems and are encased in bristly husks, and it is here that the two species become quite distinct from one another. The husk of the American hazelnut is open at the bottom, so it only partially encloses the nutshell; the bottom of the husk often flares away from the nutshell, looking like a fringe or skirt. The husk of a beaked hazelnut completely encases the nutshell and, in fact, extends beyond the nut to form a sort of neck (this is the "beak" that gives the species its common name). The beaked hazelnut has a unique growth form; nuts frequently grow as twins, connected to the stem at their bases.

HARVESTING TIPS

The husks of both hazelnut species are well-armed with tiny bristles, which don't seem to detract the deer, bears, squirrels, birds and other wildlife in the least. The bristles are, however, a nuisance to humans who want to harvest the nuts. Wear leather gloves when picking hazelnuts. You may also want to pick them while they are still a bit underripe, and let them fully ripen at home; wild animals seem to strip the shrubs of nuts the moment they turn ripe.

MORE ABOUT HAZELNUTS: The nuts of wild hazelnuts are extremely similar to domestic hazelnuts, which are also called filberts (they're those little round, brown-skinned nuts you get in frosty drinks sometimes). Wild hazelnuts are generally a bit smaller than their domesticated relatives. They're delicious raw, and make a wonderful addition to baked goods; in addition, they pair well with meats, grains and other savory foods, so they are extremely versatile. Native peoples in British Columbia, where beaked hazelnuts are the only edible nut that grows in the wild, pounded hazelnuts with berries and meat into cakes; they also boiled crushed nuts to extract the oil.

Husks and shells of hazelnuts are green when the nuts are maturing; the husks turn tan and become dry when the nuts are ripe, and the nutshell becomes brown. Harvesting hazelnuts successfully is a matter of good timing. If you see almost-ripe hazelnuts in late August or early September, you might want to pick some and let them ripen at home, because they may not be there a week later. Hazelnuts grow in profusion on some land I own on Minnesota's North Shore, on a high hill overlooking Lake Superior. When I am there in the summer, I'm always excited to see how many hazelnuts there are on the shrubs; however, I seldom get a really good harvest because the critters usually beat me to them. I've read that squirrels and deer can completely strip the nuts from the shrubs in a wide area on the day they ripen, and I believe it.

If you've picked underripe hazelnuts, set them in boxes in a cool location until the shells turn brown and the husks dry out; this could take several weeks. Once the nuts have ripened—whether on the tree or in your garage—they are ready to process. The husks are a bit of a nuisance to remove, especially those of beaked hazelnuts. Native peoples used to bury the whole nuts until the husks rotted, then dig them up and shell them. A friend who spends a good bit of time on Minnesota's Leech Lake Reservation tells me that they some-times put the nuts in burlap bags, then place them on rooftops and let the fall rains rot the husks (he didn't mention how they protect the nuts from squirrels, though, and I have visions of a bunch of fat and happy squirrels up there).

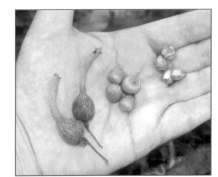

Beaked hazelnuts: In husk, husked, shelled

I know of no tricks to coax off the dried husks; I simply put on the leather gloves and go at it, sometimes using a pliers to break away the dried husk. Once the husks are off, you'll have a pile of round hard-shelled nuts. These can be stored for a long time in a cool area, and shelled as needed; or you may prefer to get it all over with at once and shell the nuts right after husking them. Shelled nuts should be stored in the refrigerator or freezer; if you roast them in a 350°F oven for 10 to 15 minutes, they can be kept at room temperature for several weeks.

The brown skin that covers the nut is completely edible, although it is slightly bitter; it is sometimes removed before cooking for aesthetic reasons as well as for a sweeter taste. To remove the skins, roast the nuts as described above, then place them while they are still warm in the folds of a coarse, thick towel and rub vigorously; the skins should come off fairly easily.

QUICK IDEAS FOR USING HAZELNUTS
- Use wild hazelnuts exactly as you would use domestic hazelnuts. They also make a good substitute for chopped or slivered almonds in most dishes; chop the hazelnuts to the appropriate consistency in a food processor.
- Chop the nuts to the consistency of coarse meal, and add to baked goods such as pancakes or muffins.
- Coarsely chopped or broken hazelnuts are delicious in vegetable stews.
- I love to use finely chopped hazelnuts, mixed with a little flour or cracker crumbs, to dredge fish that I am pan-frying.

OTHER RECIPES IN THIS BOOK FEATURING HAZELNUTS
- Pesto with Basil and Ramp Leaves (page 30)
- Baked Asparagus with Hazelnut Breadcrumbs (page 78)
- As a substitute in Browned-Butter Hickory Nut Pie (page 133)
- Wild and Brown Rice Casserole with Mushrooms (page 389)

Hazelnut and Parsley Pasta

2 or 3 servings; easily increased Preparation: Under 30 minutes

Here's an easy, quick and delicious recipe that I made up when I was harvesting the herbs from the garden before a killing frost one fall. Wild hazelnuts are the perfect accent; they are harvested several weeks earlier, and blend beautifully with the sharp, clean taste of garden-fresh parsley.

6 to 8 ounces uncooked fettuccini
   or linguini
2 tablespoons unsalted butter
¼ cup coarsely chopped wild hazelnuts
3 or 4 cloves garlic, minced

½ cup chicken broth
A handful of fresh parsley, preferably
   Italian flat-leaved parsley
Salt and pepper
Grated Parmesan cheese for serving

In large pot of lightly salted boiling water, begin cooking pasta according to package directions. While pasta is cooking, melt butter in medium skillet over medium heat. Add hazelnuts; cook, stirring frequently, until they become fragrant and lightly brown, about 5 minutes. Add garlic; cook for about 2 minutes longer. Add broth; increase heat to medium-high and cook until liquid has reduced to about 2 tablespoons. Meanwhile, chop parsley to medium consistency in food processor or by hand.

When pasta is cooked but still firm to the bite, scoop out a bit of the water and set it aside, then drain pasta and return to cooking pot. Pour reduced hazelnut mixture over pasta. Add chopped parsley, and toss everything together to mix well. If it appears too dry, add a little of the pasta cooking water (this is not a saucy dish; it should be moist but not wet). Season to taste with salt and pepper. Serve immediately, passing grated Parmesan to add at the table.

Hazelnut-Chocolate Gelato

About 1 quart   Preparation: Involved (requires ice-cream maker)

Gelato is a style of ice cream that is popular in Italy (and becoming more popular here as people discover it). It's denser than regular ice cream, and has a smooth, silky texture.

3 cups whole milk, divided
¾ cup unsweetened cocoa powder
¾ cup sugar
3 tablespoons cornstarch

A generous pinch of salt
¾ cup coarsely chopped hazelnuts, skinned if you like

If using ice-cream maker that requires pre-freezing, place it in freezer as directed by manufacturer, generally 12 to 24 hours.

In medium saucepan, heat 2 cups milk just to boiling over medium heat. While milk is heating, combine remaining 1 cup milk with cocoa powder, sugar, cornstarch and salt in small bowl; whisk to blend. Add cocoa mixture to boiling milk; reduce heat and simmer, stirring constantly, until cocoa powder and sugar dissolve and mixture thickens, about 3 minutes. Transfer mixture to large bowl. Stir in hazelnuts and set aside to cool, then cover and refrigerate for at least 4 hours or as long as overnight.

When you're ready to churn, start ice-cream maker (if using electric machine); pour chilled mixture into container. Churn until gelato holds a soft shape, 15 to 20 minutes. Transfer gelato to plastic container; cover and freeze until hard, at least 4 hours. To serve, let soften at room temperature for 5 minutes before scooping.

Apricot and Hazelnut Biscotti

About 60 biscotti

2 cups all-purpose flour, plus additional for working with dough
2 teaspoons baking powder
1/2 teaspoon salt
1/4 cup (half of a stick) unsalted butter, softened

1/2 cup sugar
1/2 teaspoon vanilla extract
2 eggs, lightly beaten
3/4 cup whole or halved hazelnuts, toasted and cooled
3/4 cup diced dried apricots (about 5 ounces)

Heat oven to 350°F. Spray baking sheet with nonstick spray; set aside. Combine flour, baking powder and salt in wire-mesh strainer or sifter; sift into large mixing bowl and set aside. In food processor fitted with metal blade, combine butter and sugar; process until light and fluffy. Add vanilla and 1 egg; process until just blended. Add remaining egg; process until just blended. Add flour mixture; pulse on-and-off just until flour is incorporated.

Turn dough out onto lightly floured worksurface. Knead a few times, then divide in half. Roll a portion into a rectangle that is about 8 inches wide and 3 or 4 inches long. Scatter half of the nuts and half of the apricots evenly over the rectangle, keeping the back inch clear of nuts or fruit. Roll up rectangle into a log, patting firmly. Place on prepared baking sheet. Repeat with remaining dough, nuts and fruit; place second log on baking sheet 3 inches from first log. Pat each into a flattened, rounded rectangle that is about 10 inches long and 2½ inches wide. Bake until very lightly colored and firm to the touch, about 25 minutes. Remove from oven, then reduce the temperature to 300°F.

Cool logs on baking sheet for 10 minutes, then use 2 spatulas to transfer each log to a cutting board. Using serrated knife, cut logs diagonally into 3/4-inch-wide slices. Transfer slices to same baking sheet. Bake for 15 minutes. Turn biscotti over, and bake for 15 minutes longer, or until firm and dry (biscotti will become harder as they cool off). Transfer to wire rack to cool. Store in airtight container at room temperature.

Sunflower Nuts (Helianthus annuus)

Eat the toasted seeds, or sprout them for a delicious, nutritious salad addition.

HABITAT, RANGE

The sunflower is a native prairie plant that is found in most of our region. Their range extends from Michigan and Indiana westward to Idaho, and from the Canadian border all the way down to the Gulf states. Look for them in waste fields, on prairies and at the edges of agricultural areas, in disturbed spots, in ditches and on sunny hillsides. They require full sun.

PARTS USED

Seeds, generally toasted

SEASONS

Late summer

Sunflowers

IDENTIFICATION TIPS, DANGEROUS LOOKALIKES

There are many types of sunflowers in the United States. All produce edible seeds, but some species have seeds that are too small to bother with. Sunflowers are quite familiar in appearance, with golden petals and brown centers. Many wildflowers have this color pattern and general appearance, but none grow so large as the sunflower, which can reach heights of 9 feet; individual blooms can be as wide as 6 inches. Domestic sunflowers are much larger, attaining heights up to 15 feet and sporting blossoms up to a foot wide.

The sunflower is a coarse plant, with hairy stems that are stiff and upright. Leaves are alternate and heart-shaped, broadest near the base with a toothy, pointed tip; they feel like sandpaper when touched. Sunflowers have a large central disk that is brown or purplish brown and is surrounded by golden-yellow rays (commonly called petals) that are 1 to 2 inches long. The flower heads rotate to face the sun all day. In mid- to late summer, the central disk produces hundreds of seeds, each encased in a brittle, papery husk. These can be black, gray or striped with white.

HARVESTING TIPS

Cut off the entire flowering head, with about 4 inches of stem, after the seeds have formed but before they are dry enough to fall out. In our area, this is generally in late August or early September.

SPECIAL CONSIDERATIONS

Sunflower seeds are relished by all wild birds, and by many other critters as well. Be sure to leave some for the wildlife, and also to propagate for next year.

People who are allergic to pollen will react to sunflower pollen found in the flower heads, whether in the field or after harvesting; the seeds don't seem to cause a problem once they've been removed from the flower heads.

NUTS

MORE ABOUT SUNFLOWER NUTS: With their large, showy flowers, sunflowers are hand-some specimens no matter where they are found. They brighten the sides of roadways in both urban and rural areas, and add color to a landscape dominated by brown and green. It's really interesting to observe them several times throughout the day to note how they turn their heads to face the sun. At the end of their growing season, they provide a delicious and nutritious nut that is a small version of those we buy in the store.

Once you get the harvested sunflower heads home, hang them in a warm, dry place to cure. I sometimes hang them in mesh bags from the basement rafters to keep them out of the reach of mice that may find their way indoors as the weather cools in fall. Make sure that air can circulate freely around the flower heads as they are drying; I've had them get moldy when packed too tightly.

When the heads are dry, rub the seeds off; I hold the head over a paper grocery bag and rub into that. Spread the seeds out on a window screen and let them air-dry for a week or so, until all parts of the husk are dry and hard. They will keep in this way for months in a cool location.

To prepare the unhusked seeds for eating as an out-of-hand snack (peel-and-eat), soak them overnight in a solution of 1 gallon water to 2 cups salt. The next day, drain the seeds and air-dry them, then roast them in a 250°F oven for an hour or two, until the shells are crisp.

To prepare the seeds for use in salads or cooking (or if you prefer to eat already-shelled sunflower nuts rather than peel-and-eat), start with plain dried seeds, not salted as described above. Shell the nuts, discarding the husks (or saving them to make coffee; see below). Mix each cup of shelled nuts with a tablespoon of melted butter or oil and a scant ¼ teaspoon salt. Spread the buttered nuts on a baking sheet, and bake at 250°F until the nuts are lightly brown and crisp, about an hour and a half, stirring occasionally. If you like, you can add a little chili powder, cumin or cayenne to the butter mixture before roasting. Roasted nuts should be stored in the refrigerator or freezer.

Sprouted sunflower seeds are a delicious addition to salads, and make good use of seeds that may be too small to use in another way. Parrots and other pet birds absolutely love sprouted sunflower seeds as well. Start with dried seeds—not salted or roasted; the seeds must be whole, not cracked or broken. Soak ½ to 1 cup of sunflower seeds in a jar of cool water for 4 to 6 hours; if you're sprouting for yourself rather than a bird, it's best to husk the seeds first, but you can also remove the husks from the sprouts. Drain well, then place in a small strainer set in a bowl, and cover it loosely with waxed paper. (Sprouter kits are much easier and more efficient than this strainer arrangement. I got an excellent sprouter from The Sprout People: www.sproutpeople.com.) Rinse the sprouts several times a day, letting them drain well before returning the strainer to the bowl and re-covering it. They generally sprout in a day or two; when the seed splits open and develops a white tail that is ¼ inch long, it is ready to eat, although you can let the tail grow longer if you prefer. Experiment with longer or shorter sprouting times to determine how you like them. You can also plant the sprouted seeds in a tray of dirt and let them grow until they have tiny leaves, then cut these off to use in salads.

JUST FOR FUN

Sunflower Art Projects

Get a reproduction of one (or more) of Vincent Van Gogh's paintings of sunflowers. He painted a series of these while living in Arles, France in 1888 and 1889, and they are as beautiful and important today as they were then. Get watercolors, tempera paints, chalk or crayons, and a supply of drawing pads. Take the kids on a field trip to see growing sunflowers, then back home to study Van Gogh's paintings; you might want to pick a sunflower to bring back and put in a vase also. Let the kids create their own artwork of sunflowers. Sunflowers are an excellent subject for kids to paint or sketch because of the bright colors and interesting shapes.

QUICK IDEAS FOR USING SUNFLOWER NUTS

- To make sunflower butter, grind raw or roasted sunflowers in a food processor, adding a little peanut oil if necessary, until smooth; sweeten with honey or maple syrup to taste and store in the refrigerator.
- Sprinkle roasted sunflower nuts on salads for a nice crunch.
- For sunflower shell coffee, roast the husks in a 350°F oven until browned, 15 to 20 minutes. Cool and grind in a coffee grinder; brew as you would coffee, or mix with ground coffee as an extender. It doesn't taste quite like coffee, and it is caffeine-free, so it will not replace your morning espresso; but it's interesting to try if you are shelling a pile of sunflower nuts.

Homemade Granola

About 4½ cups   Preparation: Over an hour

3 cups old-fashioned rolled oats (not instant)
1¼ cups whole wheat flour
½ cup (packed) golden brown sugar
½ cup slivered almonds
½ cup chopped butternuts, black walnuts or other nuts
½ cup dry nonfat milk powder
⅓ cup roasted sunflower nuts

½ teaspoon salt
½ cup vegetable oil
½ cup water
¼ cup honey
2 tablespoons maple syrup
¾ teaspoon vanilla extract
¾ cup dried blueberries, huckleberries or cranberries

Heat oven to 300°F. In 13 x 9 x 2-inch baking dish, combine oats, flour, sugar, almonds, butternuts, milk powder, sunflower nuts and salt; stir to mix. In small bowl, whisk together oil, water, honey, syrup and vanilla. Pour evenly over oat mixture, stirring to coat. Bake until granola is crunchy and golden brown, about 45 minutes, stirring frequently. Turn off oven and let baking dish sit in oven for 20 minutes. Stir in dried berries; let baking dish sit in oven for about 20 minutes longer. Remove baking dish from oven and cool granola completely. Store at room temperature in airtight containers.

Spaghetti with Ramp Leaves and Sunflower Nuts

2 or 3 servings; easily increased   Preparation: Under 30 minutes

6 to 8 ounces uncooked spaghetti
10 to 20 ramp leaves, fresh or previously frozen
1 tablespoon butter
3 tablespoons roasted sunflower nuts

¼ teaspoon hot red pepper flakes
½ cup chicken broth
Salt and pepper
Parmesan or Romano cheese for serving

Heat large pot of salted water to boiling. Add spaghetti and cook according to package instructions.

Meanwhile, pat ramp leaves dry if still wet from washing. Cut leaves into ¼-inch-wide strips, cutting across the width rather than from top to bottom. In medium skillet, melt butter over medium heat. Add sunflower nuts and hot pepper; sauté until sunflower nuts are just beginning to color. Add sliced ramp leaves and sauté for about 2 minutes. Add chicken broth; increase heat to medium-high and cook until broth reduces to about half. Remove from heat; add salt and pepper to taste.

Drain spaghetti and pour into a warmed bowl, or return to empty (but still warm) cooking pot. Pour ramp mixture over spaghetti and toss thoroughly. Pass Parmesan or Romano cheese separately, preferably grating freshly onto each serving.

GREENS & FLOWERS

FLOWERS ARE a relatively small category in this book, so I am lumping them together with greens because with some plants, both the flowers and the greens are used as food. In several cases, the root of a flowering plant is also eaten, but I have chosen to cover roots as a separate chapter because their harvest and preparation are so different from flowers and greens.

There are a number of wild plants with non-showy flowers whose greens are used as vegetables, and these make up the bulk of this section. Included here are two of the most commonly used wild foods: curly dock and nettles. You'll also find the "edible lawn weeds" here, including purslane, lamb's quarters, plantain and the sorrels—sheep and wood sorrel. Dandelions, an honorable member of the "edible lawn weeds" clan, are handled separately in the Top Ten chapter. In addition, several wildflowers have leaves that are edible, even though the flower is not (usually) used. I've lumped a few of these together under the heading of Edible Flower Leaves.

A section called Tea Flowers includes three plants whose flowers are commonly used for tea: chamomile, red clover and pineapple weed. Wild roses are discussed in the Fruits and Berries chapter; although the rose petals are edible, the rose hips are really the story, so I felt that this plant should be in with the other fruits. Uses for rose petals are discussed in the Wild Roses listing that begins on page 240.

Curly Dock *(Rumex crispus)*

Abundant and easy to find, dock is probably the most commonly harvested wild green. Its lemony taste is welcome in braises and simmered dishes.

HABITAT, RANGE

Curly dock is an introduced plant that has naturalized throughout the United States. It is one of the most easily recognizable and commonly found edible green plants, and grows in agricultural fields and nearby ditches, along roads, in vacant lots and on waste ground. It prefers moist, sunny areas, but will tolerate poor soil and partial shade.

PARTS USED

Young leaves, raw or cooked; stalks, cooked

SEASONS

Spring and summer

IDENTIFICATION TIPS, DANGEROUS LOOKALIKES

Curly dock

Curly dock—also called curled dock, yellow dock or sour dock—is a member of a large family of docks, including patience dock (*R. patientia*) and greater water dock (*R. orbiculatus*), both of which also grow throughout our region and are also edible. Curly dock has paddle-shaped, coarse, deep blue-green leaves that are 5 to 10 inches long and have deeply curled edges (rather like lasagna noodles). Leaves have a deep central midrib, with numerous smaller veins branching out to the edges. The leaf attaches to the stem in a distinctive way—the base of the leaf clasps the stem with a papery straw-colored sheath. The leaves form a rosette at the base of the plant; further up the plant, they grow opposite one another on a coarse, stiff central stem that may appear ribbed. The plant can reach as much as 6 feet in height after flowering.

Dock is a biennial, flowering in its second year. In mid-summer, the tops of the second-year plants develop long clusters of densely packed green flowers that develop into flattened seed husks, each about ¼ inch across and containing 3 seeds. The seed husks turn brown in the fall, and persist to the following spring, making early-spring identification of a dock patch easy. No species of dock is toxic, although some are too sour or bitter to be of interest to the cook. Curly dock is generally regarded as the best for eating.

Young burdock (page 392) may be confused with young dock; however, burdock leaves are covered with fine hairs on the undersides, and the leaves are broader and coarser than dock leaves. Burdock leaves resemble rhubarb leaves (but much coarser), while young dock look more like large, narrow, thick spinach leaves.

HARVESTING TIPS

Look for last year's old brown dock plants to find young, edible dock in the spring. The seed clusters of the old plants are recognizable even from a distance. When the midrib of each leaf becomes red in summer, the leaf is too sour to be used raw in salads; it's still fine for cooking.

Dock is a vigorous grower, and the seeds are designed by nature to blow away, helping to propagate the plant; in addition, the plants spread by underground roots. Don't worry about over-harvesting dock; it is a survivor, and will continue to flourish even if picked heavily.

SPECIAL CONSIDERATIONS

Some people may get an upset stomach from eating large quantities of dock. As with all unfamiliar foods, eat a reasonable portion, especially the first time, until you know if you will have an adverse reaction. Dock has the reputation of causing kidney problems due to soluble oxalates in the plant, but it's unlikely that the amount eaten by any forager would cause these problems. However, if you have kidney problems, this is something to consider.

In *Identifying and Harvesting Edible and Medicinal Plants in Wild (and Not So Wild) Places,* Steve Brill reports that eating very young, unwashed dock leaves causes a persistent numbing sensation on the tongue. Washing takes care of the problem.

MORE ABOUT CURLY DOCK: Curly dock, along with lamb's quarters and dandelion, was introduced to the East coast by colonists who brought seeds over from across the Atlantic. All these plants flourished in the New World, and are now found throughout the country. Dock is probably the most popular of these as a green vegetable. It grows in large stands, making it easy to gather a meal's worth. It has a deep green flavor with lemon overtones, and provides good amounts of calcium, iron and trace minerals, as well as respectable amounts of vitamins A and C.

Very young dock leaves that have no trace of red on the veins can be used raw in salads. They are a bit coarse, and there are other wild greens that I enjoy far more in salads, but you may like to try this. I prefer to cook the greens; young greens can be simply boiled, sautéed or steamed. Older greens that have red midribs may be fairly sour; par-boiling them, then draining before using in the final dish, helps eliminate this sourness. Dock doesn't cook down as much as other greens, so you don't need to gather as much as you would of, say, sorrel. Because dock is easy to harvest in large quantities, you may find yourself with more than you can eat. Par-boil the leaves, then pack them into freezer-weight plastic bags and freeze.

Stems can be harvested all spring and into the summer, and are easy to prepare. Peel away the tough outer layer, starting at the base, then simmer in a skillet of water for a few minutes until tender. They can be served as a sour vegetable (good with lots of butter), or added to soups and stews. Don't add them until the end, because they get mushy if cooked too long.

You'll often read that dried dock seeds can be ground in a spice grinder or blender to make a meal that can be added to muffin batter and the like; it has no natural thickening power so it can't be used entirely in place of flour, and it will make the final product denser. It's a lot of work to separate the seeds from the inedible dried husks, and I've never thought the resulting product was worth all that effort. It is an interesting experiment to try with the extremely plentiful dock seeds, but may yield disappointing results.

JUST FOR FUN

Dried Dock Flower Arrangements
The dried seed heads of dock make an interesting addition to a vase of fall wildflowers.

QUICK IDEAS FOR USING CURLY DOCK
- Substitute dock leaves, picked before the midribs turn pinkish, for kale (or broccoli di rabe) in any recipe. Reduce or eliminate any lemon juice or vinegar called for in the dish; curly dock contributes its own sour flavor to the dish.

OTHER RECIPES IN THIS BOOK FEATURING CURLY DOCK
- Vegetable Terrine with Mushrooms (page 382)

Pasta with Dock and Sausage

4 servings   Preparation: Under an hour

1 pound orecchiette, small shells or other relatively small "shaped" pasta	2 cloves garlic, minced
12 ounces dock leaves	1 can (8 ounces) tomato sauce
1 pound bulk Italian sausage*	2 teaspoons mixed Italian herb blend
1 medium onion, chopped	1½ cups shredded mozzarella cheese

Heat oven to 350°F. Spray medium casserole with nonstick spray; set aside. In large pot of lightly salted boiling water, begin cooking pasta according to package directions. Begin heating another large pot of lightly salted water to boiling. Cut dock leaves in half lengthwise; if the midrib is thick and tough, cut it away and discard. Cut leaf halves into ½-inch strips, cutting across the length so you have short strips (rather than with the length to get long strips). Add to second pot of boiling water, and cook until just tender, generally 5 to 10 minutes. Drain dock leaves and refresh in cold water. When pasta is cooked, drain that also, and return to cooking pot.

In medium skillet, cook sausage over medium heat until lightly browned and cooked through, stirring to break up. Drain excess grease; add onion and garlic and cook, stirring frequently, until onion is tender, about 5 minutes. Stir in tomato sauce and herb blend; cook for a minute longer. Transfer sausage mixture and drained dock leaves to pot with pasta; stir to combine. Transfer mixture to prepared casserole; top with shredded cheese. Bake until cheese melts and casserole is bubbly around edges, about 20 minutes.

*If you can't find bulk sausage, simply buy uncooked Italian sausages and remove the casings.

Dock and Chickpea Soup

4 servings   Preparation: Under an hour

You may substitute other greens, such as sheep sorrel or lamb's quarters, for the dock; if using greens that reduce significantly in volume as they cook, use about 6 cup of cut-up greenss. For a nice flavor, try a mix of greens.

2 uncooked bratwurst or Italian sausages
1 tablespoon olive oil
2 medium yellow onions, diced
10 cloves garlic, minced
½ teaspoon hot red pepper flakes
½ cup dry sherry
1 teaspoon dried oregano
½ teaspoon paprika
½ teaspoon ground cumin
3 to 4 cups cut-up young dock leaves

1 quart chicken broth
1 can (16 ounces) chickpeas, drained
    and rinsed
3 tablespoons tomato paste
½ teaspoon salt
1 tablespoon cornmeal
Freshly ground black pepper
2 hard-cooked eggs, optional, chopped
Grated Parmesan cheese for garnish,
    optional

Remove casings from sausages; crumble meat into large pot or small Dutch oven. Cook over medium heat, stirring frequently to break up, until sausage loses pink color. Add oil, and heat briefly. Add onions, garlic and pepper flakes; reduce heat to medium-low and cook until onions are very soft and beginning to color, about 10 minutes, stirring frequently. Add sherry, oregano, paprika and cumin; stir to loosen browned bits on bottom of pan. Increase heat to medium and cook until sherry cooks away, about 5 minutes. Add dock, broth, chickpeas, tomato paste and salt. Heat to boiling over high heat; reduce heat so mixture bubbles gently and cook for about 5 minutes. Sprinkle cornmeal over the top, then stir in; continue cooking for about 10 minutes longer, stirring occasionally. Spoon into individual soup plates; grind some fresh black pepper over each serving. Top each serving with a sprinkling of egg and some Parmesan cheese, if using.

Greens and White Beans

2 main-dish or 4 side-dish servings; easily increased   Preparation: Under an hour

Serve with crusty bread to soak up the savory juices in this Italian-style dish.

1 tablespoon olive oil
1 small onion, diced
4 to 6 cloves garlic, chopped
¼ teaspoon hot red pepper flakes
10 to 12 ounces fresh dock leaves
1 can (15 ounces) cannellini beans, white
    kidney beans or great northern beans

1 cup chicken broth
½ teaspoon mixed Italian herb blend, or
    herbs of your choosing
¼ teaspoon salt
A few grinds of fresh black pepper
Grated Parmesan cheese for serving

Heat oil over medium heat in small soup pot. Add onion and garlic; cook, stirring frequently, until beginning to color, about 5 minutes. Add red pepper flakes; cook for a few minutes longer. Meanwhile, rinse the dock very well in cold water; shake to dry somewhat, but don't try to dry completely; the leaves should retain some water. Cut dock crosswise into 1-inch strips. Add to pot. Cook, stirring frequently, for about 5 minutes. Drain beans; rinse briefly and drain again (some of the bean liquid should remain clinging to the beans). Add beans, broth, herbs, salt and pepper to pot. Adjust heat so mixture bubbles gently. Cook for about 15 minutes, stirring occasionally. Serve in soup plates, passing Parmesan cheese separately.

Impossible Greens Pie

4 servings   Preparation: Under an hour

"Impossible pies" were developed by the good folks who make Bisquick baking mix. A mixture of Bisquick, eggs and milk is poured over other ingredients; during baking, the mixture forms a soft crust underneath the rest of the ingredients. This easy pie features wild greens and cottage cheese.

½ cup diced onion
2 teaspoons chopped garlic
1 teaspoon olive oil, butter or margarine
2½ cups chopped dock, or 4 cups of any
    more-tender wild greens such as sheep
    sorrel, lamb's quarters or dandelion
1 cup cottage cheese (cottage cheese with
    chives is a nice variation)

1 cup milk (lowfat or skim works fine)
½ cup Bisquick
3 eggs, or ¾ cup liquid egg substitute
¼ cup grated Parmesan or Romano cheese
½ teaspoon salt
½ teaspoon dried oregano
½ teaspoon dried marjoram
A good pinch of freshly grated pepper

Heat oven to 350°F. Spray 2-quart casserole with nonstick spray; set aside. In large skillet, sauté onion and garlic in oil over medium heat until just soft. Add greens; sauté until greens are tender, adding a little water if necessary. Scrape mixture into prepared casserole. Spoon cottage cheese evenly over greens. In blender, combine remaining ingredients; process until smooth. Pour evenly over greens. Bake for 35 to 40 minutes, or until set and golden brown. Let stand for 5 minutes before serving.

Day Lilies *(Hemerocallis fulva)*

A lovely flower that lasts but a single day; the spent blossoms can even be gathered the next day. The unopened buds can be battered and fried like zucchini blossoms.

HABITAT, RANGE

The day lily is an introduced plant that now grows wild in the majority of our region, although it is scarce to non-existent in the Dakotas. It is found on abandoned homesites and waste ground, along roadsides, on the edges of farm fields, and in empty lots. Day lilies prefer a good amount of sun.

PARTS USED

Ripe flowers, cooked (often dried); tubers, raw or cooked

SEASONS

Flowers, mid- to late summer; tubers, spring through summer

IDENTIFICATION TIPS, DANGEROUS LOOKALIKES

Day lilies

Day lilies are a common and familiar garden plant that has escaped into the wild. Leaves grow from the base of the plant and are long, narrow and swordlike with veins running from base to tip. They resemble the leaves of iris (*Iris* spp.), but iris leaves tend to be more upright while the leaves of day lilies bend and arch downward at the ends. Iris roots are poisonous, but the plants are easy to identify when flowering as the iris doesn't resemble the day lily at all.

Day lily flowers are distinctive and easy to distinguish. Each blossom is 4 to 6 inches long; it has 6 petals that form a deep vase-like shape, and the petals are orange with a yellow stripe down the center. Flowers grow in multiples on a leafless stalk, and face upwards. The petals have no spots, which helps distinguish them from the Turk's cap lily (*Lilium superbum*), an edible flower whose tubers can also be cooked and eaten. As a further point of distinction, the flower stalks of the tiger lily have leaves on them, while flower stalks of the day lily are leafless. Iris flower stalks have leaves also, and as noted, this is a plant you want to avoid.

HARVESTING TIPS

The best day lily flowers are those that are fully open; if you prefer to eat the buds, gather them when they are about half-open, before the petals flare. Each day lily lasts but a single day; however, fallen day-old blossoms can be gathered and cooked the same day, or dried for later use.

If you are planning to harvest the roots of day lilies in the spring before the plant is in bloom, I recommend doing so only when you have positively identified a patch of flowers the previous summer, to avoid digging poisonous iris tubers.

SPECIAL CONSIDERATIONS

Field Guide to North American Wild Plants cautions that the day lily should be eaten in moderation, to avoid a possible laxative effect.

If you are tempted to eat the day lilies in your garden, consider first that any chemicals you—or the nursery from which you bought the plants—may have put in the soil will be in the plant's system. Allow several years of growth with no chemicals before eating garden day lilies.

MORE ABOUT DAY LILIES: Day lilies reproduce by underground tubers, and can form large colonies over the course of years. However, these tubers aren't exactly mobile, so the plants aren't seen as frequently as plants that spread by seeds (although somehow, day lilies do manage to spread to new areas occasionally). I see them primarily on abandoned homesteads, at the edges of civilization, and along freeways (where I wouldn't harvest them even if I could get at them, due to concerns about fumes). I have eaten the tubers, and they're delicious, with a sweet, almost corn-like flavor and a wonderful crunch. However, I don't dig them up except when I see a really large colony; in these cases, it helps the colony to break up and loosen some of the tubers, allowing the choked roots to expand.

The flowers, however, can be harvested freely; they last just a day, and they don't contribute to reproduction so you're not harming the resource by taking them—you're just depriving the landscape of a lovely flower that would be gone the next day.

Day lily buds (the unopened flower head) are delicious, with a taste that seems like a cross between a green bean and a zucchini. You can boil or braise them by themselves, then serve them as a solo vegetable; however, their soft texture—like cooked zucchini—seems less interesting to me than other vegetables, and like zucchini, day lilies seem best to me in a mixed dish.

Dried day lilies are used in Chinese cooking; they're called golden needles, and are an integral ingredient in several famous dishes including Hot and Sour Soup (see page 358 for my recipe). To dry the flowers, choose fresh or day-old flowers. Place them on wire racks and dry at room temperature until leathery and shrunken; you can also dry them in a food dehydrator or in the oven on the lowest setting, where they will be dry in 3 or 4 hours (see pages 420-422 for information on drying foods in a dehydrator or oven). Store dried day lilies in glass jars in a cool cupboard; they don't take up much room because the volume of the flower is considerably reduced by drying. Re-hydrate the dried flowers before use; it takes 20 to 30 minutes in tepid water. After soaking, I prefer to tear them into halves or quarters along the length; if the base seems woody after soaking, I cut that away before tearing them. If you prefer, you can add the entire dried blossom to soups or stews, where they will contribute a subtle floral tang.

Raw day lily petals can also be eaten, but I've honestly never tried this. Like rose petals, the day lily petal is likely to be bitter at the base where the petal joins the stem; you may want to cut this lighter area away before adding the raw petals to salads or the like. Some people report a mild reaction to the raw petals, which may irritate the throat slightly.

QUICK IDEAS FOR USING DAY LILIES
- Simmer day lily buds (unopened flowers) in lightly salted water for 15 minutes, then serve as you would cooked zucchini.
- Slice peeled raw tubers very thinly and add to green salads for a sweet, crunchy sensation. The tubers are quite small, but luckily a little goes a long way.
- Make pickled day lily buds, following any recipe you have for pickled zucchini.
- Add day lily buds to stir-fries.
- Chop up day-old flowers and add to stews or soup.

OTHER RECIPES IN THIS BOOK FEATURING DAY LILIES
- Hot and Sour Soup (page 358)

Frittata with Day Lily Flowers

A frittata is an Italian-style flat (not rolled) omelet. This one is great for a nice brunch; serve with fresh fruit and muffins or tea bread.

1 medium zucchini, halved lengthwise and
    sliced ⅛ inch thick
Half of a red bell pepper, diced
Half of a medium onion, cut in half across
    the equator and then into thin strips
1 tablespoon olive oil
1 garlic clove, finely chopped
6 eggs, or 1½ cups liquid egg substitute

¼ cup whole milk or light cream
1 teaspoon chopped fresh oregano, or
    ½ teaspoon dried
½ teaspoon salt
A few grindings of black pepper
6 day lily flowers, green bases removed
¼ cup crumbled feta cheese

Heat oven to 450°F. In large oven-proof skillet, sauté zucchini, bell pepper and onion in oil over medium heat, stirring frequently, until vegetables are just tender. Add garlic and cook for about a minute longer. While garlic is cooking, combine eggs, milk, oregano, salt and pepper in mixing bowl; beat well with whisk. Pour egg mixture into skillet; stir to allow egg to flow around and under vegetables. Arrange day lily flowers in an attractive pattern on top. Cook without stirring for about 3 minutes; the top should still be moist, but the bottom should be well set. Sprinkle feta cheese evenly over the top. Place skillet in oven; cook until eggs are set and top is puffed and bubbly, 5 to 10 minutes. Remove from oven; cool slightly before cutting into wedges to serve.

Batter-Fried Blossoms

Variable servings; make as much as you wish   Preparation: Under 15 minutes

Serve these as an appetizer, or as an unusual side dish. The amount of batter given will coat about 6 flowers; make more as you need it.

Peanut oil for frying
¾ cup beer or club soda
⅔ cup all-purpose flour
⅛ teaspoon salt

A few grindings of black pepper
Fresh day lily flowers, green bases removed
Garlic salt or other salt blend

In deep skillet or large saucepan, begin heating 1 inch of oil over medium-high heat; it will need to be at 375°F for frying. While oil is heating, whisk together beer, flour, salt and pepper in large mixing bowl. When oil reaches 375°F, dip flowers, one at a time, in batter, turning to coat; allow excess to drip back into bowl. Add battered flowers to hot oil, 2 or 3 at a time. Cook until golden brown on all sides, turning carefully as needed. Drain on paper towel-lined plate; sprinkle with a little garlic salt to taste. Serve hot.

Shrimp Salad-Stuffed Day Lilies

4 servings (appetizer or luncheon)   Preparation: Under 15 minutes

Try this same technique with any stuffing mixture that sounds good to you. It's a lovely presentation, and makes a smashing centerpiece on a luncheon buffet.

½ pound peeled and deveined cooked
    shrimp
3 tablespoons minced red bell pepper
2 green onions, thinly sliced (whites and
    most of the greens)
3 tablespoons mayonnaise (reduced-fat
    works fine)

1 teaspoon rice vinegar or white wine
    vinegar
Salt and pepper
8 fresh day lily flowers, green bases
    removed
Sesame seeds for garnish

Chop shrimp to medium consistency. Place in mixing bowl; add bell pepper, green onions, mayonnaise and vinegar. Stir to combine well; add salt and pepper to taste. Just before serving, divide mixture evenly between flowers, packing into center; sprinkle filling with sesame seeds. Serve immediately.

Lamb's Quarters *(Chenopodium album)*

Sometimes called "wild spinach," lamb's quarters is common and easy to harvest in quantity. One of the first wild foods that beginning foragers learn.

HABITAT, RANGE
Lamb's quarters grows throughout the United States. Look for it on waste ground, in abandoned fields and vacant lots and in your own back yard; it is one of the most common edible "garden weeds."

PARTS USED
Leaves, raw or cooked; seeds, ground as flour substitute

SEASONS
Spring through fall

Lamb's quarters

IDENTIFICATION TIPS, DANGEROUS LOOKALIKES
Lamb's quarters is a tender annual herb that can grow as tall as 2 feet, although it is usually much shorter. Distinctive triangular leaves with large, rounded teeth give the plant one of its common names, goosefoot, as the leaves resemble the ribbed foot of a goose or duck. Leaves grow alternately on somewhat hairy stems that appear ridged or grooved; stems of larger plants may have a reddish tinge to them. The undersides of the leaves are powdery white or silvery, and covered with very fine hairs; the leaves seem water-resistant even on the top sides. Lamb's quarters have no perceptible odor; if you find a plant that looks like lamb's quarters but smells strong, this isn't lamb's quarters.

HARVESTING TIPS
In early spring, pick entire plants; the tender stems are delicious when steamed, boiled or sautéed, so the entire plant can be cooked without pulling off the leaves. Later in the season, when the stems become tough, harvest only leaves or the tender new growth at the tops of the plants.

SPECIAL CONSIDERATIONS
Lamb's quarters absorbs toxins from contaminated soil more readily than some other wild plants, so it is particularly important to forage well away from roadsides or other sources of pollution when harvesting this plant.

Lamb's quarters is a vigorous grower that spreads easily. You don't have to worry too much about overharvesting this plant, as it will pop back up the next year—even where you may not want it (like in your petunia bed).

MORE ABOUT LAMB'S QUARTERS: One summer, I was at the house of Ron Berg, a well-known chef in the Gunflint Trail area of northeastern Minnesota. His wife Keli was with us as we were inspecting Ron's garden, and she pointed to a neatly tended row of lamb's quarters in the garden bed. "I thought they were weeds," she said, "and was starting to pull them out when Ron got all upset because he had *planted* those things in the garden!" Turns out that the previous fall, Ron had painstakingly gathered seeds from lamb's quarters so that he could have a ready crop of this, one of his favorite greens.

Ron's not the only one to value this particular plant. Like curly dock, lamb's quarters was introduced to the United States by European settlers; both plants have spread and are now naturalized throughout most of the country. Lamb's quarters is one of the best of the wild greens, with a mild flavor similar to spinach. Unlike spinach, lamb's quarters doesn't bolt or get bitter in warm weather, making it an excellent green for summer use. It's rich in calcium, iron and potassium, and has good amounts of vitamins A and C as well as trace minerals.

The leaves have a rough, almost fuzzy coating on the undersides, and this can be a turn-off when they are used raw in a salad. Young, small leaves have less of this, so are the best choice for eating raw; I often gather a few handfuls of young lamb's quarters to toss into a mixed salad in the spring.

Cooked lamb's quarters is delicious, and can be handled just like spinach. Like spinach, lamb's quarters leaves cook down to a fraction of their raw volume, so you need to gather a quart or more of raw leaves for each serving of cooked leaves you want. I often snip off the entire plant when it is young and tender in the spring, and cook it whole without picking the leaves off; the stem is tender and tasty at this stage, and it's easier to prepare the greens for cooking if you don't have to fiddle around pulling off individual leaves.

In the fall, lamb's quarters produces many tiny black seeds. These can be shaken from the dried plants into a paper bag, then ground and added to breads and baked goods. Like most of the seeds that can be gathered from wild plants to use as a flour substitute, lamb's quarter seeds can't replace white flour as they don't have gluten; they are also dark and will add noticeable flecks to your baked goods (so don't add them to an angel-food cake!). I've heard about cooking the seeds down as a sort of gruel, but have never tried this.

QUICK IDEAS FOR USING LAMB'S QUARTERS
• Pick tender young leaves to add raw to green salads.
• Steam or lightly boil leaves, or entire tender young plants, and serve as you would spinach.

OTHER RECIPES IN THIS BOOK FEATURING LAMB'S QUARTERS
• Salade Sauvage (page 54)
• As substitute in Dock and Chickpea Soup (page 299)
• Impossible Greens Pie (page 300)

Steam-Sautéed Lamb's Quarters

General instructions; make as much as you wish   Preparation: Under 15 minutes

For each serving, you will need:

1 teaspoon butter, margarine or olive oil
½ teaspoon minced garlic
3 to 4 cups (tightly packed) lamb's quarters leaves or whole young plants, wet from washing

½ teaspoon freshly squeezed lemon juice
Salt
A pinch of cayenne pepper or black pepper

In medium or large skillet, melt butter over medium heat. Add garlic; cook for about a minute, stirring frequently. Add lamb's quarters; they should still have water clinging to them from washing (if they are dry, add a few teaspoons of water to skillet with greens). Sprinkle with lemon juice. Cook, stirring frequently, until greens lose much of their volume. Cover skillet and cook for about 3 minutes, stirring several times. Remove cover; sprinkle greens with salt and cayenne or black pepper to taste. Cook until liquid in skillet reduces to almost nothing, which should take just a minute or two. Taste for seasoning and adjust if necessary; serve immediately.

Variation: Steam-Sautéed Sheep Sorrel
Follow recipe above, substituting 4 cups sheep sorrel leaves for the lamb's quarters. Eliminate the lemon juice. Proceed as directed.

Homemade Wild Greens Pasta

About 1 pound fresh pasta (enough for 4 servings)   Preparation: Over an hour

1 cup (tightly packed) lamb's quarters,
   ramp greens, dandelion greens or
   other greens
2 eggs
2 teaspoons olive oil

½ teaspoon salt
2 cups all-purpose flour, approximate, plus
   additional for rolling dough
1 tablespoon water, approximate
A little butter or olive oil, optional

Heat large pot of salted water to boiling. Add greens; return to boiling and cook for 1 minute. Drain immediately and refresh with plenty of cold water. Roll greens up in a towel and squeeze to remove as much moisture as possible. Add greens to food processor and chop as finely as possible. Add eggs, oil and salt to food processor and process for about a minute. Add 2 cups of the flour and process until a ball forms; if mixture is too crumbly, add a little water. Process for about 1 minute; dough should be smooth and resilient. Wrap dough in plastic wrap and set aside for about 30 minutes.

Divide dough into 4 balls, and re-wrap to prevent dough from drying out until you're ready to roll and cut it. If you have a pasta machine, roll to ¹/₁₆ inch thickness and cut as desired. Otherwise, on lightly floured surface, roll each ball to a ¹/₁₆-inch-thick rectangle. Cut into ¼-inch-wide noodles, or as desired. Transfer to pastry cloth or cutting board that has been generously dusted with flour while you roll out remaining pasta.

You can cut the pasta an hour or 2 in advance of cooking time; to keep noodles from sticking together, you need to "fluff" them every 15 minutes or so. To do this, gently pick up a loose handful of noodles with your fingertips, separating the individual noodles by shaking gently or pulling apart as necessary; let the fluffed noodles fall gently back onto the floured pastry cloth, a few noodles at a time. The noodles should be lightly coated with flour; sprinkle a little additional flour over the noodles before fluffing if necessary.

To cook the pasta, heat large kettle of salted water to boiling. Add pasta and stir gently with wooden spoon. Cook for about 2 minutes (slightly longer if your noodles are somewhat uneven in thickness); drain well. Toss with a little butter or oil to prevent sticking, or mix gently with sauce as desired.

Eggs Baked on Lamb's Quarters Nest

4 servings Preparation: Under an hour

These make a lovely brunch dish, and also work well as a starter or light supper.

4 slices bacon
¼ cup diced onion
7 to 8 cups (tightly packed) lamb's quarters
  greens
⅓ cup heavy cream
¼ teaspoon salt

A few grindings of black pepper
¼ cup finely grated Parmesan or Romano
  cheese
4 eggs*
Hot toast points

Heat oven to 400°F. Lightly spray 4 ramekins or 8-ounce baking dishes (such as small Pyrex bowls) with nonstick spray; arrange on baking sheet and set aside. In large skillet, cook bacon over medium heat until crisp; transfer to paper towel-lined plate. Pour off and discard all but about a tablespoon of bacon drippings from skillet. Add onion to skillet; cook over medium heat, stirring frequently, until tender. Add lamb's quarters to skillet; cover and cook until wilted and reduced in volume, stirring several times; this will only take a few minutes. Remove cover; if the greens have released much liquid, cook, uncovered, until liquid cooks away. When greens are dry, add cream, salt and pepper to skillet. Cook, stirring occasionally, until mixture is somewhat thickened, about 5 minutes.

Divide lamb's quarters mixture evenly between prepared ramekins. Crumble a slice of bacon over each; sprinkle a tablespoon of Parmesan over each. Use a spoon to make an indentation in center of lamb's quarters mixture; carefully break an egg into each indentation. Bake until egg whites are just set, about 15 minutes; yolks should still be runny. Serve with hot toast points.

*If you are concerned about salmonella, use pasteurized eggs for this dish, as the yolks are not fully cooked.

Nettles (wood nettle, *Laportea canadensis*; stinging nettle, *Urtica dioica*)

Amaze your friends by serving them (cooked) nettles…most people will be shocked to learn that they are edible—and delicious to boot!

HABITAT, RANGE

Nettles are fairly common throughout our entire region, except that wood nettles don't grow in hot, sunny plains such as those in the Dakotas. Stinging nettles thrive in sunny locations, while wood nettle prefers areas of dappled shade. Look for stinging nettle in disturbed areas, waste fields, along trails, fences and roads, and along streams and rivers that are not too overgrown. Wood nettle prefers moist areas such as forested riverbanks and stream corridors, and old riverbottom areas.

PARTS USED

Young leaves and shoots, cooked (stinging nettle is often dried)

SEASONS

Spring is the prime time for both species; stinging nettles produce another crop in the fall, and young stinging-nettle leaf tips can be gathered all summer (however, see Special Considerations below)

IDENTIFICATION TIPS, DANGEROUS LOOKALIKES

Both species of nettles are well-armed with fine hairs that can inflict a painful sting, and both have toothed, somewhat coarse leaves. Wood nettle plants have alternate leaves on a solid, rounded stem, while the longer, narrower leaves of stinging nettle are opposite on a hollow, squared stem (the stems are similar in appearance to mint stems). Wood nettle grows to perhaps 4 feet tall when mature, while I've walked in patches of stinging nettle that were over my head. Both species have clusters of tiny pale-greenish flowers in the leaf axils; the wood nettle has a cluster at the top of the stem as well, while stinging nettle does not. There are no toxic lookalikes.

Wood nettle

Stinging nettle

HARVESTING TIPS

The base of each nettle hair has a small bulb that is filled with irritating fluid; when the delicate but sharp hair enters the skin and the bulb is squeezed, the fluid is injected under the skin. Although there are foragers who pride themselves on picking nettles with bare hands, I recommend that you use gloves if you wish to avoid getting stung.

If you do get stung, take comfort from the fact that usually the pain goes away shortly (although I have felt a tingling numbness as much as 24 hours later, and know someone else who reports the same phenomenon). To relieve the sting, crush some dock or jewelweed on the affected area.

Nettles are vigorous growers; it's difficult to overharvest them, especially since you'll usually be taking just the top part of the plant.

SPECIAL CONSIDERATIONS

Herbalists and natural medicinalists use nettles to treat a variety of conditions ranging from gout, congestion and anemia to asthma and kidney problems. However, like many herbal supplements, nettle is subject to many conflicting opinions. The best advice I can give is that if you have concerns, ask your doctor. Noted naturalist Steve Brill, in his book *Identifying and Harvesting Edible and Medicinal Plants in Wild (and Not So Wild) Places*, says that nettle leaves should be collected "before they flower in the spring. They may be bad for the kidneys after they flower." This may be helpful advice to consider if you have concerns. Never eat nettle leaves raw.

MORE ABOUT NETTLES: Many people are astonished when they learn that nettles are edible. The common names used for nettles exemplify the typical attitude towards these plants: itch weed, fireweed, burn weed and seven-minute weed (the itch supposedly lasts for seven minutes). But in fact, nettles are one of the most commonly used wild greens; once they are cooked, the lose their sting entirely. They retain their bright green color even when cooked, a true rarity among greens. They are extremely nutritious, providing rich amounts of vitamins A and C, as well as calcium, iron, potassium and other trace minerals. Stinging nettle is easy to dry, and the reconstituted nettles retain the color and vitamins of the fresh leaves.

Several types of nettles grow in our region. All are edible when cooked; some are better than others (never eat any nettle leaves raw). Wood nettle is probably the best; it has a rich, warming, wholesome taste, and a bit more flavor than stinging nettle; it's also more tender than stinging nettle, which has a tendency to be stringy even early in the season. Stinging nettle appears in the woods a few weeks earlier than wood nettle, and flowers earlier. Once the plants start to flower, most foragers stop picking nettles. Some foragers, however (including me), continue to pick the tender new leaves at the top of the plant all summer; these leaves are fairly stringy but still tasty, and they work just fine for dishes such as Seven-

Minute Dip (page 315) or Nettle Soufflé (page 317), for which the cooked nettles are puréed. The tougher leaves also make a perfectly delicious tea or broth any time of the year; simply discard the leaves after brewing. Stinging nettle produces another crop in the fall, and will continue to produce even after a light frost or two.

Nettles are easy to cook. First, wash the stalks well in several changes of water, then pluck the leaves from the stems, toss them in boiling water to cover and cook for a few minutes; drain and use as you would cooked spinach (if you're like me and prefer to handle nettles with rubber gloves, you'll want to wear them while handling the uncooked leaves). The cooking water can be used as the base for a vegetable broth, or drunk as a tea; it's particularly delicious when sweetened with maple syrup. I tried chilling some nettle broth once to drink as an iced tea; it was not bad, but not something I would make again. If you plan to substitute nettles for cooked spinach in a recipe, it might be helpful to know that nettles lose about half their volume when cooked, so plan on cooking twice as much as required for the dish. If you're going by weight, plan on about 6 cups of fresh nettles, fairly tightly packed, to yield 10¼ ounces of squeezed, cooked nettles.

Wood nettles have tender stalks, and the entire plant can be eaten when young. Look for wood nettles that are 5 or 6 inches tall; they will have just a crown of leaves at the top, with few or no side leaves. Cook this stalk whole with its leafy crown intact, and serve simply with butter, salt and pepper.

Stinging nettles dry very well, and once they're dry, most people can handle them without gloves (however, if you have very sensitive skin, you may still want to wear rubber gloves until you've cooked the dried nettles). The easiest way to dry nettles is to gather together a half-dozen stalks and tie them tightly at the end; hang the bundle in a breezy screened porch or a dry spot like the attic. Once they're dry, pull the leaves from the stems (wearing gloves if you've got sensitive skin) and let them air-dry on a baking sheet for a few more days until they are quite brittle, then pack in jars, seal tightly and store in a dark area. Two cups of packed dry nettle leaves, weighing about 1½ ounces, will yield about ⅞ cup (about 3¾ ounces) when cooked. I've never dried wood nettles, but have read that they do not dry as well as stinging nettle (Kay Young, *Wild Seasons*). Leaves from both stinging nettle and wood nettle can be frozen; simply blanch briefly in boiling water, pack into appropriate containers, and freeze.

JUST FOR FUN
Nettle Research
This would be a good learning project for kids. Research at the library, in books and on the internet, and see how many unusual uses you can find for nettle. Here are some to get you started:
- The leaves of stinging nettle are used to wrap certain cheeses in England.
- Some people like to beat themselves with nettle stalks, to stimulate the skin (I'll bet it does, too).
- Nettle stalks have been used to make cords; wood nettle makes finer cordage than stinging nettle because the fibers are shorter.
- In Finland, a fine cloth is made from nettle fibers.
- Pacific Northwest Native American tribes used nettle stings to stay awake while whaling.
- In Nepal, nettle is believed to act as a moth repellent; small amounts of nettle are sometimes mixed with wool in blankets, rugs, and storage bags to provide protection.
- Nettle tea is beneficial to growing plants, and is used in gardens and for houseplants.
- Nettle roots were used by native peoples and pioneers to make a yellow dye.

QUICK IDEAS FOR USING NETTLES
- Boil a handful of fresh or dried nettle leaves in water to cover generously for 10 minutes, or until desired strength; strain. Serve hot as tea, with or without lemon and sweetened if you like (maple syrup or honey are particularly good); or salt lightly and use as a vegetarian broth.
- Add crumbles of dried stinging nettle leaves (such as may be found at the bottom of your storage container) to soups and stews for flavor, color and nutrition.

OTHER RECIPES IN THIS BOOK FEATURING NETTLES
- Vegetable Terrine with Mushrooms (page 382)

Seven-Minute Dip

About 3 cups (10 to 12 appetizer servings)　　　Preparation: Under 30 minutes, plus chilling

2 cups (tightly packed) fresh nettle leaves
　　(about 1½ ounces, weighed prior to
　　washing)
3 slices bacon, finely diced
3 tablespoons minced red bell pepper
1½ cups sour cream (reduced-fat works
　　fine)
½ cup mayonnaise (reduced-fat works
　　fine)

½ cup shredded cheddar cheese
1 envelope (1 ounce) dry onion soup mix
½ teaspoon dried basil
½ teaspoon dried oregano
1 round loaf sourdough bread (about
　　1½ pounds)
Raw vegetables for dipping

Cook nettle leaves for 10 minutes in large pot of lightly salted boiling water; drain well, rinse with cold water and gently press to remove excess moisture. Set aside to cool completely. (If you are starting with nettles that have been dried, frozen or previously cooked, you'll need about 1 cup of cooked greens, which should weigh just under 4 ounces.)

While nettles are cooling, fry bacon until crisp in skillet over medium heat. Transfer with slotted spoon to paper towel-lined plate. Discard all but a film of drippings from skillet; add pepper and sauté until just tender. Transfer with slotted spoon to paper towel-lined plate and drain very well.

When nettles are cool, chop to medium-fine consistency in food processor or by hand; transfer to mixing bowl. Add sour cream, mayonnaise, cheese, soup mix, basil, oregano, and cooled bacon and bell peppers to mixing bowl. Stir gently but thoroughly to combine. Cover and refrigerate for at least 1 hour.

Just before serving, cut 1½-inch slice from top of bread. Pull out insides of loaf, leaving 1-inch-thick shell. Cut top slice and bread removed from center of loaf into bite-sized pieces. Place hollowed loaf on serving platter; surround with bread chunks and vegetables. Spoon chilled nettle mixture into center of loaf; serve immediately.

Nettles with Ginger

2 servings; easily increased   Preparation: Under 15 minutes

4 cups tender nettle leaves
1 teaspoon peanut oil or canola oil

1 tablespoon chopped fresh wild gingerroot, or 1 teaspoon chopped domestic
Salt or soy sauce

Heat large pot of water to boiling. Add nettle leaves. Return to boiling; cook for 2 minutes, stirring occasionally. Drain, reserving liquid if you like for nettle tea.* Let nettle leaves stand in colander to drip dry while you begin cooking the gingerroot.

In medium skillet, heat oil over medium heat. Add gingerroot; cook, stirring constantly, for about 2 minutes. Add drained nettle leaves. Cook, stirring frequently, for about 5 minutes. Sprinkle with salt or soy sauce to taste.

*After draining the leaves, return liquid to pot. Add nettle stems, cut into smaller lengths to fit pot. Heat to boiling; cook for about 5 minutes. Remove from heat and set aside to steep until desired strength, 5 to 15 minutes. Serve warm as a tea, sweetened with maple syrup, honey or sugar if you like; or use as a broth.

GREENS &
FLOWERS

Nettle and Potato Chowder

4 servings   Preparation: Under an hour

4 or 5 ramps with greens (roots trimmed),
   or 1 tablespoon minced shallot
1 rib celery, cut into ⅛-inch dice
1 tablespoon olive oil or vegetable oil
1 quart chicken or vegetable broth, divided
2 pounds Idaho or other starchy potatoes,
   peeled and cut into ⅜-inch dice

1 to 1½ cups (tightly packed) fresh nettle
   leaves
¼ teaspoon freshly ground black pepper,
   or to taste
Grated Asiago or Romano cheese for
   serving, optional

Chop bulbs and maroon stems of ramps; slice leaves into strips. Set leaf strips aside. In large pot over medium heat, sauté chopped ramps (or shallot) and celery in oil for about 5 minutes. Add 3½ cups of the broth and the potatoes; increase heat to high. Heat to boiling. Reduce heat so broth bubbles gently, and cook until potatoes are tender, stirring occasionally. Meanwhile, heat a large pot of water to boiling. Add nettle leaves. Return to boiling and cook for 1 minute; drain. Combine in blender with remaining ½ cup broth; pulse until finely chopped but not puréed.

When potatoes are tender, use a potato masher or large spoon to mash up some of them; don't mash them all, just enough to thicken the broth. Stir in chopped nettle mixture, sliced ramp leaves and pepper. Return to a gentle bubble and cook for about 5 minutes, stirring occasionally. Pass grated cheese separately so each person can add some to their soup if they wish.

Nettle Soufflé

4 servings   Preparation: Under an hour

This light and airy soufflé makes a wonderful accompaniment to ham or other roasted meats or poultry. Larger stinging nettle leaves, as you'd pick in midsummer, work fine for this dish since they get chopped finely (if served whole, these larger leaves have a coarse, somewhat stringy texture).

1 quart (tightly packed) fresh nettle leaves (about 3 ounces, weighed prior to washing)	1 teaspoon dry mustard powder, optional
	¾ teaspoon salt
1 cup milk (2% or skim milk work fine)	½ teaspoon white pepper
1 tablespoon plus 1½ teaspoons cornstarch	A pinch of ground nutmeg
¼ cup minced onion	6 large eggs
1 teaspoon dried thyme	½ cup shredded Parmesan cheese, divided
	¼ teaspoon cream of tartar

Heat oven to 375°F. Spray 1½- to 2-quart soufflé dish (or other straight-sided casserole) with liberal amount of nonstick spray; set aside. Cook nettle leaves for 10 minutes in large pot of lightly salted boiling water; drain well, rinse with cold water and gently press to remove excess moisture. Set aside to cool while you prepare other ingredients. (If you are starting with nettles that have been frozen or previously cooked, you'll need about 2 cups of prepared greens, which should weigh just under 8 ounces.)

In saucepan, combine milk and cornstarch, blending with fork. Add onion, thyme, mustard, salt, pepper and nutmeg. Heat over high heat, stirring constantly, until mixture thickens and bubbles. Remove from heat.

Separate eggs, placing all 6 whites into a large bowl and transferring 2 of the yolks into blender container; reserve remaining yolks for another use. Add ¼ cup of the Parmesan cheese to blender, along with milk mixture. Process until smooth. Add drained nettle leaves; pulse on-and-off until nettles are very finely chopped and mixture is smooth.

Add cream of tartar to bowl with egg whites. Beat at highest speed of hand mixer until soft peaks form. Fold nettle mixture into whites; scrape into prepared dish. Sprinkle remaining ¼ cup of Parmesan cheese over top. Use tip of sharp knife to lightly score a circle on top of soufflé mixture, 1 inch from edge of dish. Bake in center of oven, without disturbing or opening door, until puffed and rich golden brown, about 25 minutes; the center should jiggle just a bit when you gently shake the dish. Serve immediately.

Nettle Risotto

4 servings

5 quarts water	1 large shallot, minced
6 to 8 nettle tops and stems, or 1 cup dried nettles	1 cup arborio, carnaroli or other short-grain rice suitable for risotto
½ teaspoon salt	¼ cup dry sherry
2 teaspoons butter	A good pinch of nutmeg
2 teaspoons olive oil	3 tablespoons grated Parmesan cheese

In large, heavy-bottomed saucepan, heat water to boiling. Add nettles and salt. Boil gently for 5 minutes; remove from heat and let steep for at least 10 minutes. Strain cooking liquid into another saucepan; set nettles aside to cool. Place saucepan of nettle liquid over medium heat; keep at a simmer during the entire rice-cooking period. Rinse and dry saucepan used to cook nettles.

In rinsed saucepan, melt butter in oil over medium heat. Add shallot; cook, stirring frequently, until just tender, 3 to 4 minutes. Add rice and cook, stirring frequently, for about 5 minutes; the rice will look chalky. Add sherry and cook, stirring frequently, until sherry cooks away. Add about ¼ cup of the simmering nettle broth and cook, stirring frequently, until the liquid cooks away. Continue to add broth in small batches, stirring frequently, until the rice is almost tender, about 15 minutes. Total cooking time will be about 20 minutes; you may not need quite all the broth, or you may need a bit more (use hot water if you run out of broth near the end.)

While rice is cooking, separate and discard nettle stems. Chop cooked greens finely. When rice is almost tender, stir nettles and nutmeg into rice. Continue cooking, adding liquid as necessary, until rice is just tender but still firm to the bite in the center. Add a bit more broth if necessary, until rice is proper consistency; it should be creamy but not soupy. Remove from heat; stir in Parmesan cheese and serve immediately.

Purslane (Portulaca oleracea and others)

This small, inconspicuous plant is rather homely, but makes a great addition to the salad bowl. When cooked, it acts as a thickener, and is frequently used in stews.

HABITAT, RANGE

Purslane grows as a succulent groundcover throughout our region, as well as throughout most of the United States. It prefers sandy soil, but will grow in a wide variety of conditions; its succulent stems and leaves retain moisture, allowing it to grow in dry areas. Look for it on waste ground, in disturbed areas and vacant lots, and in your own back yard; I often see it growing from sidewalk cracks.

PARTS USED

Leaves and stems, raw or cooked

SEASONS

Late spring through fall

Purslane

IDENTIFICATION TIPS, DANGEROUS LOOKALIKES

Purslane creeps low to the ground, often forming dense mats the size of a piece of typing paper. Stems are fleshy and often reddish. Thickened paddle-shaped leaves, ½ to 1½ inches long, grow along the stem in both alternate and opposite fashion, and form a small rosette at the end of the stem. The tiny yellow flowers are inconspicuous, opening only on sunny days. There are numerous varieties of purslane; all are edible. Purslane has smooth stems; if you find something that you think is purslane but the stems are hairy, pass it by.

I've read several warnings to watch out for members of the spurge family (*Chamaesyce* spp. or *Euphorbia* spp.), which often grow among purslane. The plants don't look similar at all, but if you're not paying attention you could accidentally harvest some spurge in with your purslane. Spurge emits a milky sap when the stems are broken, while purslane sap is not milky; spurge stems are thin and wiry, not fleshy like purslane. Spurge is poisonous, but it really is easy to distinguish from purslane.

HARVESTING TIPS

If you're picking purslane in mid- or late summer for use in salads, pick only the tender new leaves at the tip of the plant; larger leaves and the stem are tough at this time of year. Purslane is a vigorous grower, and it seems hard to over-harvest it; even if an individual patch is wiped out, the plant will sprout with vigor nearby. Just ask any gardener.

MORE ABOUT PURSLANE: According to the National Gardening Society, some weed scientists rank purslane as the most frequently reported weed species in the world and the ninth most detrimental weed to world agriculture. Be that as it may, purslane is a highly edible "weed" that is often one of the first plants learned by foragers. Cooks in Italy, Greece, France, the Netherlands and Turkey have been using purslane for centuries.

Purslane reminds me a bit of okra; it has a mucilaginous quality to it, and the same ability to thicken soups and stews. I prefer the taste of purslane to that of okra, however; its flavor is somewhat like a lemony green bean, and it goes well with many other foods. It's high in vitamin A; a 3½ ounce serving contains 1,300 IUs (about 3 times as much as spinach), as well as over 100mg of calcium and a good amount of iron.

One of the most common uses for purslane is to add raw leaves to a salad; the thick leaves are a pleasant contrast to thin lettuces. They can also be chopped and mixed with other vegetables to make a more substantial salad. Added to soups and stews, purslane becomes a thickener that adds a slightly lemony overtone. It can also be boiled for 10 minutes and served with butter and seasonings, but in this fashion purslane is less interesting to me than as part of a chorus in a mixed dish. I particularly enjoy it with tomatoes, but it goes well with garbanzo beans, green beans, zucchini and many other vegetables as well.

Always wash purslane well, using several changes of water if it seems particularly gritty. The fleshy leaves seem to hold dirt and fine sand well. This is especially important if you'll be eating the purslane raw; boiling helps remove some of the fine grit that clings to the plants.

QUICK IDEAS FOR USING PURSLANE
- Add a handful of purslane leaves and chopped tender stems to soup or stew in the final 20 minutes of cooking, to thicken and enrich the broth.
- Purslane stems can be pickled in the same ways used for cucumbers; try it as a refrigerator-type pickle rather than a fully processed pickle.
- Add purslane to bread dressings for an interesting flavor and texture.

OTHER RECIPES IN THIS BOOK FEATURING PURSLANE
- Salade Sauvage (page 54)
- Red Potato Salad with Purslane (page 336)

Greek Country Salad

1¼ cups plain yogurt
Salt
2 cups purslane leaves and tender stems
1 clove garlic
1 tablespoon olive oil

1 cup cooked garbanzo beans, drained and rinsed if canned
3 tablespoons chopped flat-leaf (Italian) parsley

Line wire-mesh strainer with a triple thickness of cheesecloth; set over mixing bowl. Add yogurt; let stand at room temperature for 30 minutes (or as long as an hour in the refrigerator, loosely covered). Meanwhile heat a large saucepan of salted water to boiling over high heat. Add purslane; return to boiling, adjust heat so mixture boils gently and cook for 2 minutes. Drain purslane and refresh immediately with cold water; let drain until yogurt is ready.

With mortar and pestle, crush garlic with a little salt (coarse salt works best) until smooth paste forms. Add olive oil; mix well. Transfer garlic paste to glass or Pyrex mixing bowl. Add drained yogurt, discarding the thin greenish liquid that will have dripped from the yogurt. Add garbanzo beans, parsley and well-drained purslane to mixing bowl; stir gently to mix well. Serve at room temperature.

Stewed Tomatoes with Purslane

I love this served over a big bowl of crushed saltines—the wild version of comfort food.

1 can (14.5 ounces) diced tomatoes in their own juice
⅓ cup finely minced green bell pepper
¼ cup finely minced celery, including a few of the leaves if possible
2 tablespoons minced onion
2 teaspoons dried basil

1 teaspoon sugar
1½ cups purslane leaves and tender stems, chopped coarsely
Salt and pepper
Saltine crackers for serving (6 to 8 individual crackers per serving)

In medium nonreactive saucepan, combine tomatoes and their juices, bell pepper, celery, onion, basil and sugar; fill tomato can a quarter full of water, swish it around, and pour into saucepan. Heat just to boiling over medium-high heat; adjust heat so mixture bubbles gently and cook for 10 minutes, stirring occasionally. Add purslane; continue cooking for 15 to 20 minutes longer, stirring occasionally; mixture should be juicy but not soupy. Season with salt and pepper to taste. To serve, crush crackers coarsely into individual soup bowls; spoon stewed tomatoes over crackers.

Purslane and Tomato Salad

Make this in summer, when tomatoes are fresh from the vine. At that time of year, gather your purslane from the tops of the plants only; older leaves will be a bit too tough to eat raw.

2 large ripe tomatoes
Salt
2 tablespoons balsamic vinegar or
   red wine vinegar
¾ cup well-washed tender purslane leaves,
   halved or quartered if large

¼ cup crumbled feta cheese
8 fresh basil leaves, coarsely chopped
2 tablespoons olive oil

Cut tomatoes in half across the equator. Scoop out and discard seeds; sprinkle tomatoes with salt and place upside-down in strainer for 10 minutes. After tomatoes have stood for 10 minutes, cut into ½- to ¾-inch pieces and place in glass or Pyrex mixing bowl. Add vinegar, stirring to combine. Let stand for 10 minutes, or as long as 2 hours (stir occasionally if lengthy standing is used).

When tomatoes have marinated as long as you'd like, add purslane, feta, basil and olive oil; stir gently to combine. Taste for seasoning, and add salt and pepper if necessary. Serve at room temperature.

GREENS & FLOWERS

Sheep Sorrel (*Rumex acetosella*)

When you find a patch of sheep sorrel, it's easy to harvest a good quantity for use in salads or as a delicious cooked vegetable. A few raw leaves make a refreshing trail nibble.

HABITAT, RANGE

Sheep sorrel is an introduced perennial herb that grows throughout our area; in fact, it is found throughout the United States. It likes sunshine and prefers acid soil that is somewhat sandy. Look for it in empty fields and on vacant land; it grows well in areas that have been disturbed.

PARTS USED

Young leaves, raw or cooked

SEASONS

Spring through fall

IDENTIFICATION TIPS, DANGEROUS LOOKALIKES

Sheep sorrel is named for the shape of the leaf, which resembles a sheep's head with outstretched ears. Note that not every leaf on a sorrel plant will have the ears, but many will; don't pick from a plant that has no leaves with this distinctive characteristic. The leaves of sheep sorrel are generally 1 to 3 inches long (plus the length of the leafstalk), and have a shimmery quality to them, giving you another good field mark to look for. They also are somewhat fleshy—not thick like purslane, but not as thin as dandelion leaves.

Young sheep sorrel

In spring, the leaves grow on short stalks close to the ground in a basal rosette. In late spring, the plant sends up a stiff flower stalk that tops out at perhaps a foot and is mostly leafless, although a few leaves grow alternately on the stalk, clasping it with a papery sheath like those of curly dock (page 296). Tiny flowers, which may be green, red, reddish brown or pinkish purple, cluster on the stalk in the summer. There are no dangerous lookalikes if you follow careful identification practices. Remember to always look for the sheep's ears on at least some of the leaves, and remember that sheep sorrel grows in a basal rosette—not as a vine or shrub. Another interesting characteristic that helps separate sheep sorrel from some similar leaves (such as nightshade, *Solanum* spp.) is that the 2 ears of sheep sorrel sometimes don't line up with one another across the leaf; they're often off kilter. Bindweed (*Convolvulus* spp.) has small ears, but the lobes are directly opposite one another (plus, bindweed is a vine, so is fairly easy to distinguish). The ears on nightshade are usually separate from the rest of the leaf, looking like an arrow-shaped leaf with 2 separate lobes.

HARVESTING TIPS

Sheep sorrel grows by spreading rhizomes. Each time the soil is disturbed, the broken rhizomes create new patches of sheep sorrel. This means that you will find sheep sorrel in colonies, especially on disturbed ground. Sheep sorrel seed stalks have a reddish hue; look for patches of pinkish red in sunny fields to locate possible colonies of sheep sorrel.

To keep sheep sorrel fresh when harvesting in the sunny locations it prefers, carry a small cooler, or a bucket with a little cold water. If the leaves are wilted when you get home with them, soak them in a sinkful of cold water—preferably with a few ice cubes added—for 20 to 30 minutes; this usually revives the leaves quite nicely.

SPECIAL CONSIDERATIONS

Like other members of the *Rumex* family, sheep sorrel contains a fair amount of soluble oxalates; avoid sorrel if you have kidney problems. Over-indulging in sheep sorrel may cause stomach upset (but then, so will over-indulging in ice cream).

MORE ABOUT SHEEP SORREL: If you're out hiking in the spring on a warm day, a patch of sheep sorrel is a welcome sight. The leaves are very tart and lemony, and cause your mouth to water when you chew them. Actually, the sight of a patch of sorrel causes my mouth to water when I just look at it, for it is a delicious vegetable.

Sheep sorrel is excellent eaten raw in salads; to compensate for its tart taste, reduce the amount of vinegar or lemon juice that may be called for in the recipe. It makes a wonderful cooked green as well, but you'll need to gather at least 5 times as much as you want because it cooks down so much. When you're washing the sorrel, pluck off and discard the leafstems, which are much tougher than the leaves.

Like many greens, sheep sorrel turns a disappointing army green when its cooked. But the flavor is so good that this can be overlooked. When steamed or simply sautéed, sheep sorrel tastes a bit like spinach that has been spritzed with lemon juice. Sheep sorrel freezes well; simply blanch, drain, pack into freezer bags and freeze.

QUICK IDEAS FOR USING SHEEP SORREL
- Tuck a few sheep sorrel leaves in a sandwich; it's particularly good, I think, on cheese sandwiches that have a little mayo and mustard.
- Add sheep sorrel leaves to mixed green salads, especially those that include a bit of tart apple.
- Substitute sheep sorrel for spinach in any recipe; reduce or eliminate any lemon juice called for in the recipe.

OTHER RECIPES IN THIS BOOK FEATURING SHEEP SORREL
- As substitute in Dock and Chickpea Soup (page 299)
- Impossible Greens Pie (page 300)
- Steam-Sautéed Sheep Sorrel (page 308)
- Vegetable Terrine with Mushrooms (page 382)

Sorrel and Rice Side Dish

4 servings   Preparation: Under 30 minutes

1 large onion, chopped	4 cups cooked long-grain rice
Half of a red bell pepper, finely diced	2 tablespoons minced fresh basil, or
1 tablespoon minced garlic	1 tablespoon dried
1 tablespoon olive oil	Salt and pepper
4 cups sheep sorrel leaves	¼ cup crumbled feta cheese

In large skillet, sauté onion, bell pepper and garlic in oil over medium heat until tender, 5 to 10 minutes. Add sorrel; cook for about 2 minutes or until well wilted, stirring constantly. Add rice; cook until rice is heated through, about 5 minutes, stirring frequently. Stir in basil, and salt and pepper to taste. Transfer to serving dish; sprinkle with feta cheese.

Sorrel Soup with Chicken Meatballs

4 or 5 servings   Preparation: About an hour

This takes a bit of time, but the resulting soup is really delicious. The sorrel adds a nice tart accent to the soup.

Meatballs:
⅓ cup Italian-flavored breadcrumbs
⅓ cup milk
5 cloves garlic
4 sprigs fresh parsley, stems removed
2 chunks of Parmesan or Romano cheese, each about 1 inch square
¾ pound boneless, skinless chicken, cut into 1-inch chunks
1 egg, beaten
½ teaspoon salt
A few grindings of black pepper

Soup:
2 teaspoons olive oil
6 cups sorrel leaves
2 quarts low-salt chicken broth
1 cup cooked rice
Grated Parmesan cheese for garnish

In mixing bowl, combine breadcrumbs and milk; stir and let stand for about 5 minutes. Meanwhile, chop garlic finely in a food processor. Remove half the chopped garlic and set aside in small bowl. Add parsley tops to workbowl with remaining garlic and pulse on-and-off a few times. With motor running, drop Parmesan through feed tube; process until finely chopped. Add chicken and pulse a few times. Add egg, salt and pepper and pulse until chicken is chopped to medium-fine consistency; don't chop the meat to mush, or the meatballs will be too dense. Add meat mixture to bowl with the soaked breadcrumbs; mix gently but thoroughly. Shape into 1-inch balls, rolling firmly between your palms. Place chicken balls on a plate in a single layer; cover and refrigerate while you prepare soup.

In large pot, heat oil over medium heat. Add reserved garlic and sauté, stirring frequently, for about a minute. Stir in sorrel and continue cooking until wilted, 4 to 5 minutes. Add chicken broth. Heat to a strong simmer and cook, uncovered, for about 15 minutes. Stir rice into broth. Gently drop meatballs into simmering broth in single layer. Cover the pot and simmer for 15 minutes, turning meatballs once midway through cooking. Serve with additional Parmesan cheese.

Fish Poached with Sorrel

3 or 4 servings   Preparation: Under 30 minutes

Sorrel is frequently used in simple fish dishes. Here's a good start; once you've prepared this, you will probably come up with your own variations.

Half of a small white onion, cut into
    thin strips
2 tablespoons chopped shallot
2 teaspoons olive oil
1 cup white wine
½ cup orange juice

1 to 1½ pounds boneless, skinless firm
    white fish fillets such as sea bass or
    halibut
Salt and pepper
3 cups chopped sheep sorrel leaves
1 tablespoon cornstarch dissolved in
    2 tablespoons cold water

In skillet that is sized to hold fish comfortably in a single layer, sauté onion and shallot in oil over medium heat until tender, about 5 minutes. Add wine and orange juice to skillet; heat to boiling, and cook for about 3 minutes, stirring occasionally. Sprinkle fish with salt and pepper to taste. Gently lay fish in skillet; reduce heat so liquid is just simmering. Cover and poach for about 4 minutes. Add sorrel. Re-cover and cook just until fish is opaque; plan on 10 total minutes cooking time for an inch-thick fillet, or slightly less if fillet is thinner.

Use slotted spoon to transfer sorrel to serving plate; top with fish fillets. Cover plate loosely and keep warm. Stir cornstarch mixture; add to liquid in skillet, whisking constantly to prevent lumps. Cook, whisking constantly, until sauce thickens somewhat; it won't be as thick as gravy. Taste sauce for seasoning, and adjust if necessary. Strain sauce into sauceboat or serving bowl; serve with fish and sorrel.

Violets (Viola spp.)

Add a lovely touch—and a goodly amount of vitamins—to springtime salads by including some violet leaves and a few flowers for garnish. The flowers can also be used to make a lovely purple syrup—quite a conversation starter.

HABITAT, RANGE
Many species of violet live throughout the entire United States. Most prefer moist soil and a bit of shade, but others can be found in dry, sunny areas with poor soil.

PARTS USED
Flowers, raw, candied or infused; leaves, raw or cooked

SEASONS
Spring

IDENTIFICATION TIPS, DANGEROUS LOOKALIKES

Common blue violet

The USDA Plants Database lists over 100 species of violets in the United States. All are more or less edible; some taste better than others, but none are toxic. The common blue violet (*V. sororia* or *V. papilionacea*) is the familiar purple flower, but the pale-purple birdfoot violet (*V. pedata*) is also found in most of our region (it does not grow in the Dakotas, and may be locally scarce elsewhere). The downy yellow violet (*V. pubescens*) has, as you might guess, a yellow flower, and grows throughout our region. The flower is similar in shape on all these violets, although leaf shape may vary quite a bit. Leaves of the common blue violet and the downy yellow violet are the familiar heart shape, while leaves of the birdfoot violet are shaped as the name implies—like a bird's foot with extra toes.

Birdfoot violet

Violet leaves are an excellent spring green, but can be confused with other plants if the flower is not blooming. The safest way to gather violet greens is to wait until the plants are flowering; that way, you know that the leaves you are picking are, indeed, violets.

Flowers have 5 petals and a symmetrical butterfly-like shape; the stem is bent at the point of attachment, making the flower appear to droop. As noted, there are many species of violets; exact flower and leaf characteristics as well the hues vary quite a bit, but all have the familiar violet "look." For specific identification, consult a good wildflower identification guide.

You may see a few other plants with flowers that somewhat resemble violets, but they have characteristics that help distinguish them. The larkspur (*Delphinium tricorne*) has a 5- to 7-petalled purple, blue or white flower that is violet-like; however, the larkspur has a long horn or spur growing from the back of the flower, making it easy to avoid. In addition, the larkspur grows on a stem that has multiple flowers and leaves attached to it, while most violets are simpler in their growth. Buttercups (*Ranunculus* spp.) have 5- to 7-petalled yellow flowers, but the flowers are symmetrically cup-like rather than butterfly-shaped like violets, and the stems are hairy, while those of violets are smooth. Monkshood (*Aconitum* spp.) looks like a purple violet that has not unfurled yet; the petals curl around to form a hood or shield. An important point is that the leaves of all 3 of these plants resemble those of birdfoot violets, not the heart-shaped leaves of the common blue violet. All 3 of these plants are toxic (the monkshood in particular is highly poisonous), so must be avoided. Violet roots are also toxic; harvest only the leaves and flowers.

HARVESTING TIPS

Violet flowers are small, and it takes a lot of them to make something like syrup. I gather flowers as I find them and freeze them in plastic containers, adding to my stash as I find more flowers. When I have enough, I thaw the whole container out and proceed with the infusion. This won't work if you're gathering flowers to candy; the flowers are wilted when they thaw out.

SPECIAL CONSIDERATIONS

There seems to be some debate about the edibility of yellow-flowered violets. I've eaten a few downy yellow violet flowers in my time and have suffered no ill effects; however, Steve Brill reports in *Identifying and Harvesting Edible and Medicinal Plants in Wild (and Not So Wild) Places* that yellow violets should not be eaten because they may be cathartic (and also because they are somewhat rare). If there is an abundance of yellow violets in your area, it might be a good idea to check with a local forager to determine edibility of the particular species, or sample just a few until you know if you will have a problem with them.

MORE ABOUT VIOLETS: Wild violets are a popular flower. One species or another of wild violet is the state flower in Illinois, Wisconsin, New Jersey and Rhode Island. Fresh violet flowers are showing up at trendy restaurants in salads these days. They're also well-known to pastry chefs and brides alike; candied violets are probably one of the best-known edible flower garnishes in use, and are traditional on wedding cakes.

Fewer people know, however, that the leaves of violets are an excellent spring green. A few raw leaves tossed into a mixed salad will add a peppery snap, and they can be cooked alone or as part of a mixed-greens pot to be eaten like spinach (the stems are tough; remove them before using). Each spring, as I head into my yard with the colander to gather violet greens, one of my neighbors occasionally comes up to tell me about the fond memories they have of collecting violet flowers and greens for the kitchen with their grandmother.

The leaves become tough in the heat of summer, but fall may bring a crop of new and tender leaves. Be sure that you are picking from known violet beds in the fall, so you don't accidentally pick a dangerous violet lookalike; the safest way to gather violet leaves is to do so when the plants are in flower. If you note the location of beds in the springtime, you can harvest leaves from them in the fall even when no flowers are present.

The best violet flowers have a sweet perfume, and make a delightful trail nibble as well as a spectacular garnish for salads and other foods. An infusion of violet flowers can be used to make a brilliantly colored syrup.

JUST FOR FUN
Wildflower Bath Tea
Pack this into a pretty jar to keep on the bathroom counter, or to give as a gift. To get started, air-dry a cup of violet flowers and a cup of wild rose petals on a screen for a week. In a large mixing bowl, combine the dried violet flowers and rose petals with ¼ cup dried lavender flowers (available at floral, bath or craft shops), 2 tablespoons dried rosemary leaves (whole needle-like leaves, not crushed; found in the spice aisle), and 2 tablespoons dried mint leaves (preferably dried whole). Mix gently. Scatter 20 drops of rose-scented essential oil and 20 drops of lavender-scented essential oil over the flowers (essential oils are found at bath-and-body shops or craft stores), mixing gently to disperse the oils evenly. Pack into glass jars and seal tightly. To use, place a tablespoon in a metal tea ball; hang it under the running faucet when filling the bathtub, or float it in the tub. Feel free to vary this formulation based on your own preferences. You could add dried chamomile or pineapple weed, for example, or use different essential oils; a few drops of patchouli oil give a deeper, muskier fragrance (don't use very much patchouli, however; it can be quite overpowering).

QUICK IDEAS FOR USING VIOLETS
- Add a handful of violet leaves to a mixed green salad, or to a batch of spinach that you are cooking.

- Scatter a few fresh violet flowers over salads, or use to garnish other foods.
- Fill an ice cube tray one-quarter full with water and freeze solid. Add a violet flower to each compartment; fill completely with water and re-freeze. Use these "violet cubes" in fruit punches, where they will add an elegant air.

OTHER RECIPES IN THIS BOOK FEATURING VIOLETS
- Springtime Torte (page 50)
- Salade Sauvage (page 54)
- Wild Fruit Gels (page 260)

Violet Syrup

About 1 pint   Preparation: Over an hour

Use this startlingly purple syrup on pancakes, as an ice cream topping, or to saturate layer cakes; or, mix 2 tablespoons with a glass of sparkling water for a light, refreshing drink. The higher amount of sugar makes a thicker syrup, but the extra sugar somewhat overpowers the delicate floral taste.

2½ to 3 cups de-stemmed purple violet   2½ to 3 cups sugar
    blossoms, well washed*   1 tablespoon freshly squeezed lemon juice

2 cups water   1 tablespoon rose-flower water, optional

Combine violet blossoms and water in nonreactive saucepan. Heat to a full boil over medium heat, stirring several times. Remove from heat and let stand for 30 minutes. Strain through cheesecloth-lined strainer. Gather up the cheesecloth and squeeze gently to extract more of the liquid, then discard the cheesecloth and blossoms. Strain the liquid through a paper coffee filter (I place the filter into a small mesh strainer) to remove any small particulate matter.

Combine strained violet "tea" with sugar in a heavy-bottomed saucepan. Place over medium heat and stir constantly until sugar dissolves. Heat to boiling, then stop stirring. When the mixture comes to a full boil, start timing. Cook for 2 minutes, then remove from heat. Set aside to cool.

When syrup is lukewarm, stir in lemon juice and rose-flower water. The lemon juice will make the syrup turn a bright purple color (prior to this, it will probably be a muddy blue color). Pour syrup into a clean bottle and store in the refrigerator.

*You may gather the violet blossoms over the course of days (or weeks). Simply snip the blossoms off into a wire-mesh colander. Rinse well and drain, then place into a plastic container and freeze. Add to your frozen stash until you have enough to make syrup.

Candied Violets

Preparation: About an hour

Use these as a garnish for ice cream, cake or other desserts. They also look very pretty on a breakfast platter, especially if you're serving pancakes with Violet Syrup (page 331).

Fresh violets on the stem   **Superfine sugar**
Egg white (1 will do 15 to 20 violets)

Wash violets well. Allow to dry on paper towels. Heat oven to 250°F. Line baking sheet with waxed paper. Beat egg white(s) with whisk until foamy. Place ½ cup of sugar in flat dish. Dip violets, 1 at a time, into beaten egg whites; use small brush to ensure that all sides of the petals are coated. With a toothpick, gently open petals into original shape of flower, then place face-down in the sugar; spoon additional sugar over back. Use the toothpick to keep the petals open and separate, and make sure that each is well-coated with sugar. Place flower onto prepared baking sheet, arranging the flower so the "face" is up and the stem side down. Use toothpick to re-shape petals, and sprinkle with sugar if there are bare spots. Repeat with remaining flowers. Place baking sheet into oven. Prop oven door open several inches with a ball of foil. Bake until the sugar is crystallized, about 30 minutes. Store in an airtight container.

Skillet Salmon with Violets

4 servings   Preparation: Under 15 minutes

Dressing: **Salmon:**
3 tablespoons balsamic vinegar   4 boneless, skinless salmon fillets (4 to 6
3 tablespoons extra-virgin olive oil   ounces each)
1 tablespoon freshly squeezed lemon juice   Salt and pepper
1½ teaspoons minced garlic   2 teaspoons olive oil or canola oil
½ teaspoon dried thyme   3 to 4 cups violet greens
¼ teaspoon salt   ¾ cup water
A few grindings of black pepper   8 to 12 violet flowers

In small jar, combine all dressing ingredients; seal tightly and shake well to blend. Set aside. Season salmon fillets with salt and pepper to taste. In large skillet, heat oil over medium-high heat until shimmering. Add salmon to skillet; reduce heat to medium and sauté until golden brown on bottom, about 5 minutes. Turn salmon so the browned side is up. Scatter violet leaves around edges of skillet; stir for a minute or 2 until leaves begin to wilt. Add water around edges of pan (don't pour water over salmon, or you will lose some of the nice color). Cover skillet and cook until salmon is just opaque, about 5 minutes longer.

To serve, place a piece of salmon on each individual plate. Use slotted spoon to transfer greens to plates, mounding greens alongside and slightly overlapping salmon. Shake dressing again and pour over salmon and greens. Garnish with fresh violet flowers; serve immediately.

Watercress *(Nasturtium officinale; also listed as Rorippa nasturtium-aquaticum)*

Peppery and delicious, watercress is welcome in salads and other dishes. Wild watercress is the same as that sold in the grocery store—at a much better price!

HABITAT, RANGE

Watercress grows throughout our region except in the arid portions of the Dakotas. It thrives in clear, cold, slow-moving water; look for it on the edges of small streams and coldwater springs.

PARTS USED

Leaves, raw or cooked

SEASONS

Spring through fall

IDENTIFICATION TIPS, DANGEROUS LOOKALIKES

Wild watercress looks exactly like the kind you can buy in the store, so if you're familiar with that, you know what to look for. It often grows in a tangle or mat; on

Harvesting watercress along stream

closer inspection you'll see the compound leaves that grow alternately on fleshy, grooved floating stems. Each compound leaf has 3 to 11 small, rounded, dark-green leaflets with a larger terminal leaf; the compound leaves can be as long as 6 inches, although they are frequently shorter. Watercress is found floating on the surface or laying flat in the mud; delicate white roots can be seen growing from the floating or submerged stems. Clusters of tiny white 4-petalled flowers appear later in the season, followed by slender seed capsules along the stems that contain several tiny reddish brown seeds. There are no dangerous lookalikes.

HARVESTING TIPS

Watercress is best in the spring, but it can be harvested through summer and fall if you are selective in what you take. Once the plants start to flower, look for tender young growth to cut rather than the flowering portions. The leaves become very pungent once the plants bolt (develop seeds), but new growth in the fall is milder and worth harvesting.

Take only the part of the plant that is above the water; portions below may have tiny snails and slime that can be hard to remove. Also, if you take just the above-water portion, the plant will continue to grow, so you don't have to worry about over-harvesting.

SPECIAL CONSIDERATIONS

Harvest watercress only from unpolluted water sources. If you'll be eating it raw (which is the best way to eat it), you may wish to soak it in water that has camper's water-purifying tablets added. Handled like this, watercress is completely safe.

MORE ABOUT WATERCRESS: Watercress is peppery and pungent, and adds a delightful twist to salads. It's also the main ingredient in the famous British tea snack, watercress sandwiches. You may find watercress—at hefty prices—in the grocery store; this is a commercially cultured version that has a milder flavor, but wild watercress can be used in any recipe calling for domestic watercress.

Watercress is rich in vitamin A, with 4,700 IUs in a 3½ ounce serving. It also provides lots of calcium, as well as good amounts of iron and trace minerals. It is used throughout the world, making it one of the most popular culinary plants. The stems are edible as well as the leaves, although they may get tough during the summer.

QUICK IDEAS FOR USING WATERCRESS

- Add well-washed watercress to salads or sandwiches (if you have concerns about microscopic parasites, cleanse the watercress in water containing camper's water-purifying tablets).
- Toss a handful of watercress into soups and stews; it's particularly good with potatoes.

OTHER RECIPES IN THIS BOOK FEATURING WATERCRESS

- Salade Sauvage (page 54)

Watercress Tea Sandwiches

6 to 8 appetizer servings   Preparation: Under 15 minutes, plus 2 hours chilling

¼ cup (half of a stick) butter, softened
½ cup finely chopped watercress
12 slices firm, thinly sliced white sandwich
   bread (don't use soft white bread)
8-ounce container whipped cream cheese
   (plain, salmon or chive-and-onion
   flavored)

Half of a cucumber, very thinly sliced
A few sprigs whole watercress leaves and
   stems, for garnish

In mixing bowl, cream butter with electric mixer. Add watercress; stir in with wooden spoon. Divide watercress mixture evenly between 6 of the bread slices, spreading to edges. Spread cream cheese on remaining 6 bread slices. Arrange cucumber slices over buttered slices; top with cream-cheese-covered slices, putting the covered sides together. Press together firmly. Wrap in plastic wrap; refrigerate for at least 2 hours and as long as 6 hours.

When ready to serve, unwrap sandwiches; trim and discard crusts. Cut sandwiches diagonally into 4 triangles each. Arrange on serving platter; garnish with watercress sprigs.

Variation: Watercress-Salmon Tea Sandwiches
Follow recipe above, using plain or chive-and-onion cream cheese. Use 3 or 4 ounces thinly sliced lox (smoked salmon) in place of the cucumbers. Proceed as directed.

Red Potato Salad with Watercress or Purslane

6 servings   Preparation: Under an hour

I developed this recipe one day when I had a pile of fresh watercress, and some red potatoes in the pantry that needed to be used. I dug around in the cupboard and fridge, looking for things to go along with them, and came up with this absolutely delicious recipe.

1¼ to 1½ pounds small red-skinned
   potatoes, about 2 inches in diameter
2 tablespoons olive oil
1 teaspoon mustard seeds
⅓ cup diced onion
1 tablespoon minced shallot
⅔ cup chicken broth
2 tablespoons drained capers

1 tablespoon Dijon mustard, or a bit more
   to taste
1 tablespoon seasoned rice vinegar
2 cups watercress or purslane leaves
   (removed from stems before measuring),
   halved if large
½ teaspoon salt
A few fresh grindings of black pepper

In large pot of boiling water, boil potatoes over high heat until just tender, 20 to 25 minutes. Meanwhile, heat oil in medium skillet over medium-high heat. Add mustard seeds. Cook, shaking pan occasionally, until mustard seeds begin to pop and dance. Add onion and shallot; reduce heat to medium and cook until onion is tender-crisp, about 5 minutes, stirring occasionally. Add chicken broth and capers. Cook until broth has reduced to about 2 tablespoons, about 10 minutes. Stir in mustard and vinegar; cook until liquid boils. Add watercress; cook, stirring frequently, until wilted, about 2 minutes. Remove from heat; stir in salt and pepper.

When potatoes are tender, drain and cool briefly in colander. Cut into quarters, placing into large mixing bowl. Add watercress mixture; stir with wooden spoon to combine thoroughly. Allow to cool slightly; serve warm. Leftovers may be served cold, or the entire dish may be refrigerated after making to be served cold if you prefer (although it is very good when served warm).

Composed Salad with Peppers, Mozzarella and Warm Mushrooms

2 servings; easily increased   Preparation: Under 30 minutes

If you have watercress or wild mushrooms, but not both, you can still make this delicious salad by following the substitutions noted. The recipe may look complicated, but it really is simple and most of the work can be done in advance.

Pepper mixture:
2 bell peppers, preferably of different colors
2 small cloves garlic, chopped
1 teaspoon chopped fresh rosemary or
    other fresh herb of your choice
2 tablespoons extra-virgin olive oil
Salt and freshly ground pepper to taste

Mushroom dressing:
2 tablespoons balsamic vinegar
2 tablespoons dry sherry
1 teaspoon Dijon mustard

Salad:
2½ to 3 cups watercress (substitute mixed
    baby greens if you can't get watercress)
8 ounces fresh water-packed mozzarella
    cheese*
10 to 12 ounces chanterelles, oyster
    mushrooms, hen of the woods or
    hedgehog mushrooms (substitute baby
    portabellas or crimini mushrooms if
    you don't have wild mushrooms)
1 tablespoon butter
1 tablespoon extra-virgin olive oil

The following steps can be done earlier in the day. Roast the peppers under the broiler or by holding them over a gas flame until skins are completely blackened. Transfer to paper bag; seal and let stand for 10 minutes, then peel off charred skin. Remove and discard core and stem. Cut peppers into ½-inch dice; transfer to mixing bowl. Add remaining pepper-mixture ingredients. Stir well and set aside to marinate at room temperature for 30 minutes to 4 hours, stirring occasionally. Combine mushroom dressing ingredients in small bowl; stir together and set aside. Arrange watercress on 4 individual salad plates; slice mozzarella ½ inch thick, and divide evenly between salad plates (if you prepare the plates more than 15 minutes in advance, cover and refrigerate until serving time).

When you are ready for final preparations, slice the mushrooms ¼ inch thick. In large skillet, melt butter in oil over medium heat. Add mushrooms; sauté until mushrooms are tender and any juices have been absorbed. Stir the mushroom dressing and pour into skillet. Cook until liquid has reduced to about a tablespoon. Season with salt and pepper to taste.

Spoon equal portions of the hot mushrooms evenly over the cheese and greens on the salad plates. Spoon a line of peppers over the top of each portion. Serve immediately.

*Use the fresh mozzarella that is packed in water or a sealed pouch with a little water; American-style mozzarella is not the right texture for this dish. If you find water-packed mozzarella in small balls (about 1 inch across), these work well also; use 2 per serving, slicing them ½ inch thick.

Wood Sorrel (yellow or common wood sorrel, *Oxalis stricta*, and others)

With its lemony flavor and cheerful leaves, wood sorrel is a favorite lawn nibble of kids and adults alike. It makes a wonderful addition to salads, and a handful steeped in boiling water makes a lemony tea.

HABITAT, RANGE

Yellow wood sorrel is widespread, growing in every state except Nevada, California, Alaska and Hawaii. It thrives in lawns, disturbed areas, abandoned fields and parkways, on shaded slopes, and along trails and sidewalks. It prefers moist soil and dappled shade, but can survive in dry, sunny areas.

PARTS USED

Leaves, seed pods

SEASONS

Spring through fall

IDENTIFICATION TIPS, DANGEROUS LOOKALIKES

Wood sorrel has a slender, ropey stem topped with three heart-shaped leaflets joined at a central point; each leaflet is creased, and the leaflet folds upward along this crease in the evening or during stormy weather. Tiny 5-petalled flowers bloom from spring through early fall. Yellow wood sorrel has yellow flowers.

Wood sorrel

The mountain wood sorrel (*O. montana*), which is found occasionally in Minnesota, Iowa, Michigan, Indiana and states east of there, is quite lovely—white with pink stripes that run down the petals to a pink ring in the center of the bloom. The violet wood sorrel (*O. violacea*) has, as you might imagine, pale violet flowers; it is found throughout our region but is not as common as yellow wood sorrel. All the wood sorrels noted above are edible; there are no dangerous lookalikes.

HARVESTING TIPS

Pick wood sorrel on a sunny day, when the leaves are open; if you look for it in overcast or stormy weather, it's hard to see because the characteristic leaves are folded up.

SPECIAL CONSIDERATIONS

Wood sorrel contains a fair amount of soluble oxalates. People with kidney disease, kidney stones, rheumatoid arthritis, or gout probably should avoid eating wood sorrel. For others, the amount that will be eaten over the course of the season is unlikely to cause problems.

MORE ABOUT WOOD SORREL: What a charming little plant wood sorrel is. I love to see its cheerful little blooms and delicate, heart-shaped leaves peeking out from the midst of other plants, and its lemony flavor is delicious. It was first catalogued for science by the Swedish botanist Carl von Linne (Linnaeus) in 1753, but the plant has been used by cooks, philosophers and children since medieval times (it is said that St. Patrick used wood sorrel to demonstrate the concept of the Holy Trinity). It is a favorite of children, who find it easy to identify and, frankly, get a kick out of eating lawn weeds! Savvy hikers look for wood sorrel along the trail; a few bites of wood sorrel will freshen a dry, hot mouth.

The casual observer may readily mistake wood sorrel for a member of the clover family. Both plants sport a triple cluster of leaves, and grow in disturbed places, meadows and waste ground. Closer observation, however, reveals wood sorrel's distinctive heart-shaped leaves, which are easy to distinguish from clover's rounded leaves. Wood sorrel has tiny 5-petalled flowers, while clover has globe-shaped compound flowers (typically pink or white) that are generally ½ to 1 inch across. In full sun, during stormy or windy weather, and in the evening, wood sorrel's leaves fold in upon themselves along the midrib, looking like a tiny umbrella.

Wood sorrel can grow as tall as 15 inches, but is generally smaller. Stems at the base of the plant usually have a purplish hue. After flowering, the plants develop 5-sided seed pods, which will eventually dry and scatter their contents. In the yellow wood sorrel (*O. stricta*), the seedpods stand upright; in other wood sorrels, the seedpods point sideways or downward. The young, green seedpods are delightfully crisp; I love to pick them off and munch on them as I am washing a batch of wood sorrel at the sink.

The leaves of wood sorrel are tender and are wonderful added to green salads. Wood sorrel can be cooked in any recipe calling for spinach or other tender leaves, but like many greens it turns a disappointing olive-drab color; I prefer it raw.

QUICK IDEAS FOR USING WOOD SORREL
- Add wood sorrel leaves to any green salad for a tangy taste.
- Make wood sorrel tea by pouring boiling water over a handful of plants (no need to pull the leaves away from the stems—just remove the roots). Let steep for 15 to 20 minutes. Strain and sweeten to taste; enjoy hot or as a delicious iced tea.
- When you're hiking, add a few freshly picked wood sorrel leaves to your sandwich.
- Substitute wood sorrel leaves for fresh parsley in any recipe; it will add a lemony flavor.

OTHER RECIPES IN THIS BOOK FEATURING WOOD SORREL
- Salade Sauvage (page 54)
- Morels with Crème Fraîche (page 69)

Couscous Salad with Wood Sorrel

6 servings   Preparation: Under 30 minutes

1¼ cups chicken broth, vegetable broth or water

¾ cup couscous

4 sun-dried tomato halves, finely diced

¼ cup pine nuts or slivered blanched almonds

½ teaspoon ground cumin

½ teaspoon ground coriander seed

3 tablespoons olive oil

1 tablespoon white wine vinegar

½ teaspoon salt

½ cup (tightly packed) wood sorrel leaves

3 tablespoons finely diced red onion

Half of a small apple, diced

In saucepan, heat broth to boiling over high heat. Add couscous and diced tomatoes. Stir well; cover and remove from heat. Set aside for 5 to 10 minutes while you prepare remaining ingredients.

In small heavy skillet, toast pine nuts over medium heat, stirring constantly, until beginning to color. Add cumin and coriander seed; remove from heat and stir for about a minute to toast spices. Transfer nut/spice mixture to mixing bowl. Add oil, vinegar and salt to mixing bowl; stir vigorously with fork to blend. Fluff couscous with fork; add to mixing bowl and stir well. Set aside until couscous cools to room temperature, stirring occasionally to help it cool. Meanwhile, chop wood sorrel leaves to medium-fine consistency. When couscous is room temperature, stir in wood sorrel, onion and apple. Serve immediately.

GREENS & FLOWERS

Green Sauce with Wood Sorrel

About ⅔ cup (6 to 8 servings)   Preparation: Under 15 minutes

This simple but fabulous sauce is based on chimichurri, *a classic Argentinian herb sauce. Serve it with grilled meat, poultry or seafood; use it as a marinade; or add a few spoonsful to potato salad or bean dishes for extra flavor.*

1 small jalapeño pepper	⅔ cup (tightly packed) wood sorrel leaves
4 to 6 cloves garlic	⅔ cup (tightly packed) parsley leaves
2 bay leaves, broken up	¼ cup white wine vinegar
1 teaspoon fresh bergamot or marjoram leaves	2 tablespoons extra-virgin olive oil
	½ teaspoon salt, or to taste

Cut off stem of jalapeño; remove seeds and veins if you prefer a less spicy sauce. In food processor, combine pepper, garlic, bay leaves and bergamot or marjoram. Pulse until finely chopped, scraping down as needed. Add wood sorrel and parsley; pulse until finely chopped. Add vinegar, oil and salt; pulse until well blended. Taste for seasoning and adjust salt if necessary. Serve at room temperature; refrigerate leftovers for up to 5 days.

Edible Flower Leaves

Here are just a few of the edible flower leaves you'll find in our area. Toss a few into a mixed salad for extra flavor and a unique appearance.

The leaves of many beautiful wildflowers are edible. Generally, you won't harvest enough to make a complete dish from any one kind, but they can be added raw to salads as an accent; many can be included in a pot of mixed greens for cooking. Here are a few of the wildflowers whose leaves are used in these ways. Also see Minor Greens on page 344; these plants also have flowers, but as they are less conspicuous, I am not including them with the showy flowers listed here.

Also see Minor Greens on page 344

CHICORY *(Cichorium intybus)*

Chicory

You may be familiar with this cheery blue daisy-like flower, but may not realize that the greens are a delicious edible, prized for their bitter tang. Harvest young greens before the flower stalk develops; at that time, they closely resemble dandelion greens, and grow in the same type of basal rosette. Unlike dandelion leaves, chicory leaves have fine hairs on them; these are noticeable along the edges of the leaves. Once the plant sends up flower stalks, the leaves become too bitter to eat (although hardy souls may boil them in several changes of water to make them edible if not palatable). If you see a patch of chicory flowers in the summer, note the location so you can return the following spring to harvest the leaves. The long taproot of chicory can be handled just like dandelion roots (pages 46-47), and is often used as a coffee substitute or extender. Chicory grows throughout the United States, in habitat similar to that favored by dandelions.

Clintonia

CLINTONIA *(Clintonia borealis)*

This plant, also called bluebead lily or corn lily, is found primarily in the northern part of our region; it lives in the boreal forest and deep woodlands with rich soil. Each clintonia plant has 2 or 3 large, shiny leaves (sometimes up to 5) that grow in a basal rosette and are deeply cleft by the vertical midrib; they resemble ramp leaves, but lack the narrow maroon neck that characterizes ramps. A leafless flower stalk arises from the center and is eventually crowned with 3 to 5 yellow nodding bell-shaped flowers. The crisp leaves have a delicious cucumber-like taste; I love to tuck a few into a sandwich, or slice them into ribbons to add to salad. Clintonia leaves resemble those of some poisonous lilies; the flower is the surest way to identify clintonia. Once the plant flowers, the leaves tend to taste too strong, but not all plants in a patch flower at once. Wait for a few flowers to appear, confirming the identity of the plants, then harvest young leaves from other plants in the colony that have not yet flowered. Clintonia leaves can be boiled like spinach, but I don't care for the flavor of the boiled leaves; I really enjoy this plant raw, fresh and crisp.

OXEYE DAISY (*Chrysanthemum leucanthemum*)

Oxeye daisy

Here's a true daisy that is an interesting salad green. It grows throughout the country in fields and waste ground, requiring sunny locations. The 2-inch-wide flower has white petals surrounding a yellow central disk that appears depressed in the center. The narrow dark-green leaves are alternate on the stems, and have irregularly lobed edges. A few leaves added to a salad will add a peppery flavor; the leaves are strong, so don't use too many or you will overpower the rest of the salad. Some people enjoy the leaves boiled, although I've never tried this.

SPRING BEAUTY (*Claytonia* spp.)

One of the loveliest of the early flowers, spring beauty is scattered throughout our region with the exception of the Dakotas. Look for it in moist woods, often alongside violets; I've

Spring beauty

also seen it growing near wood nettle patches. The most distinctive feature is the lovely 5-petalled flower, which is white (or light pink) with pink stripes. Each plant has 2 leaves from 2 to 5 inches long; the leaves are attached halfway up the stem. Leaves of Carolina spring beauty (*C. caroliniana*) are broad in the middle, with slender leafstalks; leaves of the Virginia spring beauty (*C. virginica*) are much narrower, almost sword-like but with the same slender leafstalk. Leaves have a sweet, "green" taste, and can be harvested in limited numbers to add to salads (take only 1 leaf from each plant, and only from large colonies; if the colony is small, simply enjoy it for its beauty and leave it untouched).

Spring beauty tubers are edible and delicious, although quite small (about the size of a marble). They can be eaten raw, or boiled just like potatoes, and are often called "fairy spuds." Spring beauty is threatened by deer predation and habitat encroachment, and is rare in much of its range; harvest tubers only out of a large colony, and then, only sparingly.

Minor Greens

These plants go well in a mixed pot of stewed greens.

Just because I've classified these greens as minor doesn't mean they aren't worth looking for. In general, they have limited use, or are small enough that they are not going to provide the major component of a dish. Most are good for salads, and also can be added to a greens pot (generally in combination with other greens). The plants here all have flowers, but they tend to be inconspicuous; for showy wildflowers with edible greens please see Edible Flower Leaves on page 342.

CHICKWEED (common chickweed, *Stellaria media;* star chickweed, *S. pubera;* mouse-eared or big chickweed, *Cerastium vulgatum*)

Common chickweed

These plants grow throughout our region in disturbed areas and yards, next to roads and cultivated lands, and in ditches, meadows and sparse woodlands; they prefer moist soil. Chickweed is a sprawling plant, sometimes forming mats. All species have paired leaves on weak stems. Common chickweed is the smallest, with leaves that are generally about an inch long on noticeable leafstalks. Leaves of star chickweed are stalkless, and may be up to 3 inches in length. Mouse-eared chickweed is covered in tiny hairs that some people find objectionable when the leaves are served raw. Chickweed has a mild, sweet flavor and a tender-crisp texture that is welcome in salads; the entire young tips can be used, or the leaves pulled off to use without the stems. Tender tips and young leaves can be cooked like spinach—steamed, sautéed or boiled for just a few minutes, then dressed with butter or other flavorings. It can be harvested any time of year it is growing; the last 2 or 3 inches of the plant are best, as older growth is stringy and tough.

Black mustard

MUSTARD (*Brassica* spp.)
Members of the mustard family can be recognized by their symmetrical, 4-petalled yellow flowers that grow in clusters at the tops of the branching stems. Leaves at the base of the plant are deeply lobed or irregularly jagged. Mustard can grow to 4 feet in height, and is found throughout the country in fields, disturbed areas, and waste ground. Young leaves have a sharp taste that is welcome in a salad (don't use too many, though, or they will

overpower everything); they can also be added to a pot of mixed greens for cooking. Unopened flowering heads can be boiled for a few minutes and served like tiny broccoli; really quite interesting. Once the flowers open completely, the leaves become too bitter to be of much interest; try boiling the leaves in several changes of water to reduce bitterness. In summer, mustard seeds can be harvested from the narrow, brittle seed pods, then dried and used like the grocery-store variety.

PLANTAIN *(Plantago major)*

This is one of the most common "edible garden weeds," and grows throughout the country in yards, vacant lots, fields, playgrounds and just about anywhere you look. It is recognized by the rounded, heavily veined leaves, generally 2 to 4 inches long but as long as 8 inches, that grow as a basal rosette; in late spring the plant develops a skinny flower spike that is probably the most recognizable feature of this plant (it looks like a cross between a banana and a green pinecone, and can be up to 8 inches in height). In early spring, harvest young plantain leaves to use sparingly in salads, or, preferably, as an addition to the cooked-greens pot. If the midrib is tough, fold the leaf in half

Plantain with seed stalks

and snip away the rib. The seeds can be harvested and ground to add to baked goods, but I find them uninteresting at best. It also takes quite a few to do much with; one fall, I processed 50 stalks and ended up with ¾ ounce of seeds.

Wintercress

WINTERCRESS *(Barbarea vulgaris)*

Also called garden yellow rocket, this plant is similar to the mustards (above). It has the same type of clustered 4-petalled flowers and deeply lobed leaves; however, the leaves near the bottom of the plant have separate lobes at the base that look like ears, while those higher up on the main stem have rounded teeth and grow around the stem in a clasping fashion. Leaves and unopened flowering heads can be used as described in the listing for mustard.

Wintercress Vinegar

Prepare the vinegar with leaves that have been harvested before the plants flower. A month later, when you gather plants to place into the strained vinegar, choose those that have flowered; they'll look very pretty in the final product.

2 cups gently packed wintercress leaves

2 cups white wine vinegar or champagne vinegar

1 stalk wintercress, with both leaves and flowers

Sterilize a 1-quart canning jar in boiling water (page 418). Pack well-washed wintercress leaves into jar. Add vinegar; cover and seal tightly. Place in cool cupboard for 3 to 4 weeks, shaking jar occasionally.

For final preparation, sterilize a 1-pint bottle (I like to use a shaker-top bottle that originally held soy sauce or vinegar). Wash the wintercress stalk well and force it into the bottle. Strain vinegar through fine-mesh strainer; pour into bottle with wintercress stalk. Cap or cork bottle and store in pantry, where it will keep its flavor for 6 months.

Mixed Greens with Black-Eyed Peas

4 servings Preparation: Under an hour

This is a nice way to use a bag of mixed greens; if you don't have quite enough wild greens, use Swiss chard or beet greens from the supermarket to make up the amount needed.

4 cups (tightly packed) mixed wild greens
½ cup diced fennel bulb
½ cup chopped onion
2 tablespoons olive oil
¾ cup chicken broth
1 can (14.5 ounces) diced tomatoes,
  drained

1 teaspoon dried oregano
½ teaspoon salt
¼ teaspoon black pepper
1 can (14.5 ounces) black-eyed peas,
  drained and rinsed

If greens seem bitter, cook in a large pot of boiling water for 5 minutes, then drain, rinse with cold water and set aside to drain thoroughly (you may want to do this with just part of the greens, or with none of them, depending on what you've picked). In small soup pot, cook fennel and onion in oil over medium heat until fennel is tender, about 10 minutes, stirring frequently. Add chicken broth; cook for about 10 minutes longer, stirring occasionally. Add greens, tomatoes, oregano, salt and pepper. Cook for 10 minutes, or until greens are tender, stirring occasionally. Add black-eyed peas. Reduce heat and simmer for about 10 minutes to blend flavors.

GREENS & FLOWERS

Tea Flowers

These contribute a mild fragrance to mixed teas; chamomile can be used alone to make a stomach-soothing tea.

Here are three wildflowers that are often used for tea. They can be used alone or in combination with other flowers or leaves; see the recipe that follows for a tea blend you might enjoy.

CHAMOMILE *(Matricaria chamomilla)*

Chamomile

This is probably the best-known of the wild teas; in fact, chamomile is grown commercially to make tea that is available in the supermarket. Chamomile grows in the wild throughout our region with the exception of the Dakotas; look for it on roadsides, in waste ground and old fields, and in disturbed areas. The flowers are small and daisy-like, with fine white petals that tend to hang down below the yellow central disk; they sit atop multiple-branched stems on plants that are between 7 and 12 inches tall. The sparse leaves are bright green and feathery. Flowers and leaves have a distinct pineapple scent when crushed. To use for tea, harvest flowers in the height of bloom. Snip from the stems and place on a screen, then let air-dry completely; this may take up to a week. Store dried flowers in sealed glass jars in a dark cupboard. Brew by pouring boiling water over a handful of flowers in a teapot (or use a tablespoon per cup) and steeping for 5 minutes; strain and enjoy as is, or sweeten to taste. I drink chamomile tea when I have an upset stomach; others use it for mild headache.

Pineapple weed

PINEAPPLE WEED *(Matricaria discoidea* or *M. matricarioides)*
This plant resembles its relative, chamomile, but the flowers are lacking the white petals, consisting of a proportionally large rounded yellowish greenish head set into a cup. Pineapple weed is much leafier than chamomile. It's also called the disc mayweed, and grows in the same types of habitat where chamomile is found. It is more widespread throughout the country, however; whereas chamomile is largely an Eastern plant, pineapple weed's range extends to the West coast and down to most of the southern states. The plants are 6 to 18 inches tall, and as with chamomile, the flower heads and leaves smell strongly of pineapple when crushed. Harvest and use as described for chamomile, above.

RED CLOVER *(Trifolium pratense)*

Clovers are common and easy to recognize, with their round, ball-like flowerheads and 3-part leaves. Red clover has a pinkish red to purplish red flower that is ½ to 1 inch across; leaves are marked with conspicuous whitish chevrons, making this plant easy to identify. It is found throughout the United States, in fields, ditches, waste and disturbed ground and yards. Flowerheads can be used raw as a salad garnish; a scattering of the leaves can be eaten raw in salads (they have a somewhat coarse feeling in the mouth, so don't use too many). Flowerheads really shine, though, as an ingredient in mixed teas. Harvest, dry and brew as described in chamomile, above. Note: When harvesting red clover, don't pick from plants whose leaves are spotted or have rings; they may be infested with a fungus that produces slaframine, a toxic alkaloid that can sicken horses (and probably is none too good for people). This is called black patch disease; affected plants show black, gold or brown spots or rings (from an article in *Equinews*, Volume 6 Issue 3, 2003).

Red clover

Wildflower Tea Blend

Yields 2 cups dried blend; enough for 6 to 8 pots of tea

Preparation: Under 15 minutes
(once flowers have been dried)

1 cup dried red clover blossoms
½ cup dried chamomile or pineapple-weed blossoms
¼ cup dried whole mint leaves, or 1 tablespoon crumbled

¼ cup dried strawberry, raspberry or blackberry leaves*
¼ cup dried rose petals, optional

In mixing bowl, combine all ingredients; mix gently with your hands. Transfer to glass jar; seal tightly and store in a dark, cool place. To make tea, place a tablespoon per cup in a teaball (if using a teapot, use ¼ cup of the blend). Pour boiling water over tea blend; steep for 5 minutes (or to taste). Strain and sweeten if desired.

*If you've used raspberry or blackberry leaves, don't let the tea steep too long before straining, or the tea may become bitter due to tannin in these leaves.

WILD MUSHROOMS

MOREL MUSHROOMS are what got me into foraging, and are still my favorite thing to go after in the woods. They have a short season, however, growing for just a few weeks (in a good year!) in the spring. Luckily, there are other mushrooms that appear in summer and fall, so the mushroom enthusiast has other quarry to hunt.

Mushroom identification is critical; a mistake made here can be fatal. Some mushrooms take on different forms throughout their growth cycle, or may appear slightly different in various habitats; with some, spore prints are needed for unequivocal identification. As noted in the introduction, this book is not a field guide, so I am not going to attempt to explain what various mushrooms look like; instead, I refer you to a good field guide (see bibliography for recommendations). The mother of all mushroom books is *Mushrooms Demystified,* by David Arora, but you'll also want some smaller, more portable books to take out into the field (at 960 pages, my paperback edition of *Mushrooms Demystified* weighs in at 3¼ pounds). If there is a local chapter of the Mycological Society of America, you might want to join it; the best way to learn mushroom identification is from an expert, and the MSA is a great place to start your search for wild mushrooms. Visit their website at http://www.msafungi.org/ to look for a chapter near you.

In the kitchen, I approach mushrooms based on their texture and cooking characteristics. I've divided some of the more common (and more safe-to-harvest) wild mushrooms into categories based on these criteria. In general, any mushroom within a category can be substituted for any other in the same category. You'll also find notes about each mushroom species discussed, including information on season, habitat and other tips.

Thin-Walled, Flexible Mushrooms

These mushrooms may look delicate, but they pack plenty of flavor. In addition, their unique shapes add interest to a variety of dishes.

This is a small group of mushrooms, but includes my favorites: cauliflower fungus, black trumpet (also called horn of plenty), and that perennial favorite, the morel. These mushrooms shrink quite a bit during cooking, and release a fair amount of flavorful liquid; be sure to cook them long enough that the mushrooms re-absorb the liquid, or use the liquid as the base for a flavorful sauce.

BLACK TRUMPET (Craterellus cornucopioides)

Also called the horn of plenty or black chanterelle, this exquisite mushroom has a rich, almost smoky flavor and very dramatic appearance. It looks like a miniature woodland trumpet that is grayish on the outside with a hollow black interior. They're found in small colonies in mixed woodlands and mossy areas; look for them from midsummer through fall. They are relatively small, generally 2 to 3 inches in height, and their dark color makes them blend into the forest floor, so finding them can be a bit of a challenge. Because they shrink quite a bit, you'll need to gather a good number to enjoy them as a simple sauté on their own, although a few can do wonders as an accent in a dish (especially one that has a cream sauce). I generally cut these in half from top to bottom before cooking, or chop them as required by the recipe. They dry very well, and retain their flavor when rehydrated.

CAULIFLOWER FUNGUS (Sparassis crispa and S. radicata)

Look for this distinctive cream-colored fungus from late summer through fall in our area; they're typically found at the base of pine trees, but also appear occasionally under oak trees. Cauliflower clusters consist of multiple, wavy-edged, fan-like sheets that grow together in a fairly tight head; clusters generally range in size from baseball- to basketball-size (although *S. radicata* can grow to very large size, reportedly as large as a bushel basket). The wavy edges discolor to brown as the fungus ages; trim away any darkened or dried edges before using. They store well in the refrigerator, unwashed and loosely wrapped in plastic; be sure to wash them well just before using to remove dirt trapped in the folds. Cut into strips, or break into small clusters, for cooking. Cauliflowers are very fragrant, with a nutty flavor. Stomach upset has been reported when cauliflower fungus is combined with red wine, although I have never had this problem.

MOREL FAMILY *(Morchella* spp.)

Please see the morel section starting on page 56 in the Top Ten chapter for detailed information on this premiere wild mushroom.

OTHER RECIPES IN THIS BOOK FEATURING THIN-WALLED, FLEXIBLE WILD MUSHROOMS

- Morel recipes on pages 60-69
- Surprise Stuffing (page 126)
- Autumn Mushroom Soup with Carrots and Leeks (page 372)
- Mushroom-Cornmeal Biscuits (page 373)
- Polenta Stuffed with Mushrooms (page 374)
- Wild Mushroom Soup Gratinée (page 378)
- Salisbury Steaks with Mushroom Gravy (page 379)
- Mushroom "Baklava" (page 380)
- Vegetable Terrine with Mushrooms (page 382)
- Mushroom Consommé (page 385)
- Pork and Mushroom Pie (page 388)
- Wild and Brown Rice Casserole with Mushrooms (page 389)
- Mushroom Fried Rice (page 401)
- Wild Rice and Mushroom Soup (page 409)
- Dried mushrooms (page 422)

Black Trumpet Risotto

4 servings   Preparation: Under 30 minutes

Black trumpet mushrooms pair perfectly with creamy short-grain rice in this Italian classic. Their rich flavor and intense perfume come through nicely in this simple preparation, and their dark color contrasts nicely with the rice. Morels, boletes or chanterelles would work well as substitutes.

1 cup chopped black trumpet mushrooms (about 2 ounces)
5 teaspoons butter, divided
3 cups chicken broth, approximate
1 clove garlic, finely minced

1 cup arborio, carnaroli or other short-grain rice suitable for risotto
1/3 cup dry sherry or white wine
2 tablespoons finely chopped Parmesan, Romano or Asiago cheese, optional

In heavy-bottomed medium saucepan, sauté mushrooms in half of the butter over medium heat for 5 minutes; any juices released by the mushrooms should have cooked away during this time. While mushrooms are cooking, heat chicken broth to simmering in another pot; adjust heat to maintain simmer throughout cooking. Transfer mushrooms to a small bowl, spooning them out carefully to leave as much of the melted butter in the pan as possible; set mushrooms aside.

Melt remaining butter in same saucepan over medium heat. Add garlic and sauté for about a minute. Add rice and cook, stirring frequently, for about 5 minutes; the rice will look chalky. Add wine and cook, stirring frequently, until wine cooks away. Add about 1/4 cup of the simmering broth and cook, stirring frequently, until the liquid cooks away. Continue to add broth in small batches, stirring frequently, until the rice is almost tender, about 15 minutes. Add mushrooms to saucepan with rice and continue to cook, adding broth as needed, until rice is just tender but still firm to the bite in the center. Total cooking time will be about 20 minutes; you may not need quite all the broth, or you may need a bit more (use hot water if you run out of broth near the end). Rice should be creamy but not soupy; stir in a bit more broth as needed. Remove from heat; stir in Parmesan and serve immediately.

Cheesy Mushroom Crisps

55 to 60 crackers

Serve these rich crackers as an appetizer, or to accompany soup and salad for a light supper. These are best when prepared with highly flavored mushrooms that are relatively low in moisture, such as morels, black trumpets, white truffles or chanterelles.

1 cup coarsely chopped black trumpets
  or substitute (see note above), about
  2 ounces
3 tablespoons butter
¾ cup grated Parmesan, Romano or
  Asiago cheese

¼ teaspoon salt
⅛ teaspoon coarsely ground black pepper
⅔ cup all-purpose flour
3 tablespoons cream or milk, approximate

In medium skillet, sauté mushrooms in butter over medium heat for about 5 minutes; any juices released by the mushrooms should have cooked away during this time. Transfer mushroom mixture to medium mixing bowl; set aside until completely cool and butter is no longer liquid. (Note: If it is warm in your kitchen, you can refrigerate the bowl of mushrooms, but don't let it get too cold; the butter should be congealed but not so cold that it is hard.)

In food processor, combine mushroom mixture, Parmesan cheese, salt and pepper; pulse on-and-off a few times to chop mushrooms and mix everything. Add flour and pulse until well combined. Add enough cream to form a dough that holds together but is not wet; be careful not to overmix the dough. Shape dough into a tightly packed 1-inch cylinder. Wrap in waxed paper and chill for an hour or longer.

When you're ready to bake, heat oven to 375°F. Slice dough ⅛ inch thick. Place on ungreased baking sheets. Bake until nicely browned around the edges and firm to the touch, about 15 minutes. Loosen from baking sheet while still warm.

Chicken and Polenta with Mushrooms

4 servings   Preparation: Under 30 minutes

2 large cloves garlic
2 cups chicken broth
1 bay leaf
4 boneless, skinless chicken breast halves
    (about 6 ounces each)
Salt, pepper and dried thyme
1 tube (1 pound) prepared polenta, or
    equivalent in homemade (see page 374)

½ cup finely grated Parmesan cheese
8 ounces black trumpets, cauliflower fungus,
    morels or other wild mushrooms
2 teaspoons butter
2 teaspoons olive oil

Heat oven to 425°F. Spray baking sheet with nonstick spray; set aside. Partially crush garlic cloves with flat side of knife; you don't want to pulverize them, just break them open and flatten them somewhat. Combine crushed garlic cloves with chicken broth and bay leaf in small saucepan. Heat to boiling over medium-high heat, and cook until broth reduces to about ¾ cup.

While broth is reducing, pound thick end of chicken breast halves to even thickness. Sprinkle with salt, pepper and thyme to taste; set aside. Slice polenta into 12 slices. Arrange polenta slices on prepared baking sheet in a single layer. Spray top sides of polenta slices with nonstick spray, or brush lightly with oil if you prefer; sprinkle Parmesan cheese evenly over slices. Set aside.

Chop mushrooms coarsely. In small skillet, sauté mushrooms in butter over medium heat, stirring occasionally, until juices released by mushrooms have cooked away. By now, the chicken broth should have reduced to ¾ cup. Remove and discard bay leaf. Remove garlic cloves and transfer to cutting board to cool; pour reduced stock into skillet with mushrooms. Set aside and keep warm.

Place baking sheet of polenta slices in oven, and set a timer for 10 minutes so you don't forget them. Heat oil in large skillet over medium-high heat. Add chicken breasts in single layer and cook until nicely browned on both sides and cooked through. Don't overcook the chicken; it should have just a bit of spring to it when pressed with a fingertip. Set aside and keep warm for the few minutes it will take to finish the polenta.

If you like, place polenta under broiler for a few minutes to crisp cheese on top; otherwise, let bake until cheese is bubbly. Now, assemble individual portions: Place one piece of chicken on each serving plate (wide, shallow soup plates work well). Arrange 3 slices of polenta around the edges of each piece. Cut garlic cloves in half and place one half in each plate. Spoon an equal amount of mushrooms on top of each portion. Pour the broth evenly over the 4 servings. Serve immediately.

Potato-Mushroom Cake

4 main-dish servings; 10 to 12 appetizer servings   Preparation: Under an hour

In Spain, frittata-like dishes like this are served at room temperature as a snack with drinks. For a light, delicious vegetarian supper, serve warm with a salad of baby greens topped with sliced pear, some crumbled blue cheese, and Honey-Roasted Nut Clusters (page 282).

1 tablespoon olive oil, approximate, divided
1 pound russet potatoes, peeled and shredded
Salt and freshly ground black pepper
1½ cups cut-up or sliced black trumpets, morels or other wild mushrooms

1 or 2 cloves garlic, minced
4 eggs, or 1 cup liquid egg substitute
¾ cup whole or 2% milk
½ cup sour cream (reduced-fat works fine)
3 to 4 ounces soft cheese such as Brie, Camembert or similar,* cut into 1-inch slices

Heat oven to 375°F. In well-seasoned medium cast-iron skillet, heat about a teaspoon of the oil over medium heat, swirling skillet to completely coat bottom. Add potatoes, spreading evenly. Cook for about 15 minutes, turning in large chunks several times; each time you turn potatoes, drizzle a little more oil over potatoes before turning them. When potatoes have started to become browned throughout, sprinkle with salt and pepper to taste. Add mushrooms and garlic. Drizzle with a little more oil and turn potatoes again. Cook for about 5 minutes longer, turning one more time. Meanwhile, beat together eggs, milk and sour cream in mixing bowl. When potatoes and mushrooms have cooked together for 5 minutes, pour egg mixture over potatoes; don't stir it in, just pour it evenly over the top. Place skillet in oven and bake for 20 minutes. Arrange cheese evenly over top of cake. Return to oven and bake for 5 minutes longer. Serve hot, or allow to cool somewhat and serve warm.

*I have sometimes used a wonderful double-cream Champignon cheese from Bavaria for this. It's a soft, ripened cheese that is studded with bits of mushroom, and goes perfectly with this dish.

Hot and Sour Soup

4 servings

Cauliflower fungus is a perfect substitution for the dried cloud ears traditionally used in this classic Chinese recipe. The subtle perfume of the cauliflower fungus adds a new layer of flavor to this vinegary, peppery soup.

¼ cup dried day lily flowers (page 302), or golden needles (dried tiger lily flowers; available at Chinese markets)

4 to 5 ounces fresh cauliflower fungus (a clump that is a bit bigger than a softball)

Half of an 8-ounce can sliced bamboo shoots

¼ pound pork tenderloin

1 tablespoon cornstarch

1 tablespoon dry sherry

6 ounces firm tofu (bean curd)

2 tablespoons tapioca starch, or 1 tablespoon plus 1½ teaspoons cornstarch

⅓ cup rice vinegar (I use seasoned rice vinegar)

1 teaspoon soy sauce

1 teaspoon salt

½ teaspoon finely ground white pepper

1 quart chicken broth

1 egg, lightly beaten

2 scallions, sliced ⅛ inch thick

Add dried day lily flowers to large bowl of boiling water; set aside for 20 minutes. Meanwhile, prepare the other ingredients. Clean cauliflower fungus, then slice into ½-inch strips; set aside in large bowl. Cut drained bamboo shoots along their length into ⅛-inch-wide strips. Add bamboo shoots to a small pan of boiling water and cook for about a minute, then drain and add to bowl with cauliflower fungus. Cut pork into ⅛-inch-thick slices across the grain; cut each slice into ⅛-inch-wide strips. Combine cornstarch and sherry in a small mixing bowl; add pork strips and stir to coat. Slice tofu into strips that are about 3/16 x ½ x 2 inches. In small bowl, combine tapioca starch with ¼ cup water. In measuring cup, combine vinegar, soy sauce, salt and pepper, stirring until salt dissolves.

When dried flowers are swollen and soft, drain well. Cut away and discard any hardened base, then cut or tear each blossom into 3 or 4 strips, adding them to bowl with cauliflower fungus.

In soup pot, heat chicken broth to boiling. Add cauliflower fungus mixture. Heat to boiling, then reduce heat and simmer for about 5 minutes. Stir in vinegar mixture. Rapidly add pork strips a few at a time, stirring constantly to separate strips. Simmer for about 5 minutes. Increase heat slightly so mixture boils gently. Add egg in a thin stream, stirring constantly. Cook for about a minute. Add tofu strips to pot. Stir tapioca starch mixture, then pour into pot and cook, stirring constantly, until soup thickens and becomes translucent. Stir in scallions and serve immediately.

Variation: Hot and Sour Soup with Fresh Day Lily Flowers

Substitute 1 packed cup of withered fresh day lily flowers for the dried flowers. Tear each into 4 strips. There is no need to soak these in boiling water; add them to the soup just after you add the pork strips.

MUSHROOMS

Twice as Curly Noodles and Mushrooms

4 side-dish servings   Preparation: Under 30 minutes

Cauliflower fungus lend their interesting, curly shape to curly pasta in this easy dish. The wonderful flavor and fragrance of the cauliflower fungus really comes through in this simple dish, too. If you don't have cauliflower fungus, morels would be a good substitution.

8 ounces curly pasta such as curly egg noodles, spirals, cavatappi or mini lasagna

4 to 5 ounces fresh cauliflower fungus (a clump that is a bit bigger than a softball)

2 tablespoons butter, divided

¼ cup coarse dry breadcrumbs*

1 vegetable bouillon cube, dissolved in ¼ cup hot water

Grated Romano or Asiago cheese for serving, optional

Heat large pot of salted water to boiling over high heat. Add pasta; cook according to package directions. While pasta is cooking, clean cauliflower fungus carefully and tear into bite-sized pieces (this makes a much more attractive dish than slicing the fungus).

In medium skillet, melt 1 tablespoon of the butter over medium heat. Add breadcrumbs. Cook, stirring constantly, until deeply golden and toasted. Transfer to small bowl and set aside. Melt remaining 1 tablespoon of butter in same skillet. Add cauliflower fungus. Cook, stirring occasionally, until juices released by the cauliflowers have cooked away, about 5 minutes. Add vegetable bouillon mixture and cook until liquid has reduced to just a small amount, about 5 minutes longer.

When pasta is tender but still firm in the center, drain. Add cauliflower fungus mixture, tossing well to coat. Sprinkle toasted breadcrumbs over the top; toss gently and serve immediately, passing grated cheese for those who would like it.

*Tip: Use a hand-held grater to grate dried slices of hearty bread, such as Italian country-style bread. The consistency is just right. If you prefer, you can chop dried bread coarsely in a food processor, or even smash it up with a rolling pin.

Mushroom Pasta Pillows (Gnocchi)

4 servings Preparation: Over an hour

The gnocchi are wonderful, but the rich sauce made from the mushroom-soaking liquid is what makes this dish exceptional.

2 cups chicken broth
1 clove garlic
½ ounce dried black trumpets, morels or
other dried wild mushrooms
2 russet potatoes (1 to 1½ pounds total)
1½ teaspoons unsalted butter

1 egg
½ teaspoon salt
⅔ to 1 cup all-purpose flour, plus
additional for shaping dumplings
1 tablespoon snipped fresh chives
Freshly grated Parmesan cheese for serving

Note: You will be boiling potatoes and preparing the mushrooms at the same time. The mushrooms can be chopped while the potatoes are still boiling, or after the potatoes have been riced, depending on how the timing works out.

Begin heating large pot of water to boiling; on another burner, heat chicken broth to boiling in small saucepan. Add garlic to broth and cook for 5 minutes. Add mushrooms to broth. Remove from heat and set aside for about 15 minutes, or until mushrooms are soft. Keep an eye on the large pot of water; when it boils, add unpeeled potatoes and cook until just tender, 30 to 35 minutes.

When mushrooms are soft, return to heat and boil gently for about 5 minutes. Use slotted spoon to transfer mushrooms and garlic to paper towel-lined plate; set aside to cool. To make the sauce, strain chicken broth through funnel lined with paper coffee filter. Rinse any grit from small saucepan, and return strained broth to saucepan. Cook broth at a gentle boil until it has reduced to about 3 tablespoons, adjusting heat as necessary (keep an eye on the broth while you are fiddling with the potatoes, to make sure it doesn't cook away!). Remove from heat. Stir in butter; set sauce aside and keep warm.

Check potatoes for doneness; when they are tender, remove from boiling water, then peel while still hot (I wear rubber gloves and hold the hot potato under a stream of cold water in the sink; the skin slips off easily). Process potatoes and cooked garlic clove through food mill or potato ricer, or mash by hand to fine consistency (do not use a food processor, which causes the gnocchi to be tough). Set potatoes aside in a large bowl to cool to warm room temperature.

Chop mushrooms finely, and stir into potatoes (note: if you're ready for this step and the potatoes are still cooking, go ahead and chop the mushrooms, then transfer them to the large bowl that will later hold the potatoes). Make a well in cooled potatoes and break egg into the well. Add salt to egg and beat together in the well with a fork. Add flour to the well, a few tablespoons at a time, and incorporate it into potatoes and egg until the entire mixture has been combined. Add just enough flour to produce a soft dough that is no longer sticky. Turn out on generously floured worksurface, and knead gently several times to make a smooth dough. Working with about one-quarter of the dough at a time, roll with your palms on floured worksurface to form a rope that is just over ¾-inch thick. Cut into 1-inch pieces. Place a piece on your left hand (if you are right-handed), on the fingertips; press the tines of a fork into the piece to make ridges, rolling the piece as you press the fork into it (this is much easier and more natural than it sounds). You want the gnocchi to be nicely ridged over about half of its surface; I usually end up with a slight lip where I pull the fork away from the gnocchi after rolling. In addition to adding visual interest, the ridges and lip will catch the sauce. Transfer shaped gnocchi to floured baking sheet and repeat with remaining dough; keep shaped gnocchi in a single layer.

Heat large pot of salted water to boiling. Add 8 to 10 of the gnocchi and stir very gently to prevent sticking. The gnocchi will sink to the bottom, but soon will float to the surface. Boil for about a minute after they float, then transfer with slotted spoon to warm serving bowl; cover bowl to keep warm while you cook remaining gnocchi. When all gnocchi are cooked, pour sauce over the top. Sprinkle with chives; serve with freshly grated Parmesan cheese.

Deluxe Scrambled Eggs

2 or 3 servings   Preparation: Under 15 minutes

Deceptively simple, and absolutely delicious. Although any wild mushroom can be used here, cauliflower fungus or morels are most suited. Their texture and woodsy perfume make them a perfect partner with the rich eggs and cheese. The dish will be most luxurious if you use cream, but if you are cutting calories, use milk instead of cream.

1 tablespoon butter or margarine
2 cups cut-up cauliflower fungus or morels
   (bite-sized pieces; 3 to 4 ounces)
4 eggs, or 1 cup liquid egg substitute
3 tablespoons cream, half and half, milk or
   evaporated skim milk

1 tablespoon snipped fresh chives
¼ teaspoon salt
A few grindings of black pepper
1 sandwich-sized slice of muenster or
   Swiss cheese, cut into smaller pieces
   (about 1 ounce)

Melt butter in large skillet over medium heat. Add mushrooms and cook, stirring frequently, until softened and reduced in volume, 5 to 7 minutes. Meanwhile, beat together eggs, cream, chives, salt and pepper in a small bowl.

When mushrooms are ready, pour egg mixture into skillet. Reduce heat to medium-low and cook, stirring constantly, until eggs are softly set, about 5 minutes. Stir in cheese and cook until just melted, about 1 minute. Serve immediately.

Solid, Soft Mushrooms

Mushrooms in this category are very common in our area, so it's easy to harvest enough for a meal.

Besides puffballs, which are covered in the Top Ten section on pages 118-127, this is a very small category of edible mushrooms. They tend to produce lots of liquid during cooking, and are softer than commercial species such as the common white button mushroom; they lose a good bit of volume during cooking. Most cooks sauté them, allowing plenty of time for the liquids released during cooking to be re-absorbed.

INKY CAP FAMILY (*Coprinus* spp.)

Shaggy mane

These mushrooms have a unique "self-digesting" feature: as specimens mature, they *deliquesce,* emitting a blackish liquid before completely disintegrating. Specimens for the table should be gathered before this occurs. The most common of these in our region are the inky cap *(C. atramentarius)* and the shaggy mane or lawyer's wig *(C. comatus)*. Alcohol of any type should be avoided when eating inky caps; some people have a severe reaction to the combination. Both species fruit in spring and fall, in habitats as diverse as city parks and sidewalks, to edges of agricultural areas, to forests and shelterbelts. These mushrooms are easiest to identify when they are deliquescing; identification at the earlier, edible stage can be a bit tricky. Be sure to consult with an expert or to observe a full growth cycle, including deliquescing specimens, before harvesting. If you want to try drying these mushrooms, use a food dehydrator or slow oven (see page 422 for dehydrating information); air drying reportedly does not work well.

PUFFBALL FAMILY (various species)

Please see the puffball section starting on page 118 in the Top Ten chapter for detailed information on this delicious group of wild mushrooms.

WAXY CAP (*Hygrophorus russula*)

Edibility of this species is a matter of some debate. Alexander Smith, in his generally reliable guidebook *The Mushroom Hunter's Field Guide*, lists it as "edible and one of the best." However, Dr, Michael Kuo, in his excellent MushroomExpert.com website,* declares this mushroom as downright awful, stating that "the texture is slimy and insipid, and the taste is foul." I've never eaten this mushroom, so have no opinion to offer; however, any mushroom that inspires such a broad range of opinions is worth a mention. If you want to see for yourself, look for it in the fall, in hardwood forests (particularly oak) and open, grassy woods. According to all accounts, it is often wormy, so specimens should be cut lengthwise in the field to inspect them. It reportedly dries well.

Kuo, M. (2003, October). Hygrophorus russula. Retrieved from the MushroomExpert.Com Web site: http://www.bluewillowpages.com/mushroomexpert/hygrophorus_russula.html

RECIPES IN THIS BOOK FEATURING SOLID, SOFT WILD MUSHROOMS
- Puffball recipes on pages 121-127
- Chicken and Polenta with Mushrooms (page 356)
- Potato-Mushroom Cake (page 357)
- Polenta Stuffed with Mushrooms (page 374)
- Pork and Mushroom Pie (page 388)
- Wild and Brown Rice Casserole with Mushrooms (page 389)
- Wild Rice and Mushroom Soup (page 409)
- Dried mushrooms (page 422)

MUSHROOMS

Relatively Firm, Meaty Mushrooms

Here are some of the best-known—and most delicious—wild mushrooms. They can be substituted for domestic mushrooms in almost any recipe you have.

This is the largest category of wild edible mushrooms. From the cook's perspective, species listed here are most similar to cultivated mushrooms available in the grocery store, such as white button mushrooms and cremini. Feel free to substitute mushrooms from this group for domestic mushrooms in any recipe you have, although expect the finished dish to have more flavor than it would if domestic white button mushrooms were used. You also may need to increase cooking time slightly. Note: unlike domestic mushrooms, virtually all wild mushrooms should be cooked before eating.

MUSHROOMS

BOLETUS FAMILY (*Boletus* spp.; also *Leccinum* spp.)

Mushrooms in this family have pores rather than gills on the undersides of the caps. The cèpe or porcini (*B. edulis*) is the best-known of this group, and is considered one of the premier wild mushrooms both here and in Europe. Boletes can be difficult to identify, as there are many members in this large family. For some excellent information, visit Dr. Michael Kuo's "An Introduction to Boletes" at http://www.bluewillowpages.com/mushroomexpert/boletes.html. Boletes are found in summer through fall, in both hardwood and coniferous woodlands. They are excellent when dried; in fact, dried porcinis from Italy and elsewhere command high prices in American gourmet shops.

CHANTERELLES (*Cantharellus* spp.)

One of my favorite wild mushroom families. Colors range from creamy white to golden to deep orange, but all have a trumpet-like shape with ridges (sometimes called folds or veins) rather than true gills; these ridges extend partway down the stem, unlike the distinct demarcation where the gills of other mushrooms stop at the stem. The golden chanterelle, also called girole or pfifferling *(C. cibarius),* is often considered the best of this choice group; its golden to orangeish color and subtle apricot-like taste make it a favorite in the kitchen,

Golden chanterelle

where it enlivens sautés, stews and many other dishes. Look for it from summer through fall in open areas of woodlands and parklands. The yellow-foot chanterelle (*C. tubae-formis)* is not quite as flavorful as the golden chanterelle, but still well worth seeking out.

It appears from mid- to late fall in hardwood or coniferous woodlands. The lovely red chanterelle *(C. cinnabarinus)* is smaller than the golden or yellow-foot; its striking reddish orange color makes it relatively easy to spot under mixed hardwoods in the fall. All chanterelles listed here dry well; cut in half or quarters from top to bottom before drying.

HEDGEHOG *(Hydnum repandum;* also called *Dentinum repandum)*

Hedgehogs get their name from the small teeth that protrude from the underside of the cap (in place of gills). Look for them from midsummer through late fall, particularly in coniferous woodlands but also in mixed hardwood-conifer forests. They tend to grow in large colonies, often in beds of moss or leaf litter. The teeth often separate from the cap during cooking, flecking the dish with little cream-colored bits. I've read that hedgehogs can be bitter if not thoroughly cooked, but have not had this experience. Hedgehogs dry well; slice them ⅛ to ¼ inch thick before drying.

HEN OF THE WOODS *(Grifola frondosa;* also called *Polypilus frondosus* and *Polyporus frondosus)*

Also called maiitake, sheep's head mushroom or kumotake, hen of the woods is highly prized for its rich, distinctive flavor, which works well in casseroles, sautés and sauces. (Do not confuse hen of the woods with chicken of the woods, a very different fungus which is discussed on page 386.) Hens grow in clusters that typically range from grapefruit- to soccerball-sized, although I've read reports of clusters approaching 25 pounds (boy, I wish I had found *that* one!). Each cluster is comprised of many individual brownish caps growing from a fleshy central core. They grow at the base of oaks, primarily, but can also be found under beech, elm and maple. Look for them in the fall; young specimens are best, as they can get tough when mature. I like to separate individual caps from the cluster before cooking them, although you can also slice across the cluster (be sure to look for dirt that may be trapped between individual caps). Hens dry well; prepare as you would for cooking by separating or slicing.

HONEY MUSHROOM *(Armillaria mellea)*

Honey mushrooms are very widespread and are considered excellent by many; however, some people may get stomach upset from them, so always eat just a small portion at first. They grow in large clusters at the bases of both hardwoods and conifers, and are also found growing from buried wood or decaying stumps; look for them from late summer through fall. They are often called "shoestrings" because of the black strands that connect the base of the stem to the host wood (in fact, this is one of several identification keys). You may want to peel the stems of older specimens to remove tough and fibrous material; some people eat only the caps of older specimens. Honey mushrooms don't dry well, but are excellent when pickled or canned.

OYSTER MUSHROOM (*Pleurotus ostreatus;* also related *P. cornucopiae*)

Also called abalone mushrooms or pleurotte, oyster mushrooms have been successfully domesticated, so you may see them in the supermarket (usually at hefty prices). Their pleasant, mild flavor and meaty texture make them a good choice for almost any mushroom recipe; as a bonus to the forager, they are abundant growers and easy to identify. Look for oyster mushrooms from spring through late fall, growing in clusters or shelf-like arrangements directly on standing or fallen trees; they have little or no stalk to speak of, and the veins extend down the length of whatever stalk is present. To prepare for cooking, separate the clusters into individual caps, then slice if necessary.

Oyster mushrooms

The bases are tough, but can be used in stock. The separated caps dry well.

PINE MUSHROOM (*Tricholoma ponderosus;* also called *T. magnivelare* or *Armillaria ponderosa*)

Also referred to as the American matsutake, this mushroom is highly prized for its spicy yet fruity aroma. (The true matsutake, T. matsutake, apparently doesn't grow in our region.) Pine mushrooms are typically thought of as a species of the Pacific Northwest, where they are eagerly harvested by foragers and often end up in Asian markets both in the U.S. and abroad. They do grow in our region, however, and in fact are commercially harvested in Quebec. Look for them from late summer through fall near jack pine *(Pinus banksiana)*, often partially concealed by beds of moss. Because of their remarkable aroma, pine mushrooms are best in simple preparations that allow their characteristics to shine. They're used extensively in Japanese cooking; they're also excellent broiled with a little soy sauce and butter, or simply sautéed. They are one of the very few wild mushrooms that can be eaten raw. Caps of large specimens may be stuffed and baked. I've heard that they dry well, but I've never tried this.

OTHER RECIPES IN THIS BOOK FEATURING RELATIVELY FIRM AND MEATY WILD MUSHROOMS

MUSHROOMS

Potato-Mushroom Chowder

6 servings   Preparation: Under an hour

Many chowder recipes rely on cream for their rich, soothing texture. This low-fat version uses natural potato starch instead; you'll never miss the cream (or the calories!), and the mushroom flavor comes through nicely. A mix of several types of mushrooms is really good in this chowder; and if you're short on wild mushrooms, use a few domestic mushrooms to fill out the total. For a vegan dish, use a total of 5½ cups of mushroom or vegetable stock, omitting the milk and ham.

1 cup diced onion (½-inch dice)
¼ cup finely diced celery (¼-inch dice)
¼ cup finely diced carrot (¼-inch dice)
¾ pound firm, meaty wild mushrooms, sliced or diced into small bite-sized pieces
1 pound Yukon gold or other potatoes

1 quart mushroom broth, vegetable broth or chicken broth
½ teaspoon rubbed sage leaves
¼ pound thinly sliced ham (the kind used for sandwiches)
1 can (12 ounces) evaporated skim milk
1 teaspoon salt
¼ cup minced fresh parsley

Spray small Dutch oven with nonstick spray, and sauté onion, celery and carrot over medium heat for about 5 minutes. Add mushrooms and cook, stirring occasionally, until any liquid released by mushrooms has cooked away, about 10 minutes. Meanwhile, peel potatoes; chop them medium-coarse in food processor, or cut by hand into ¼-inch dice.

When mushroom liquid has cooked away, add potatoes, broth and sage to Dutch oven. Heat to boiling. Reduce heat to a gentle bubble and cook for about 15 minutes, stirring occasionally. While soup is cooking, cut ham into ½-inch strips, then cut strips into 1- or 2-inch-long pieces. Spray medium skillet with nonstick spray, and cook ham over medium-high heat until it crisps up, stirring frequently to separate slices.

When soup has bubbled for 15 minutes, add crisped ham, milk and salt, stirring well. Heat until milk is hot, but don't boil. Stir in parsley and serve.

Pork, Cabbage and Mushroom Hot Pot

3 or 4 servings

Inspired by Japanese cooking techniques, this comforting hot pot is easy and delicious. Use any mushrooms you like, from sturdy chicken of the woods, to softer types such as puffballs, hedgehogs or oyster mushrooms ... the matsutake, or pine mushroom, would be most authentic.

2 tablespoons soy sauce

1 tablespoon sake or dry sherry

1 teaspoon grated gingerroot

1 teaspoon minced garlic

12 to 14 ounces pork tenderloin, sliced
 $\frac{1}{8}$ inch thick

1 small head Chinese cabbage (about
 $1\frac{1}{2}$ pounds)

8 to 12 ounces pine mushrooms or other
 mushrooms

2 or 3 carrots

1 cup chicken broth

1 teaspoon sugar

$\frac{1}{2}$ teaspoon salt

1 tablespoon cornstarch mixed with
 2 tablespoons cold water

2 green onions, sliced

Hot cooked white, brown or sushi-style
 rice for serving

In mixing bowl, combine soy sauce, sake, gingerroot and garlic; mix well. Add pork, stirring to coat. Set aside for 20 minutes or so, while you prepare remaining ingredients.

Slice Chinese cabbage across the head into 1-inch-wide pieces; break cabbage slices apart somewhat with your hands. Slice or cut mushrooms into bite-sized pieces. Peel carrots and cut into matchstick pieces, about $\frac{1}{8}$ x $\frac{1}{8}$ x 2 inches. In measuring cup or small bowl, blend together chicken broth, sugar and salt.

When all ingredients are ready, place a third of the cabbage into Dutch oven or other large pot. Top with a third of the mushrooms, a third of the carrots and half of the pork. Repeat layers, ending with vegetables (so you will have 3 layers of vegetables, 2 of which also include pork). Pour chicken broth mixture over all. Heat to a gentle boil over high heat (you won't be able to see the liquid, but you should be able to hear it bubbling). Cover pot and adjust heat to medium, or a bit lower; the mixture should bubble gently. Cook for 20 to 25 minutes. Stir cornstarch slurry and pour into pot, stirring very gently. Sprinkle green onions over the top. Cook for a few minutes longer, until the liquid thickens somewhat. Serve over rice in wide, shallow soup plates.

MUSHROOMS

Autumn Mushroom Salad

4 servings

Feel free to substitute other varieties of mushrooms for those noted; honey mushrooms or cauliflower fungus would be good choices. If you're short on wild mushrooms, you may use domestic mushrooms such as cremini, shiitake or portabella in place of one of the wild mushrooms.

1 loaf Italian or French bread, sliced
   1/4 inch thick
Olive oil spray*
3 tablespoons grated Parmesan cheese
6 cups mixed salad greens
1/4 cup olive oil
3 large shallots, thinly sliced
1/2 pound chanterelles, sliced lengthwise

1/2 pound oyster mushrooms, sliced
   lengthwise
1/2 pound hen of the woods, sliced across
   the cluster
1 tablespoon freshly squeezed lemon juice
2 teaspoons red wine vinegar
1/2 teaspoon salt
Freshly ground black pepper

Heat oven to 375°F. Lightly spray both sides of the bread slices with olive oil, and place in single layer on baking sheet. Sprinkle lightly with Parmesan cheese. Bake until bread is lightly browned, about 10 minutes.

Meanwhile, arrange salad greens in strips down the center of 4 serving plates; set aside. Heat oil in large skillet over medium heat. Add shallots; sauté for about 2 minutes. Add chanterelles. Increase heat to medium-high and sauté for 3 to 4 minutes. Add oyster mushrooms and hen of the woods; sauté for about 5 minutes longer. (Don't forget about the bread during this time; check it occasionally and remove it from the oven when it is golden brown.)

When mushrooms have cooked as noted, remove from heat and add lemon juice, vinegar, salt and a good grinding of black pepper. Toss gently to mix. Divide mushrooms evenly between the 4 plates. Arrange toasted bread slices along the sides. Serve immediately.

*I use a mister-type device called a Misto to spray the olive oil (the sprayer is great for coating pans etc.). You can also buy olive oil cooking spray such as Pam. If you prefer, simply brush a light coating of olive oil over the bread, using a pastry brush.

Chanterelles and Dumplings

3 or 4 servings   Preparation: Under an hour

Chanterelles are perfect for this hearty soup; they won't fall apart while the dumplings are simmering. Other good choices would be boletes, oyster mushrooms or chicken of the woods.

2 or 3 medium carrots, peeled and sliced
⅛ inch thick
1 small onion, diced
2 teaspoons vegetable oil
10 to 12 ounces chanterelles or other firm,
    meaty mushrooms
¼ teaspoon dried thyme
1 quart vegetable broth or chicken broth
Salt and pepper to taste

Dumplings:*
1½ cups all-purpose flour
2 teaspoons baking powder
½ teaspoon salt
½ teaspoon dried sage, optional
⅔ cup milk
3 tablespoons butter or margarine, melted

In medium soup pot, sauté carrots and onion in oil over medium heat for about 5 minutes, stirring occasionally. Meanwhile, cut chanterelles into large bite-sized pieces; small to medium chanterelles can simply be cut in half vertically, but larger ones should also be cut crosswise. Add chanterelles and thyme to pot and cook for about 5 minutes longer, stirring occasionally. Add broth. Increase heat and cook until broth comes to a gentle boil. Cook for about 5 minutes.

While mixture is cooking, prepare dumplings: In medium mixing bowl, combine flour, baking powder, salt and sage, stirring to blend. Stir milk and melted butter together in measuring cup and add to flour mixture. Stir until flour is moistened; don't overmix or dumplings may be tough.

Taste broth, and add salt and pepper if necessary. Use tablespoon to scoop up a ball of dumpling dough that is just a bit larger than a golfball. Gently drop dumplings on top of simmering broth, arranging them evenly across the top. Cook at a gentle boil for 10 minutes. Cover and reduce heat slightly; cook for 10 minutes longer. Serve in soup plates or bowls.

*For an easier version, substitute 1½ cups buttermilk biscuit mix, prepared according to package instructions, for the dumpling dough. Proceed as directed.

Autumn Mushroom Soup with Carrots and Leeks

2 main-dish or 4 starter servings   Preparation: Under 30 minutes (plus broth)

When you're ready for a mushroom soup that is not cream-based, try this simple and delicious version. I like to use a mix of two mushrooms, such as chanterelles and cauliflower fungus.

1 medium carrot, peeled
1 medium leek
1½ teaspoons olive oil
¼ cup white port or sherry, optional
A pinch of ground turmeric, optional (adds a wonderful color)
8 ounces trimmed and cleaned chanterelles, oyster or hedgehog mushrooms, or cauliflower fungus, or a mix of these

1 quart vegetable broth (see recipe below, or use purchased vegetable broth)
½ teaspoon salt, or to taste
Optional serving garnishes: Toasted croutons, chopped fresh parsley

Cut carrot into short julienne pieces (⅛ x ⅛ x 1 inch). Trim root end from leek; cut off bulb at the point where it is medium green (use the trimmings in the vegetable stock, below). Split bulb in half from top to bottom, and hold under running water to wash out any dirt. Slice bulb halves across the rings into half-moon strips (⅛ inch or slightly thinner).

In small stockpot, heat oil over medium-low heat for about a minute. Add carrot and leek pieces. Cook, stirring frequently, for 5 minutes. Add port and turmeric; increase heat slightly and cook until liquid cooks away (if you are not using the wine, skip this step, adding turmeric with vegetable broth). Meanwhile, cut mushrooms into ½-inch strips or other bite-sized pieces.

After wine has cooked away, add mushrooms and vegetable broth to stockpot, stirring well. Heat to a very gentle boil and cook for 15 minutes, stirring occasionally. Add salt to taste. Serve garnished with croutons and/or parsley if you like; it's also delicious without any garnish.

Homemade Vegetable Broth

If you have any trimmings from domestic mushrooms (such as the stems from shiitake mushrooms), by all means add them to the stock.

8 cups water
4 medium carrots, cut into 1-inch pieces (unpeeled but washed)
2 stalks celery, cut into 2-inch pieces

The green necks and tops from 1 or 2 medium leeks, cut into 1-inch pieces
1 medium tomato, cut into eighths
2 bay leaves

Combine all ingredients in small stockpot. Heat to boiling. Reduce heat so liquid is barely boiling. Cook for 1½ hours, stirring occasionally. Strain and discard vegetables. You should have 4 cups stock; boil to reduce, or add water as necessary, to equal 4 cups.

Mushroom-Cornmeal Biscuits

15 biscuits

Chanterelles have an earthy, meaty flavor that's wonderful in these biscuits. I prefer to use dried chanterelles rather than fresh; the slightly chewy texture of the reconstituted mushrooms adds a nice texture to the biscuits.

½ ounce dried chanterelles (about ¾ cup) or other dried wild mushrooms

2 cups boiling water

1 green onion, minced

1 teaspoon butter

2 cups all-purpose flour, plus additional for working with dough

¼ cup masa harina* or fine cornmeal

1½ teaspoons baking powder

¾ teaspoon salt

½ teaspoon baking soda

¼ teaspoon white pepper

¼ cup chilled unsalted butter, cut into ½-inch pieces

1 cup buttermilk

In bowl, combine mushrooms and water. Let stand for 20 to 30 minutes, or until mushrooms have softened and expanded but are still somewhat firm. Drain, saving liquid for use in other recipes. Chop mushrooms to medium texture. In skillet, sauté mushrooms and green onion in butter for about 3 minutes. Remove from heat and set aside to cool.

Heat oven to 425°F. Spray baking sheet with nonstick spray; set aside. In large bowl, combine flour, masa harina, baking powder, salt, baking soda and white pepper; mix well. Add butter; cut mixture together with pastry blender or two knives until mixture resembles coarse meal. (You can use a food processor for this step if you prefer. Pulse dry ingredients a few times to blend, then add butter and pulse until the mixture resembles coarse meal. Transfer mixture to a bowl for final mixing.) Add mushroom mixture and buttermilk; stir until dry ingredients are just moistened and starting to clump together.

Turn mixture out onto generously floured worksurface. Knead lightly for a minute or so, until mixture comes together in a loose ball; don't overwork the dough or the biscuits will be tough. Roll dough to ½-inch thickness. Cut with 2½-inch round cookie cutter or drinking glass. Arrange biscuits on prepared baking sheet. Bake for 15 minutes, or until golden brown.

*Masa harina is corn flour, used to make tortillas, tamales and other Mexican specialties. It is sometimes found with the flour in large supermarkets and co-ops. It can also be found at a Mexican specialty grocer.

Polenta Stuffed with Mushrooms

4 servings   Preparation: Over an hour

If you don't have time or inclination to make the polenta, this mushroom sauce is also wonderful served over pasta, rice or biscuits.

- 1 bay leaf
- ¼ teaspoon salt
- 1 cup polenta
- 10 to 12 ounces cleaned, trimmed fresh mushrooms (a mix of two types is best)
- 1 to 2 tablespoons olive oil, divided
- 3 tablespoons sweet (red) vermouth, sherry or apple juice
- 1 teaspoon plus 1 tablespoon unsalted butter, divided

- ½ cup diced carrot
- ¼ cup diced white onion
- 2 cloves garlic, minced
- ¼ teaspoon dried thyme
- 1 medium tomato, peeled, seeded and diced
- 1 cup chicken broth or vegetable broth
- 3 tablespoons grated Pecorino or Romano cheese

In heavy saucepan, combine 3½ cups water, the bay leaf and salt. Heat to boiling over medium-high heat. Sprinkle polenta into boiling water, stirring constantly with long-handled spoon. Continue to stir constantly until water comes to a boil again, then reduce heat to low. Cooking time for the polenta will be 30 minutes; it's helpful to set a kitchen timer so you remember when to take it from the heat, since you will be working on the mushrooms while the polenta cooks. Stir polenta occasionally while it is cooking.

While polenta is cooking, cut mushrooms into ¼- to ½-inch pieces.* Heat heavy-bottomed large skillet over medium heat. Add about 1½ teaspoons of the oil and heat until shimmering. Add enough mushrooms to just cover bottom of skillet. Let them cook without stirring until they have begun to brown, then stir and continue cooking until nicely browned on both sides. Push mushrooms to sides of skillet, add a little more oil, and cook another batch of mushrooms in similar fashion. Repeat until all mushrooms have been browned; you will probably have 3 batches. (If you cook all the mushrooms at once, they release a lot of liquid and will steam rather than brown.) Once all mushrooms have been browned, add vermouth and stir well. Cook, stirring frequently, until vermouth has cooked almost completely away. Transfer mushrooms to a bowl and set aside. Heat oven to 375°F.

Add 1 teaspoon of the butter to same skillet and heat until butter stops foaming. Add carrot and onion to skillet and cook, stirring occasionally, for about 5 minutes. Add garlic and thyme, and cook for a few minutes longer. Stir in tomato and cook for a few minutes longer. Add broth, stirring to loosen any browned bits. Increase heat to high and cook until most of the broth has cooked away and mixture is saucelike, about 10 minutes. (Don't forget to stir the polenta during this time, and also to keep an eye on the clock to be sure you don't cook the polenta too long.) Return mushrooms and any juices to the skillet. Reduce heat and cook for a minute or two, just to warm the mushrooms.

When polenta has cooked for 30 minutes, remove from heat. Remove and discard bay leaf. Stir remaining 1 tablespoon butter into polenta. Spray 8-inch-square baking dish with nonstick spray. Spoon half of the polenta into dish, spreading evenly with wet spoon. Spread half of the mushroom mixture evenly over polenta. Top with remaining polenta, again smoothing with a spoon. Spread remaining mushrooms over polenta. Sprinkle with cheese. Cover dish with foil and bake for about 20 minutes. To serve, cut polenta into squares and dish out with a spatula.

*Thick or solid mushrooms such as puffballs or chicken of the woods should be cut into cubes that are about ⅜ inch thick. Mushrooms with typical caps, such as hedgehogs and honey caps, should be sliced ¼ inch thick; if the slices are longer than 1 inch, cut slices into shorter pieces. Small morels can be cut in half or quartered, while larger morels should be quartered, then cut crosswise into ⅜-inch pieces. Loosely formed mushrooms such as oyster mushrooms and hen of the woods can be cut across the length into ½-inch pieces.

Scallops and Chanterelles

4 servings   Preparation: Under an hour

1¼ pounds chanterelles or substitute (hedgehog mushrooms work well)
1 tablespoon butter
2 medium tomatoes, peeled, seeded and diced
½ cup dry sherry or white wine

½ teaspoon salt, plus additional for sprinkling scallops
¼ teaspoon white pepper
1 to 1¼ pounds fresh scallops
¾ cup heavy cream
Hot cooked rice for serving

Heat oven to 425°F. Lightly grease 1½-quart casserole or baking dish; set aside. Slice larger chanterelles in half vertically, then cut all chanterelles into pieces that are roughly an inch across, slicing stems on an angle to yield wider pieces. Melt butter in heavy-bottomed large skillet over medium-high heat. Add chanterelles and cook, stirring frequently, until juices released by mushrooms have cooked away, about 5 minutes. Transfer chanterelles to a bowl; set aside.

Add tomatoes to skillet and cook, stirring frequently, for about 2 minutes. Add sherry; increase heat to high and cook until most of the liquid cooks away, stirring frequently. Return chanterelles to skillet, and add salt and pepper; stir to mix well with tomatoes. Scrape mixture into prepared casserole. Arrange scallops over mushroom mixture. Sprinkle lightly with salt and set aside.

Add cream to skillet and cook over high heat, stirring constantly, until reduced to about half volume. Pour cream over scallops. Bake until scallops are just cooked through and cream is beginning to brown in spots, about 10 minutes; sea scallops will take slightly longer than bay scallops. Serve immediately with hot cooked rice.

Rabbit with Two Mushrooms

2 servings   Preparation: Under an hour

This recipe uses two types of mushrooms—dried boletes and fresh oyster mushrooms. The bolete family has no gills; instead, the cap has a spongy underside with thousands of tiny pores. Don't feel odd about straining out and discarding the chopped-up boletes after cooking them; the flavor has been captured in the soaking water and the sauce base.

½ ounce dried bolete slices* (typically
   ½ to ⅔ cup, loosely packed)
1 cup water
½ pound boneless meat from a
   young rabbit
3 tablespoons all-purpose flour
1 teaspoon salt
½ teaspoon white pepper

1 tablespoon butter
1 tablespoon olive oil
3 ounces fresh oyster mushrooms, cut into
   ½-inch strips (about 2 cups of strips)
3 tablespoons chopped shallots
¼ cup sweet (red) vermouth
1 cup chicken broth
Hot cooked wavy noodles

Combine boletes and water in small saucepan. Heat over medium heat until bubbles begin to come up around the edges. Reduce heat and simmer for about 2 minutes. Remove from heat and set aside for about 20 minutes while you prepare rabbit.

Slice rabbit meat across the grain into ⅛-inch-thick slices; they should be no bigger than 1 x 2 inches, and probably will be much smaller. Lay strips in single layer on worksurface. In small shaker bottle, combine flour, salt and pepper; shake to mix well. Sprinkle over rabbit strips and pound in lightly with meat mallet. Turn strips; flour and pound second side.

In large skillet, melt butter in oil over medium heat. Add rabbit pieces in single layer, and turn as soon as the first side has browned slightly (you will probably just get done arranging the strips in the skillet when it will be time to turn the pieces that went in first). Cook on second side until lightly browned. Use tongs to transfer rabbit to a dish; set aside and keep warm.

Add oyster mushrooms to skillet. Cook, stirring occasionally, for about 10 minutes. While oyster mushrooms are cooking, remove boletes from soaking water and set aside on paper towels to drain. Strain soaking water through a paper coffee filter into small bowl and reserve.

When oyster mushrooms have cooked for about 10 minutes, use slotted spoon to transfer them to dish with rabbit; set aside. Add chopped boletes and shallots to skillet and cook, stirring constantly, for about 2 minutes. Pour in vermouth and stir to loosen any browned bits. Increase heat to medium-high and cook for about a minute, stirring constantly. Strain through wire-mesh strainer into bowl with mushroom soaking liquid; discard solids in strainer. Rinse skillet briefly and return to stove.

Pour mushroom soaking liquid into skillet and cook over medium-high heat until reduced to a thin layer. Add chicken broth and cook, stirring occasionally, until reduced to about 3 tablespoons; this will take about 5 minutes. When liquid has reduced and is becoming syrupy, return rabbit and oyster mushrooms to skillet and cook for about a minute over medium-low heat. Serve with wavy noodles.

Variation: Chicken with Two Mushrooms
Substitute ½ pound boneless, skinless chicken meat for the rabbit. Proceed as directed.

*If you don't have wild-harvested boletes, use purchased dried porcini.

Sweet Autumn Pasta Toss

3 or 4 servings   Preparation: Under an hour

Sweet vermouth lends a wonderful taste to this dish of wild mushrooms and garden squash; you might almost think there are apples in the dish. Orecchiette pasta—"little ears"—are cup-shaped pasta that mimic the shape of the oyster mushroom caps, and also work well to capture the full-bodied sauce. Any small pasta shape can be substituted.

6 ounces orecchiette or other small pasta shapes like shells
Half of an acorn squash or substitute*
2 tablespoons unsalted butter
4 ounces oyster mushrooms or other firm, meaty wild mushrooms

3 tablespoons sweet (red) vermouth
1 tablespoon liquid chicken bouillon, such as Bovril
2 teaspoons balsamic vinegar
3 tablespoons chopped fresh parsley
Salt and pepper

Heat large pot of salted water to boiling over high heat. Add pasta; cook according to package directions. While pasta cooks, scoop out and discard seed cavity from squash. Peel squash, and cut into ¼-inch dice. In large skillet, melt butter over medium heat. Add squash; sauté for 5 minutes. Meanwhile, cut mushrooms into strips that are about ½ inch wide and 2 inches long; you should have about 1½ cups. When squash has cooked for about 5 minutes, add mushrooms; cook, stirring constantly, for about a minute. Add vermouth, chicken bouillon and vinegar. Cook until most but not all of the liquid has cooked away, about 3 minutes; the mixture should be somewhat syrupy.

If pasta is tender before squash mixture is cooked, reserve a few tablespoons of the pasta cooking water and drain pasta; set aside. If squash is cooked before pasta is tender, remove from heat, cover and set aside. When pasta is drained and squash mixture is cooked down, add a tablespoon or 2 of the pasta-cooking water to squash to moisten. Toss drained pasta with squash mixture and parsley; add a bit of salt and pepper if needed.

*Substitute 6 ounces butternut squash or pumpkin, peeled and cut into ¼-inch dice before measuring (about 1½ cups of diced squash).

Wild Mushroom Soup Gratinée

4 servings   Preparation: About an hour

If you enjoy French onion soup, try this mushroom variation. Serve with a green salad and some hearty bread for a perfect autumn supper. Note: You will need broiler-safe serving bowls for the final cooking stage.

1 large yellow onion
1 tablespoon butter
2 teaspoons olive oil
3 cloves garlic, coarsely chopped
1 teaspoon sugar
¾ to 1 pound hen of the woods, oyster
   mushrooms or chanterelles

1½ quarts mushroom broth, vegetable
   broth or chicken broth
Salt and pepper
4 slices Italian or French-style bread*
½ pound Gruyère or Swiss cheese,
   shredded

Cut peeled onion into quarters from top to bottom, then slice each quarter crosswise about ⅛ inch thick. In medium soup pot, melt butter in oil over medium heat. Add onion and garlic, stirring to coat with butter. Cook for about 5 minutes, stirring occasionally. Sprinkle sugar over onions; reduce heat to low and cook, stirring occasionally, until onion has turned rich golden brown and is very tender, about 30 minutes.

While onion is cooking, cut mushrooms into bite-sized pieces. Hen of the woods or oyster mushrooms should be cut into ½-inch strips across the caps and tender stem portion. Small to medium chanterelles can be halved or quartered lengthwise; larger specimens should be halved and cut across the length. Set cut-up mushrooms aside.

When onion is rich golden brown, add mushrooms to soup pot and cook for about 5 minutes, stirring occasionally. Heat broiler. Add broth to soup pot and heat to a gentle boil. Cook for about 10 minutes, then taste for seasoning and add salt and pepper if necessary. While soup is cooking, lightly toast bread slices under the broiler.

For final cooking, divide soup evenly between 4 broiler-safe individual serving bowls. Float a piece of toasted bread on top of each, then divide cheese evenly over the top of the bread. Broil until cheese melts and bubbles. Serve immediately, warning diners to be careful because the bowls will be very hot!

*Hearty country-style bread works best. Ideally, the slices should be about ¾ inch thick, and just a little smaller in size than the top of your soup bowls.

Salisbury Steaks with Mushroom Gravy

4 servings   Preparation: Under an hour

Many recipes for Salisbury steaks use canned mushroom soup. This one uses dried wild mushrooms instead, to produce a richer and more flavorful gravy.

½ ounce dried wild mushrooms,
   any variety
3 cups beef broth
1 egg
¼ cup milk
⅓ cup breadcrumbs (whole-grain
   breadcrumbs are very good)
2 teaspoons Dijon mustard
½ teaspoon salt

¼ teaspoon pepper
1 pound lean ground beef or venison
¼ cup finely chopped onion
1 teaspoon vegetable oil
1 small tomato, peeled, seeded and
   chopped (or ¼ cup drained canned
   diced tomato)
1 tablespoon cornstarch blended with
   2 tablespoons water

In saucepan, combine mushrooms and beef broth. Heat to boiling. Reduce heat and cook at a gentle boil for 5 minutes. Remove from heat and set aside to cool.

In mixing bowl, beat together egg and milk. Add breadcrumbs, mustard, salt and pepper, stirring to mix. Let stand for about 10 minutes. Add ground beef and onion to soaked breadcrumb mixture; mix thoroughly but gently with your hands. Shape into 4 oval patties.

In large skillet, brown patties on both sides in oil over medium heat. While patties are browning, remove mushrooms from broth, squeezing to remove excess liquid. Strain broth through paper coffee filter to remove any grit. Trim any woody parts from mushrooms if necessary, then chop mushrooms medium-fine and return to strained broth. Add tomato to broth and stir well.

When patties are nicely browned, add broth mixture and heat just to boiling. Reduce heat and cover; simmer for 15 minutes, turning patties every 5 minutes. Transfer patties to serving dish; cover to keep warm. Add cornstarch mixture to skillet and cook, stirring constantly, until sauce thickens. Serve sauce with patties.

MUSHROOMS

Mushroom "Baklava"

4 servings as a first course or light main dish; 8 appetizer servings   Preparation: Over an hour

Baklava is a traditional Greek dessert consisting of multiple layers of ground nuts and flaky phyllo (a tissue-thin pastry), all layered with lots of butter and honey. This mushroom version makes a spectacular appetizer, first course or light main course. The rich, earthy flavor of hen of the woods mushrooms works particularly well in this recipe, but you can use any mushrooms you have.

1½ cups chopped onion

2 tablespoons butter, divided

3 cups coarsely chopped or sliced hen-of-the-woods, oyster mushrooms or substitute (about 9 ounces)

½ teaspoon salt

¼ teaspoon dried thyme

¼ teaspoon freshly ground pepper

Olive oil cooking spray or butter-flavored cooking spray

About half of a 1-pound package phyllo pastry,* thawed according to package directions if frozen

1 cup finely shredded Monterey Jack cheese

Heat oven to 350°F. In large skillet, cook onion in 1 tablespoon of the butter over medium-low heat for about 15 minutes, stirring occasionally; onions should be slightly caramelized. Add mushrooms; increase heat to medium and cook for about 5 minutes longer. Stir in salt, thyme and pepper. Remove from heat and set aside to cool slightly.

Spray 11 x 7-inch baking dish liberally with cooking spray. Unfold phyllo on worksurface, and trim into a rectangular stack that is just slightly larger than baking dish; depending on the brand of phyllo you have, you may get 2 rectangular stacks from the unfolded phyllo. Cover phyllo with waxed paper, then place lightly dampened dishtowel on top to prevent phyllo from drying out. As you remove each set of phyllo sheets from the stack, re-cover remaining phyllo.

Place 2 sheets of phyllo in prepared baking dish, patting edges up sides of dish slightly. Spray top phyllo sheet with cooking spray (use enough cooking spray to just lightly film the phyllo, about a 1-second burst; you don't need to saturate the phyllo, just coat it lightly but thoroughly). Place 2 more phyllo sheets into dish and spray the top sheet; place 2 more phyllo sheets into dish and spray the top sheet (so you have a total of 6 phyllo sheets in the dish, and have sprayed every other sheet with cooking spray). Spread one-quarter of the mushrooms over the phyllo, spreading all the way to the edges; the mushrooms will not cover the phyllo in a solid layer, so be sure to spread them evenly. Sprinkle with one-third of the cheese.

Repeat this layering twice (six sheets of phyllo with spray on every other sheet, then a layer of mushrooms and a sprinkle of cheese); after the third layer, you should still have some mushrooms left but should have used up all the cheese. Melt remaining 1 tablespoon of butter. Place a single sheet of phyllo on top of the last layer, and brush lightly with melted butter. Repeat 5 more times, so the top layer will be 6 phyllo sheets that have all been brushed with butter. Spoon remaining mushrooms around the edges only, forming a border; this helps prevent the top layer of phyllo from curling up during baking.

Cover dish with foil. Bake for 30 minutes, then remove foil and bake for 15 minutes longer. To serve, cut into squares or strips using a very sharp knife; be sure to cut all the way through the bottom layer of phyllo. Remove pieces from dish with spatula. Serve immediately, or allow to cool slightly and serve warm.

*Look for phyllo in the freezer case of well-stocked supermarkets, or at specialty grocers that carry Mediterranean foods (where you may be able to find fresh, unfrozen phyllo).

Potato-Mushroom-Ham Gratin with Blue Cheese

4 servings   Preparation: Over an hour

2 cups low-salt chicken broth or
    mushroom broth
3 or 4 fresh sage leaves, or ½ teaspoon
    crumbled dried sage
⅛ teaspoon white pepper
1 tablespoon butter
¾ pound hedgehog or oyster mushrooms
    or chanterelles, sliced ¼ inch thick
    (3½ to 4 cups after slicing)

½ pound sliced Black Forest or other
    hearty ham, cut into ¼-inch-wide
    strips
1½ pounds russet potatoes, peeled and
    thinly sliced (about 2 medium)
4 ounces crumbled blue cheese

Heat oven to 425°F. Lightly grease 8-inch-square baking dish or comparably sized casserole; set aside. Combine chicken broth and sage in small saucepan. Heat to boiling over high heat, and cook until reduced to about 1 cup (to make this easier, pour 1 cup water into the saucepan first, and note the level; pour out the water, add the broth and reduce to the noted level). When broth has reduced, remove from heat. Pull out sage leaves and discard (if you used crumbled dried sage, there's no need to remove it). Stir in pepper; set aside.

In large skillet, melt butter over medium heat. Add mushrooms; sauté until juices released by mushrooms cook away, about 10 minutes. Stir in ham strips; remove from heat. Arrange half of the potatoes in prepared dish. Top with mushroom mixture, spreading evenly. Scatter half of the blue cheese over mushrooms. Top with remaining potatoes. Pour broth over potatoes; sprinkle remaining blue cheese on top. Cover dish with foil. Bake for 30 minutes. Uncover and bake until potatoes are tender and top is nicely browned, about 30 minutes longer. Let stand for 10 minutes before serving.

Vegetable Terrine with Mushrooms

10 slices

Colorful vegetables are layered with two kinds of mushrooms in a light batter; when sliced, this terrine is a visual stunner, and it tastes as good as it looks. Although the preparation is a bit involved, it's worth every minute. Serve 1 slice per person as an appetizer, or 2 slices per person as a side or light main dish.

Butter for greasing loaf pan
5 ounces tender greens such as dandelion, nettle or sheep sorrel, or a mix*
6 ounces peeled baby carrots (about 1¼ cups)
4 to 5 ounces fresh cauliflower fungus (a clump that is a bit bigger than a softball) or morels†
4 ounces fresh chanterelles, hedgehog mushrooms or other firm, meaty mushrooms
2 tablespoons butter or margarine, divided
Salt and pepper

Batter:
3 eggs, or ¾ cup liquid egg substitute
1 cup whole or 2% milk
½ cup all-purpose flour
1 teaspoon salt
¼ teaspoon ground nutmeg
A small handful of fresh parsley leaves

Heat oven to 400°F. Generously grease standard-sized loaf pan with butter; set aside. Coarsely chop greens; you should have about 4 cups tightly packed. Set aside.

Cook carrots in large saucepan of boiling water just until tender, 6 to 8 minutes. Drain water into another saucepan. Refresh carrots under cold running water; drain well and set aside. Return water to boiling. Add greens and cook until tender, 3 to 5 minutes.* Drain greens in wire-mesh strainer and hold under cold running water until completely cool; this sets the color as well as stops the cooking. Fill saucepan with fresh water and place over medium-high heat; you will need some boiling water just before the terrine goes into the oven.

Break well-washed cauliflower fungus into bite-sized pieces, or cut into ¾-inch-wide strips (if using morels, slice into halves or quarters, depending on size). Slice chanterelles or other mushrooms ¼ inch thick. In large skillet, melt half of the butter over medium heat. Add cauliflower fungus and cook, stirring frequently, until juices released by fungus have cooked away, about 5 minutes. Transfer cauliflower fungus to a dish; salt and pepper lightly and set aside. Melt remaining butter in same skillet. Add chanterelles and cook, stirring frequently, until juices released by mushrooms have cooked away and mushrooms have browned slightly, 5 to 8 minutes. Salt and pepper lightly and remove from heat.

Prepare batter: In blender container or food processor workbowl, combine eggs, milk, flour, salt and nutmeg. Process until smooth. Add parsley. Pulse on-and-off a few times, just until parsley is chopped finely; don't liquefy the parsley.

MUSHROOMS

Pour about ¼ cup of the batter into prepared loaf pan. Arrange cauliflower fungus evenly over batter. Arrange carrots evenly over cauliflower fungus, laying them lengthwise so they are parallel to the long sides of the pan. Pour another ¼ cup of the batter over carrots.

Squeeze greens lightly, then arrange evenly over carrot layer. Top with chanterelle slices. Press gently but firmly to even the layers. Pour remaining batter evenly over all. Shake pan gently to distribute batter evenly, then knock pan on counter a few times to dislodge any air bubbles.

Place pan in larger baking dish. Set dish on oven shelf. Add boiling water to come halfway up the loaf pan. Bake until loaf is firm and beginning to brown around edges, about 40 minutes; a cake tester inserted into the center of the loaf should come out cleanly. Carefully remove loaf pan from water bath. Allow to cool for about 45 minutes, or longer if you wish to serve the terrine at room temperature. Remove from loaf pan and slice 1 inch thick. This can be served warm or room temperature.

*If you have greens such as plantain, curly dock or other greens that require longer simmering to become tender, simply cook the greens until they are tender, drain, and continue as directed. For a non-wild substitution that works perfectly well, use fresh spinach.

†Cauliflower fungus and morel mushrooms both add wonderful fragrance to this dish, and the cauliflower fungus, in particular, has a firm texture that is just perfect. However, these mushrooms can be hard to find, and morels are generally not available in the fall when the other wild mushrooms are found. You can use reconstituted dried cauliflower fungus or morels, although the texture is not quite as good; frozen would be a better choice. If you don't have either of these, substitute wild or cultivated oyster mushrooms (or domestic cremini or baby portabella mushrooms), sliced ¼ inch thick.

Warm Mushrooms with Greens and Toasts

2 servings; easily doubled   Preparation: Under 30 minutes

One autumn afternoon, I returned home with a small haul of mushrooms and a huge appetite. There wasn't much in the fridge or pantry, and I ended up throwing together a sort of wilted lettuce salad featuring the fresh mushrooms. After that first time, I did a little fine-tuning to get the dish just the way I like it. Try it; I hope you'll enjoy it as much as I do.

6 to 8 ounces chanterelle or oyster
  mushrooms, or other firm, meaty
  wild mushrooms
2 tablespoons butter, divided
2 thick slices country-style Italian bread,*
  cut into halves (4 pieces total)
¼ cup diced white onion
6 cups torn tender salad greens
3 tablespoons chicken broth or water

2 tablespoons balsamic vinegar or
  red wine vinegar
2 tablespoons extra-virgin olive oil
1 teaspoon honey
½ teaspoon Dijon mustard
Salt and freshly ground pepper
A few shavings of Parmesan cheese for
  garnish, optional

Slice mushrooms just under ¼ inch thick, or into whatever type of bite-sized pieces you prefer; set aside. In large skillet, melt 2 teaspoons of the butter over medium heat. Add bread slices, turning to coat both sides. Cook until golden on both sides, turning once or twice. Arrange 2 slices in each of 2 large soup plates; set aside.

Melt remaining butter in same skillet over medium heat. Add onion; sauté for about 5 minutes. Add mushrooms; sauté until any juices released by mushrooms have cooked away and mushrooms begin to color, 5 to 10 minutes. Meanwhile, place salad greens in large mixing bowl; set aside. When mushrooms are nicely browned, add chicken broth, vinegar, oil, honey, mustard, and salt and pepper to taste. Cook for about 1 minute longer, stirring to loosen any browned bits; the liquid will reduce somewhat, but the mixture should not become dry. Pour mushroom mixture over salad greens in mixing bowl, and toss gently but thoroughly. Divide mushrooms and greens evenly between the 2 soup plates, with the toasts standing upright against the rims of the plates. Top each serving with a few shavings of Parmesan cheese.

*Use good-quality Italian- or French-style bread that has a chewy crust, porous interior and sturdy crumb; softer bread won't be very good in this dish. Day-old bread actually works better than a very fresh loaf. The bread I use slices into ovals that are about 6 inches wide and 3 or 4 inches tall; I cut these in half so each toast is about 3 x 4 inches. If your bread is smaller—or larger—adjust your cutting accordingly. I like the slices to be ¾ to 1 inch thick.

Mushroom Consommé

Egg white is used to clarify a rich mushroom broth, leaving a lovely, clear consommé. Fresh mushrooms add additional appeal to this elegant soup, which makes a great first course.

2 quarts unsalted chicken broth or vegetable broth

2 ounces dried wild mushrooms, any variety (a mix works well)

1/4 cup minced shallots or onions

1/4 teaspoon freshly ground black pepper

3 tablespoons dry sherry

2 tablespoons soy sauce

3 egg whites

1/2 pound fresh wild mushrooms, any variety

A few drops of lemon juice

In small stockpot or large saucepan, heat broth until simmering; remove from heat. Add dried mushrooms; soak until soft, 20 to 45 minutes depending on variety and size of dried mushrooms. When mushrooms are soft, remove from stock and mince; return minced mushrooms to stock. If the fresh mushrooms have stems, mince them and add to the broth. Add shallots and black pepper to broth.

Heat to simmering over medium-high heat; reduce heat and simmer for 40 minutes, skimming occasionally and keeping level of liquid constant by adding water as necessary. Remove from heat; stir in sherry and soy sauce.

Beat egg whites in large bowl and gradually add broth to whites, whisking constantly. Return mixture to pot. Place over medium heat and whisk gently until mixture is simmering. Stop stirring; let simmer for 15 minutes (do not boil).

Line strainer with double layer of cheesecloth, and set over large bowl. If necessary to get at consommé, carefully cut a hole in the egg white raft and remove that segment. Ladle consomme into strainer carefully (do not pour directly from stockpot or broth will be cloudy). Taste broth; adjust seasoning if necessary. Discard egg whites.

Slice fresh mushrooms thinly. Heat a small saucepan of water to boiling and add lemon juice. Add sliced mushrooms and cook for 2 minutes, or until tender. Drain well. Transfer to clean saucepan; add consommé. Heat to simmering. Ladle into bowls and serve immediately.

Solid, Firm to Tough Mushrooms

These substantial mushrooms soak up flavors during the slow cooking needed to tenderize them.

This group includes one of the most common and easy to identify mushrooms, chicken of the woods. The mushrooms in this group require longer cooking times than the other, more tender mushrooms covered previously. They work well for braises, stews and other moist, slow-cook methods.

BEEFSTEAK FUNGUS *(Fistulina hepatica)*

This fungus, which resembles raw beef liver (and even oozes a reddish liquid when squeezed), typically grows as a *bracket*—a shelf or projection—on dead oak trees. It is also found on chestnut trees, and occasionally on living oak trees as well. Look for it from late summer through fall; with its red color and somewhat sticky surface, it's hard to miss. Some cooks parboil it in several changes of water before cooking in other dishes to remove sourness; this also removes much of the red color. Soaking in milk is said to accomplish the same thing, but I've never tried this. Beefsteak fungus can be grilled like steak, and I've read that in England, it is sliced raw and added to salads. It does not dry well.

CHICKEN OF THE WOODS *(Laetiporus sulphureus)*

Also called sulphur shelf, this easy-to-identify fungus looks like a shelf or series of shelves, and is found on deciduous trees, particularly oak. It is harvested from midsummer through fall, and often reappears on the same tree year after year. This mushroom gets its name not only from its yellow color but from its firm, almost chicken-like texture. The soft edge of the cap is the best part; older chickens and the center of large specimens are too tough to eat. It can be grilled like steak, but I think it's best when cooked in a braise or stew. Chicken of the woods can cause intestinal upset in some people. It does not dry well.

Chicken of the woods

ORANGE MILKY CAP *(Lactarius deliciosus)*

This mushroom is a member of the *Lactarius* family, all of which exude milky, latex-like sap when cut. The orange milky cap, which is also called saffron milky cap, is bright orange with orange sap; the flesh and gills quickly show a green stain when bruised. Edibility varies from specimen to specimen, with some being tasty and others somewhat sour (this may depend on specific habitat where the mushroom is found; if you find good-tasting orange milky caps in one area, others from the same area will probably also be good). Look for the orange milky cap in coniferous woodlands and sandy areas from summer through late fall. Milky caps may be infested with insects; slice lengthwise to check the interior of the stem. The orange milky cap dries well, and is often pickled.

OTHER RECIPES IN THIS BOOK FEATURING SOLID, FIRM TO TOUGH WILD MUSHROOMS
- Pork, Cabbage and Mushroom Hot Pot (page 369)
- As substitute in Chanterelles and Dumplings (page 371)
- Polenta Stuffed with Mushrooms (page 374)
- Mushroom Consommé (page 385)

Pork and Mushroom Pie

4 servings Preparation: Over an hour

Similar to a traditional "pub pie," this hearty dish can be made with any mushrooms you have. Even firm mushrooms like chicken of the woods will be tenderized by the lengthy oven-braising. Serve with mashed potatoes, to sop up the abundant and delicious gravy.

1 can (10.5 ounces) beef consommé
2 tablespoons tomato paste
¼ cup all-purpose flour
½ teaspoon dry mustard powder
¼ teaspoon dried rosemary
1¼ pounds boneless pork loin, cut into
    1-inch cubes

10 to 12 ounces chicken of the woods,
    chanterelles or other wild mushrooms,*
    cut into large bite-sized chunks
¾ cup frozen pearl onions, thawed
1 sheet puff pastry (half of a 17-ounce
    package), thawed if frozen
1 egg beaten with 1 tablespoon water

Heat oven to 350°F. Lightly grease 1½-quart casserole dish; set aside. In large mixing bowl, combine consommé, tomato paste, flour, mustard and rosemary; whisk to blend. Add pork, mushrooms and onions, stirring to combine. Transfer mixture to prepared casserole, mounding slightly if necessary (casserole will be quite full, but the mixture will cook down). Cover casserole; bake for 2 hours, stirring several times (place a sheet of foil on a lower oven rack underneath the casserole, to catch any drips).

After 2 hours of baking, remove casserole from oven and uncover. Cut puff pastry sheet slightly larger than top of casserole dish. Place on top of casserole, pushing edges down into dish slightly; be careful not to burn yourself! Brush top of pastry lightly with beaten egg. Return to oven and bake for 30 minutes longer; pastry will be deep golden brown and very puffy. Serve immediately. (If there are going to be leftovers, it's best to eat the pastry in the first serving, as it will get quite soggy afterwards. The pork-and-mushroom mixture makes a wonderful leftover, however; try serving it over mashed potatoes.)

*If using beefsteak fungus, parboil it in several changes of water before adding to the pork mixture.

Wild and Brown Rice Casserole with Mushrooms

4 servings   Preparation: Over an hour

I love recipes that use more than one wild ingredient. This one uses three: wild rice, mushrooms and hazelnuts. Of course, you can substitute domestic ingredients for any of these, depending on the season and your larder.

½ cup diced onion
1 tablespoon olive oil
½ cup ready-to-cook wild rice
¼ cup uncooked brown rice
1½ cups cut-up chicken of the woods or
    other fresh wild mushrooms* (cut into
    ¼-inch dice or slices before measuring)

¼ cup dry sherry, optional
1½ cups chicken broth
¼ cup coarsely chopped hazelnuts or other
    nuts, or slivered almonds
½ teaspoon salt
A few grindings of black pepper

Heat oven to 350°F. In oven-safe pot, sauté onion in oil over medium heat for about 5 minutes, stirring occasionally. Add wild and brown rice and cook, stirring constantly, for about 3 minutes. Add mushrooms and cook, stirring occasionally, for about 5 minutes. Add sherry carefully (to avoid steam) and cook, stirring frequently, until sherry has been absorbed by rice. (If you are not using sherry, skip this step.) Stir in chicken broth, nuts, salt and pepper and heat to boiling. Cover and place in oven. Bake for 1 hour.

Note: Some types of wild rice—in particular, paddy-grown commercial rice—require a longer cooking time than others. If your rice is not yet tender after 1 hour, add a little more chicken broth or water and continue baking until the rice is tender, checking every 15 minutes.

Variation: Wild and Brown Rice Casserole with Dried Mushrooms

Substitute 1 cup dried wild mushrooms for the fresh mushrooms. Soak in 1½ cups boiling water for 15 to 20 minutes, or until softened. Drain mushrooms, reserving liquid, and chop as necessary. Strain soaking liquid through paper coffee filter into 2-cup measure; add chicken broth or water to equal 1½ cups and use in place of the broth in the recipe. Proceed as directed.

*If using beefsteak fungus, parboil it in several changes of water before adding to the pork mixture.

ROOTS & STARCHES

Roots from flowers and vines, and starches such as wild rice, were important foods for Native Americans. Along with nuts, these foods supplied much-needed carbohydrates to a diet that was often heavy on meats, fruits and greens. Serious foragers still rely on roots and wild grains for bulk in the diet; however, for the casual to moderate forager, these foods play a much less important role than other wild foods.

Harvesting roots obviously requires digging, and in many places this is not allowed; even where it is allowed, digging can cause erosion if the soil is not replaced properly. To me, most roots are less accessible and, frankly, less interesting than wild fruits, mushrooms or greens. I dig a few roots for use, but in general, I prefer to spend my foraging time looking for other plants rather than digging up the countryside or marsh.

Seeds of wild plants are even harder to come by in quantities that make them interesting to the casual forager. One that can be harvested in quantity is wild rice; its harvest is regulated by state wildlife agencies, and may not be permitted in some locations such as Native American reservations.

A few roots have already been discussed; for information on these, please see the listings for ramps (page 22), dandelions (page 44), cattails (page 80), day lilies (page 301) and spring beauty (page 342).

Burdock (common burdock, *Arctium minus*; great burdock, *A. lappa*)

Used extensively in Japanese cooking, burdock root has an earthy, sharp taste that works well in stews. It's a job to dig it up, so plan on some hard work before planning your meal.

HABITAT, RANGE

Burdock grows throughout out region and, indeed, throughout most of the United States, in agricultural areas, on waste ground, along roadsides and in vacant lots. It seems to thrive in a variety of soil types and conditions.

PARTS USED

Roots, raw or cooked; flower stalk, cooked

SEASONS

Roots, summer through fall; flower stalk, spring

IDENTIFICATION TIPS, DANGEROUS LOOKALIKES

First-year burdock

Burdock is a biennial plant. In its first year, it grows as a cluster of rhubarb-like leaves in a basal rosette. In its second year, the plant produces a single flower stalk topped with numerous purple-topped burry flowers that dry into the "prickle burrs" often found in a wandering dog's coat (or a kid's hair). Great burdock can get over head height, while common burdock is shorter, generally under 4 feet tall.

The taproot of first-year plants is what we're after; second-year taproots are apparently too tough to eat, although I've never tried it. First-year burdock is easy to identify; on first glance, it looks like rhubarb that has escaped someone's garden. The leaves are up to 2 feet long and as much as a foot wide, and have very wavy, curly edges—like rhubarb leaves, but with shorter stalks. The underside of the leaves, however, are covered with downy white hair. There are no dangerous lookalikes that sport this hairy underside. Young burdock leaves resemble those of young dock; however, dock leaves are hairless (and edible).

The flower stalk of the second-year plant is delicious before the plant has flowered. Find the fattest flower stalks you can (with no flowers), and cut them off at the base.

Second-year burdock

HARVESTING TIPS

Look for last year's withered, brown flower stalks to locate patches of burdock in the spring, before the second-year plants have flowered; then look for the first-year plants which will consist solely of the basal rosette. Once you've found first-year burdock, the work begins. It's easiest to harvest when the soil is soft, a day after a rain. Even then, you'll need a lot of elbow grease to dig up the long root, which is brittle and will snap off if you try to pull it before digging enough. Push the tip of a narrow-bladed shovel in a circular pattern around the base of the plant to loosen the soil, then pry the root out and shake off the dirt. Burdock roots range from the thickness of a pencil to an inch or more across in a large specimen.

Burdock often grows along the edges of cultivated fields, and the soil seems somewhat softer in such places, so it pays to ask a farmer if you can dig the field edges for burdock. Burdock reproduces by seed, incidentally; those prickle-burrs attach to passing deer and other animals, spreading the plant far and wide. You don't have to worry about over-harvesting burdock; it has a very good method of propagating itself and will survive even the most determined forager's harvesting.

MORE ABOUT BURDOCK: Here's a plant that most farmers will gladly let you dig; it's considered an agricultural pest, and it seems to thrive in and around tilled fields. The root, however, is a delicious vegetable —rather like a long, cream-colored carrot, with a nutty, sweet flavor that reminds me a bit of parsnips. It is used extensively in Asian cuisine; Japanese cooks call the root "gobo" and use it in dishes ranging from tempura to soup to sushi. In the Zen macrobiotic diet, gobo root is the most "yang" of all vegetables.

Scrub the roots very well to remove side hairs and clinging dirt, as well as the outer layer of skin; you can use any abrasive pad that doesn't have soap embedded in it. If the roots are large, you can peel them, but it's not necessary with smaller roots. I always keep a pan of acidulated water (with a little lemon juice or vinegar added) and put the roots into this immediately after scrubbing, to prevent them from turning brown. If the roots are very large, split them vertically and check for a tough core in the center; it can be pulled out easily.

Burdock can be thinly sliced and added raw to salads; it's much more common, however, to boil the roots before serving them alone or combining them with other ingredients. Smaller roots can be boiled whole (cut into convenient lengths), for use in salads, sushi or other dishes; larger roots are usually sliced before boiling. I slice them ⅛ inch thick, generally cutting on an angle to get a wider slice if the roots are narrow.

The flower stalk of the second-year plant makes a delicious vegetable. Peel the thick stalk, then par-boil it for 5 minutes in boiling water; this reduces bitterness. After that, use as you would celery.

QUICK IDEAS FOR USING BURDOCK

- Add burdock roots, cut into convenient lengths if small or thinly sliced if larger, to stews and soups. Cooking time should be about the same as carrots, parsnips or other firm root vegetables.
- Several sources I've checked talk about boiling sliced burdock root until tender, then mashing it and making patties. I've never tried this, but perhaps you would like to so I pass it along.
- If you've got any Italian recipes for cardoon (a vegetable that is related to the globe artichoke), substitute peeled, par-boiled burdock flower stalks for the cardoon. Both have a celery-like texture and can be used in the same ways: cooked in casseroles and soups, or blanched and added to salads.

OTHER RECIPES IN THIS BOOK FEATURING BURDOCK

- Vegetable Fried Rice (page 401)

Burdock with Indian-Style Spices

4 side-dish servings   Preparation: Under 30 minutes

8 ounces burdock roots	½ teaspoon cumin seeds
1 tablespoon vegetable oil	¼ teaspoon hot red pepper flakes
2 teaspoons sesame seeds	2 teaspoons soy sauce
1 teaspoon mustard seeds	¼ cup water or chicken broth

Peel burdock root and shred coarsely (I use a food processor, laying the roots sideways in the feed tube; I press hard so the shreds are a bit thicker than usual). Moving quickly to avoid discoloration of shredded roots, add oil to medium skillet and place over medium heat until warm. Add sesame seeds, mustard seeds, cumin seeds and pepper flakes; shake skillet to spread spices evenly. Cook, stirring frequently, until mustard seeds begin to pop, about 1 minute. Add burdock shreds and stir well. Cook for about 5 minutes, stirring frequently. Add soy sauce and water to skillet. Cover and continue cooking for about 15 minutes, stirring occasionally. Remove cover and cook until any remaining liquid is absorbed. This is good served hot, but also is tasty at room temperature.

Burdock and Carrot Stir-Fry

4 servings   Preparation: Under an hour

Burdock makes a wonderful stir-fry ingredient. It has a clean, mellow, earthy taste and stays pleasingly crunchy. This recipe is based on a traditional Japanese dish, kimpira gobo.

1 tablespoon white vinegar
¾ pound burdock roots
4 large carrots
1 teaspoon vegetable oil
¼ to ½ teaspoon hot red pepper flakes

⅓ cup mirin (Japanese sweetened rice wine used for cooking)*
2 tablespoons soy sauce, preferably a lighter type such as Kikkoman
½ teaspoon dark (Asian) sesame oil
Hot cooked rice

Add vinegar to bowl of cold water. Scrub burdock roots well with non-soapy scouring pad under running water; as each root is cleaned, place it into the pan of vinegar water (this prevents discoloration). Working with 1 root at a time, slice burdock thinly, cutting at a diagonal so slices are wider. Place slices into the vinegar water as you go, and continue until all roots have been sliced. Set burdock aside. Peel carrots and cut into julienne strips (⅛ x ⅛ x 3 inches). Set aside.

Heat oil in a wok or large skillet over medium-high heat. Add hot pepper and stir-fry for about a minute. Quickly drain burdock and add it to wok. Stir-fry for about 5 minutes. Add mirin to wok. Cook until mirin has cooked away, about 5 minutes, stirring occasionally. Add carrots and stir-fry for about 3 minutes. Add soy sauce and stir-fry for about 3 minutes longer, or until carrots are tender-crisp. Stir in sesame oil and remove from heat. Serve with hot cooked rice.

*If you can't find mirin, substitute cream sherry with 1 tablespoon sugar added.

Burdock Stalk Soup

3 or 4 servings   Preparation: Under an hour

1 pound burdock flower stalks (8 to 15, depending on size)
2 ribs celery, sliced ⅛ inch thick
2 carrots, sliced ⅛ inch thick
1 onion, diced

2 tablespoons butter
6 cups chicken broth
½ teaspoon dried thyme
Salt and pepper

Peel flower stalks and cut into 2-inch lengths. Heat large pot of water to boiling. Add stalks. Cook for 10 minutes. Drain and rinse in cold running water; set aside to drain completely.

In small soup pot, sauté celery, carrots and onion in butter over medium heat until tender, stirring occasionally. Add drained burdock flower stalks, broth and thyme. Heat to boiling, then reduce heat and simmer for 30 to 40 minutes. Remove from heat and let cool slightly, then purée in blender or food processor. Add salt and pepper to taste; serve hot.

Jerusalem Artichokes *(Helianthus tuberosus)*

This knobby tuber can be dug all winter where the ground does not freeze; in fact, the tuber becomes sweeter with the cold. Domesticated Jerusalem artichokes are sometimes found in supermarkets or specialty greengrocers; the wild ones are the same but smaller.

HABITAT, RANGE
This Great Plains native grows throughout our region, preferring full sun in moist but not wet soil. Look for it alongside agricultural fields, in thickets and ditches, and on prairies and waste ground.

PARTS USED
Tubers, raw or cooked

SEASONS
Fall through winter

IDENTIFICATION TIPS, DANGEROUS LOOKALIKES
Jerusalem artichoke looks like a rougher version of its cousin the sunflower (*Helianthus annuus*), with similar yellow rays (petals) around a central disk. The disk of the Jerusalem artichoke is yellowish brown, however, while sunflowers have darker reddish to brownish disks. Jerusalem artichoke flowers are smaller than sunflowers as well, generally 2 inches across or smaller.

Jerusalem artichoke flowers

Jerusalem artichokes can grow over 9 feet tall, but are generally 6 feet or less. Each plant has a central stalk that branches near the top, and each of these branching stems is crowned with the flower. Leaves are oval-shaped with slightly toothed margins and pointed tips; they generally grow alternately on the stem, but are sometimes opposite near the base of the plant. The entire plant has a rough, coarse feel during the growing season; in fall, when the plant has dried out (but the tubers are ready for harvesting), the stem is woody, and the leaves and flowers remain as brown, brittle remnants. There are no dangerous lookalikes, as long as you can see the full plant (whether growing or dried up). If you dig tubers from plants that have been cut down, be sure to dig only where you know no iris (*Iris* spp.) is growing; Jerusalem artichoke tubers look somewhat similar to iris bulbs on first glance, and iris is poisonous. Remember that bulbs are layered, however, while tubers are solid throughout, giving another point of distinction between the two roots. Iris tends to prefer wetter areas, although Jerusalem artichoke may be found in the same vicinity.

HARVESTING TIPS

Locate stands of Jerusalem artichoke in the summer, when the yellow flowers on tall stalks provide clear identification. Return in fall—and even through winter if the ground is still workable—to dig the tubers.

If the ground is soft, you may be able to simply pull up on the stiff stem of the plant to pull out the tubers; generally, you'll have to dig a bit with a trowel or small spade. The tubers don't go very deep, so they are much easier to dig than, say, burdock root. Jerusalem artichokes spread by tubers (not by seeds), so be sure to leave some in the ground to allow the plant to return the following year.

SPECIAL CONSIDERATIONS

Jerusalem artichokes may cause flatulence in some people, especially if eaten in quantity.

MORE ABOUT JERUSALEM ARTICHOKES: When it comes to foraging for roots, Jerusalem artichoke is my favorite. It's easy to harvest, requiring just a hand trowel or small spade. It grows in agricultural areas and other places where it is often considered a pest, so landowners generally don't mind if you dig it up. I don't feel like I am damaging the habitat when I dig Jerusalem artichoke, as the fields I dig in are generally disturbed or tilled anyway.

The tubers grow as swellings at the ends of the stringy, rope-like rhizomes. They're lumpy and misshapen, usually creamy beige or white but sometimes tinged with pink. Tubers range from the size of very small red potatoes, down to disappointingly tiny lumps no bigger than a short piece of young string bean. If you've found nothing but the tiny ones, you can still cook them—but it will take quite a few to amount to a meal, and they seem too tough to eat raw.

Scrub the tubers well to remove the fine hair-like roots that sprout from them, as well as to clean off a bit of the thin skin; also cut away and discard the ropey rhizome. Larger tubers can be peeled with a sharp swivel-bladed peeler. Raw tubers can be sliced and added to salads, where they contribute a sweet, nutty crunch that reminds me of jicama (or water chestnuts). Jerusalem artichokes can also be pickled by following recipes for pickled cauliflower.

Add Jerusalem artichokes to any stew or pot-roast, as you would use potatoes. You can boil them until tender, then slice or mash them; however, they are watery and don't mash up fluffy like potatoes. Slices can be pan-fried, but again, they're not potatoes, and don't get crisp in the same way.

The carbohydrate in Jerusalem artichokes is *inulin*, a soluble dietary fiber that is non-digestible. Diabetics and people with hypoglycemia who can't tolerate potatoes and other starchy foods can generally eat Jerusalem artichokes, so they provide an important food option for some people. (If you are diabetic or have hypoglycemia and wish to make Jerusalem artichokes a part of your diet for this reason, you may wish to check with your health care professional.)

Jerusalem artichokes store well in the refrigerator; simply put them in a plastic bag and keep in the crisper drawer, where they'll stay fresh for weeks. You can also peel them and keep them in a container of water in the refrigerator; that way, they're ready for use any time the urge hits.

QUICK IDEAS FOR USING JERUSALEM ARTICHOKES
- Peel tubers that are at least ½ inch across, then slice thinly and add to salads for a delicious, nutty crunch.
- Toss a few Jerusalem artichokes into soups or stews to complement other vegetables.
- Boil tubers, then cream or scallop as you would potatoes.
- Peel tubers, then soak in any pickling liquid you like; refrigerator-pickle type liquid works well.
- Add some peeled burdock root to the fryer next time you are making tempura.

OTHER RECIPES IN THIS BOOK FEATURING JERUSALEM ARTICHOKES
- Wild-Root Soup (page 404)

Farmhouse Field Vegetable Stew

4 servings   Preparation: Over an hour

Jerusalem artichokes are often considered a nuisance weed in agricultural areas. This recipe proves that they are every bit as useful and delicious as the cultivated crops they grow alongside. Serve this with a big green salad and a loaf of hearty bread.

8 ounces bulk Italian or country-style
    sausage (if using cased sausages,
    remove the skins)
1 large onion, cut into 1½-inch chunks
1 small rutabaga (1 to 1¼ pounds)
2 medium turnips (about 8 ounces total)
2 cloves garlic
¾ pound Jerusalem artichokes
1½ to 2 cups baby carrots, or 3 regular-
    sized carrots

1 cup chicken broth
½ teaspoon salt
¼ teaspoon crushed black pepper
¼ teaspoon dried oregano
¼ teaspoon dried thyme
A good pinch of dried rosemary leaves,
    crushed between your fingers

Heat oven to 375°F. In Dutch oven, cook sausage and onion over medium heat until sausage is browned, stirring to break up sausage. While sausage is cooking, prepare vegetables, adding them to Dutch oven as each is ready. Peel rutabaga and turnips, and cut them into 1½ inch chunks. Peel garlic and slice it thinly. Peel Jerusalem artichokes and cut in half if large. Baby carrots can be added to the pot with no further preparation; regular carrots need to be peeled and cut into 1-inch chunks.

When all vegetables have been added to the Dutch oven, stir in chicken broth, salt, pepper and herbs. Heat to boiling, stirring several times. Cover Dutch oven and bake until vegetables are tender, stirring several times; this will take 1 to 1¼ hours.

Variation: Vegetarian Farmhouse Field Vegetable Stew
Omit sausage; use 2 teaspoons vegetable oil to cook the onions and other vegetables as directed. Substitute vegetable broth for the chicken broth. Proceed as directed.

Pan-Roasted Jerusalem Artichokes

3 servings as written; easily increased   Preparation: Under 30 minutes

If you've never had Jerusalem artichokes before, this is a good introduction. The simple cooking method brings out their natural sweetness, and gives them a handsome glazed, browned appearance.

1 pound Jerusalem artichokes, at least ½ inch across
⅔ cup chicken broth or vegetable broth

2 cloves garlic, sliced
2 teaspoons butter
Salt and pepper

Peel Jerusalem artichokes, dropping them into a bowl of water as they are peeled (this helps remove any dirt or grime from the peeled surface, and also keeps them from turning brown). When all are peeled, drain and place them into heavy-bottomed medium skillet with broth, garlic and butter. Heat to boiling over medium-high heat. Cover and reduce heat so broth is bubbling gently, and cook until Jerusalem artichokes are just tender, 7 to 10 minutes. Remove cover and increase heat slightly. Cook until liquid has evaporated and Jerusalem artichokes are nicely browned, shaking pan frequently to prevent burning and sticking. Sprinkle with salt and pepper to taste before serving.

Bacon-Wrapped Chokes

4 appetizer servings; easily increased   Preparation: Under an hour

These were inspired by rumaki, a common appetizer in Chinese restaurants. Rumaki is usually made with chicken liver and a water chestnut that have been wrapped in bacon. I eliminated the liver and used Jerusalem artichokes in place of the chestnuts; for a flavor boost, I season the chokes with sweet-and-sour sauce. The end result is delicious.

8 to 12 peeled Jerusalem artichokes, about 1 x ¾ inches
¼ cup purchased sweet-and-sour sauce
4 to 6 slices bacon

3 tablespoons soy sauce
1 tablespoon rice vinegar
½ teaspoon sugar
1 teaspoon sesame seeds

Heat oven to 375°F. Spray small baking sheet with nonstick spray; set aside. In small bowl, combine Jerusalem artichokes and sweet-and-sour sauce; stir to coat. Set aside for 10 or 15 minutes if you have time; otherwise, proceed directly to the next step.

Cut each bacon slice in half across the length to make 8 to 12 shorter pieces. Wrap a half-slice around each choke, securing with a wooden toothpick. Place on prepared baking sheet. Bake until bacon is crisp and golden brown, about 25 minutes. While chokes are baking, combine soy sauce, vinegar, sugar and sesame seeds in small decorative bowl. Serve soy sauce mixture with warm bacon-wrapped chokes.

Vegetable Fried Rice

4 servings   Preparation: Under 30 minutes

This recipe calls for both burdock root and Jerusalem artichokes, but gives substitutes for either of these ingredients so you can make it even if you have just one of them. It makes a nice light lunch or supper dish, or a good side dish to accompany other stir-fried dishes. Use cooked rice that has been refrigerated until cold, rather than freshly cooked rice; refrigeration gives the rice the proper dry, chewy texture.

1 teaspoon rice vinegar or white vinegar

2 ounces Jerusalem artichokes or canned, sliced water chestnuts

2 teaspoons peanut oil or vegetable oil, plus additional if needed

¼ cup broth or water

2 to 3 ounces burdock root or parsnip

¼ cup finely diced celery (¼-inch dice)

¼ cup finely diced red bell pepper (¼-inch dice)

½ cup diced onion (½-inch dice)

¼ cup frozen green peas (thawed or still frozen; don't substitute canned peas)

1 egg (omit if you prefer a vegan dish)

2 to 3 cups leftover cooked white or brown rice

2 tablespoons soy sauce

¼ teaspoon 5-spice powder (found with Chinese staples), optional

¼ teaspoon sugar

Add vinegar to small bowl of cold water. Peel Jerusalem artichokes and cut them into ⅛-inch-thick matchstick pieces or small slices, adding them to vinegar water as you cut. Set aside. (If you're using water chestnuts, simply drain them and cut into matchsticks.) Combine oil and broth in wok, and heat over medium heat while you prepare burdock root. Peel burdock root and slice ⅛ inch thick, adding to wok as you slice. When all has been sliced, increase heat to medium-high and cook until liquid boils away, stirring frequently. Add celery and bell pepper; stir-fry for about 3 minutes. Add onion and peas; stir-fry for about 3 minutes longer, adding oil if needed.

Push vegetables up the sides of the wok. Break egg into center of wok, and scramble immediately with a fork. Continue stirring egg with the fork until it is cooked and in small pieces; some of the vegetables will get mixed in with the egg and that's OK. When egg is cooked, add rice, breaking up large clumps. Stir-fry for about 3 minutes. Quickly drain Jerusalem artichokes and add to wok along with soy sauce, 5-spice powder and sugar. Stir-fry for about 2 minutes. Serve hot.

Variation: Mushroom Fried Rice
Use one of the following: ½ cup finely diced chicken of the woods (¼-inch-dice); ¾ cup diced puffballs (½-inch-dice); 1 cup sliced cauliflower mushrooms or morels; or ¾ cup of any other mushroom variety, sliced or otherwise cut up into small pieces before measuring. If using chicken of the woods, add them to wok along with celery and bell pepper. If using any other mushroom species, add them to wok along with onion and peas. Proceed as directed.

Variation: Chicken, Pork or Shrimp Fried Rice
Follow main recipe or mushroom variation above, adding ¼ pound diced chicken or pork to wok along with celery and bell pepper; or, add ¼ pound sliced or diced raw shrimp to wok along with onion and peas. Proceed as directed, adding a little more oil if needed.

Other Roots

Here is a small selection of roots that can be foraged and eaten. I think of these roots as curiosities rather than the main quarry when I go out; if I were living off the land, I would no doubt feel differently. For the casual forager, a few of these roots make an interesting addition to a stew or mixed vegetable dish, but it is unlikely that enough will be gathered to form a solo dish.

EVENING PRIMROSE (*Oenothera biennis*)

Evening primrose flower

This lovely yellow flower grows throughout our region in wastelands, fields and disturbed sites, as well as on prairies and along roadsides. It's also common along the beaches of Lake Superior. It can live in poor soil, and tolerates a variety of moisture conditions. Like burdock, it is a biennial, living 2 years and taking a different form in its second year. In its first year, it has long, narrow leaves that form a basal rosette; in its second year, it sends up a flowering stalk that has numerous alternate leaves and several cup-shaped yellow flowers. Dig the root of the first-year plant from late summer until the ground freezes. It can be boiled and served like parsnips; a better use is to add it to mixed-vegetable stews or stir-fry dishes. It has a peppery taste that is welcome in casseroles and soups.

GROUNDNUT (*Apios americana*)

Also called hopniss, this is a twining vine that is often seen covering fences and shrubs. It

Groundnut flower

grows throughout our region, and favors streamside locations and other moist places with sandy soil. It has compound leaves, with 5 to 9 oval leaflets with sharp points; maroon or purplish flowers that resemble pea flowers grow in the leaf axils. The plants develop tubers that are strung along the cord-like roots; an individual root may have numerous tubers, and can stretch out for some distance. Tubers produce a sticky liquid when cut; this is not noticeable when the tubers are cooked, and may help thicken dishes in which the tubers are used. Add the peeled tubers to stews and soups, as you would potatoes; they can also be boiled, then mashed and seasoned to make an interesting side dish. The roots can be harvested any time you can dig the soil; dig at the base of the plant and follow the ropey roots to locate the tubers. Since groundnuts grow in sandy areas and often near streams, be sure to replace the soil where you've dug to prevent erosion.

SOLOMON'S SEAL, GREAT OR TRUE (*Polygonatum canaliculatum*)

Great or true Solomon's seal grows throughout out region in moist woods and fertile ditches. It resembles the false Solomon's seal (*P. biflorum*) until you look under the leaves; on great Solomon's seal, flowers (and later, berries) grow from each leaf axil on the underside of the plant, while on false Solomon's seal, the flowers and berries grow in a cluster at the end of the stem. Here is a little rhyme to help you remember this: "Solomon's seal, to be real, must have flowers along the keel." The distinction is important, because the roots of great Solomon's seal are edible, while those of false Solomon's seal are poisonous except with very special, precise preparation. Roots of great Solomon's seal are white, and have a round "seal" where the previous year's shoots grew; roots of false Solomon's seal are

Great Solomon's seal

yellowish and show no circular patch. Harvest the roots of great Solomon's seal in the summer, when the flowers and berries make identification easy; scrub well (or peel) and add to stews and soups in place of potatoes. I've frozen the roots successfully after boiling; although they do get a bit watery when thawed, they are still fine for stews and the like. Note that great Solomon's seal is protected in some of its range and should not be dug; in other places, it should be harvested selectively and only where abundant.

WAPATO (*Sagittaria* spp.)

Also called duck potato or arrowhead, wapato was a mainstay in the diets of Native Americans even through the time of the Lewis and Clark expedition; they wrote of Native

Wapato leaf and flower

American women harvesting the tubers of this plant by wading chest-deep in ponds and dislodging tubers with their toes. Fortunately, wapato can be harvested with the aid of a hoe rather than by wading into cold water; once the tubers are loosened, they float to the surface and can be drawn in with the hoe. The plants actually benefit from having their roots broken up, although you should not harvest more than 10% of the plants in a given area (and then, only when abundant). Look for the arrowhead-shaped leaves floating on the surface of cool, still ponds and small lakes; it grows throughout our region. Peel the roots and prepare like potatoes; they have a muddy taste if eaten raw.

WILD GINGER (*Asarum canadense*)

Wild ginger grows throughout our region, in moist woods and rocky areas with rich soil. Two heart-shaped leaves on long, thick leafstalks have a brownish, 3-petalled cup-like flower at the base where the stems join. The underground tuber is knobby and grows sideways from the leaves rather than downward like a carrot. The root is juicy and aromatic, with a scent and flavor like commercially available gingerroot only much milder. Dig the root from spring through fall, and substitute it for domestic gingerroot in any recipe, but double or triple the amount called for. Wild gingerroot is used in Fiddlehead Stir-Fry (page 43) and Nettles with Ginger (page 316); as noted, it can also be used in any recipe in this book that calls for gingerroot by increasing the quantity.

Wild ginger in flower

Wild-Root Soup

4 servings   Preparation: Under an hour

1 pound Jerusalem artichoke tubers, wapato (duck potato) tubers or groundnut tubers
1 quart chicken broth or vegetable broth
½ cup finely diced carrot
¼ cup finely diced red bell pepper
¼ cup finely diced onion

1 tablespoon minced shallot
1 tablespoon butter or olive oil
1 teaspoon fresh thyme leaves, or ½ teaspoon dried
1 cup cooked wild rice
Salt and freshly ground black pepper

Peel tubers, cutting larger pieces into sizes to match smaller chunks. As you peel them, add them to a saucepan with the chicken broth. When all have been peeled, heat just to boiling over medium-high heat. Cook at a gentle boil until tubers are tender, 15 to 20 minutes. Remove from heat and set aside to cool somewhat.

In medium skillet, sauté carrot, bell pepper, onion and shallot in butter over medium heat until tender, 5 to 10 minutes; stir thyme in during the last minute. Meanwhile, pour cooled broth and roots carefully into blender; purée on high speed. Return broth mixture to saucepan. Add wild rice and sautéed vegetables. Cook over medium heat for a few minutes, until soup is hot and flavors have blended a bit. Taste for seasoning, and add salt and pepper as needed. Serve hot.

Solomon's Seal and Potato Pan-Fry

2 or 3 servings   Preparation: Under an hour

Solomon's seal root has a flavor that is somewhat reminiscent of turnips. The roots are sticky when you peel them, but this is not noticeable in the finished dish.

2 ounces greater Solomon's seal root (about 4 pieces that are 3 inches long each)

2 tablespoons olive oil

¾ pound small red or Yukon gold potatoes, halved and sliced ⅛ inch thick

Half of an onion, diced

1 or 2 cloves garlic, minced

¼ teaspoon hot red pepper flakes

Salt and pepper

Heat saucepan of water to boiling over high heat. Peel Solomon's seal roots, discarding peels. Add peeled roots to saucepan of boiling water; cook for 15 minutes, or until just tender. Drain and refresh in cold running water; set aside.

In heavy-bottomed large skillet, heat oil over medium-high heat until shimmering. Add potato slices; reduce heat to medium and cook for 10 minutes, stirring and turning potatoes occasionally. While potatoes are cooking, slice boiled Solomon's seal root into ⅛-inch-thick disks. When potatoes have cooked for about 10 minutes, add sliced Solomon's seal root; cook for about 5 minutes longer, stirring occasionally. Add onion, garlic and hot pepper; cook for 10 minutes longer, or until potatoes are crisp and nicely browned, stirring and turning several times. Season with salt and pepper to taste; serve immediately.

Wild Rice *(Zizania aquatica or Z. palustris)*

Wild rice is still an important food for native peoples; its harvest is a ritual with cultural importance. True wild rice differs markedly from paddy-grown, commercially available wild rice; it has a mellower, nuttier fragrance and is lighter in color.

HABITAT, RANGE
Wild rice inhabits marshes, shallow lakes and ponds, and bays of larger lakes throughout most of our region, but is concentrated in the states around the Great Lakes.

PARTS USED
Seeds, processed and cooked

SEASONS
Fall

IDENTIFICATION TIPS, DANGEROUS LOOKALIKES
Wild rice is relatively common in our region, particularly in the northern part. It grows in the shallows as a 3- to 8-foot-tall aquatic grass; in the fall, the plants develop hanging seeds that

Wild rice plants

Unhusked wild rice

are the kernels of "rice" encased in husks. Leaves are long and very narrow, and float on the water next to the stalks. There are no dangerous lookalikes.

HARVESTING TIPS
Look for the distinctive narrow, floating leaves to identify stands of wild rice. The harvest of wild rice is controlled by state law in most places, and even the method of harvesting and craft used to harvest it may be regulated. The basic idea is to pole a canoe or shallow-draft boat through the stands of rice, then gently bend a ripe stalk over the boat and beat or shake the stalks to dislodge the grains into the bottom of the boat. Wild rice has sharp barbs that may annoy your skin; most ricers wear gloves, hats and long-sleeved shirts.

SPECIAL CONSIDERATIONS
Wild rice occasionally develops a pink or purple fungus that can cause illness or delirium. Avoid stands containing misshapen or colored kernels, and pick out any that you may find in your harvest.

ROOTS & STARCHES

MORE ABOUT WILD RICE: Wild rice was one of the major food staples of Native Americans in the Great Lakes area, who introduced it to traders and colonists. Paddy-grown wild rice is now available, but most people agree that it is not as delicious as the wild-grown kind. Native American tribes in Minnesota, Wisconsin and Michigan still harvest and sell truly wild rice; it is worth seeking out if you are buying wild rice.

Harvesting and processing wild rice is not a casual undertaking; I've never done it, although I have seen it done when I was living in Wisconsin, and have eaten wild rice that was hand-harvested and processed by individual foragers. The grains must be harvested—often over the course of several days or a week, as not all grain ripens at once. Then it must be air-dried before being parched at low temperatures (175°F to 300°F, depending on what source you check) in a cast-iron kettle or oven. Next, it is pounded to separate the husks from the grains; some ricers place the parched grain in a large container and jump in it (with clean moccasins on their feet) to separate the husks from the grain. After that, it must be winnowed to separate the chaff from the grain; the standard procedure is to put the pounded rice in a large basket and toss it in the air, letting the breeze carry away the husks as the rice falls back into the basket. All of this is quite labor-intensive, and is generally more work than the casual forager will wish to undertake. Serious foragers in this region, however, rely on wild rice as a staple carbohydrate, and often harvest it in large quantities.

The harvest of wild rice is controlled by state Natural Resources Departments; in some areas such as Native American reservations, harvest is restricted to band members. If you want to try your hand at wild rice harvesting, follow state and local regulations, and obtain the proper permits. You may be able to strike a deal with the local band or a local commercial harvester to have them process your grain in exchange for a portion of the harvest or for payment.

Once you've got the grain processed, it can be cooked like domestic rice; it has a much nuttier taste, and a more interesting texture than domestic rice. It's higher in protein than even brown rice (to say nothing of white rice, which has been stripped of many nutrients), and has more iron and copper than brown rice.

How to boil wild rice: In saucepan, combine 1 part ready-to-cook wild rice to 3 parts water or chicken broth. Add a good pinch of salt, perhaps ⅛ teaspoon per cup of rice. Heat to boiling, then reduce heat and boil gently until the rice grains just begin to pop open slightly, about 20 minutes;* don't cook it so long that the grains open completely and turn inside-out. Drain the rice if necessary, and serve or use in recipes calling for cooked rice. Cooked wild rice can be frozen in convenient portions, then thawed and used as needed. (*Hand-processed wild rice cooks more quickly than commercially grown wild rice, which may take as long as an hour to become tender.)

QUICK IDEAS FOR USING WILD RICE
- Use cooked wild rice in dressings and casseroles that call for brown rice.
- Mix chopped hazelnuts with cooked wild rice; top with a little butter and serve hot.
- Add cooked wild rice to soups to provide texture and body.

OTHER RECIPES IN THIS BOOK FEATURING WILD RICE
- Waldorf Salad with Wild Rice (page 86)
- Wild Rice-Walnut Pilaf (page 278)
- Wild and Brown Rice Casserole with Mushrooms (page 389)
- Wild-Root Soup (page 404)

Wild Rice Dressing

4 to 6 servings   Preparation: Under 30 minutes

Serve this alongside the Thanksgiving turkey, or with any roasted or grilled meats.

½ cup diced onion
¼ cup diced celery
1 tablespoon butter or vegetable oil
½ cup slivered almonds, chopped pecans or other nuts

¼ cup dried cranberries or golden raisins
½ cup dry sherry or chicken broth
2½ to 3 cups cooked wild rice, or a mixture of wild and white rice if you prefer
Salt and pepper

In large saucepan, sauté onion and celery in butter over medium heat until tender, stirring occasionally. Add almonds, cranberries and sherry. Increase heat slightly and cook, stirring occasionally, until sherry has reduced to about a tablespoon. Add wild rice. Reduce heat and cover; cook until rice is heated through, about 10 minutes. Season with salt and pepper to taste. Serve hot.

Wild Rice and Mushroom Soup

6 servings   Preparation: About an hour

¾ cup ready-to-cook wild rice
1½ cups chicken broth or water
¾ cup diced red onion
¾ cup diced or thinly sliced celery
½ cup diced or coarsely chopped carrot
2 tablespoons butter
1 to 1½ cups sliced or cut-up mushrooms,
   any variety*

2 tablespoons freshly squeezed lemon juice
2 tablespoons dry sherry
¼ cup all-purpose flour
1 quart mushroom broth, vegetable broth
   or chicken broth
1 cup half-and-half or light cream
Salt and pepper

In medium saucepan, combine rice and chicken broth. Heat to boiling, stirring several times. Cover and reduce heat; simmer until water is absorbed and rice is just tender, about 15 minutes for hand-harvested wild rice. Remove from heat and let stand while you cook the other ingredients.

In small soup pot or large saucepan, sauté onion, celery and carrot in butter over medium heat until just tender, 5 to 10 minutes, stirring occasionally. Add mushrooms; sauté until just tender, about 5 minutes. Add lemon juice and sherry, stirring to combine. Sprinkle flour into pot, stirring constantly; cook, stirring constantly, for 10 minutes. Add mushroom broth, stirring constantly; cook for about 10 minutes, stirring occasionally. Stir in cooked wild rice and cream. Heat just to simmering; do not boil. Add salt and pepper to taste; serve immediately.

*If using extremely firm mushrooms such as chicken of the woods, dice them finely and add to pot during the preliminary sautéing of the vegetables (rather than after the vegetables have already been sautéed).

"Many Things Wild" Casserole with Wild Rice

6 servings   Preparation: About an hour

This versatile casserole lets you combine several different wild foods in a simple side dish. If you're making it in the spring, try morel mushrooms; in the fall, oyster mushrooms, cauliflower mushrooms or puffballs work well, but any mushroom can be used. If ramps are out of season, substitute leeks; simply cut the white part in half lengthwise and then slice thinly (you could even use regular onions in place of the ramps or leeks).

½ to ¾ cup sliced ramps or leeks (see note above)

2 teaspoons butter, margarine or oil

2 cups cut-up mushrooms

1 cup chicken broth

⅔ cup crabapple quarters, or diced wild apples or pears, optional

3 cups cooked wild rice (page 407)

¼ to ⅓ cup broken or chopped hazelnuts, black walnuts or other nuts

¼ teaspoon salt

Heat oven to 350°F. Lightly grease a 1½-quart casserole; set aside. In large skillet, cook ramps in butter over medium heat, stirring occasionally, for about 5 minutes. Add mushrooms and continue cooking until mushrooms have softened somewhat, about 5 minutes. Add chicken broth, and apples if using; increase heat to medium-high and cook for about 5 minutes, stirring occasionally. Stir in the wild rice, nuts and salt. Transfer mixture to prepared casserole. Cover with lid or foil and bake for 30 minutes if the rice was warm when you started; if the rice was refrigerator temperature, bake for 45 minutes.

MISCELLANEOUS WILD EDIBLES

This short chapter is a catch-all for a few things that didn't fit anywhere else. Maple syrup is the biggest item here, but you'll also find a bit of information on a handful of other plants that can be foraged and put to good use in the kitchen.

Maple Syrup

More than most other foods, maple syrup evokes memories of time spent in the woods. This is particularly true if you've ever been involved in collecting sap and processing it; the memory stays with you forever, and each time you dig into a stack of pancakes dripping with maple syrup, you will recall those crisp mornings gathering and boiling sap in the sugarbush.

Making maple syrup is a lengthy process; it takes 40 gallons of sap to produce one finished gallon of syrup, and all that sap has to be collected from the trees and then boiled down. The process isn't complicated, however, and if you want to try your hand at small-batch syruping, it's a fun and interesting project.

It's best to work with trees that grow in your own yard or on other private property to which you have access and permission; it takes days to gather enough sap to work with, and if you drill into a tree on public land, it is a sure bet that someone will mess with your gear while you are not there (and there may be regulations against it). Also, if the trees grow in your own yard, you'll have one puzzle solved from the start: identifying a maple tree when it has no leaves. Experienced syrupers learn quite quickly how to identify a maple tree in the barren woods, but for your first attempt, it's easier to work with trees you have identified in other seasons. The best is the sugar maple (*Acer saccharum*); this is the tree whose leaves provide a most stunning display of fall color, with hot-poker-orange leaves. The black maple (*A. nigrum*) also is a good sap producer. Softer maples such as the silver maple (*A. saccharinum*) and the red maple (*A. rubrum*) yield sap with a lower sugar content, and it may take as much as 75 gallons of sap to yield a gallon of syrup. You can also make syrup with the sap from birch (*Betula* spp.) and other trees; simply follow the same procedures outlined below.

Maple sap dripping through spile

Each maple tree of the proper sort will produce about a gallon of sap per day, but you can store the sap in a clean, covered 5-gallon food-grade pail on a cold porch until you have enough to work with. You'll need some sort of tap—commonly called a *spile*—for the sap to flow through, and a collection bucket to catch the sap. You can make your own spiles with pipe from the hardware store. Each spile should go 2 inches into the tree, and you'll want it to hang out by another 2 or 3 inches, so a 5-inch length of ½-inch-diameter copper tubing will make a dandy homemade spile (I bet you could use PVC pipe sold for plumbing also, but I haven't tried this). A 1-gallon ice cream pail makes a fine collection bucket.

Wait until the weather warms to the 40s during the day (but drops below freezing at night), generally mid to late March depending on your exact location. Drill a ½-inch hole into the tree (tap trees that are a foot in diameter or larger), at about waist level and 2 inches into the wood, at a slightly upward angle. Use a wooden mallet to pound your spile into the hole; then, pound a long, heavy nail at a downward angle above the spile and hang your collection bucket so the sap will drip from the tube into the bucket. Check the bucket several times each day, especially as the weather warms; empty the accumulated sap into a larger bucket, then re-hang the collection bucket and move on to the next tree. If you've never seen maple sap before, you may be surprised; it looks just like water, and has just a subtle, sweet taste.

Store the sap on a cold porch or unheated garage until you have 5 gallons. Each 5-gallon batch will yield only about a pint of syrup, but for the home processor, that's about as much sap as you can handle at a time. Start boiling the sap in a large canning kettle, but don't do it in your kitchen; I've heard stories of wallpaper peeling off after an individual tried to make maple syrup inside. (Think about all that water being boiled off in the winter, when you can't open the windows, and you begin to see how something like this could happen.) When the sap reduces in volume and looks lost in the large kettle, transfer it to a smaller pot and continue boiling. When the sap reduces to a quart or so, finish the boiling inside.

To check for doneness, dip a clean, room-temperature metal spoon into the boiling mixture. Move it away from the steam, and hold it sideways over a plate. The sap has been sufficiently reduced when it forms two thick beads that drip off the spoon together; if they drip alternately, the sap needs further reducing. Pour the finished syrup—strained if there seem to be impurities from the trees—into a sterilized canning jar (see page 418 for information on sterilizing). Store it in the refrigerator, where it will keep for many months.

For more information on making maple syrup, I recommend the book *Sugartime,* by Susan Carol Hauser. It's a delightful book, with useful information as well as lots of memories and stories about time spent in the sugarbush.

Other Tree Products

Syrup, nuts and fruit are the most obvious foods that come from trees; however, other parts of certain trees are edible or otherwise useful as well. Here are a few things you can do with these other tree products.

AMERICAN BASSWOOD *(Tilia americana)*

Young leaves of this graceful tree are a well-known wild edible in the early spring, and the flowers can be used later in the spring to make tea. Basswood trees have multiple trunks with light gray bark and large, heart-shaped leaves. The leaves are not quite symmetrical; the rib doesn't bisect the leaf evenly, so one side is larger than the other. Pick leaves when they are just unfurling and are still light green; they should be sweet and tender, and make a delicious addition to salads or a nice trail nibble. If the leaves are too old, they'll be tough to chew; they won't hurt you, but they aren't any fun to eat either. In late spring or early summer, basswood trees develop large off-white flowers on long stalks. Place a half-dozen flowers in a tea pot, add boiling water, and steep for 2 or 3 minutes, or until the tea is lightly colored and fragrant. Strain and sweeten to taste.

BIRCH *(Betula* spp.)

The twigs and inner bark of birch trees makes a delicious tea; sweet or black birch *(B. lenta)* is particularly favored. Never harvest bark from a standing, living tree; if you come upon one that has been downed by a storm (or by a logger, perhaps), you can peel the bark to get at the sticky inner bark. Otherwise, use only twigs, preferably fresh. Peel the bark off the twigs, then boil the peeled twigs in a saucepan of water, using a half-dozen small twigs

Basswood leaf

Birch trees

Eastern hemlock

Black spruce

per quart (if you're using inner bark, boil it in the same way). Note that this tea is actively boiled rather than just steeped, as are herbal or flower teas. Inner bark from the birch tree can also be scraped to yield a mass of spongy, spaghetti-like strands; these can be cooked and eaten as emergency food (again, don't remove bark from a standing, living tree).

As noted on page 412, birch sap can also be used to make syrup. Follow the same procedures used for making maple syrup; a simple home method is described on pages 412-413.

EVERGREENS (Eastern hemlock, *Tsuga canadensis;* black spruce, *Picea mariana*)
The young tips of these trees, which grow only in the northern part of our range, can be used to make a tart tea. Simmer a few tips in a saucepan of water over low heat for 5 to 10 minutes, then strain and sweeten to taste. Like birch (above), the inner bark of the hemlock can be used as a survival food in dire need, or if you find a freshly downed tree in the forest.

JUST FOR FUN
Wild Potpourri
Gather small pinecones and a few evergreen tips next time you're in the pine woods. At home, combine them with whole dried wild rose flowers, dried red clover flowers, and a few small pieces of sumac-tree berry clusters. Sprinkle with a few drops of pine-scented essential oil (available at craft stores and bath-and-body shops), or any scent you prefer. Display it in a wide, shallow bowl to add subtle fragrance to a room, or pack in a jar and dress with a ribbon to give as a gift.

Spice Plants

Here are a few plants that produce berry-like fruits that are used as a spice or seasoning. These are easy to harvest, and can be kept in a dark, cool cupboard to use as needed.

COMMON JUNIPER *(Juniperus communis)*

This flattened, low-growing shrub is found throughout most of our region with the exception of southern Iowa; it prefers poor soil, often growing in rocky areas and on clifftops overlooking the Great Lakes. It produces hard, dark-blue berries that are covered with a whitish dusty powder. Use these hard fruits in any recipe calling for commercial juniper berries; they're excellent in marinades for meat (particularly venison) and are used to make sausages. Juniper is one of the main ingredients used in the distillation of gin; the juniper scent is what we smell when we sniff a bottle of gin.

Juniper berries

SPICEBUSH *(Lindera benzoin)*

Spicebush grows in the southern part of our region, primarily in Illinois and Ohio but also in parts of southeastern Iowa and southern Michigan. It favors rich, moist woodlands and streambanks. The fruit is a small oval berry that turns bright red when ripe in the fall. Spicebush berries taste quite a bit like allspice, and can be substituted for whole allspice

berries in recipes for jam, chutney, marinades and sauces; it can also be ground and used much like ground allspice. Spicebush berries tend to develop a slightly off flavor if stored at room temperature too long; for lengthy storage, keep in the refrigerator or freezer. For the best taste in recipes that call for ground or crushed berries, keep them whole until just before use. The leaves of the spicebush plant also can be used for seasoning; dry them for storage, and crush them into marinades and stews for a subtle sweet-and-spicy flavor. For recipes in this book that use spicebush berries, see pages 117, 152, 156, 159, 185, 198, 217 and 220.

Spicebush berries

PRESERVING & GENERAL TECHNIQUES

HERE IS some general information that applies to a number of recipes throughout this book.

Canning Information, Sterilizing Jars

The method given below for sterilizing jars and lids is the way I always work when canning, but it does require care to avoid a nasty burn. If you have a different way of handling jars, please feel free to do what is comfortable for you. These instructions are provided for cooks who may not be familiar with canning procedures, and will ensure safe canning.

Modern canning jars have two-piece tops, consisting of a flat lid and a screw-on band. When canning, you must always start with new lids. It's OK to re-use a lid if you're just covering a jar of something that will be placed in the cupboard (for example, a jar of dried fruit) or stored in the refrigerator; be sure to wash it very well. The bands can be re-used a number of times, but if the insides start to get corroded and the band becomes hard to screw on the jar, recycle it and buy new bands.

Always use jars specially made for canning; old mayonnaise jars and the like are not strong enough. Canning jars can be re-used indefinitely, unless they develop a nick or crack. Always inspect each jar by holding it up to the light, looking for cracks or fractures. Then, when you are washing the jar prior to sterilizing it, run your wet finger over the top rim of the jar, checking for nicks. Even a small nick will cause canning failure; if you find jars like this in your collection, recycle them or put them in a special place away from your canning jars.

HOW TO STERILIZE CANNING JARS AND LIDS
Wash jars, bands and new lids in hot, soapy water; rinse very well. Place washed jars on a rack in a water-bath canner, and cover with 1 inch of water; for smaller batches of jam that will go into half-pint jars, you can use a Dutch oven instead of the water-bath canner, but be sure to line the bottom with a thick towel or place a rack in it to keep the jars away from the hot metal on the bottom of the pan. Heat the water to boiling over high heat, then boil for 10 minutes. Turn off burner and allow the jars to stand in the hot water while you prepare the food to be canned. Meanwhile, place lids and washed bands in a saucepan; cover with water. Heat to a vigorous simmer. Cover and remove from heat.

Using long tongs and commonsense care, quickly remove one jar from the canner (or Dutch oven), pouring its water back into the canner. Fill the jar with food as indicated in the recipe, leaving the amount of head space indicated ("head space" refers to the empty area at the top of the jar). Wipe the jar rim and threads with a clean towel. Place a lid and band on top, and screw the band on so it is just finger-tight. Return the jar to the canner and repeat with remaining jars and food (unless you won't be processing the food; then, just proceed as directed in the recipe).

HOW TO PROCESS FOOD IN A HOT-WATER BATH

Once you've got the sterilized jars filled with food and returned to the canner (or Dutch oven), add additional hot water if necessary to cover the filled jars by 1 inch. Heat to boiling over high heat, then begin timing and boil for the amount of time indicated in the recipe. Use a canning tongs or long-handled tongs to remove the jars from canner (grasp them below the bands rather than grasping the bands, which might break the seal). Place jars on a thick towel on the countertop, away from drafts, to cool. (You'll hear each jar "ping" as it seals—a most satisfying sound.) When cool, check each jar for a proper seal. The center of the lid should be depressed, and it should not move up and down when pressed with a finger. If any jars are improperly sealed, refrigerate and enjoy as you would any opened jam (or other food). Sealed jars can be stored in a cool, dark place for up to a year.

ABOUT PRESSURE CANNING

Hot-water bath canning works fine for fruits and high-acid foods such as tomatoes and pickled foods; however, if you're canning vegetables (such as cattail stalks), you *must* use a pressure canner. Since I haven't used a pressure canner in any recipes in this book, I will not go into the details here; if you have a pressure canner, follow the instructions that came with it, or check in a good book on home canning.

Dehydrating Wild Foods

Home drying, or dehydrating, is an excellent preservation method for many wild foods such as fruits, greens and mushrooms. Instructions for some specific foods that require different techniques than those here have been given throughout the text, in the write-up of that specific food. For general dehydrating, follow these techniques. Much of this information came from my book, *The Back-Country Kitchen;* if you're interested in learning more about dehydrating foods, you might be interested in this book.

Home drying works on a simple principle: warm air is circulated over prepared foods to remove the moisture. Food is generally held on a tray that allows maximum air flow. A number of home dehydrators are available; your oven can also be pressed into service. Dehydrators come with their own trays. For oven dehydrating, stretch a piece of bridal-veil netting over a cake-cooling rack, then secure it to the rack with twist-ties. Fruit leathers, need to be dried on a solid liner sheet (dehydrator) or plastic-lined baking sheet (oven); see page 263 for information on fruit leathers.

Fruits, greens and mushrooms can generally be dried with no preparation other than washing and perhaps slicing. (In comparison, vegetables generally need to be blanched or par-boiled before dehydrating.) As a general rule, if a fruit can be frozen with no special preparation, it can also be dried with no special preparation. Some fruits dehydrate better if they are first syrup-blanched; the dried fruit will be softer and stickier than untreated fruit, and will have more vibrant color. To prepare the syrup, combine 1 cup sugar and 1 cup white corn syrup with 2 cups water. Heat to boiling, stirring until sugar dissolves. Add fruit; reduce heat and simmer for 5 minutes. Drain and rinse fruit in cold water before drying.

Arrange foods on the trays in even layers, ideally with air space between each piece. However, keep in mind that the food will shrink as it dries, so the spaces between the foods will grow. Stir or rearrange the food periodically during drying, to separate pieces that may be stuck together and to promote even drying.

Quality home dehydrators have thermostats; in general, 145°F is a good temperature for fruits, while mushrooms and greens can be dried at a slightly lower temperature—perhaps 130°F to 140°F. If you're drying in the oven, set it to the lowest setting possible, and prop the door slightly ajar with a ball of foil or an empty can; this allows moisture to escape, and also keeps the temperature down.

To check foods for dryness, remove a piece or two from the dehydrator or oven, and cool to room temperature before judging doneness. (If you're making fruit leather, remove the entire tray and let it cool slightly before checking.) Some individual pieces may be dry sooner than others; simply remove them from the trays and continue drying the rest until everything is finished. Let the food stand at room temperature for an hour or so, then pack into clean glass jars, seal tightly and store in a cool, dark location (freeze dehydrated foods for optimum quality). Check it several times over the next few days to be sure that moisture isn't developing inside the jars; if you see any moisture, take the food out and dry it some more in the dehydrator or oven. Properly dehydrated foods retain their quality and freshness for a year or longer. If you notice any mold, however, discard the entire contents of the jar without tasting; moisture has gotten in somehow and compromised the food, and it is no longer safe.

Blueberries: Frozen or fresh blueberries both dry well, and require no pretreatment; fresh blueberries can be dipped briefly into boiling water to "check" (break) the skin, which reduces drying time. *Doneness test:* Hard, dark, wrinkled; frozen or "checked" blueberries will be slightly flattened when dry. *Drying time:* 6 to 8 hours.

Crabapple wedges: Crabapples can be dried with no additional preparation, or syrup-blanched first. To prepare either blanched or unblanched crabapples, quarter washed fruit, removing seeds and blossom end if large. Syrup-blanch for 5 minutes if you like. *Doneness test:* The blanched crabapples will be glossy and slightly sticky, with dark-red peels and pinkish flesh; they are rather like a leathery candy. Unblanched crabapples are dry and leathery and have a duller appearance, with tan flesh and brick-red skins. *Drying time:* 4 to 5½ hours, depending on size of crabapples.

Currants or gooseberries: Frozen or fresh berries both dry well, and require no pretreatment; fresh berries can be dipped briefly into boiling water to "check" (break) the skin, which reduces drying time. Don't dry prickly gooseberries; the prickles become stiffer, making them very unfriendly to eat. *Doneness test:* Hard, dark, wrinkled; frozen or "checked" berries will be slightly flattened when dry. *Drying time:* 8 to 10 hours.

Elderberries: Spread washed elderberries (stemlets removed) on mesh liners over drying trays (elderberries get quite small when dried, and will fall through normal ventilated dryer trays). *Doneness test:* Shrunken and hard. *Drying time:* 4 to 5 hours.

Ground cherries: Frozen or fresh ground cherries both dry well. Wash and cut into halves; arrange, cut-side up, on dryer trays. *Doneness test:* They will shrink and flatten quite a bit, becoming leathery. Color of dried ground cherries is a deep gold. *Drying time:* About 5 hours.

Mountain ash berries: These mealy berries dry well at room temperature; simply spread them on baking sheets and let stand at room temperature until dry, stirring several times a day. To hasten drying, spread individual berries, or even small berry clusters, on the tray of a food dehydrator or baking sheet for oven drying. *Doneness test:* Leathery and hard, deep brick color. *Drying time:* 3 to 4 hours.

Mulberries or raspberries: Spread in single layer on solid liner sheets or baking sheets (for oven drying) to catch drips; no pretreatment is needed. If you like, transfer fruits to regular (ventilated) dryer trays after an hour or two, after any juices have been released, to hasten drying. *Doneness test:* Leathery and shrunken. *Drying time:* 4 to 10 hours; raspberries dry more quickly than mulberries.

Mushrooms: Wash mushrooms to remove any grit; morels need particular attention. Solid-capped mushrooms like honey mushrooms and chanterelles can be sliced, halved or quartered, depending on size. Morels should be cut in half. Fleshy mushrooms such as chicken of the woods should be sliced ⅛ to a scant ¼ inch thick. *Doneness test:* Morel halves and thin slices of meaty mushrooms will be crispy and lightweight; halved solid-capped mushrooms and thicker slices with be leathery and spongy. all mushrooms lose a lot of weight when dried. *Drying time:* 3 to 24 hours, depending on thickness and variety.

Pawpaw slices: Peel and remove seeds. Slice pawpaws ¼ inch thick; arrange slices in single layer on dryer trays. *Doneness test:* Dried pawpaw slices are leathery and somewhat shrunken; they turn light tan. *Drying time:* 4 to 5 hours.

Prickly pear cactus fruit: Peel and cut into ¼-inch slices. Arrange in single layer on solid liner sheets or baking sheets (for oven drying) to catch drips. If you like, transfer slices to regular (ventilated) dryer trays after an hour or two, after any juices have been released, to hasten drying. *Doneness test:* Leathery and firm; bright reddish or rich gold (depending on variety) even when dry. *Drying time:* 5½ to 6½ hours.

Plums: Halve plums and remove pit. Plums can be dried with no further pre-treatment, or syrup-blanched first. Arrange plum halves, blanched or not, cut-side up, on dryer trays. *Doneness test:* Shrunken firm and leathery; blanched plums will be softer and stickier when dry, while untreated fruit will be harder and more chewy. *Drying time:* 8 to 24 hours, depending on size of fruit.

Serviceberries (juneberries): Remove stem and blossom ends. Cut fruits in half for quicker drying, or dry whole. Arrange in single layer on trays. If it's not too humid, you can also spread whole serviceberries on baking sheets in a single layer, and dry on a screen porch or other enclosed, airy spot; they will take a few days, during which time they should be stirred occasionally. *Doneness test:* Shrunken and leathery. *Drying time:* 6 to 10 hours.

Strawberries: Wash and remove cap. Arrange on dryer trays no more than 2 deep. *Doneness test:* Leathery and somewhat spongy. *Drying time:* 4 to 8 hours, depending on size.

General Winemaking Notes

Winemaking can be a bit confusing to the beginner. Many recipes assume that the reader already knows the basics, and give little in the way of details or specific instructions. On the opposite end of the spectrum are books that delve so thoroughly into the science of wine-making that they completely bewilder the beginner with formulations and calculations. Following is a step-by-step description of the winemaking process. Hopefully, it is enough to guide the beginner through the process without being overly complex. To put it all together, I've included notes I took while making a batch of dandelion wine in 2003.

You will need:

Ingredients specified in individual recipe*
2-gallon (or larger) stoneware crock
Sodium metabisulphite (often just called "sulphite" at winemaking stores)
Muslin or cheesecloth
Glass gallon jug

Air lock
Siphon hose
Clean wine bottles
New corks
Corking device

*Specific recipes may call for the following specialty winemaking ingredients (available at any winemaking supply store):

Wine yeast (don't use baker's yeast)
Yeast nutrient (to encourage yeast growth)
Campden tablets (a convenient form of sodium metabisulphite)
Pectic enzyme (used with fruits that may be high in pectin, to prevent cloudiness)

Acid blend, including malic acid (to adjust acid balance)
Tannin (added when the fruit is lacking in natural tannin; assists in clarification and adds depth of flavor)

A note about cleanliness: You must be rigorous about sterilizing all your equipment during all steps of winemaking; otherwise, the wine may be contaminated by bacteria, wild yeast, fungus or other undesirables. To sterilize, you can boil spoons, straining cloths etc. for 5 minutes, but boiling is not practical for jugs and larger equipment. Most home winemakers use a solution of sodium metabisulphite. Keep a batch of sulphite solution on hand in a stoppered gallon jug during the entire winemaking process, mixing it according to the instructions on the package. Follow any safety precautions on the packet, and use in a well-ventilated area; this is a strong solution, and deserves respect.

The primary ferment: Prepare ingredients as directed in recipe. Rinse stoneware crock with sulphite solution. Place prepared ingredients in crock as directed in recipe. Cover crock with muslin and let stand in a warm location as directed in recipe, stirring as directed (sterilize your stirring spoon by rinsing with sulphite solution, or by boiling, each time). After the yeast has been added according to the instructions, the wine will begin to ferment and bubble; solid ingredients will form a cake on top, and the liquid underneath will be carbonated. The fermenting wine will smell like alcohol and yeast; this is normal.

When the wine is ready for straining, clean the glass gallon jug and rinse with sulphite. Strain wine through cheesecloth into the jug; discard solids. If you don't have a full gallon of liquid, add white grape juice or water to "top off" the liquid to equal 1 gallon. Sterilize the air lock with sulphite solution; fill partway with water (or a mild sulphite solution) and use to seal the jug. Let stand in a cool location for secondary fermentation.

The secondary ferment: During fermentation, the yeast converts the sugar to alcohol. As the yeast works, the wine will produce gas, which is manifested by bubbles rising to the surface. You want the wine to ferment until most of the sugar has been converted and the wine has developed a good flavor. You need to allow time for this to happen, but you don't want the wine to sit on a batch of "dead yeast" or it will develop off-flavors.

The wine should ferment actively for approximately a week; the water in the air lock will bubble frequently at the beginning, and you may see bubbles rising to the top of the liquid in the jug (similar to those in a glass of carbonated beverage, except smaller). As the wine ferments, it will also "throw" a sediment consisting of dead yeast and other particles, which will settle to the bottom of the jug. To help the wine to clear, and to ensure a better flavor, the liquid should be separated from the sediment once vigorous fermentation has stopped; this technique is called "racking".

Racking the wine: During secondary fermentation, the wine separates into two layers: a top layer of liquid (which may still be cloudy) and a thin bottom layer of sediment. When this first happens, the wine will still be quite active, and should be left undisturbed until fermentation slows considerably. When the water in the air lock remains pushed up on the release side, and a bubble comes through only once every minute or two, it's time for the first racking. Use a food-grade hose (or winemaker's siphon), sterilized with sulphite solution, to siphon the liquid into a clean, sterilized jug, leaving behind the sediment. Top off the wine with water to within ½ inch of the top of the jug; you want as little air in the jug as possible. Seal the jug with the air lock again (after re-sterilizing it), and return it to the cool location.

Note: Beginning winemakers often don't rack wine at all, simply waiting until the wine has settled completely before bottling. The wine may still be drinkable without racking; however, you are far more likely to get a decent wine if you rack when the wine throws a large amount of sediment.

Clarification: After the first racking, the wine will continue to ferment slowly, throwing sediment as it clarifies. At this point, the technique becomes less precise. You may want to rack the wine again after a month or two; this is especially important if the wine continues to throw a large amount of sediment. Top the wine off with water each time you rack, to minimize the amount of air at the top of the jug.

Serious winemakers use hydrometers to check the sugar content of the wine (and also the alcohol content), and if you decide to turn this into a hobby, you would do well to invest in this simple piece of equipment. When the hydrometer indicates that the sugar has been consumed, fermentation has ceased. If you don't have a hydrometer, simply watch the bubbling of the water in the air lock; when the wine stops fermenting, it will stop producing gas, so there will be no more bubbles rising through the air lock. The liquid in the air lock will be level on both sides; if the water in the air lock remains pushed up on the release side, fermentation is still occurring, although it may be almost unnoticeable.

Most recipes for homemade wine call for a fermentation period of several months, with at least one racking; however, you could keep the wine in the fermentation jug for up to 6 months—some have kept it as long as a year—as long as you rack it whenever it throws a noticeable amount of sediment.

Even after fermentation ceases, the wine may still be slightly cloudy. If you bottle wine while it is still cloudy, there will be sediment in the bottle; careful pouring will allow you to leave most of the sediment in the bottle, but you lose some wine in the process. For this reason, most winemakers allow the wine to rest in the gallon jug, racking as necessary, until it is clear.

Bottling the wine: When you decide that the wine is ready to bottle, use the siphon hose to transfer the wine into clean, sterilized wine bottles. Cap each with a new cork that has been boiled for 5 minutes; use the corking device to force the corks down into the neck of the bottle. Many home winemakers run a piece of sterilized string alongside the cork, push the cork halfway in, then pull out the string. This releases the pressure from inside the bottle, allowing you to push the cork all the way in.

Rest the bottles on their sides, and let the wine age in the bottle for at least a month; longer aging will produce a wine with more character, but if the wine is left in the bottle too long, it will eventually start to fade. Most homemade wines are best drunk within a year of being bottled, although I've had 12-year-old homemade wine that was exceptional.

KEYS TO WINEMAKING SUCCESS
- Use winemaking yeast (available from winemaking stores) rather than baker's yeast.
- Sterilize all equipment with sulphite or boiling water.
- Once the wine is in the fermentation stage, never let the air lock dry out; it must always have some water in it to prevent bacteria and wild yeasts from getting into the wine.
- Rack the fermenting wine periodically to remove sediment.

PUTTING IT ALL TOGETHER

It may be interesting to read the following records I kept for a batch of Dandelion Rosé Wine I made in 2003 (the recipe is on page 53).

May 16: Warm and sunny. Picked 3½ quarts dandelion flowers. Spent 3 hours plucking to get 2 quarts petals; some flowers left over. Added boiling water to petals in crock at 5:00 p.m.

May 18: Added Montrachet yeast, raspberries, raisins, citrus juice, nutrient and sugar to petal mixture at 6:00 p.m. Hydrometer reading 13% on alcohol scale; specific gravity 1000; brix 25.

May 22: Strained into clean jug at 5:00 p.m. Nice rosy-pink color. Hydrometer reading 0% alcohol, specific gravity 1000. Added 1½ cups white grape juice to fill jug. By 9:00 p.m., vigorous ferment going; air lock bubbling continuously, with millions of tiny bubbles rising.

May 23: Moved jug to basement (66°F) this morning.

May 24: Sediment beginning to form; liquid still very cloudy. Counted 27 bubbles per minute through air lock at about noon.

May 25: 13 bubbles per minute through air lock at 9:30 a.m. About ¾ inch light-colored sediment at bottom of jug.

May 26: 5 bubbles per minute through air lock at 4:00 p.m. Should be ready to rack in a day or two. Sediment layer becoming more distinct, although liquid is still very cloudy.

May 27: Bubbling 2 or 3 times per minute now. Liquid clearing a bit more.

May 28: Bubbling about once per minute now, so we racked the wine at 7:00 p.m. Hydrometer reading was at the very top, so all sugar has been consumed. Tasted wine; pleasant flavor, tastes like dandelion wine with a hint of raspberry. Still a bit cloudy, but by the color it looks as though it will have a nice rosé hue. Topped off with about 8 ounces water.

July 20: Racked wine (it could have been racked several weeks sooner, just didn't get around to it). Wine fairly clear, very pleasant flavor. Color is peachy-orange; very pretty. There was about ⅛ inch of firm sediment at bottom, so we left some liquid in bottom of jug when racking. Topped off with 9 ounces water. Would like wine to clear a bit more before bottling.

December 20: Bottled wine; cleared up nicely, has lovely peach-pink color. Will let sit in bottles for a month or more before sampling. Note: Wine could have been bottled sooner, or could have waited a bit longer. All fermentation had ceased some time before, so there was nothing going on; we bottled it because we needed the jugs for a new batch of wine.

March 25: Sampled the first bottle today. Very pleasant wine. Raspberry flavor is definitely there, but it also has the "dandelion" taste, although not as strong as a straight dandelion wine. Pretty color, nice to sip. Did not seem to be overly high in alcohol. A success!

Simple Sugar Syrup

This basic blend is used for making sorbets, and occasionally, for topping off wine during racking. A slightly stronger solution is used for sorbets, while a lighter formulation is used for wine. Here are formulations and instructions for two different kinds of syrup. Yields are approximate, but give you an idea of how much to expect.

Simple Sugar Syrup for Sorbet (Heavy)

Sugar:	1 cup	$1\frac{7}{8}$ cups	$3\frac{3}{4}$ cups
Water:	$\frac{5}{8}$ cup	$1\frac{1}{4}$ cups	$2\frac{1}{2}$ cups
Yield:	1 cup	2 cups	4 cups

Simple Sugar Syrup for Winemaking (Light)

Sugar:	$\frac{1}{3}$ cup	$\frac{5}{8}$ cup	$1\frac{1}{4}$ cups
Water:	1 cup	$1\frac{7}{8}$ cups	$3\frac{3}{4}$ cups
Yield:	1 cup	2 cups	4 cups

Combine sugar and water in saucepan. Heat to boiling, stirring just until sugar dissolves. Remove from heat; cool to room temperature. Transfer to sterilized canning jar and store in refrigerator for up to 3 weeks.

Sources & Bibliography

NUTRIENT CONTENT
U.S. Department of Agriculture Nutrient Database for Standard Reference, Release 15 (http://www.nal.usda.gov/fnic/foodcomp/Data/SR15)

PLANT RANGES, DISTRIBUTION AND GENERAL INFORMATION
U.S. Department of Agriculture, NRCS. 2002. The PLANTS Database, Version 3.5 (http://plants.usda.gov). National Plant Data Center, Baton Rouge, LA 70874-4490.

U.S. Department of Agriculture, Forest Service, Rocky Mountain Research Station, Fire Sciences Laboratory (2002, April). Fire Effects Information System. (http://www.fs.fed.us/database/feis/)

Burns, Russell M. and Honkala, Barbara H., technical coordinators. *Silvics of North America, Volume 2: Hardwoods.* Washington, DC: U.S. Department of Agriculture, Forest Service, 1990.

Little, Elbert L., Jr. *Atlas of United States Trees Volumes 1 and 4.* U.S. Department of Agriculture Miscellaneous Publications, 1971 and 1977.

Russell, Dr. Alice B. *Poisonous Plants of North Carolina.* Department of Horticultural Sciences, North Carolina State University. (http://www.ces.ncsu.edu/depts/hort/consumer/poison/poison.htm)

Vines, Robert A. *Trees, Shrubs, and Woody Vines of the Southwest.* Austin, TX: University of Texas Press, 1960.

FIELD GUIDES
Angier, Bradford. *Field Guide to Edible Wild Plants.* Harrisburg, PA: Stackpole Books, 1974.

Arora, David. *Mushrooms Demystified.* Second edition. Berkeley: Ten Speed Press, 1986.

Elias, Thomas S. and Dykeman, Peter A. *Field Guide to North American Edible Wild Plants. New York: Outdoor Life Books, 1982.*

Hosie, Robert C. *Native Trees of Canada.* Ottawa: Canadian Forestry Service, Department of Fisheries and Forestry; re-published by Fitzhenry & Whiteside, 1979.

Miller, Orson K. and Miller, Hope H. *Mushrooms in Color.* New York: E.P. Dutton, first edition (no date).

Newcomb, Lawrence. *Newcomb's Wildflower Guide.* Boston: Little, Brown and Company, 1977.

Oslund, Clayton and Oslund, Michele. *What's Doin' the Bloomin'?* Duluth, MN: Plant Pics LLP, 2002.

Peterson, Lee Allen. *A Field Guide to Edible Wild Plants of Eastern and Central North America.* Boston: Houghton Mifflin Company, 1977.

Smith, Alexander H. *The Mushroom Hunter's Field Guide.* Ann Arbor: The University of Michigan Press, 1977.

Symonds, George W. D. *The Shrub Identification Book* and *The Tree Identification Book.* New York: Harper Collins, 1963 and 1958.

Tekiela, Stan. *Wildflowers of Minnesota* (and *Michigan, Ohio* and *Wisconsin*). Cambridge, MN: Adventure Publications, Inc., 1999–2001.

COMBINATION BOOKS (FIELD GUIDE/COOKBOOK/GENERAL INFORMATION)

Brill, Steve. *Identifying and Harvesting Edible and Medicinal Plants in Wild (and Not So Wild) Places.* New York: William Morrow, 1994.

Gibbons, Euell. *Stalking the Wild Asparagus.* New York: David McKay Company, Inc., 1962.

Hamerstrom, Dr. Frances. *The Wild Food Cookbook.* Amherst, WI: Amherst Press (A Division of Palmer Publications, Inc.), 1989.

Jordan, Peter and Wheeler, Steven. *The Ultimate Mushroom Book.* London: Anness Publishing Limited, 1999.

Krumm, Bob. *The Great Lakes Berry Book.* Helena, MT: Falcon Press Publishing Co., Inc, 1996.

Lyle, Katie Letcher. *The Wild Berry Book: Romance, Recipes and Remedies.* Minnetonka, MN: NorthWord Press, 1994.

Nyerges, Christopher. *Guide to Wild Foods and Useful Plants.* Chicago: Chicago Review Press, 1999.

Shanberg, Karen and Tekiela, Stan. *Plantworks.* Cambridge, MN: Adventure Publications, Inc., 1991.

Szczawinski, Adam F. and Turner, Nancy J. *Wild Green Vegetables of Canada* and *Edible Garden Weeds of Canada.* Ottawa, Canada: National Museums of Canada, 1980.

Tatum, Billy Joe. *Wild Foods Cookbook & Field Guide.* New York: Workman Publishing Company, 1976.

Young, Kay. *Wild Seasons.* Lincoln, NE: University of Nebraska Press, 1993.

COOKBOOKS OR INSTRUCTIONAL BOOKS

Berry, C.J. *First Steps in Winemaking.* Great Britain: Standard Press (Andover) Ltd., 20th impression (no date given).

Duncan, Peter and Acron, Bryan. *Progressive Winemaking.* Great Britain: The Amateur Winemaker Publications Ltd., 1981 (17th impression).

Farges, Amy. *The Mushroom Lover's Mushroom Cookbook and Primer.* New York: Workman Publishing, 2000.

Hunt, David, Ed. *Native Indian Wild Game, Fish & Wild Foods Cookbook.* Edison, NJ: Castle Books, 1992.

Kimball, Yeffe and Anderson, Jean. *The Art of American Indian Cooking.* New York: Lyons & Burford, 1965.

Liddell, Caroline and Weir, Robin. *Frozen Desserts.* New York: St. Martin's Griffin, 1995.

Marrone, Teresa. *The Back-Country Kitchen: Camp Cooking for Canoeists, Hikers and Anglers.* Minneapolis: Northern Trails Press, 1996.

Marrone, Teresa. *The Seasonal Cabin Cookbook.* Cambridge, MN: Adventure Publications, Inc., 2001.

OF GENERAL INTEREST

Gunderson, Mary. *The Food Journal of Lewis & Clark: Recipes for an Expedition.* Yankton, SD: History Cooks, 2003.

Hauser, Susan Carol. *Sugartime.* New York: The Lyons Press, 1997.

Madsen, Lynn. *Fit For Life: Exercise for Everyday People.* Minnetonka, MN: National Health & Wellness Club, 2003.

Ortiz, Beverly R., as told by Julia F. Parker. *It Will Live Forever: Traditional Yosemite Indian Acorn Preparation.* Berkeley: Heyday Books, 1991.

Index

NOTE: Please also see listings with the copy for each species, listing other recipes in this book that use that species.

Teresa Marrone (shown above harvesting wild grapes) has been gathering and preparing wild foods for more than 20 years, and brings her knowledge and warm writing style to her newest book, *Abundantly Wild*. She is the author of *The Seasonal Cabin Cookbook* and *The Back-Country Kitchen*, and has also written or edited numerous other cookbooks on outdoor cooking, fish and wild game. She lives in Minneapolis with husband Bruce and their Senegal parrot, Tuca.